IN MANCHURIA

*The Last Days of Old Beijing: Life in the Vanishing
Backstreets of a City Transformed*

IN MANCHURIA

A Village Called Wasteland
and the Transformation of Rural China

MICHAEL MEYER

BLOOMSBURY PRESS
NEW YORK • LONDON • NEW DELHI • SYDNEY

Bloomsbury Press
An imprint of Bloomsbury Publishing Plc

1385 Broadway
New York
NY 10018
USA

50 Bedford Square
London
WC1B 3DP
UK

www.bloomsbury.com

First published 2015

ISBN: HB: 978-1-62040-286-3
PB: 978-1-62040-288-7
Trade PB: 978-1-63286-056-9
ePub: 978-1-62040-287-0

LIBRARY OF CONGRESS CATALOGING-IN-PUBLICATION DATA

Meyer, Michael J., 1972-
In Manchuria / Michael Meyer. —First U.S. edition.
pages cm
Includes bibliographical references.
ISBN: HB: 978-1-62040-286-3
PB: 978-1-62040-288-7
Trade PB: 978-1-63286-056-9
ePub: 978-1-62040-287-0
1. Manchuria (China)–Description and travel. 2. Meyer, Michael J., 1972–Travel–China–Manchuria. 3. Farm
life–China–Manchuria. 4. Rice farmers–China–Manchuria. 5. Rice farming–China–Manchuria. 6. Manchuria
(China)–Social life and customs. 7. Manchuria (China)–Rural conditions. I. Title.
DS782.3.M47 2014
951'.80612–dc 3
2014017907

2 4 6 8 10 9 7 5 3 1

Typeset by Hewer Text UK Ltd, Edinburgh
Printed and bound in the U.S.A. by Thomson-Shore Inc., Dexter, Michigan

For Benjamin, our 路客

Wasteland 荒地

→ To Songhua River

Rice Fields

Rice Fields

Airfield

Rice Fields

Elementary School

Shop

Eastern Fortune Rice

My House

San Jiu's House

New Apartments

Rice Fields

Auntie Yi's House

Gas Station

→ To Jilin City

Bank

Shops

Food

Red Flag Road

Hot Spring

W.C.

Rice Station

Police Station

Rice Fields

Foothills

Rice Fields

Clinic

Market & Shops

Rice Fields

Train Station

Middle School

To Changchun ←

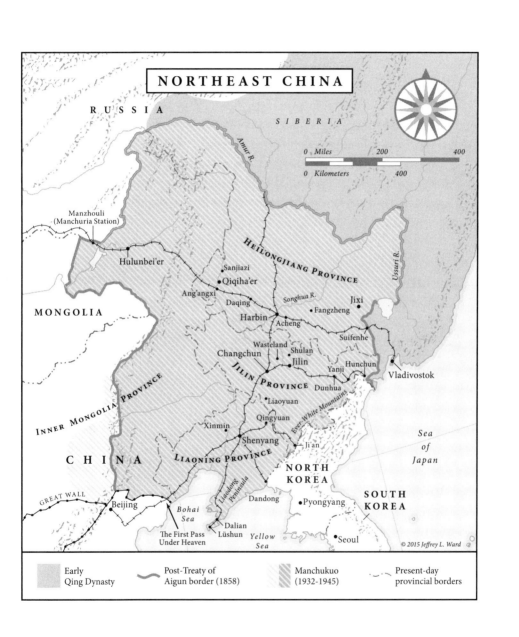

NORTHEAST CHINA

RUSSIA

SIBERIA

0 Miles 200 400

0 Kilometers 400

Amur R.

Ussuri R.

Manzhouli
(Manchuria Station)

Hulunbei'er

HEILONGJIANG PROVINCE

Sanjiazi

Qiqiha'er

Ang'angxi

Daqing

Songhua R.

Jixi

MONGOLIA

Harbin

Acheng

Fangzheng

Wasteland

Shulan

Suifenhe

Changchun

Jilin

JILIN PROVINCE

Dunhua

Hunchun

Yanji

Vladivostok

INNER MONGOLIA PROVINCE

Liaoyuan

Qingyuan

Ever-White Mountains

Xinmin

Shenyang

Ji'an

Sea
of
Japan

CHINA

LIAONING PROVINCE

NORTH
KOREA

GREAT WALL

Beijing

Liaodong Peninsula

Dandong

Pyongyang

SOUTH
KOREA

Bohai
Sea

Dalian

Lüshun

Yellow
Sea

The First Pass
Under Heaven

Seoul

© 2015 Jeffrey L. Ward

Early
Qing Dynasty

Post-Treaty of
Aigun border (1858)

Manchukuo
(1932-1945)

Present-day
provincial borders

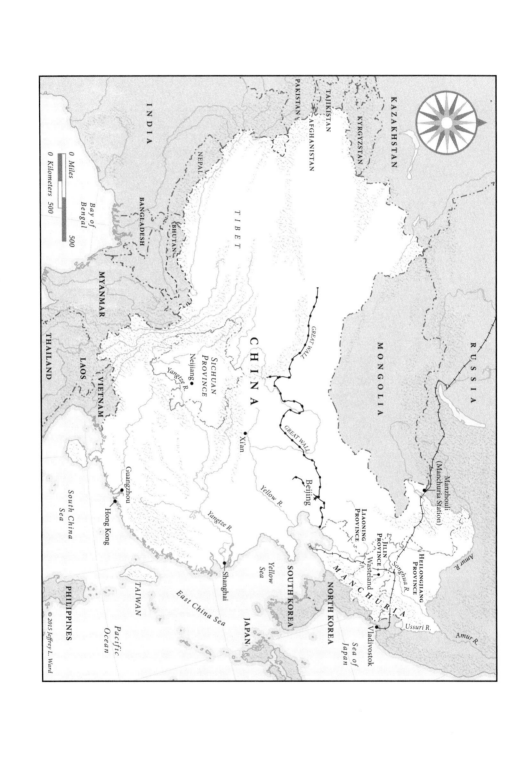

© 2015 Jeffrey L. Ward

CONTENTS

Wasteland

In Manchuria

*Could it be that all the elegance of heaven and earth
is stored north of the Wall?*

From "Guarding the Pass," a nineteenth-century *zidishu*,
a folktale performed in Manchu and Chinese.

*Every piece of duckweed floats down to the sea;
People will always meet each other somewhere.*

From the classic Chinese novel *Journey to the West.*

CHAPTER I

WINTER SOLSTICE

I N WINTER THE land is frozen and still. A cloudless sky shines off snow-covered rice paddies, reflecting light so bright, you have to shield your eyes. I lean into a stinging wind and trudge north up Red Flag Road, to a village named Wasteland.

The view is flat, lifeless, and silver fresh. The two-lane cement road slices through the paddies like the courses plowed across frozen lakes in my native Minnesota, but there are no icehouses to shelter in here. Ten minutes ago, I set off from the coal-fueled warmth of Number 22 Middle School, where I volunteer as an English teacher. Already my beard is beaded with ice.

Tufts of dry husks sprout through the snow, resembling ripening brooms. To my left, the sun sinks over the far horizon. It is 3:22 p.m. at December's end—or, as Chinese farmers know it, *dongzhi* (Winter Solstice), one of twenty-four fortnight-long periods describing the seasons based on the sun's longitude. The previous solar term was Major Snow, which fell on schedule, blanketing Wasteland in white. Next up, in early January, is Slight Cold, which, given today's high temperature of minus 8 degrees Fahrenheit, makes me fear what "slight" will feel like. At school, a red nylon propaganda banner lashed to the accordion entrance gate urges us to PREVENT HAND, FOOT AND MOUTH DISEASE and, less helpfully, announces that WINTER BRINGS THE BIGGEST CHANGE IN TEMPERATURE.

Red Flag Road's single traffic sign displays a speed limit of forty kilometers an hour. On school days I never see anyone break it; bicycles and three-wheeled motorcycles saunter and sputter to the crossroads' Agricultural

Bank, seed store, noodle shops, and train station. Painted bright pink and crowned with a peaked tin roof whose cobalt-blue matches Wasteland's usual sky, the station has been rendered all but obsolete: the new high-speed trains that cover the seventy miles between the cities of Jilin and Changchun do not stop here. For passengers in the sealed compartment, Wasteland whooshes by in a silent four-second blur, looking like any other village in northeast China.

Closer inspection reveals a dotted line of trash aside Red Flag Road: empty boxes of expensive Panda brand cigarettes and bottles of Moutai brand liquor; broadsheets of stock tips, real estate flyers, and fortune-telling booklets advising the most auspicious days to buy property; and self-published circulars, sold in big cities, with titles such as *Intriguing Stories* and *Strange Affairs*. In addition to the latest gossip about the private lives of top officials, the pamphlets answer questions such as *Will our capital be moved from Beijing?* (No.) *Did the 1989 student protest movement fail?* (Yes.) *How many people were killed during the Cultural Revolution?* (Lots.)

Today the only sound on Red Flag Road comes from another banner, strung between two Manchurian ash seedlings, whipping in the wind. The cloth twists and unfurls, then twists again. Between gusts spin the Chinese characters for *plant*, then *seeds*, then *record* and *yield*. I pass the banner every day and, unlike the farmers, study its message. In the Chinese countryside—free of newsstands and street signs—propaganda is my primer, even when written by Comrade Obvious. This red ribbon teaches me the characters that form: PLANT QUALITY SEEDS TO PRODUCE A RECORD YIELD.

For decades, the three-story middle school was Wasteland's tallest structure. From my English classroom window I can see all the village's homes, whose clusters make an archipelago across the fields. Now I walk toward a billboard whose message I can read a mile away: BUILD THE NORTHEAST'S TOP VILLAGE. It was erected by Eastern Fortune Rice, a private agribusiness company based in Wasteland. I never thought about this propaganda—just another exercise in blatancy—until Eastern Fortune began making it come true.

Gossip says that, like the railroad, Red Flag Road will be upgraded, too. Locals wonder if it's their way of life that will be made obsolete. There's even talk of changing the village's name.

No one can say for certain why the place is called Wasteland. It may have been a ploy by homesteaders to discourage other migrants from moving to this fertile floodplain, stretching from the western banks of the Songhua (Pine Flower) River to forested foothills. Neighboring hamlets, also comprising a few dozen single-story homes abutting table-flat rice paddies, include Lonely Outpost, Zhang's Smelly Ditch, the Dunes, and Mud Town.

In the movie *Caddyshack*, Rodney Dangerfield boasts that he and his partner, Wang, just bought some land at the Great Wall: "On the *good* side!" Wasteland is in the other direction. Beyond the wall begins China's northeast, or *Dongbei* (rhymes with *wrong way*). Chinese say a map of their country resembles a chicken, which makes the Northeast its head, squeezing between Mongolian grasslands and the Ever-White Mountains before bumping up against Siberia.

Perhaps no other region has exerted more influence on China across the last four hundred years. Historically, the West referred to the Northeast as Manchuria, homeland of the Manchu, tribes that for centuries alternated between independence from and vassalage to the Chinese emperor before uniting to storm through the Great Wall in 1644 and seize the Beijing throne. The Manchu's Qing dynasty ruled China for nearly three hundred years, doubling its territory—adding Tibet, Xinjiang, and Inner Mongolia—to form the borders of today's multiethnic nation. But the regime's center could not hold. On her deathbed in 1908, the empress dowager Cixi chose a two-year-old boy named Puyi for the throne. The toddler bawled during his coronation. "Don't cry," his father consoled. "It will be over soon." Four years later, the increasingly dissolute Qing crumbled, and Puyi became China's last emperor, forced to abdicate in 1912 after the revolution led by Sun Yat-sen that created the Chinese republic.

By then, the nation's gains were the Manchu's loss: more Manchu lived south of the Great Wall than in their former homeland, and culturally they had all but assimilated with the Han Chinese they once ruled. Today, most Manchu look indistinguishable from other Northeasterners. Though their court was bilingual—Mandarin remained China's lingua franca; a Manchu emperor even named Tiananmen, Chinese for "the Gate of Heavenly Peace"—most Manchu no longer spoke their mother tongue. The language, which sounds nothing like Mandarin and is written in a Mongolian-based script, began a fade toward extinction.

Eroding, too, was the Manchu's hold on the Northeast, which their emperors had attempted to maintain as a cultural reserve. Countermanding centuries of edicts restricting migration to Manchuria, Han Chinese homesteaders flooded the region. Between 1927 and 1929 alone, an estimated one million settlers arrived each year, surpassing the number of Europeans who landed annually in the United States at the peak of its immigration wave.

Most new arrivals didn't call the land Manchuria, or the Northeast, or "east of the barrier" (the Great Wall), or even the "three eastern provinces," as redistricting had it rendered on maps. They called their new home what it looked like: the Great Northern Wasteland.

"Although it is uncertain where God created paradise," wrote a French priest crossing Manchuria during this era, "we can be sure He chose some other place than this."

But I found it beautiful and unique, a land worthy of its evocative names.

The wind whips across the scalloped snow, slashing through my four layers of clothes. I imagine the gale born to neglectful parents named Gobi Frost and Siberian Tundra. My neighbors call their seething offspring the Torturer, constantly driving needles into our bones no matter how much we pad them.

And yet, the sky stretches from horizon to horizon, a fresh prairie sky without pause. In Chinese cities you do not stop to appreciate the sky; you can rarely see it through the smog. Other parts of rural China feel stooped and low ceilinged, with clouds sagging from age. But at China's Northeastern frontier, the sky's incandescent blue is as much of the landscape as the dark earth below. Farmers here seldom call the dirt mere "soil." Unlike elsewhere in China, where fields have been turned and tilled for thousands of years, in the Northeast they farm comparatively virgin "black earth" using "sweet water." When thawed, a handful of loam feels as rich and saturated as spent coffee grounds.

Wasteland is a typical rural Chinese community, even if its fields are not. Instead of working terraced hillsides year-round, farmers harvest a single annual crop of rice from paddies that run to the distant foothills, surrounding us on three sides.

Beijing is a twelve-hour train ride southwest, a trip equal in distance to the six-hundred mile journey between central Maine and Washington, D.C. Wasteland is closer—by half—to Vladivostok and Pyongyang, if logistical and cultural worlds away. On my classroom blackboard, the "map" I often chalk to explain our village's location is labeled:

Russia

Mongolia

Wasteland

North Korea

The Great Wall

The middle white space, China's Northeast, is equal in population and area to Germany and France combined. The analogy also evokes its recent past: while late-nineteenth-century Western travelers who journeyed to Manchuria compared this frontier to Alaska's, the next generation wrote that they had arrived in a "cradle of conflict" that was Asia's Alsace-Lorraine.

For the first half of the twentieth century, Manchuria was the prize in battles between China, Japan, and Russia. Brokering the end of one war earned President Theodore Roosevelt the Nobel Peace Prize but gave Japan control of much of Manchuria's railroad—China's longest and most lucrative—linking its mineral-rich heartland to Pacific Ocean ports. Russia had failed to yoke Manchuria to eastern Siberia; Japan tried shaping it into the toehold for its imperial dream of the "Greater East Asia Co-Prosperity Sphere."

Due to its similarity to *Manchukuo*, the name of the puppet state Japan founded here in 1931, the term *Manchuria* fell from use after Japan's surrender, ending the Second World War. But *Manchuria* long predates the Japanese invasion, appearing on nineteenth-century Chinese maps and in European atlases—often replacing *Tartary*. Even the Communist Party's regional office once used it, in publications with names such as the *Manchurian Worker*.

Western press reports revived the term during the Korean War, but *Manchuria* faded from use after Soviet advisers withdrew from the region in 1955 and it was—at last—wholly controlled by the central government in Beijing.

But as its status as geopolitical hot spot dimmed, the Northeast still retained its Otherness. China is a patchwork of places as diverse as America's, each with its own local language, cuisine, and character. Append *Dongbei* (*Northeast*) before any of these nouns, and it will, to a Chinese person, evoke a ringing lilt of elongated vowels, sour cabbage served with potatoes and boiled pork dumplings, and tough, yet self-effacing, people known for eccentricity. A recent national pop hit, "All Northeasterners Are Living Lei Fengs," poked fun at the natives' overcompensating virtu-ousness, familiar to anyone who has experienced the placating temperament known as "Minnesota Nice."

I'm attracted to all of this, especially the eccentrics, who remind me of my childhood neighbors. And unlike in China's other borderlands, where the native mother tongue is Tibetan, Uighur, or Cantonese, the Northeast today uses standard Mandarin Chinese—which I speak and read fluently—and a closely related dialect. But it was the region's history that drew me here most.

Chinese civilization, as my middle school students have been taught to recite with stentorian solemnity, "has five thousand years of history." In their textbooks, the Northeast claims only a sliver of that time line, making its past feel comparatively intimate. The bulk of its recorded antiquity began in the early seventeenth century, around the time—on the other side of the world—that Shakespeare wrote his plays and the Pilgrims landed at Plymouth Rock.

Anyone who has spent time in contemporary China knows the feeling of traditions slipping away, of old landscapes remade. In Beijing you could return to a neighborhood where you ate noodles the week before and find it flattened to a field of rubble. A decade ago, at a Buddhist nunnery that would be submerged by the Three Gorges Dam, I met an elderly novitiate who said she wanted to live there forever. She asked if I could put her into a story so she always would.

But the Northeast's history still seems near. Its artifacts spill across the region like playing pieces left on a board game named Empire. You can travel on railways built in the name of the czar; pace not through ancient Buddhist temples but into onion-domed Russian Orthodox cathedrals; walk down boulevards lined with Japanese pines and colonial ministries constructed in an architectural style dubbed Rising Asia; tour Puyi's "Puppet Emperor's Palace"; visit sites where the Japanese held Allied prisoners, including Bataan Death March survivors; and stand on the bridge—reaching halfway across the Yalu River, separating China and North Korea—that American pilots dive-bombed during the Korean War. I saw these sites—and the stories missing from their official plaques—as markers that charted the rise and fall of the Manchu, and the nadir and ascent of modern China. Uniquely for a Chinese region, foreigners played a prominent role on its stage.

Other than Harbin city's famous Ice Lantern Festival, a monthlong winter carnival around life-size replicas of famous buildings made from blocks of frozen Songhua River water, the Northeast remained to most Chinese "the land beyond the pale," as the expanse north of the Great Wall was historically known. Winter is the barrier today; skiers and masochists aside, who sets off for a subzero holiday? Summers are mild and bright, but even then I often feel like I have this upper-right-hand corner of the nation to myself: no scrums at train ticket windows, no need for hotel reservations, no dodging tour groups. On the twenty-five thousand miles that I've traveled on side trips from Wasteland, I've often sat alone in a train car, unlike in the south, where the compartments could be so crowded, I have spent rides standing in the toilet or lying on newspapers spread beneath the bench seats.

At Manchuria's de facto border, the First Pass Under Heaven—where the Great Wall tapers into the Bohai Sea—a rebuilt section of the wall extends five hundred yards west before ending abruptly at a cinder block barrier. It obstructs any view; the visitor is stuck facing a gray curtain of cement. But set in its middle is a normal-size door, the kind that separates rooms in an apartment. Push hard and it opens to reveal the unimproved Great Wall, crumbling and crowned by tall grasses and mature elms, scaling the mountains wild. Traveling in the Northeast feels like stepping through that door.

*

On a farm, weather is the fourth dimension. The icy wind burns my cheeks on Red Flag Road. Ahead, in the distance, moving closer and sputtering like a shot-up biplane, I see a three-wheel tractor. Oversize sunglasses and a white cotton surgical mask obscure the driver's face, which is further shrouded by a fur-lined People's Liberation Army hat. Its earflaps bounce rhythmically over the black ice. The driver honks, a limpid squawk that sounds like the tractor's battery is conserving energy. The driver lays into it harder. One rule of the Chinese countryside is that the more peaceful the surroundings, the more noise people make.

The driver stops, and the tractor idles roughly, as if stamping its feet in the cold. I have no idea who is under the hat, those glasses. Through the face mask comes the dialect-inflected demand: "*Ga ha'me'ne ni!*"

What am I doing? "I'm walking."

The driver asks, in the singsong Northeastern way: "*Shei jia'di'ah?*"

"To whose family do you belong?" is a standard greeting here—even to a foreigner—unlike elsewhere in China, where strangers ask if you've eaten, or what country you're from.

"The Guans," I reply, naming my Manchu landlords.

"Correct!" the man laughs. "Get on!" He kicks the tractor into gear. It leaps like it's been defibrillated.

I tuck my head behind his shoulder as the driver put-puts a mile north, turning off Red Flag into a huddle of two dozen single-story brick homes. He stops at the last one, with sodium lights shimmering through the windows and a stream of smoke flowing from its chimney. My house is another mile north, but tonight is the weekly meal with my closest friend in Wasteland.

I thank the unknown driver, who won't accept payment, though I know that one day he will identify himself and the favor I can return. I push open the never-locked front door, stomping the snow off my jeans in the vestibule, then opening a door to the home's main room and climbing on the *kang*, a brick platform bed two feet high that runs the length, and nearly the width, of the room. Heated by burning dried rice stalks, the *kang*'s linoleum covering is hot to the touch but feels comfortable when covered with cotton bedrolls. The house smells pleasantly of toasted grain, like we're lounging atop baking bread, and I am always happy to step over its threshold.

Next to the *kang* is a round table laden with steaming plates of twice-cooked pork, flash-fried mushrooms, garlic-sautéed wild greens, and rice grown in the paddy just outside these wall-size windows, weatherproofed with plastic wrap. The dishes have been cooked in a large wok sunk into a cement stove, fired by burning rice stalks.

"*Mai'er*," the family's patriarch says with a nod.

"San Jiu," I say, nodding back. The lack of formality—of *You must be cold; have you eaten? you're not wearing enough layers; eat; take a smoke; drink some tea; you must be cold, it's winter now and cold outside, you have to wear more; eat; have some beer; you look cold; eat, eat, eat*—means that I'm home.

"I cooked," he says. "It's the two of us tonight. Everyone else had to go to"—and here he says the term for Fourth Cousin, Second Nephew, or some other title which I can never keep straight without a diagram. Every branch of a Chinese family tree has its own name indicating not only which side you come from but in what order. In English we say *aunt*, but in China she was, for example, *the wife of my father's oldest brother*. One's cousin could be *your mother's younger sister's second-born son*. San Jiu (pronounced *San Joe*) means "Third Uncle on Mother's Side."

I know his given name, but have always called him San Jiu. He is a sixty-six-year-old ruddy-cheeked man who never seems to age but rather hardens, like the Manchuria ash lining Red Flag Road. He still opens beer bottles with his teeth, shoulders fifty-pound sacks of seed, and weeds his paddy by hand, stooping low in the muck. He smokes Changbaishan, a brand named for the perpetually snow-covered peaks on this province's border with North Korea. The name translates as Ever-White Mountains, but when we share one together, I just see a lump of tar.

"It's your Christmas, right?"

"In two days," I reply.

"My wife is gone tonight," he says, resolute. "So we can drink."

San Jiu fills two rice bowls with Snow brand beer (often the only cups in a farmer's home are for tea). After he finishes his bowl, he splashes in a bit of the hard stuff from a plastic gallon jug and sips loudly. None is offered: San Jiu remembers the last time he served me sorghum liquor.

That was seven years ago, when I had visited Wasteland for the first time. I was alone, on a *National Geographic* assignment about historical

Manchuria. After rolling two hours east from the provincial capital of Changchun on a bus that smelled of feet, the driver pulled to the edge of the two-lane road, stared out the windshield into the darkness, and said, gravely: "Are you sure you want to get off here?"

After he pulled away, I stood alone in the subzero air, regretting the decision. There were no taxis, no dumpling restaurants or shops to wait inside—no streetlights, even. A calf-high granite slab said, in Chinese characters, that I had arrived in Wasteland.

With chattering teeth, I walked up Red Flag Road under a black dome thick with stars. The Big Dipper bent low over snow-covered paddies. Complete silence. Plumes of breath. The smell of burning rice stalks wafting from chimneys. San Jiu stood on the road with a flashlight, waiting. He led me to his house and into a room full of people raising glasses over a table full of steaming food.

"What if I moved here?" I had asked, after too many shots of 120-proof liquor.

"You live in Beijing!" he said. "Everyone wants to be there. No one moves here."

But I could, I thought, keeping the notion to myself.

After dinner, San Jiu stretched me on the *kang* next to him. We slept side by side, as rigid as mummies. Through the night, I dreamed of moving to Manchuria.

But I had stayed in Beijing, living in the capital's oldest neighborhood with several Chinese families in a courtyard home that lacked heat, hot water, and a toilet. Beijing was tearing down its traditional lanes—*hutong*—at the heart of its Old City, and before it vanished I wanted to experience a life that tourists, foreign students, and journalists (I had been, in order, all three) only viewed in passing. For two years I taught English in the local elementary school and to retired seniors, giving me a purpose and place in the community. Life in the lanes was not postcard pretty—poverty never is—as I wrote in *The Last Days of Old Beijing,* a book detailing the neighborhood's layered history and daily routines. Much of what I saw on my *hutong* had Manchu origins, including the bamboo whistles fastened to the feet of the pet pigeons that dopplered mournfully overhead every afternoon; the names of lanes with *banner* in them, for a military division; the silk cheongsam (*qipao*, "banner robe") dresses being hand-sewn at the tailor's; and the Peking opera clanging at all hours on my elderly neighbor's television.

Throughout those years, I held Wasteland in reserve. The dominant narrative of modern China is told from its capital and coastal cities. Those shiny cities! Those new cities! Those Olympics-hosting cities! Those car-choked, class-divided, and overcrowded cities! Most foreign correspondents live in cities, and Chinese writers have long focused on urbanity and urban intellectuals—one reason some contemporary Chinese scholars feel that Pearl Buck's 1931 novel *The Good Earth* should be taught as Chinese literature.

I had written about change in urban China, and now I wondered how the other half lived. The sheer numbers of people moving off farms to urban centers had me picturing fields going to seed, as if farmers had tossed down their scythes to hop a passing bus and never return. I imagined empty houses illuminated by left-on televisions, and cows mooing plaintively with full udders.

In 1993, the U.S. Census stopped counting American farmers: the demographic had become "statistically insignificant," as less than 2 percent of the population lives on a farm. But in China nearly half the country—some 700 million people—still lives in rural areas such as Wasteland. That number was plummeting: since 2000, a quarter of China's villages had died out, victims of migration or the redrawing of municipal borders to encompass surrounding hamlets, meeting national urbanization targets. Though it sat twenty miles and an hour's bus ride away, Wasteland was recently folded into the Jilin city limits, retaining its name and—on paper, at least—offering residents the chance to become urbanites.

I knew that in the Northeast I could explore China's past. I didn't expect that in Wasteland I would glimpse the nation's future.

By 2011, China had spent more years dismantling a Marxist society than building one. Wasteland faces a new, unknown economic phase: becoming a company town.

Its largest business, Eastern Fortune Rice, began in 2000, when two village partners planted the same short-grain sticky rice as their neighbors.

The variety is commonly used in sushi, though Chinese eat it as a side dish. But unlike their hidebound neighbors, Eastern Fortune's founders experimented. They tested different seed varieties and for the first time in Wasteland grew an organic crop.

By the third harvest, government ministries began serving the rice—branded Big Wasteland—at official banquets. In 2007, China's then president, Hu Jintao, visited the village and Eastern Fortune's headquarters. A massive photo of him inspecting production hangs at the entrance to the company's new hot spring resort, which on weekends attracts a steady stream of city day-trippers who trail the jetstream of trash down Red Flag Road. The hot spring's 120 yuan ($20) entrance fee equals what local farmers earn in a fortnight.

Initially my neighbors were happy when the company announced it would buy their rice crop at above market prices and hire them to work the polishing and packaging machines it imported from Japan. As the company profited, so did the village. In the previous seven years, the number of farmers contracting their fields to Eastern Fortune doubled. The company provided rice seed and guaranteed payment of 15,500 yuan ($2,500) for a family's harvest.

That figure was twice as much as the average Chinese farmer earned annually. Eastern Fortune had contracted nearly all of Wasteland's five square miles of paddies, though a few families, including San Jiu's, still held out.

A skyline is sprouting. At the end of Red Flag Road stand cranes and the shells of five-story walk-up buildings. Eastern Fortune is offering apartments in exchange for farmers' homes, which will be razed and the land converted to paddies. Few have agreed to move: giving up their homes means losing a garden and chicken coop, which allows for self-sufficiency and a secondary income. It also takes many families' homes off the land itself, contrary to the traditional belief that health emanates from "being in contact with the earth's energy." And the elderly are worried about climbing stairs to a third-, fourth-, or even fifth-story apartment. Lastly, moving off the land means betting that the price of rice will not skyrocket by the end of the agreement. The amount promised by Eastern Fortune was, in effect, a futures contract: what seems fair today might not seem that way next year. Grain prices, like real estate, continue to soar.

The apartment project's multicolored, laser-printed billboard shows a purling stream, renamed the Revere Gentry River, an incongruously feudal term for a collectively owned farming community. Its rendition is crowned with lotuses and bordered by willow trees and apartments with indoor plumbing and central heat. The people in this future scene sit on benches and stroll under trellises with children and lovers wearing blouses and skirts and T-shirts and jeans. They look and act nothing like Wastelanders. At least, not yet.

The *kang*'s heat has me peeling layers of clothing, and San Jiu's cheeks are pink from the lukewarm Snow beer, bottles of which he pulls from a plastic crate beneath the round table. I dread a run outside to the toilet.

When San Jiu goes first, I notice a book atop the bureau, titled *Farmer Lawsuits*. It contains three hundred answers to questions that include *Can the village committee profit from individual farmer's land?* (No.); *Does the village committee have to make its books open to the public?* (Yes.); *Is it true that hitting one's wife and child is the home's concern, not the village's?* (No.); and *Do farmers have the right to petition the national government?* (Yes.). I am half expecting to read *Does winter bring the biggest change in temperature?* when San Jiu returns and says, "That book wasn't so useful. I knew all of that."

He switches on the television, showing the national broadcast of the 7:00 news. We sit with shoulders touching on the *kang*. One of the lead reports details the government's measures to rein in inflation. As it does every week at our shared meal, the mention of money leads San Jiu to ask me the price of gasoline in the United States. "What about pork? A bottle of corn oil?" For the next half hour we recount the cost of garlic, the cost of chives, the amount for tuition, the cost of rent. Everything is up, he says.

"Including the price of rice," I say. "That's good for you."

"Seed is up, fuel is up, water is up, electricity is up. It's funny that the only thing that's gone down is taxes."

In 2006, for the first time in its history, China abolished all taxes on farmers.

The landline telephone rings. San Jiu lifts the receiver. His side of the conversation sounds like this:

[Ring] Uh!

Uh?

Uhhh.

Uh. [Click]

There is no Chinese character for *Uh*, but in the Northeast it stands for many. It can mean *Hello*; *Good-bye*; *I hear you*; *I agree*; *More, please*; and *This is a difficult question to answer simply*. San Jiu turns his attention back to the evening news. He tells me that someone is coming to join us. I don't recognize the noun describing the man's place on the family tree, and San Jiu explains it slowly, in the same tone I use when diagramming a complex sentence on the blackboard for my middle school students.

"He is the son. Of the stepbrother. Understand? Of your mother-in-law. Of your wife's mother. Is it clear?"

"Uh."

And therein lies the truest answer to the question of what really led me to Manchuria, and to—of all the Northeast's villages—Wasteland. Not, initially, because of an intrinsic attraction to its history and ways. That gripped me over time. The root attraction was much simpler: a girl.

CHAPTER 2

QUID PRO QUO

T HIRTEEN YEARS EARLIER she stood in San Francisco International for the first time, thinking: *So this is what it feels like to be a foreigner.*

Frances moved through the airport cautiously, unsure where to turn. In China you just followed the crowd. But here she had to go through immigration, retrieve her bag, make a phone call, and find her connecting flight—alone. Everything was so quiet and orderly, she couldn't even hear her own footsteps. Carpeting in an airport? She watched a row of fountains sending water into the air. How wasteful. *Beijing could use that stuff*, she thought.

The people around her were patient and pleasant. The customs agent brought over his friendly dog to sniff her. There was a red channel and a green one. She didn't know where to go; she was twenty-one, and had never been outside of China. A white man in the arrow-straight line pointed and advised her to answer "No" to any questions.

She presented her passport to the officer. Its photo—taken when she was an English student at university in Beijing—showed a waif with shaved hair and sallow cheeks. The clerk looked at the long-haired, buxom woman before him. He insinuated that the passport wasn't hers at all but belonged to a man. Internally she panicked before realizing that the officer was demonstrating humor. "Ha?" she responded uncertainly. He smiled, and she tried again. "Ha ha ha!"

"Welcome to the United States."

Inside the terminal, a man in his seventies, well dressed and silver-haired, asked if she could spare a minute. He stood on a platform that said something about free speech and the First Amendment. He told Frances she should donate money to the International Association for the Something-or-Other. She didn't catch the last part. She did as she would when a beggar approached her in Beijing: she pulled out a ten-spot and put it in his hand.

"Ten dollars? That's very generous. Thank you, miss."

She froze. *Did I give him too much? Can I ask for it back?*

Instead, she asked where she could find a public phone. He pointed to a row of them.

Strange. No hovering aunties to take your money and watch the timer, calculating the fee. No receiver sitting atop a handcart of cigarettes and bottled orange soda. Just a bank of cold, shiny pay phones.

She didn't have change. The man using the phone beside her noticed her confusion. *How embarrassing—can't even figure out a telephone!* "Can you help me?" she asked.

"You need to put coins in there, then dial the number."

She opened her hand, offering a wad of bills.

"I think tens and twenties are too much," he said. "It should be fifty cents. Here, you can use my phone card. What's the number you're calling? I'll dial it for you."

My father answered in Minneapolis. He was very excited to meet her at the airport, he said. "We'll be waiting for you with bells on."

"No, no bells: I'll be embarrassed," Frances pleaded.

He thought she was in on the joke. "And horns, too! Lots of horns! We'll blow them to welcome you!"

"Please don't, please." Her voice turned serious. She listened to the uncertain silence at the other end of the line. "Wait, you were joking, weren't you?" As she walked away from the phone she had a realization— one that I had said, to her disbelief, that I felt every day in China: *These people think I'm a moron.*

She bought cigarettes to calm her nerves, managing a lighter's flick and one blissful drag before a security officer approached.

"I understand. I'll go outside. Thank you." So America wasn't a free-for-all; freedom meant something else.

*

Boarding her connecting flight to Minneapolis, she found a man occupying her seat. Frances checked her boarding pass. She had specifically asked for the window so she could watch America from above. Now an Asian man was in her way.

"Excuse me, I think you're in my place."

The burly white man beside him, in the middle, turned his sunglasses to her. "I'm sorry, you can't sit there."

She didn't know how to reply. Was this the culture? Did airplane seats in America work like hard seats on a Chinese train: first come, first grab?

"I don't mean to be rude, but I don't understand."

"I'm an immigration officer," the white man said, "and I'm transporting him. You can sit here." He motioned to the aisle seat. Frances looked at the Asian man. His left hand was cuffed to the officer's right.

She took her seat, terrified. She'd never been close to a criminal before. What if he planned an escape? With explosives! Her mind replayed the more fiery scenes from the action movie *Air Force One*. The Asian man, however, looked resigned. The officer looked tense. The plane took off. The beverage cart came around. Frances asked for a beer. The stewardess asked her age, then rattled off a list. So many choices. It was a confusing blur. "I'll have the first one you said."

After a second Budweiser, her confidence returned. She asked the officer if he liked his job. He said he had been to forty-seven countries. Had he ever been to China?

"Oh, I've been to Beijing many times. Is that where you're from?"

"I work there, but I'm from the Northeast."

The officer nodded vacantly.

"Have you heard of Manchuria?"

"I saw *The Manchurian Candidate*."

Frances had never heard of the movie. She studied the handcuffs. "How do police treat prisoners in America? If they don't tell you things, do you beat them?"

The officer thought that was hilarious. The prisoner looked out the window.

*

In Minnesota, we ate at a restaurant with *panda* in its name. "I can't think of a less appetizing image," Frances said, "than an animal known for soiling itself and smothering its offspring." She frowned at the broken English on the chopsticks packet, reading aloud, "Please try your nice Chinese food with chopsticks the traditional and typical of Chinese glorious history and culture."

She opened the menu and frowned again. "Seven bucks for garlic-fried broccoli? That's five times what it costs in China. It's just a vegetable. People pay these prices?" At meal's end, the waitress presented the check with a mound of plastic-wrapped fortune cookies. Frances had never seen one, as they had been invented by a Japanese man for American diners. The shell tasted like sugared cardboard, but much better than the mysterious orange syrup that coated our sweet-and-sour dish. Yet, to her ear, the messages within sounded overoptimistic and American. We played a game. I read the fortune, and she edited it to sound authentically Chinese.

I read: "You are one of the people who 'goes places in life.'"

"Chinese would never say that," she said. "In China, it would be: 'You're not so bad. Better than some, worse than others.'"

"Your present plans are going to succeed."

"No plan is the best plan."

"The current year will bring you much happiness."

"This is as good as it gets."

"You will step on the soil of many countries."

"The best thing to do is to stay home and serve your parents."

"You have an ambitious nature and may make a name for yourself."

"You're a woman. Be chaste and stop dreaming."

We had met in Beijing a year earlier, in 1997, teaching together at an international school located in the capital's far northern suburbs, surrounded by apple orchards and flanked by the Western Hills. I taught English to the teenagers; Frances taught the kindergarteners Chinese. Meeting her for the first time was confusing. In my two previous years as a Peace Corps volunteer in China's rural southwest, I had been ordered, in training and regular meetings, not to do three things, in order of severity:

(1) engage in politics

(2) ride motorcycles

(3) date a host country national (as locals were called)

I had arrived in 1995 as part of China's second-ever batch of volunteers. As a fluent Spanish speaker, I had hoped to be sent to Latin America, but the Peace Corps offered Vladivostok, then Turkmenistan, then Malawi, then Kiribati, then Sri Lanka. The choices kept getting further from a ¡Sí! After I refused Mongolia, the recruiter snapped, "This isn't Club Med, it's the Peace Corps." His final take-it-or-leave-us offer: China. At the time I couldn't even use chopsticks, let alone speak a word of Chinese.

Six weeks later, in a Sichuan Normal University classroom, a Peace Corps trainer warned us newcomers that a volunteer in the first group had married his college-age Chinese student. The story was related rapidly, as if it had happened during one farcical afternoon. I pictured Cary Grant as the nonplussed volunteer, doing a "spit take" and barking, "MARRIED? What, in that office? I thought she was helping me buy a TRAIN ticket!"

But Peace Corps swore it was all true. The university expelled the student, and Peace Corps the volunteer. There was more: gossip about Chinese police dragging unmarried native/foreign couples from hotel beds and tales of wily women trolling for green cards. Those came from my training-period roommate, a gruff Coast Guard veteran with a salt-and-pepper crew cut, a bulbous red nose, and a tattoo above his navel that instructed ADD OIL HERE.

We were Peace and Corps, together in one room. I was twenty-three, a freshly licensed English teacher eager to bridge cultures and study Chinese. He was in his fifties, toting a Korean War survival manual in which he underlined key passages such as "Keep a sense of humor. Americans are the most unpredictable people in the world—and methodical types like the Chinese Communists become unstrung when they cannot anticipate what we do next."

The man—I called him the Captain—watched for signs of any male volunteer "going native." My playing basketball with a female Chinese student was, for the Captain, exposure that would lead to "yellow fever." When the Captain was expelled from the Peace Corps later that year, I thought it was because he had begun a class by chalking KARL MARX on one side of the board and ADAM SMITH on the other. "This one works," he had announced, pointing at Smith. "And this one"—moving to Marx—"is full of shit." But no, the Captain had fallen in love with a host country national. Americans are the most unpredictable people in the world.

So when I moved to Beijing in 1997 after finishing my Peace Corps assignment, dating had been ingrained as Something You Just Didn't Do. But it was an untested maxim, like my mom's warning—handed down by her own mother—to never run the vacuum cleaner over its own power cord or use the blow-dryer with wet feet. You probably wouldn't get shocked, but why risk it? My students in remote Sichuan, like the isolated campus itself, had become family, and I hoped Beijing would bring the same sibling-like relationships.

I had applied to teach at the international school after reading its Help Wanted posting in the Peace Corps newsletter. Since I had no Internet access or even a cell phone, it was the only lead I had on a post-Corps life. It took an entire morning to peck out an error-free résumé on a manual typewriter. After crossing the river in a skiff with a farmer and his ox, I spent the afternoon at the post office affixing stamps brushed with fish glue and slowly writing the Beijing school's Chinese name with a leaky fountain pen. I pushed the envelope into the mailbox slot next to LOCAL, enticingly labeled OTHER PORTS.

The starting salary was $15,000 a year, an enormous increase from the $1,200 I had earned annually in the Peace Corps, and even the fact that I would have to teach grades six through eleven each day did not dampen my excitement to be able to remain in China and continue learning Chinese. On the first day of school I saw Frances, tanned from a summer hiking alone, when she arrived late to a staff meeting with a lilting apology and self-effacing laugh.

Her given name was Peony, and she hated it as much as I hated the Chinese name a teacher had assigned to me: Heroic Eastern Plumblossom. "That sounds like a girl's name," she said, a common response that always made me feel sorry for that girl, wherever she may be. "I prefer my English name, Frances," she said. "Or my nickname, Guazi." Sunflower Seed. That fit her long, slender face.

We began hanging out after school, cautiously, walking our students home, biking to Wudaokao to rifle through boxes of VCDs and remaindered cassette tapes, and playing basketball at the Language and Culture Institute's outdoor court. The first time, she out-hustled me with such spirit that it broke my heart to tell her she had to dribble. We started eating together—cautiously, again: first a McDonald's milkshake, then Korean pancakes, and finally sitting outside on one of Beijing's perfect clear autumn nights around a steaming brazier, using chopsticks to dunk lamb slices, tofu, and mustard greens in boiling water and washing the cooked food down with big bottles of Yanjing beer that chilled in an ice pail beside the table. This was 1997 B.C. (Before Cars), when Beijing life still thrived in the *hutong* and under tree-canopied sidewalks in comparably fresh air. For the first time in more than two years in China I didn't feel, no matter what our waitress had just called me, like a *laowai*, a foreigner. I didn't feel like the Other. Perhaps it was because I didn't see Frances that way. I saw many things, not least of all her beauty. Everyone saw that; heads turned to follow her curves as she passed. To me, she was quick, smart and funny—and unlike anyone I had met before, in or out of China. At her insistence, we split the dinner check. Then we said good night.

When I got home, my apartment felt unusually empty.

Frances told her roommate she had made a new friend.

Neither of us could sleep.

I was twenty-five, she was twenty. Eventually, I wanted to return to the States for graduate school. She had no interest in leaving China. We knew how it would end. But then it didn't: we spent winter nights skating at Tsinghua University's pond and spring weekends hiking the Great Wall. Peace Corps friends sent an invitation to their summer wedding in Wisconsin, and I asked Frances to go.

"I have to apply for a passport in my hometown," she said. "If I'm going to America for the first time with you, then you have to come to the Northeast for the first time with me. I want you to meet my parents."

They waited on the platform as our overnight train pulled into Liaoyuan, a small (by Chinese standards) Northeastern city of one million people. They were my first impression of Manchuria, and I liked them immediately. Frances greeted them with a "*Ma! Ba!*" and laughter. No hugs or kisses, not in public. Her father, a tall and rugged former medic in the People's

Liberation Army, pumped my hand and, unlike many Chinese on meeting a stranger, looked directly into my eyes. Her mother was a short, round bundle of welcome. She handed me a large sack of hazelnuts. "You're hungry! These are from our city!" She couldn't stop smiling.

"Yes, I'm very hungry," I lied, popping a few in my mouth. "They're delicious!"

"Oh! You like them? I'll buy you another bag! Wait here!"

Frances grabbed her arm as she bolted, saying the bag of nuts would last me a month. The four of us walked away from the station. The parents made small talk with their daughter. I wasn't the center of attention, and it felt wonderful. They didn't compliment my Chinese; they didn't ask if I could use chopsticks or how much money I made. They called me not Heroic Eastern Plumblossom but my preferred Chinese name, the transliteration of Meyer—*mai'er*—a feudal-era term that meant "a son sold in the marketplace." Her father thought it fit; here I was, thousands of miles from home, being picked up by my new family. "Sold Son! Call me Ba," he said, smacking my shoulder. Dad.

As in many Chinese families, Dad did the cooking, and he enjoyed going to the market each day, which he described as a real-life opera, awash in color and sound. I followed at his side, watching him sniff melons, poke at slabs of pork, and bargain fiercely. "In this town, people argue over pennies," he said. Despite its location on the rolling hills of a river bend, Liaoyuan looked bleak. The skyline showed a cooling tower and smokestacks surrounded by concrete walk-up apartment buildings with peeling-paint façades. Along the pitted streets, workers laid off from busted state-owned factories squatted, selling watermelon seeds and peanuts.

A century prior, during China's final dynasty, Liaoyuan ("Origin of the Liao River") had been part of the imperial hunting grounds named the Flourishing Capital Paddock, an area enclosed and offset by a fence called the Willow Palisade. Those romantic names were long forgotten. Beginning in 1931, during the Japanese occupation of Manchuria, Liaoyuan was the region's second-largest coal producer. Its only tourist "attraction" came from that era: a mass grave of forced laborers dubbed the Ten-Thousand-Person Pit that showed visitors rows of exhumed skeletons stretched on the soil around an open gash of earth. The coal seams had been stripped and the mines closed. Near the exhibit's exit, a propaganda billboard promised: LIAOYUAN TOMORROW WILL BE EVEN BETTER. It wasn't wholly empty talk: the town was transitioning to light manufacturing—and on its way to becoming one of China's leading sock producers and a maker of the MacBook computer's aluminum frame—but in 1998, it looked exhausted. No wonder Frances had graduated high school early and moved to Beijing to study English, then accepted a job at the international school.

Over dinner she recounted her day in various offices, filling out and photocopying passport forms. Around the table with us were her mother, grandmother, two cousins, and a just-arrived uncle and aunt. "He's really my uncle," Frances whispered. "She's not really my aunt but my middle school English teacher who wants to meet you." The culture shock I felt wasn't because of China: my parents had six marriages between them (no longer to each other), and a large family meal like this felt more exotic than the fried silkworms set on the table as an appetizer.

Dad worked the kitchen alone. The apartment didn't have running water or an oven, only an electric rice cooker and a single gas burner. With a cigarette clenched in his teeth and an apron around his waist, he produced braised stuffed eggplant, sweet-and-sour pork, battered lotus root, pockmarked tofu, flash-fried green beans, corn with pine nuts, and fish dumpling soup.

The English teacher raised a toast, eking out a "How do you do? Welcome you!" before knocking back 140-proof sorghum liquor. Two little-girl cousins climbed on my back, and Uncle commented on my surprising ability to use chopsticks. Dad toasted to me, then to his daughter, then to our relationship, and then . . . well, somewhere between my rendition of Fats Waller's "Everybody Loves My Baby" and Dad's performance from the People's Liberation Army songbook, Frances flashed a smile that said I was home.

Dusk faded to night. Auntie English spilled wine in her lap. One of the kid cousins fell asleep at the table. Frances's grandmother began talking about the village north of there, where she raised "Little Peony" as a girl. The village name stuck in my mind: Wasteland. What was it like to live in a place called Wasteland? "It's a very good environment," her grandmother said. For two years as a Peace Corps volunteer, I had heard Chinese sweepingly define the countryside as *luohou*—backward. "It's a better place to live than a city," her grandmother continued. "We grow rice—the best rice in China. One crop a year, when the black earth thaws after the long cold winter."

Rice tasted like rice to me, but not to her grandmother. She smacked her lips and ran her liver-spotted hands down sallow cheeks. "I can always smell and taste it. The rice from our farm is the best. I keep a sack of it here in town, even. It's the only rice I like to eat."

"I'd like to visit the village."

Frances flashed me a look that said: *Slow down.*

Her grandmother said that the village used to call her Princess.

"I'm not a princess," Frances protested.

Her grandmother swatted her head. "I say you are."

At dawn I woke heavy-headed on the apartment's wooden sofa. At Liaoyuan's train station, Frances's mother presented a pair of red wool socks she'd stayed up after dinner to knit. "I measured your foot when you were sleeping," she revealed with a sneaky grin. Dad shook my hand with a firm grip, not the usual Chinese kind, where the person cupped my palm as if it were bleeding.

"Keep calm at the American embassy when you apply for your visa," Frances's mom lectured her. "Don't lose your bad Northeastern temper." The dozen assembled relatives nodded on the platform as the conductor called for us to board the olive-green carriage. Then her mother addressed us. "Learn from each other. Help each other. You're happy together!"

Frances wept as the train pulled out. She missed them already. Her mother's head bobbed outside the window, reminding us, "You're happy together! Happy together!" The word trailed away as the train gathered speed.

For an entire summer in America, Frances subsisted on "first ones."

It was a land of decisions. At a restaurant: Eating in or taking out? Booth or table? Black or room for cream? She told the waitress she wanted a chicken burger. Roasted or barbecued? *The first one.* Whole wheat, sourdough, or French roll? *Yes.* Those are breads, which one would you like for the bun? *The first one.* And what would you like on it? *Less choices.*

After sorting out the toppings came the matter of sauce, then the option of fries, chips, or potato salad. Each carried with them several sub-choices that concerned salt content, oil variety, and entry into the Homestyle-versus-Regular debating arena. The undercard for this bout featured Pickle versus Coleslaw.

The waitress just kept coming at her. "And what would you like to drink? We have—"

"The first one."

At this point I opened the newspaper to the two pages filled with movie ads. "Let's go see a movie. You choose."

"The first one," she said.

In the car, stations crowded the radio dial: you couldn't move the tuner a bit without picking up another signal. It was just as bad as the television. Didn't Americans ever have a moment of peace and quiet? And why did everything take place indoors? Where were all the old people? She hadn't seen any grandfathers pushing infants in strollers or squatting on the curb, playing chess. No one ballroom danced on sidewalks at night or seemed to knit.

At the Mall of America, walking around the Camp Snoopy amusement park, she said: "Kids here are so lucky. When I was a kid, my toy was a pair of plastic shoes. Do they know how fortunate they are?" We studied the closest specimens, sentenced to adolescence. The boys moped past in oversize pants, too loose to cover their underwear. Metal punctured the sullen girls' noses, cheeks, and lips. They looked like they'd been condemned to Labor Camp Snoopy.

"Maybe kids in America aren't so lucky," she conceded. "There are a lot of things here to want. When I was a kid I never wanted money, because after I had a bike, there wasn't much else to buy. Movies and ice cream cost pennies."

Before the first pitch at the St. Paul Saints game, the crowd stood for the national anthem. I removed my hat. People around us sang along.

"It's very militaristic," she whispered.

The crowd drank Summit beer and munched hot dogs. Nuns gave backrubs for charity. T-shirts boomed from a cannon into the stands. A train rolled past the outfield fence. Fireworks went off after the game. It was a perfect Minnesota summer night. Frances had no idea what had transpired on the field, but even the mosquito bites dotting her exposed skin couldn't spoil her good time.

The wedding had been built up so much, months of me talking about it, expressing excitement for Frances to meet my friends, that when she arrived at the hotel, anxiety overtook her and she didn't want to leave the room. It wasn't the bitter brewery air or the way people gave us directions to avoid parts of Milwaukee dubbed "rough," "tough," and "scary"; neighborhoods in Beijing were never called that. Rather, it was the wedding itself, in particular the assembled guests. They were all strangers to her. How should she act? Would they think of her as "Chinese" and expect a certain Chinese-ness?

"I know," I said. "I hate being in these situations in China, when I only know one person in the room and they all know I am the American Guest."

"It's not the same," she argued, and she was right. In China, being the American Guest was an unearned prestige: you were temporary royalty, a grinning minor duke from a faraway land. But many of the wedding guests were Peace Corps volunteers from China. Another spoke fluent Mandarin from his studies of ancient literature at Yale.

"He'll know more about *Journey to the West* than I will and ask questions, then wonder why I'm not an expert in it," she fretted. "That was just my favorite childhood televison show, not something to analyze. The Peace Corps people will see me like their college students, not an adult. I want to go back to Beijing."

"Is this because of lunch?"

A customer in a downtown Milwaukee diner had asked if she was from China. She nodded with a smile. An opening like this usually meant the person had visited the country.

This man said: "I hope one day soon you'll be free."

Her face flashed *What?*

"Have you ever been to China?" Frances fixed her eyes on his.

"No, but I've read about it."

"Things aren't that simple. I've read about America, too."

I heard a gurgle in her voice, a more urgent tone. It was the same emotion-faster-than-words sound that had overtaken me in China when I grew weary of defending my identity.

After lunch came the wedding rehearsal. Frances saw everyone hugging, so when newcomers introduced themselves, she opened her arms to their surprised faces. Someone teased her. It stung. Back in the room, she failed to hold back tears when describing how strange it felt to be different for the first time. "So this," she said, "is why people stay home."

We drove west, camping in the Badlands, at Mount Rushmore, and in the Black Hills, then we moved across Montana, over the Beartooth Pass into Yellowstone. This was the America for her: open space, national parks, and no one looking at us twice. In Rock Springs, Wyoming, we read a plaque commemorating the 1885 massacre of twenty-eight migrant Chinese laborers killed after refusing to join their white coworkers on strike. A mob burned the Chinese workers' huts, blocked all escape routes, and fired into the panicked crowd. The survivors fled Rock Springs on foot, west along the railroad. Train conductors brought them to safety at Green River.

In a gas station Yellow Pages, I looked up "Restaurants, Chinese." Rock Springs, population 19,000, had one. Green River, population 12,000 had two. Frances chose Green River.

The waiter at China King Buffet was surprised to see her. "I'm from the Northeast," she said by way of introduction. He was from the south. Chinese people often begin a conversation with strangers this way; their Chineseness a given, the connection found by one's geographic region, or shared dialect. The waiter lobbed a *laowai* at me. Even six thousand miles away from Beijing, in my own country, I was the foreigner still. "You're the *laowai* now," I laughed. The waiter laughed, too, but his laugh said I was wrong.

After our meal, I cracked open fortune cookies, pulling out the slips to read aloud: "What's vice today may be virtue tomorrow."

"Morality is for weaklings," Frances corrected. "Do whatever it takes to get ahead."

"It is better to have a hen tomorrow than an egg today."

"Eat your eggs now as they may never hatch."

"Everything will now come your way."

"The key to happiness is to expect little from life."

"You should be able to undertake anything."

"If you never try, you will never fail."

"Your love life will be happy and harmonious."

Frances laughed, and said: "Keep one eye closed and things only look half bad."

In Santa Cruz, California, we spent the trip's final days at the beach with my grandmother, who reminded Frances of her own. For the two of them, it was love at first sight. They cooked and gardened, and my grandmother showed Frances her work from her days as a draftsman, including the design of her home. As a teenager, she had had a chance to study piano in Paris, but her father, a French immigrant with his own bakery, forbade her to go, saying, "No girl of mine is running around Paris. You'll stay and keep the books."

"He sounds Chinese," Frances said.

In San Francisco we boarded a bus for Golden Gate Park. Unlike in China, Americans didn't sing on buses. They sat guarded, or catatonic. A sign over the driver warned: Information Gladly Given but Safety Requires Avoiding Unnecessary Conversation. But soon these signs would appear on Chinese buses, too.

On Ocean Beach we watched container ships fade toward the horizon. This was the end of our road, the end of America. China, and another year of teaching—and questions about our future together—waited on the other side.

I asked: "I wonder where we'll be a year from now?"

"Maybe here."

My heart flared; she'd said it. "I hope so."

"Or maybe there." She narrowed her eyes at the wind, watching the Pacific. "But hopefully together."

Books about China can indulge an emperor's irredentist impulse to redraw a map—*This* is *China*—but our story, like Manchuria's itself, is one of blurring borders, of comings and goings, like the waves that advanced and retreated before us on Ocean Beach. I learned to read Chinese at Tsinghua

University; Frances graduated from Berkeley's law school. I wrote a book about Beijing; she worked as an attorney in Manhattan. We have long been happily married, if occasionally apart for work.

In our early years together, through graduate school and entry-level jobs and no savings, we jokingly described any unsettled, purgatorial situation as being mired "in Manchuria." It was a state that existed only in the mind, a station between what had been and what came next. *I feel like I'm in Manchuria.* Now, after moving to Wasteland, where Frances had been raised, I was actually there. But she was not about to ditch her career—let alone a good job at a firm in Hong Kong—to follow me around the Northeast, instead joining me in the village and on side trips when she could.

Thirteen years had passed since her first visit to my American home; in a sort of connubial quid pro quo I would explore where she came from. Shadowing the journey was the fear that our individual ambitions could be marking an irreversible route away from what we long wanted but also long delayed: parenthood. I was thirty-nine; she was thirty-four, and the sound of a ticking clock scored our daily long-distance conversations on Skype.

To the young man and woman sitting on the wind-blown edge of San Francisco in 1998, all of this would have sounded absurd. *What's Skype?* But when asked why I moved to Manchuria, my thoughts shift from China's edge to America's, and the woman who kindled my attraction to the Northeast. The starting point is there, at that moment of two people falling in love: looking to the horizon, leaning against one another, and holding on tight.

CHAPTER 3

LINEAGES

A SIDE FROM PASSING the bar exam, I have never been as happy as when I lived here," Frances said atop San Jiu's *kang*. "We had nothing, but didn't know it, so didn't care. We were a family."

She had made the trip north to help me find a house to rent in Wasteland. We peeled off our winter wear as San Jiu stoked the bed's brazier with dried rice stalks from the past autumn's harvest. Across the village, bushy piles of the straw rose above the single-story homes they heated.

As Frances talked, I pictured a little girl in a hand-sewn white cotton dress running through the yard as chickens scatter. "Hello, chickens!" she yells, laughing. "Hello, pigs!" She doesn't know any place beyond Wasteland, outside this yard, away from this house.

Looking back, Frances felt she was here by accident. Not San Jiu's house, where she had lived as a child—when it had an earthen floor, mud walls, and thatched straw roof—but *here* here, as in alive. In 1962 her mother woke in this home. She had tested into the region's best teachers college, but on registration day was locked inside a room by her own mother, who claimed that teaching was too difficult a job for a woman to undertake. This, after a decade of Communist Party sloganeering to abolish traditional, conservative thought. Frances's mother sat alone on the *kang*, seething. She was not one to wail; like most women of her generation, who had made the transition between old and new China, she emanated forbearance. Soon she found work outside Wasteland, clerking at a post office.

Frances's father came from far away, from the southwest province of Sichuan, and a small, steamy Yangtze River port named Yibin. He enlisted in the People's Liberation Army at age sixteen. It trained him as a "barefoot doctor," the legion of medics who delivered basic care and inoculations in the Chinese countryside, and shipped him to Manchuria. *The great northern wasteland,* he thought, concealing his disappointment. But then he was surprised at the land's beauty: prairies between foothills, forests leading to mountains. But he never got acclimated to the cold. Never. For the rest of his life, he considered it a mortal enemy. The Japanese, the Soviets? They were expelled. The cold returned every year. The army would not transfer him south, closer to home.

The mother's post office coworker knew someone who met a single soldier who was, she swore, the handsomest man she had ever seen. She arranged a blind date. At first sight, the mother thought to herself: *He is the handsomest man I have ever seen.* He had lean chiseled features, thick black hair, and a perpetual smirk that looked kind and bemused, not mean and challenging. But then, maybe men looked like this elsewhere. She had never been.

Their date consisted of walking in slow loops around the post office, chatting. They discovered that they had lost their dads when they were at the same age: eleven. They considered it a sign.

The father's transfer came through, but he was sent to an even more barren place: the steppes of Inner Mongolia. The two began exchanging letters. He got leave once a year. He asked if he could use his leave to come see her. In reply, she wrote, "I would not object."

The longer that couples were together, the shorter the telling of how they met. Here my mother-in-law always concludes: "And then we got married."

Their letters, the words they wrote while falling in love, were gone. Not seized by Red Guards during the Cultural Revolution; this is not that China story. The father was not an intellectual or "class enemy" but a soldier born to poor farmers who supported the Communists and who were largely exempt from that chaotic decade. No, the letters—written with steel nibs dipped in pots of India ink and scratched on tissue-thin sheets of onionskin and posted with stamps showing the trains and tractors of new industrial China—were just . . . gone. This frustrated only their children, who were told the past was something you reaped, not sowed.

The children's names mapped the early years of their marriage, however. The firstborn son was named for Shanxi province, where the father was stationed when he was born. The firstborn daughter, for a port in the northern coastal province of Shandong. The second-born son, for a town on the plains of Inner Mongolia. All of them arrived nine months after the father's annual leave. He was not there for their births, but then, as he said, roosters didn't watch chickens lay eggs.

Then he was offered a post in Changchun, Jilin's provincial capital, at a time when the divide between rural and urban living was even starker than it is today. A city *hukou*—the household registration file— meant better access to housing, education, transportation, and even food. The family knew it should leave the countryside when it could. Changchun was a key metropolis, a strategic Northeastern railway junc- tion, the seat of China's automotive and movie industry, and home to several universities, including the one the mother had been barred from attending.

There was a problem, however: the government preferred that farm families remained in the countryside, and so the mother's household regis- tration could not be transferred to Changchun. Again she was denied a move there. An army clerk suggested the family transfer to a second-tier city 140 miles southwest of Wasteland, named Liaoyuan. Neither mother nor father had been, but it was a city, so they went, moving into a walk-up apartment with steam radiators and indoor plumbing. Their parents had never lived in such modernity.

The mother read news and announcements over a factory's public address system, becoming a sort of teacher after all. The father worked in public health. In 1976 a nationwide campaign had begun urging urban residents— after years of being told to have multiple children—to limit their offspring to two, as China's population had doubled to 900 million since 1949, when the Communists had taken power.

Eight years after their last child arrived, the mother announced: *I'm pregnant.*

But they couldn't have another child—not with the new rule, not with his job. They scheduled an abortion for July 1976.

That month, the Tangshan Earthquake, measuring 7.8 on the Richter scale, hit northern China, killing 250,000 people. Fearing aftershocks, people in cities across the region moved out of apartment blocks and camped in makeshift tents. When city life resumed, and the mother returned home, it was too late to terminate the pregnancy. Secretly, she was relieved.

The mother would deliver the baby but agreed to give it up for adoption. She carefully screened applicants before settling on a young woman who was unable to conceive. But after the baby entered the world silent, swift, and beautiful, she could not bear to give her away. On her back in the hospital bed, she refused to let go. She named the girl Peony and declared that she would be hers forever. The father called the child Little Extra. They decided her maternal grandparents would raise her, out in Wasteland where their other kids had gone to school before moving to town.

In a Chinese family, grandparents are more than an accoutrement to be visited and nodded over on major holidays. Of course they said yes, they would take Little Extra. Though they didn't call her that. They called her Princess.

Princess rode on her grandfather's back to the paddy every summer morning. The villagers coddled and spoiled her and called her Princess, too. She was the only infant around Wasteland; the other farmers' grandkids were already old enough to write Chinese characters. Like her grandmother, they knitted clothes for her, cooked her favorite dishes, and told her stories, sitting outside in the shade of a Manchurian ash tree, or atop the *kang*. There were a few picture books inside the house—telling the names of fruit and vegetables and animals—but she didn't need books to teach her those; she saw them every day. There was no television—no one could afford one—or a mirror. Everybody told Princess she was special and beautiful, and she believed it. Her grandfather often set her in the hay next to the pigs. She climbed on and talked to them, and they responded. They told her she was a Princess. She told them they were pigs. It was a compliment.

In spring, her grandmother taught her folk songs while planting rice. Princess followed her voice through the upbeat tunes. Grandmother sang gently: *"Little sparrow, your clothes are so colorful! Why do you come here every spring?"*

"Because your spring is beautiful!" answered Little Sparrow, in perfect harmony with the world.

*

"I didn't want to leave," Frances said at San Jiu's house. "But I didn't have a choice. Because our family had been transferred to Liaoyuan, I had to enroll in school there. Now you can drive there in two hours, but back then it was a full day's journey by bus and train from Wasteland."

They sang songs in cities, too. The first one she learned at school was "Socialism Is Good." Everyone nodded their heads when they shouted it. The bouncing beat was impossible to resist.

Socialism is good!
Socialism is good!
Downplay American imperialism!
Downplay American imperialism!
Socialism is good!

As a child in Wasteland, she fell from a cottonwood tree and broke her arm. The nearest doctor was in Jilin city, twenty miles away. Her grandmother bundled her on a mule cart, which clopped through the night. The arm healed crookedly, though unnoticeably. Yet the accident had been marked in Frances's permanent record. City teachers took frowning note, but the asymmetry spared her from joining the school's rhythmic gymnastics squad or dance troupe. She never had to twirl a red ribbon to a screeching soundtrack or wave handkerchiefs for the Rice Planting Dance. She didn't even watch the performances. She knew that nobody planted rice like that. First of all, no one smiled like those dancers. Standing bent at the waist in cold, calf-deep water was hard work.

In middle school, teachers began calling her intelligent, even though she fell asleep during the class named Building Socialism. She excelled in Chinese and English. Her early-1990s textbook required memorizing such useful dialogue as:

A: Where is the Red Lobster restaurant located?
B: May I suggest our specialty: lamb chops garnished with spring peas and mashed potatoes?
A: Lobster with mayonnaise sounds inviting.
B: Permit me to pour you a glass of champagne. It's on the house.

In Chinese class, she read classic novels in which the female characters radiated beauty. They were described as looking like swallows in the branches of willow trees, with bones of jade under skin as pure as ice. They were so lovely that fish would sink and wild geese would fall out of the sky at the sight of them. But Frances had grown up on the farm. Her skin was tanned like a peasant's, not light like a city person's. She was tall. Her hair was as light-colored and brittle as the straw she shared with pigs as a child. She couldn't understand why, to be considered beautiful, a Chinese woman had to look like a foreigner. She smiled and laughed like a man, refusing to cover her mouth with her hand. She wouldn't stand like a girl, either, with arms passively at her sides. In photographs she cocked them on her hips, sharp elbows akimbo, shaping herself into a kite, waiting to fly high and far away.

"As a girl, I hated mirrors," Frances remembered. "Mirrors were all over the place in the city. At home, in the department store, at the entrance of every school." She had longed for the countryside, where her only reflection was in her grandmother's smiling eyes.

Even now, Frances remained the baby of the village. To help me find a house to rent, she had arrived on a January morning on a public minibus whose windows had frosted over from passengers' breaths, veiling the interior like tulle. Though Frances was padded in down and swaddled in a scarf and hat, an elderly passenger did a double take at her face before yelling her name in joy. On Wasteland's lanes, even after a twenty-year absence, the scene was repeated. There was no hugging, only a familiar conversation, like she had just returned from running an errand in town. Sixty-six-year-old San Jiu half skipped out his front door, calling her name.

A hot meal waited in a room filled with relatives eager to fuss. Frances lounged on the *kang* cracking sunflower seeds with them, talking about her grandmother's passing, slurping jasmine tea, and filling the room with gasps of Northeastern dialect such as *Aiya wo'de maya* (*Oh, my mother!*) and *En'e* (*All right*). The aunties warned her that she should become pregnant soon. "Mixed-blood" (*hun xue'r*) children are beautiful, they said. But be sure to eat lots of apples, a woman warned, otherwise the baby's skin would be "too yellow."

Frances rolled her eyes and shot me a grin. Her BlackBerry whirred with updates of a $300 million leveraged buyout she was working on, but she kept the device in her pocket. Lawyers had little clout in China, so no one asked her about her job. Instead her family surrounded Frances on the *kang*, demanding a child. As San Jiu and I watched the evening news in another room, I heard more laughter, more *Aiya wo'de mayas*.

We were used to complete strangers asking us about our relationship; over thirteen years, we knew these questions well enough to see them forming above a person's head, like comic strip thought bubbles. In Chinese, they read: *Married a foreigner, huh? What country? That's a good passport to have. But you couldn't find a Chinese man? Well, your children will be beautiful. Mixed-blood children are always beautiful. And smart. Beautiful and smart. But hopefully the children will look more like you.*

This silent conversation was preferable to the one Western men volunteered to me. *You know what's it's like,* it began. But I didn't. And I didn't want to know—not about enduring public tantrums or wearing matching couples' T-shirts or buying in-laws new appliances or how the 1990 Gérard Depardieu film *Green Card* explained everything. *Not our story, pal. Go eat some apples.*

With family, however, came different, well-meaning, but also loaded questions. About Frances becoming a "city girl." About how her American education had changed her thoughts. About where we would raise our child—the one we should be creating right this instant instead of idly chatting. And why didn't we move back here? The village could raise the child! What did she mean, she had to return to Hong Kong and her career? What about becoming a mother, as they had? Everything was out of context, because there was no context.

After sundown and the last good nights, Frances, looking dazed, told me, "It's amazing how coming home transforms you into a child again. I hate it. But it's also sweet." Nowadays Chinese were so focused on the future, on what lay ahead, she said. "It's nice to be able to return and see where you came from while it's still there."

The next morning we leaned into the wind and walked to see Wasteland's only vacant house. Although February brought the solar term named the Beginning of Spring, which coincided with the lunar New Year, the season felt far away.

Still, I said, the landscape looked beautiful.

"When you live in the countryside, you don't actually see it," Frances said. "You see your little slice of it: your house, your paddy, your village. None of it makes you think, 'This is beautiful.'"

She studied Eastern Fortune Rice's billboard and the sign pointing to the hot spring resort. "People travel here to soak in the water?" she asked San Jiu, who replied, *Uh*. "When I was a kid," Frances continued, "we hated going near water: the paddies were filled with fish, frogs and leeches." The countryside was romantic only to people who didn't have to live there.

The view from the top floor of Wasteland's Agricultural Bank showed shops lining a five-hundred-yard ice-covered stretch of Red Flag Road: seed stores, dumpling and hot pot restaurants, a bathhouse, a clinic, a medicine store, a funerary shop, the police station and village government office, and some brave vendors standing in olive-green great coats before boxes of candied hawthorn berries, persimmons, and arm-length saury fish—now frozen solid—pulled that morning from the Songhua River. Near the train tracks was a small fertilizer factory, a government-run grain storehouse, a rusting sign advertising Bitter Melon Beer, and a painting, on a redbrick home, of a beaming farmer under a straw hat for something named Happy Soil.

To me, this all looked charming, a respite from crowded, polluted, honking Chinese city life. Everything one needed was right here; the Agricultural Bank ATM even accepted our American debit card and spit out Chinese yuan.

Frances said: "It's charming to us now, but when you live here, it's a step down from the city. You always look to get out, to leave, and to lift your family from here, too."

I expected the village to be emptying, but Wasteland was comparatively prosperous. "If people aren't growing rice, or if they signed their crop over to Eastern Fortune, they keep their rent-free houses and commute to work in Jilin city," San Jiu said. "Or they have agreed to move to the company's new apartments, so their home will soon be razed."

Legally, Frances and I were not permitted to buy a home, since only those classified as rural residents could do so. This protected the countryside from real estate speculation, but it also kept farmers tied to their village, since they could not sell their houses and move elsewhere. But renting out a home, and even one's farmland, had recently been allowed.

One morning, as I walked alone, a Toyota Land Cruiser slowed beside me on Red Flag Road. The driver, whom I had never seen before, said, "Hey, teacher, I hear you're looking for a house."

He was the "village chief," an administrative post similar to mayor. Wasteland's leader was not a wizened farmer in a blue serge Mao suit but a thin man in his twenties who wore khakis and a puffy North Face jacket. He drove down a newly laid dirt road that cut across the paddies to a cluster of one-story cement houses. From a distance they looked like bunkers.

"You can rent one of these," he said, opening a garage door. "Eastern Fortune Rice built it as a model home. Farmers who gave up their old house could move here. But few people agreed. Now the company's building apartments instead."

"Will these newer houses be torn down?"

"Maybe," he said. It meant *Of course.*

His voice echoed in the concrete shell. It was more of a brutalist sculpture than a dwelling. Instead of brick, the *kang* was unpainted cement. The floor, wall, and ceiling were gray and unfinished, too.

"It needs flooring and all the other decor," the village chief said. "It needs furniture and probably some new window panes. And the toilet needs fixing, but it's indoor and flushes, and if you install a water heater you can shower. The kitchen needs propane tanks, and a range, and these lights don't work, so you have to fix those. *Uh,*" he said, pulling a door loose from its frame. "That needs repairing, too."

Other than that, the house was perfect.

I found myself in the situation I handled worst in China: needing to recuse myself from a suggestion without making the other person lose face. When that person was an authority figure, the stakes grew higher. I didn't want to make trouble for my family, or myself. You had to choose words carefully in the countryside, where resentments steeped like tealeaves. I panicked, and told the village chief the truth.

"I want to rent a common home, like most farmers live in. And this place needs a lot of work; I don't want to spend money repairing someone else's house, especially one that might be razed."

"That's reasonable," the village chief replied.

Then I did something even stupider. I asked whose house it was.

San Jiu called me a moron. "You should have known that he would take you to a house he owned," he said. "He's a good businessman. He also has ties to Eastern Fortune Rice. He married the sister of one of its founders. She teaches English at the elementary school." I made a mental note to visit her classroom and lead a lesson, a step toward squaring things with the chief.

San Jiu had heard of one other vacancy in the village, a home behind the police station. Without knocking, he pulled back the tall sheet-tin gate and stepped into a courtyard illuminated by hundreds of candles. They surrounded dozens of gold-painted statues of the Buddha.

"The owner's husband left her, so she became a Buddhist nun," San Jiu explained. "She's going to a convent for a while. She said you're welcome to stay here, but you have to keep the candles lit. The rent is low because of that." If I would be the village altar boy, the nun would charge the equivalent of $20 a month. An apartment half the size in Jilin city rented for ten times that amount.

"But you want to travel . . ." Frances cautioned.

"Who will know if the candles blow out?"

"Everyone will know," San Jiu said. In the village, everyone knew everything. Gossip, the original social network, was wireless, and nearly as instantaneous.

In the 1947 book *From the Soil*, a famous Chinese sociologist remembered growing up on a farm and being assigned to write a diary at school. He labored to log one entry, describing waking up, walking to class, playing at recess, walking home, doing homework, eating, and going to bed. For each successive entry he wrote, "The same as above." Even as a child he felt that countryside life made a diary, and even memory, superfluous. "The fall of the Qin dynasty, the rise of the Han dynasty—what difference does it make? People in rural society do not fear forgetfulness. People in cities need to keep address books and photo identification, but in the countryside all is known."

Historically, the inability to freely move in search of work, in addition to a village's geographic isolation, fostered a dependence on cooperation, of intimate relations with neighbors. The natural extension of this was a distrust of outsiders. Most foreigners who had visited China experienced this when a stranger shouted *Laowai!* at them. It could feel like getting soaked by a water balloon.

But Chinese could feel it, too. On the street, Frances noticed that strangers didn't exhibit a curiosity about our presence in Wasteland but rather a question mark: *Do we know those two?* Hence the usual greeting: *Whose family are you?* and the visible relief in the questioners' faces when they heard a surname they knew. That's where we fit into the puzzle. We were strangers no more.

I wanted to know where Wasteland's name came from and when the village began. The newsstand sold magazines whose covers showed Kobe Bryant and Japanese manga, but nothing on local history. This was not unusual: even Jilin city's many bookstores and its new library stocked only ideological retellings of Feudal Jilin, of Occupied Jilin, of Liberated Jilin. I broadened my search for a contemporary account of the Northeast, but that, too, yielded no results.

Beyond politics, there were other reasons such narratives were uncommon. Generations of writers born in the single-child-policy years needed to find a paying job to support their parents, rather than gamble on immersing themselves in a place, researching a book that may not even get published. Indeed, the best "memoir" I have read of a Chinese farm is a thick academic text that explains economic policy changes in the author's central China hometown. In the book, he notes that since the 1980s most Chinese villages recycled or used their archives for cooking fuel over the years, as they were seen as trivial and unworthy of preserving. (The author is now a Chinese history professor at the University of Texas.)

At Wasteland's small government office at Red Flag Road's main intersection, the friendly clerk lifted her eyeglasses to stare at a ledger. She informed me that this area had a population of 1,459. "There are 717 females and 742 men." By grade level, she broke down the 450 children attending the three schools: two elementary, and one middle. When I asked to see the town's gazetteer, which even Beijing's smallest neighborhoods have, detailing local history and color, the woman said that there wasn't one. "Look at the big stone outside," she suggested. "That has the information."

Squatting low aside Red Flag Road, I read, on the back of the slab carved with Wasteland's name: *In 1956, it became a village.*

"I love this American teacher very much. He is the tallest man which I have already seen. I think his beard is too sex. And his hair is really cool. But I love his Chinese name best. Heroic Eastern Plumblossom doesn't sound like a girl's name at all. If I saw this name first, I'll believe that will be a really cool man. I must say 'thank you' to you, Ms. Guan. Thanks for you give us a chance to speak with person who comes from America. Yours, Xue Chang."

I read the letter via Skype to Frances, who had returned to work in Hong Kong. She laughed and said, "In the States, this could be submitted as evidence at your trial."

But I was innocent. Word went out that a native English speaker and teacher had landed, and it didn't take long for my cell phone to buzz with a text from a teacher named Ms. Guan, inviting me to begin regular lessons at Wasteland's Number 22 Middle School. In Beijing, I had volunteered at an elementary school, finding it a natural entry into neighborhood life. In a small town, your work is your identity, the role you play on the community stage. To me it made perfect sense, but San Jiu thought only morons worked for free. This echoed the response I used to get as a Peace Corps volunteer when Chinese wondered what sort of a nation sent its young people abroad to work with strangers instead of staying home and providing for their own families.

I arrived at the school's electric accordion gate—a safety measure implemented nationwide after a spate of knife attacks on students elsewhere in China—and was let inside once Ms. Guan, a forty-two-year-old Wasteland native, vouched for me with the security guard, who sat inside the toasty gatehouse. "I know whose family you belong to," he said. "I heard you were wandering around."

Ms. Guan led me to a classroom packed with thirteen-year-olds and teachers. On the podium, the textbook was open to the day's lesson, "Making an Introduction":

Lucy: Hi, who are you?
Robot: Hi, I'm a robot. Glad to meet you.
Lucy: Glad to meet you, too. Let's be friends.
Robot: All right.
Lucy: I can sing. Can you?
Robot: Yes, I can. It's easy. I can see you. And I can work, too.
Lucy: That's fine.

Reciting where the Red Lobster restaurant was located seemed more useful. My robot voice elicited no laughs, instead confusing the class. *Is this what native English sounded like?* Wishing I had a different text, or at least a better robot voice, I put the kids in groups to answer discussion questions about what the lesson ominously described as "the coming control of cyberculture." Could the teens imagine a day when robots would be their singing, working friends? They could. "Well," I asked, going off book, "what if the robots turned evil? What would you do then?"

This led to a discussion of Optimus Prime's character in the movie *Transformers,* followed by pleas to end the lesson early so the male students could take me on in basketball. The court—dwarfed by the largest school-yard I had ever seen—was covered in snow, stomped to an even, Wimbledon-quality sheen. There was one ball, and fourteen kids, and soon the game more resembled a rugby scrum. The kids quickly tossed off their hats and gloves, unzipped their coats, and ran around until steam rose from their sweat-soaked heads. A group of girls in bright pink down coats that reached their calves stood to the side, tethered together with shared MP3 earbuds. They belted out Lady Gaga songs.

Frances's mother had attended Number 22 Middle School, as did Frances's sister and both brothers. The narrow single-story building where they studied was now the cafeteria and Ping-Pong room, bordered by a ten-foot-high mound of coal whose fuel made the classrooms hot enough for teachers to open the windows. White curtains swayed slowly along the classroom wall, reflecting bright sunlight.

Since Wasteland had been folded into Jilin city's administrative bound-ary, the school received faculty assigned from downtown, who commuted by bus an hour each way; they could not find a vacant house to rent, either. The school also received funds to expand. The old middle school building faced a newly built three-story elementary school. Their interiors matched the color scheme I had seen across China: seasick green to waist height, and tofu white to the ceiling.

A notice board asked: "What is modern pedagogy?" Ten framed posters down the hall's both sides showed lessons from *The Analects* of Confucius, which led to a doorway marked PARTY OFFICE. Where once it banned the Master's teachings as heterodoxy, now the government invoked them as a moral guide.

But unlike every other school in China I had visited over the previous fifteen years, no political slogans had been painted or hung on the walls. No STUDY DILIGENTLY AND IMPROVE EVERY DAY, or SEEK TRUTH FROM FACTS, or DEVELOPMENT IS THE CORRECT PRINCIPLE, or BUILD SOCIALISM WITH CHINESE CHARACTERISTICS, or STUDY THE "THREE REPRESENTS," or IMPLEMENT AN OVERALL WELL-OFF SOCIETY, or its sequel, BUILD A HARMONIOUS SOCIETY. Perhaps modern pedagogy is not hectoring children with dogma.

Instead, the walls of Number 22 Middle School had Confucius professing: "The way of the superior man is threefold, but I am not equal to it. Virtuous, he is free from anxieties; wise, he is free from perplexities; bold, he is free from fear."

After recess, in a classroom whose front blackboard was filled with the chalked content of "The Many Winter-Borne Illnesses," Ms. Guan got online and typed in a popular file-sharing site, clicking on *Night at the Museum*. Within seconds Ben Stiller's head filled the pull-down screen, then shots of Central Park West and the American Museum of Natural History. I could hear the C train screeching into the Eighty-first Street station, eight thousand miles away. As the better students scribbled down useful slang from Ben Stiller's subtitled dialogue—"Hang on one sec," "Yeah, I guess so"—I transcribed the Chinese characters for winter-borne illnesses, such as chilblains and hand, foot and mouth disease.

I sneezed, and Ms. Guan suggested eating raw garlic and drinking Coke boiled with a chunk of fresh ginger. The last time I had visited a Chinese doctor—for food poisoning—he had prescribed, on a pad, with characters written in physician scribble: "Watermelon and Pepsi." It had worked, or at least not done any harm. After school I followed Ms. Guan to the grocer for garlic and ginger.

We hit it off immediately. She talked unbidden, and nonstop. After my first day at Number 22 Middle School, I learned that though to me she looked Han Chinese, she was ethnically Manchu: her surname was a common one that meant "an official." She grew up in Wasteland, then left to study English at university in the northeast's coastal city of Dalian. She thought she had made it out of the countryside for good, but in Dalian a truck hit her as she walked across a street. The accident broke bones and her spirit; during a yearlong hospital stay, her longtime boyfriend left her, and she forgot most of her English. She was discharged to begin what she called "my life of independence."

Returning to Wasteland had felt like failure, but her mother had fallen ill, and she had no choice. That was nearly two decades ago. "I know everyone here," Ms. Guan said. It sounded like more of a lament than a boast. "My students have made it to the top universities, and some have even gone on to be teachers."

"This means you are good at your job," I said.

"No. This means I am old."

She was squat, with long black hair tinted orange at the ends, oversize pink glasses, and a kind face that could, in that teacherly way, flash into anger, which she directed at the garlic seller. "*De le ba!*" she snapped when the woman quoted the price. That was Northeast slang for "Bitch, please!"

Ms. Guan enjoyed speaking English. She talked in bursts, with the lilting cadence of a Dylan song. I finally realized Ms. Guan was speaking English as she did Mandarin Chinese, voicing its four tones: rising, falling, swooping and static. It was melodic and unique, and I hesitated to correct her.

Ms. Guan said: "But you are a very good chance to improve my spoken English."

"I need a house. Do you know of any for rent?"

"I will help you. I know everyone."

"But do you know of a house for rent?"

In a torrent of Chinese, she replied: "My father killed himself at our house. He was a teacher and threw himself down our well during the Cultural Revolution. That's why I came back here, to take care of my mother. She was alone. But she is also dead." Without even pausing long enough for me to ask a question, or say I was sorry, Ms. Guan gestured at a vendor's box and said, in English, "The price of fish isn't bad." She suggested I bring some to San Jiu: not only did she know him, she knew that he liked to eat this fish. "Here's a good one. This one, too."

Then she parried over the purchase in a rapid-fire blend of indignant dialect and teacher-perfect standard Chinese:

"*Ga ha ya?*" (Northeastern: "What's up?")

"*Duo shao qian?*" (Mandarin: "How much does it cost?")

"*Che sha ya!*" (Northeastern: "You're joking!")

"*De le ba!*"

The vendor's eyes flashed like a hockey player's before a fight. The women verbally circled one another. In the end, the vendor cut her price in half. Ms. Guan told me to pick my prize.

At the intersection of Red Flag Road, she boarded the bus to her home in Jilin city, saying good-bye before adding, "I know a house you can rent."

I stood in the fading light holding an orange plastic shopping bag filled with Coke, ginger, garlic, and six fish, as silver and stiff as broadswords. A day at school taught me 2,500-year-old Confucian sayings, how to dribble a basketball on snow, the words to Lady Gaga's "Poker Face," an underage student's opinion that my beard was too sex, the English-language learning merits of *Night at the Museum*, how to write chilblains—and cure a cold—in Chinese, and a little, then a lot, about a woman named Ms. Guan.

No one at school could tell me what I had hoped to learn when I set out to teach that day: Wasteland's history. I walked alone into the wind, past the stone that said: *In 1956, it became a village.*

CHAPTER 4

RUINS AND REMAINS

M Y WIFE'S FAMILY migrated to Manchuria in the 1930s, when her maternal grandfather left his ancestral village on the coast east of Beijing. Frances was not sure when, exactly, he went north, or why. San Jiu didn't know, either.

"There is no romance in my family," she said. "I'm sure he went north for work, and that's all. No soldiering, no joining the resistance against the Japanese, no chasing after his one true love."

"Who can say?" San Jiu added, sounding resigned, not defensive.

Her grandfather was buried here, but like all graves around Wasteland his was plowed under during the Cultural Revolution campaign to eliminate old customs, such as burying—not cremating—the deceased in the fields they tilled. The tradition lived on in other parts of China. When the snow melted, the mounded, unadorned earthen graves rose like pitchers' mounds amidst green fields latticed with trails that resembled base paths. In Wasteland the dead laid unmarked beneath the soil. Urban Chinese slandered farmers as being *tu*: soiled, or earthy. The dirt coated their clothing and burrowed into the cracks of their skin. In the end they went under and into the loam.

It had long been this way around Wasteland, where archaeologists had excavated clusters of burials, including areas of five hundred single bodies placed in stone cists dating back to the Paleolithic, Neolithic and Bronze ages. The large-scale cemeteries included foundations of solid houses, abundant farm tools, axes, fishhooks, spears and net weights and crops such as soybeans and millet. The finds evinced that the people who resided here five to seven thousand years ago lived a sedentary farming life, shattering the popular conception that the Northeast was long a vacant backwater before nomadic horsemen swept in to civilize it. Some archaeological sites even suggested habitation dating back two hundred thousand years.

Aboveground in Wasteland, we could not see any evidence of past settlements, of graves, of history that went back any further than the painted political slogans fading on redbrick walls under the bright Manchurian sun. History here was personal, and living, stretching back only as far as each resident could remember.

Scattered across the region's far north, center, and south, however, three sets of ruins explain Manchuria's deeper past.

On the train to Tonghua, a small city two hundred miles southeast of Wasteland, I sat beside a woman my age and her twenty-month-old son. The child, plump and happy, grabbed at my glasses, fingered my beard, and drooled as he pounded on the window at the passing cows. We sat in hard-seat class, on unpadded, straight-backed benches, and for stretches she asked me to hold him. The baby cooed; the voices of Wasteland's aunties rang in my ears: *You're not getting any younger.*

Tonghua was where Chinese brainwashers conditioned Sergeant Raymond Shaw for murder in the 1959 novel *The Manchurian Candidate*. His handlers brought Shaw to a room where "all of the furniture was made of blond wood in mutated, modern Scandinavian design . . . Each cubicle contained a cot, a chair, a closet, and a mirror for reassurance that the soul had not fled."

It was a perfect description of my Tonghua hotel room. The county seat, neither large nor small, was one of those places where it wasn't clear if the half-standing buildings, sprouting rebar, were being demolished or constructed.

Seventy miles further southeast down the tracks, in the border town of Ji'an, I saw both. Workers poured cement for foundations of what would become an international duty-free market. It would be sealed so North Koreans could enter via a new bridge spanning the Yalu River but not pass into greater China.

"The entire village is being torn down," a man pulling tiles off his home's roof told me. "We're being relocated so the Koreans can learn how to do business." Across the river, Koreans languidly pedaled old bicycles. Others crouched, washing clothes in the frigid water.

Two thousand years ago, this land was the seat of a kingdom named Koguryo. Koreans and Chinese debate its provenance: the former claims it as its ancient culture, while the latter—calling it Gaogeli in Chinese—holds it was "a regime established by ethnic groups in northern China, representing an important part of Chinese culture." So read the sign posted outside a royal tomb dated 37 B.C.

All museums tell stories; China's tell political ones. Often, as at these ruins, the museum or historic site is posted as a "patriotic education base." Such shrines—interpreted by the local propaganda department—present historical events as leading, inexorably, to the Communist Party's victory in the Chinese civil war. In Beijing's National Museum of China, the display concerning the nineteenth-century Taiping Rebellion against the Manchu dynasty depicts it as a pre-Marxist version of a peasant uprising without mentioning that its murderous leader believed he was the younger brother of Jesus Christ. In Tibet, museums seem to exist only to assert to visitors that the territory "had long been a part of China."

Like most frontiers, the Northeast pushed back against that neat narrative. These ziggurat-shaped tombs looked more Mayan than Manchurian: seven levels of huge stone blocks rose in receding steps. The tombs dotted the fields around the town, strung together by former castle pediments and low rock walls. The remains spilled across the Yalu River; in 2004, UNESCO added the ruins on both sides of the border to its list of World Heritage Sites, North Korea's first. In the fifth century A.D., a Koguryo ruler moved its capital to Pyongyang. In the eighth century a Chinese army toppled the kingdom, establishing a toehold in the Northeast.

I had Ji'an's ruins to myself. On a hike into a valley where once a palace stood, the only other person I saw was a farmer leading an ox. On my walk back out, the ox was tethered to the front bumper of a stuck taxi, towing it across a rocky stream. The cabbie said he was looking for me; he had heard a tourist was wandering around out here.

He dropped me off at the largest tomb, fenced and requiring an expensive ticket to enter. "These pretty ones are fake, you know," a woman selling roasted yams said. "The real ones are the mounds of rubble you see around here. These have been rebuilt."

I found no proof of this, and the woman was wearing a T-shirt that read, in English, GOD SAVE THE TEENAGERS OF AMERICA. But comparisons to old photos suggested that the photogenic ruins had been touched up. That was in line with everything I would see across the Northeast, where its history, unlike in the rest of China, felt present. Not the nation's Five Thousand Years of History, but the parts made in recent lifetimes. Even its ancient ruins looked new.

The first time I visited the city of Harbin, 160 miles northeast of Wasteland, was to update a guidebook on a job that no one else would take. It was 1998, and its tourist bureau handed out a promotional magazine meant to lure visitors. The cover story was headlined "Police, Police Vehicles, Police Dogs . . . Are So Close to Us." (I loved the tension-building ellipse.) Later, pressed between pages like a treasured leaf, I found a napkin upon which I had scrawled the word *depressing* eleven times.

Now Club Med operated a ski resort outside town, Starbucks anchored downtown's cobblestone pedestrian thoroughfare, and Disney sponsored Harbin's frenetic Ice Lantern Festival. Millions of visitors descended on the city to view two-foot-thick frozen Songhua River ice blocks fashioned into thousands of lighted designs that ranged from life-size pandas to a scale replica of the Eiffel Tower.

Frances joined me there for a long weekend. Her inner attorney marveled at what a carnival looked like in a pre-litigious society. Kids hopped across a course of three-foot-tall ice pedestals and swooped down four-story ice slides, while the adults—fueled by cheap bottles of Ice River beer—clenched knotted ropes to rappel sheer ice walls and, in go-karts, dodged the horse-drawn sleighs that jingled across the Songhua. One night we watched a large, smiling man teeter on the lip of a luge chute as his friends, who called him Fatty, urged him to go first. You got the feeling that Fatty always had to go first. He leaned forward, and was gone. His howling fur-coated mass receded into the dark.

"This place is a death trap," Frances said. But the only casualties were to our teeth, inflicted by candied hawthorn berries that somehow got even harder in the cold.

"This is really a zero-return snack." The petrified fruit stuck to my molars as their bamboo skewer jabbed the inside of my cheek, drawing blood.

"One day lawyers will put a stop to all of this fun," Frances said with a smile. "Enjoy it while it lasts."

We were in Harbin to see the remains of an all-but-forgotten dynasty that was the precursor to the Manchus' rule of China. The ruins were said to be twenty miles outside town in a place whose name sounded like a sneeze: Acheng.

Although the route took us along the expressway, the bus, like many in the Northeast, played a video showing *Er Ren Zhuan*, the regional opera. A shirtless actor in yellow silk pants asked his female counterpart—plump and shimmering in a pink silk pantsuit—her surname.

"I'm afraid I can't tell you," she replied coquettishly. "You'll want to eat it."

He guessed a name that is a homophone for rice, then one for vegetables.

"Wrong again!" the actress crowed.

"I give up. What's your name that I'll want to eat?"

"Poo!"

Clap clap clap went the recorded audience.

"I've seen this one before," Frances said. The actress gyrated comically to a hip-hop beat, exhorting the audience to *yaoqilai, yaoqilai, yaoqilai*: "Shake it!" The bus pulsed with high treble.

The driver pulled to the side of a narrow road lined with birch trees. "Here you are," he yelled above the video's din. He pointed to a small green sign that looked like it had just been clipped by a passing truck. One side was bent back, and we leaned to read, in Chinese and, instead of Manchu script, English that said: JIN DYNASTY CAPITAL SITE.

The arrow pointed at a fallow cornfield. At its edge, Frances knelt before a calf-high stone house. It was a replica of the single-story homes in the distance. Carved above its small front door were characters that read SHRINE TO THE EMPEROR OF THE SOIL. "I've never seen one of these," she said. "I thought they had all been smashed during the Cultural Revolution."

I hadn't seen any around Wasteland, either. The shrine was a relic that would have been targeted by Red Guards bent on destroying "old customs, culture, habits, and ideas."

Frances looked around at the empty plain and said, "Maybe the Red Guards never made it out here."

Who had? We walked on, toward the village, expecting a fence or a ticket taker, or at least an auntie selling postcards and socks. The only sound was a barking German shepherd chained in a courtyard. Its owner emerged from his house, asking to whose family we belonged.

"We're looking for the Jin dynasty ruins."

He pointed across the dirt lane at a chest-high gate standing alone, unattached to a wall or fence. It swung open in the wind. We stepped through, and tried to imagine the palaces of a people who, one thousand years before, ruled much of China.

The Jin (Gold) dynasty was founded in 1115 by a clan of the Jurchen, an equestrian Northeastern tribe skilled in archery and related to the Tungus, a Mongolian race. After pushing their dominion into southern China, the Jurchen moved their capital to present-day Beijing, naming it Zhongdu (Central Capital), and constructing its central chain of lakes. The city's population grew to one million. The Jin emperor ordered these Northeastern palaces razed in 1157 to show the permanence of the Jurchen migration. Six decades later the Jin fell under a barrage of flaming arrows launched by Mongolian horsemen. Their leader, Genghis Khan, marked every citizen for death; the streets of Zhongdu ran slippery with melted flesh. It would be five centuries before the Jurchen, renamed the Manchu, returned to take the throne.

All that remained of the original palaces were stones marking where building foundations once stood, and—flanked by cottonwoods standing straight as sentries—a carved tablet perched atop a stone tortoise. Facing an empty field, the inscription announced the capital's name.

At the rear of the site we found a cement slab painted with characters that said the ruins were excavated in 2000. After nearly nine centuries under the soil, all that remained were stones and the palace footprints, built at a time when Europe was emerging from the Middle Ages, developing the Gothic style, building the Arsenal of Venice, and forming the Knights Templar. The wind and light were strong on the Manchurian plain, and chips of the painted description of the Jurchen court flaked off the slab like sunburned skin.

The last legible sentence said a Jin emperor was entombed a half mile away. The grave was a three-story trapezoidal dirt mound flecked with spindly elms growing aslant from the wind. We descended into a clammy low-ceilinged room to find offerings of plastic pears and apples before a stone crypt: the final resting place of Wanyan Aguda, founder of a dynasty named for gold.

"I feel like we're intruding," Frances said. "It's so odd to be at an historic site without a ticket booth or groups following a bullhorn."

Although, this was probably not Wanyan Aguda's final resting place. History records that he was buried on a mountain near present-day Beijing. The only mention of the capital posted outside this tomb related the tale of a Chinese emperor's fishing expedition in the Northeast, before Wanyan Aguda had taken the imperial throne. He was the sole chieftain who had refused the emperor's order to dance.

"Typical stubborn pride," Frances said. She thought it masked the thin skin that came with growing up somewhere far from the center of culture and power, of feeling insignificant. "As tough as we seem, Northeasterners care about face more than other Chinese."

"You sound stubbornly proud of that."

Frances laughed. "I guess I just proved my point."

Off-site, we learned that Wanyan Aguda was a crack cavalryman, routing the superior forces of other northern tribes and allying with the Mongols to push further south into Chinese territory. His empire was the forerunner of the Manchus'.

In the shrine above his Acheng tomb, a painted cement statue depicted Wanyan Aguda as a mirthful brute in a sable-trimmed yellow silk robe, sitting on his throne. Aside from us, his audience consisted of colonies of fading red ladybugs, frozen to the ceiling.

When Manchu cavalry, assisted by a traitorous Han Chinese general, stormed through the First Pass Under Heaven, seized Beijing, and took over China in 1644, they sought to keep part of the Northeast as their cultural preserve. The Great Wall was, in fact, a series of shifting fortifications, and the previous dynasty's territory had extended north of it. To demarcate their homeland, the Manchu built a one-thousand-mile-long barrier that started at the pass and wishboned deep into the Northeast. Made from soil and trees, they called it the Willow Palisade.

This lesser wall divided Mongol, Manchu, and Han Chinese areas of settlement, protected imperial hunting lands, and secured the court's lucrative sable and ginseng trades. In 1754 the Manchu emperor Qianlong described the barrier in a five-verse poem that began:

> West reaching to the Great Wall, east connecting with the sea,
> A row of willows forms a line marking the inside and outside.
> There is no strategic fortification to guard this border,
> Nor construction of walls that exhausts the people.

Unlike the Great Wall, little of the palisade remained. I searched alone for its ruins around Wasteland, which had been within the Manchus' restricted zone, but the barrier's existence was seen only in the name of a neighboring town. The road to Ninth Platform, a former palisade signal tower, ran through villages called Birchbark Factory—for the saddle and stirrup materials it provided Manchu cavalry—and Barracks.

The palisade eroded, in part because the fence was not made of stone but of parallel dirt berms divided by a trench and topped with willows lashed in line with rope. It fell into disuse as the Manchu dynasty waned. A team of British explorers crossing Manchuria in 1886 found that the barrier had "no more existence at the present day than the Roman Wall. The wooden gateways are, however, still maintained as Customs barriers, and all traffic passing through them must pay transit dues. Only an occasional mound or row of trees marks the line where the palisade originally stood."

My students at Number 22 Middle School had never heard of it. They stared blankly when I wrote its name in Chinese, Liutiaobian, on the blackboard. No one in Wasteland knew what I was talking about, not even Ms. Guan, who was Manchu. Frances had never heard of the palisade, either. "But it's such a pretty name, like the title of a poem," she said over Skype. "School never taught us about it. Anything we learned about the Manchu was bad anyway, since their dynasty had failed. The Great Wall got all the attention. Even though the wall failed to stop the Manchu from conquering Beijing."

The Northeast held a trove of museums that were sanctioned shrines of patriotic education. They did not invite a visitor to consider a place or event's multiple and often competing narratives but rather told the one that ended in Liberation, 1949. Often, stereo speakers in the final exhibit room played the song "Without the Communist Party, There Would Be No New China." In it I heard the faint echo of the theme from *Bonanza* scoring the cowboy-celebrating museums I visited as a child in the American West. Instead of posing next to bison skulls and carved wooden Indians, Manchurian museumgoers took pictures wearing fan-shaped coronets like a Manchu princess at the Qing dynasty tombs. They rode horses at the Manchukuo Puppet Emperor's former stables and ate army rations at the Resist America and Aid Korea war memorial.

But still I visited, curious to see what contemporary China valued as history and what it discounted. Outside the capital-*m* Museums were places I came to see as lowercase sites that evinced the Northeast's past and how it shaped China's present. A Shinto shrine standing shuttered in a city park. A warlord's former mansion. A grotto not carved with Buddhist statues but topped with one of the Virgin Mary. A ghost town around a once-bustling train station. A synagogue near an onion-domed cathedral.

Collectively, these sites were unique to the Northeast, to its onetime conception as "Manchuria." On an early nineteenth-century map, the line marking the Willow Palisade drew a tent across the region's heart. I searched for it there.

Train number 7515 was a throwback to China's ancient transportation past of a decade before. The slow trains emptied in favor of high-speed lines, but a ride on those was as silent and sealed as in a Learjet's cabin. I preferred the older carriages, whose open windows and hard seats made you feel the journey as you would when flying in a prop plane. As the train rocked past a landscape that read like run-on sentences of tilled fields ending in smokestack exclamation points, I sipped a cup of Marxism brand instant coffee ("God's Favored Coffee!" the package promised in English).

Once the train passed Fushun—home to one of the world's largest open-pit coal mines—the air cleared, revealing a sharp blue sky, piles of dried cornstalks, and pine-shrouded hills. Though no modern map marked the palisade's remains, I traced its former outline by circling villages whose names ended in *men* (gate). One lay 250 miles southeast of Wasteland, in a county named Qingyuan, which meant "Origin of the Qing," or the Manchu dynasty.

Legend held that the Manchu's founding father was born there in the sixteenth century, during the Ming dynasty, which ruled part of the Northeast and its native Jurchen tribes. The boy was orphaned and raised by a Han Chinese general, who saw the child's seven birthmarks as a portent that he would usurp Beijing's Forbidden City throne. The Chinese emperor ordered the boy killed, but his adopted Han mother warned him and he fled on horseback into the thick forest with his dog. The general killed his wife, set the woods aflame, and slew the dog. As the general closed in, a flock of magpies cloaked the boy, concealing him from harm. Later he would establish sacred rites honoring his mother, anoint the magpie his lineage's patron spirit, and forbid the eating of dogs. (He also ordered that Jurchen women would never bind their feet and that his male subjects would shave their temples and braid their hair in a queue.) He would create the Manchu writing system by adapting Mongolian script, build a smaller replica of the Forbidden City palace in the Northeast, and become the first khan of the House of Aisin Gioro, the family that would rule China until 1912. His name was Nurhaci.

He died in battle against Han Chinese forces before the capture of Beijing. His son would establish the Qing dynasty and in 1635 decreed that the Jurchen were now named the Manchu, as was their homeland. The word's etymology is uncertain: it could mean "intrepid arrow." Another interpretation says it originated from Manjusri, a Buddhist bodhisattva, or enlightened being, whose name meant Gentle Glory.

Today, most of China's Manchu live in the Northeast yet make up less than 10 percent of the region's 110 million residents and less than 1 percent of China's total population. Many live in clusters such as the Manchu Autonomous County of Qingyuan, population 100,000.

It was the type of place whose first glimpse made me want to run after the train as it pulled away from the empty platform. The forlorn one-room station was a relic of the Japanese occupation. Now, with its robin's-egg-blue façade coal-stained and peeling, it looked like a forgotten toy in a dirty sandbox.

There were no taxis or a bus stop or even a traffic light in sight. Experience had taught that when I didn't know what to do in China, ceasing movement would present someone who did. I stood still in front of the train station.

Within minutes, a beefy, ruddy-cheeked man emerged from his Wholesale Tobacco/Alcohol/Sweets/Teashop. Instead of asking to whose family I belonged, he bellowed: "Today is a good day to get married! Yesterday was for funerals, today is for celebration."

He cited the folk almanac. My spirit rose: here was someone acquainted with tradition. No crowd gathered; aside from me and the man, named Li Changchun, no one else seemed to inhabit Qingyuan.

Instead of a business card, Mr. Li handed me his national identity card, which in China lists a person's ethnicity. His said "Manchu." When I asked about the Chairman Mao pin on his lapel, Mr. Li furrowed his fluffy eyebrows in the expression that meant *Why not?* "I'm Chinese!" he exulted. Mandarin didn't hyphenate a person's compound identity as American English does. Frances was Chinese-American, but Mr. Li wasn't Manchu-Chinese. He was Chinese, and a Manchu, in that order.

A thick gold loop girded his neck, looking like a felling chain around a redwood. He smoked cheap Lesser Panda cigarettes. He smelled of pine tar. He was the first person I had ever met who didn't flinch when I said "the Willow Palisade."

"*Uh*," he replied. "I've never seen it with my own eyes, but I know the village you mean: Ying'emen. I'll take you."

I liked Mr. Li.

He woke a driver—asleep on a mah-jongg table—who took us to the village, and a low brick house. "The oldest woman in the county lives here," Mr. Li said. "We'll ask her."

We entered the home without knocking to learn that the oldest woman in Qingyuan county was in the hospital. We drove back to town and found a frail woman named Yu Huifang tethered to an intravenous drip. She sat upright, expressing no surprise at the strangers who arrived to ask about a relic.

"Seventy years ago you could see the palisade here," she said. "Now it's gone; the trees were chopped down for firewood, and the moat was used for planting. It's all eroded now. No trace exists. No one cares about our Manchu history, after all."

She reclined, closed her eyes, and told us to find a man named Liu Liangjun. "He wrote a book about the palisade." Research in China is horizontal: one person passes you on to the next, like knots joining rope.

It was after dark; Mr. Li, ever the host, brought me back to town and stood rounds of Heaven Lake brand beer, named for the mythical lake atop the Ever-White Mountains. The beer tasted flat and watery. "Like the lake, maybe," he suggested.

We parted until morning. Open fires illuminated the town's curbs; it was the start of the Manchu ghost festival, when families spoke the name of the dead and air-mailed fake money to them via flames. "It's a way of remembering their spirit, to let them know you still care," a woman told me as she burned a paper sheet of gold coins. The woman didn't ask after my family, only if I could help her start a new one. "I need to find a husband. Single men leave Qingyuan to find work."

In my hotel room, the local access television channel broadcast classifieds. Kenny G's alto sax played as the ads scrolled past: a Liberation truck for sale, bags of homemade fried spiced peanuts available on Pioneer Road. A government notice urged viewers to "despise counterfeit money; cherish the people's money." Then a series of lonely-heart ads:

- Man, 76, divorced, 1.67m, owns a house with heat. No burdens. Looking for a woman 76 or younger. Beauty doesn't matter. I'll spend all my time loving you!

- Woman, 43, healthy, tender, and warm, graduated middle school. Seeking a man aged 62 or younger.

- Woman, 53, 1.55m, retired, responsible, good quality, no burdens. Wants to watch the sunset with you tonight.

Outside, the fires flickered, then died.

The historian did not own his book, so the next morning he walked us to the middle school. "They have a copy there," Liu Liangjun said. "It's only sixty-five pages, but it tells the old tales." He looked like most historians I had met in China, dressed in a polo shirt tucked into highly buckled slacks and with a graying shock of hair that suggested electrocution.

We arrived at the school to find its principal out back, hoeing a row of onions. In fluent English he asked if I knew what used to stand on the school's site. "A Buddhist temple?" I guessed correctly. In rural areas, temples had often been converted to schools and police stations. "It was pulled down during the Cultural Revolution," the teacher said, pointing at a worn cornerstone. "That's all that remains."

The principal, Mr. Li, and I followed the historian down a dirt road that we had to step off to allow a tractor to pass. The historian's book had gone missing from school, and so he would instead show us the story. We stopped at a mud embankment divided by the road. The historian pointed to a stubby, leafless willow trunk. No plaque marked the spot. "The Willow Palisade," he said.

This gate sat on the eastern flank of the barrier, which once stretched 700 miles from near Wasteland south to the Yalu River border with North Korea. It marked the imperial hunting grounds—equal in size to the state of Maine—in which Han Chinese were forbidden to settle. In the third verse of his poem about the palisade, the Manchu emperor Qianlong wrote:

> Like the fence that is seventy li long,
> The Hunting Reserve exceeds several times its confines.
> In our erection of borders and regulation of people, ancient ways are
>   preserved,
> As it is enough simply to tie a rope to indicate prohibition.

But the frontier is as much a process as a place. After the Manchu conquered Beijing, their army and its families moved to the capital in such numbers that at first the court enticed Han Chinese to repopulate the area. A 1653 decree offered seed, draft animals, and deferred taxes to farmers willing to reclaim northern land. The act was rescinded only fifteen years later, however, and by 1681 the Willow Palisade was built, sometimes incorporating walls erected in previous dynasties meant to repel the "barbarians."

Yet over the next two hundred years there were as many edicts forbidding as encouraging Han Chinese settlers (and banished convicts). Restrictions were lifted during times of southern famine, or to populate areas such as Wasteland where Russia showed territorial ambitions. Jilin city—Kirin, or Girin Ula, in Manchu—became a strategic center after the emperor opened a naval port there in 1676. A Jesuit priest who accompanied the emperor to inspect Jilin's shipworks wrote: "In this city they make their boats in a particular manner. The inhabitants always keep a great number in readiness to repulse the Muscovites, who often frequent these rivers and endeavour to take away the pearl fishery from the Kiringers."

In the end, it wasn't the Muscovites but Chinese settlers who arrived in droves. As the Qing dynasty faltered, racking up debt, local administrators needed to raise their own revenue. Their only available asset was land. In the 1870s the imperial hunting reserves and pastureland were opened to homesteaders and the palisade became superfluous.

The school principal interrupted the historian. "This area is ripe for tourism!" he said, pointing to the near distance. "You see the dip in the hills where the Willow Palisade came down? There's a lake up there where we can add tents and picnic areas and then rebuild the Willow Palisade. It's so easy: Just plant trees. I'm telling you, it's so easy. Think about it. It's willow trees! It won't cost much, it's just trees. But the local leaders won't listen to me."

Our group walked back to the school and stepped across the street to the village's only restaurant. Stacked at its entrance was a neat row of drying corncobs topped by a row of severed German shepherd paws. So much for the Manchu founding father's order forbidding his people to eat dog.

At the table, the historian sat quietly, the headmaster was talking (*"Trees! Easy! Cheap! Trees!"*), and Mr. Li held the menu. "I'm a vegetarian," I lied. A policeman in uniform joined us, said that he was Manchu, and knew the location of Qingyuan's most valuable artifact. "It's in my basement."

Grasping the type of large iron key ring I thought only existed in Westerns, the officer led me down the police station stairs. "It's in here," he said, pointing at a door. "In the boiler room." The lock clicked and the cop tugged at the metal door. On the dirt floor I saw a rusting bell as tall as my knee, inscribed in Manchu and Chinese script. "Welcome to our museum," the officer joked. "It's all that remains here of our Qing dynasty."

*

The historian suggested I look for the Willow Palisade on its western flank, where it formerly divided Manchu and Mongolian pastures. It was 120 miles from Qingyuan, and there was less development out there, the historian said—fewer roads, little construction. But more wind: surely, I thought, less of the structure would remain. Even in his eighteenth-century palisade poem, the emperor Qianlong described its diminishment:

> *I spurred my horse along the Palisade;*
> *It was so low I could have jumped over it.*
> *The deer go back and forth and can sometimes be caught outside;*
> *Building it is the same as not having built it.*

When I later made the trip west, I assumed that the bus would deposit me in an ancient village where another Manchu shop owner and another historian—distant cousins of Qingyuan's, perhaps—would step forward and show me the way. Instead, the bus discharged me in a town named New Citizen at a gleaming station as large as a regional airport. While everyone inside the terminal was friendly and engaging in the Northeastern way, offering syrupy pinecones to eat (for the seeds), asking why I didn't have kids, yelling into cell phones, and making inquiries, no one had heard of the Willow Palisade.

I asked a teller at the Agricultural Bank and a clerk at the Great Northeast Medicine Store. Unlike in other parts of China, they didn't say that I had to be mistaken, that I was pronouncing it wrong, that I didn't understand anything because I was a foreigner. Instead: blank stares, self-effacing laughter, offered cups of green tea.

The sky was high and piercingly blue, saturating everything and high-lighting a fat white moon. That feeling of open space and empty landscapes returned, and I was reminded of how much I loved traveling in the Northeast. A bus pulled up and the driver asked if I was the guy looking for the Willow Palisade. I climbed into the front seat for the full view out the windshield. It showed cornfields.

I had been up since five, and rocking along the two-lane road lulled me to sleep. The driver woke me an hour later, in a town named Zhangwu, and said, "This is the old border with Mongol lands." I didn't see the palisade, only another bus station, also large, also new. Perhaps sensing my dejection in the waiting hall, an old man wearing faded camouflage pants sidled near. I knew he was the one.

"Where is the Willow Palisade?" the man said, repeating my question. "It's thirty kilometers back the way you came. You passed it. Get off at the blue highway sign."

An hour later the same driver stopped at the sign that stretched over the road, saying "This is the only blue one, brother." The bus pulled away. The sun was high now, and sweat ran down the back of my neck. All was silent save for the patch of sunflowers rustling in the breeze. Their blossomed heads bowed toward a strip of white sand that ran fine and hot through my fingers. It felt like a dry riverbed. The blue sign posted by the local government read: IF YOU ENCOUNTER TROUBLES WHEN DOING BUSINESS IN ZHANGWU, CALL 6949006.

I thought of dialing the number and asking for help. First I followed the sand along an embankment past the sunflowers until hearing the staccato bursts of a tractor, which appeared from behind a bend of cornstalks. A farmer named Mr. Feng stopped the Taishan T-25 and asked what I was up to.

"The Willow Palisade?" he repeated. "You're standing on it."

I exhaled in relief.

"This was the moat, or part of the river, and that embankment of earth there was the barrier." Mr. Feng climbed down from his seat and led me through the corn into a clearing. "This was the barrier. But now you see that it's all broad beans, and this," he said, sinking a hand into the moist loam and ripping out a tangle of roots, "is just peanuts."

On the back of his tractor, holding on to Mr. Feng's shoulders, I bumped along the palisade's remains. He brought me back to the main road and pointed to a gully on the other side. "Didn't you see the marker there?"

I saw only a pile of trash, but Mr. Feng was off our ride and walking down to the soggy ground. He stopped at a toppled white granite plaque.

"This is the second one the government put here. The first one? It went missing." He laughed and added, "You understand, it was stolen. It's good stone."

The new stele was not properly set and lay facedown. Brushing back weeds revealed an inscription that said this was part of the western Willow Palisade. The road, it said, ran through the former gate that separated Mongol from Manchu lands.

Seeing us, another tractor stopped, and then a car, and now there were five of us standing in ankle-deep water, staring at the stone. A better marker would have included the final stanza of the emperor Qianlong's palisade poem:

> Insofar as the idea exists and the framework is there, there is no need
>   to elaborate;
> The methods of predecessors are preserved by descendants.
> When there are secure fortifications, it is peaceful for ten thousand
>   years:
> How can this be dependent on these insignificant willows?

After Mr. Feng and the other men departed, I spent an hour in the hot sun on the side of the road, caked in dirt, waiting for a bus, and happy to pass time filling an empty water bottle with the soft sand as a souvenir, thankful no one was here to hawk it. After passing me, a truck laden with watermelons shuddered to a halt and the driver hopped out of his cab and walked back along the shoulder. He said I looked like an American and asked about Obama and the economy, and how short our history was compared to theirs, and, say, what did watermelons sell for in the States? It was a conversation I could have had anywhere in China, but we were completely alone, surrounded by sunflowers, peanuts, and dragonflies, listening to different frequencies. "This is the Willow Palisade," I said with pride, and the driver replied, "The what?"

CHAPTER 5

THE WAKING OF INSECTS

At last I found a house, or should I say, a house found me. After a research trip, I had returned to Jilin city after six o'clock, too late to catch the last bus to Wasteland. That night my hotel room was freezing. Via Skype, Frances pointed at my bed and said, "Toss dried rice stalks beneath it and light them on fire."

My phone rang at six the next morning. The screen showed not Frances's number but that of Ms. Guan, the Number 22 Middle School teacher. I answered with a concerned "*Uh*," fearing something had happened.

Instead I heard: "You can live with my brother."

"When?" I said groggily.

"Now."

"I'm in Jilin."

"Meet me at the bus stop in thirty minutes."

As we waited for the Number 10 minibus, I saw that Ms. Guan had changed since our last meeting a week before. Blond streaks ran through her long black hair, her glasses now had purple-tinted lenses, and she unzipped her down jacket to reveal the top of a red rose tattooed above her left breast. It was a costume change for a new act in her life: "After the students take their high school entrance exam in spring," she said, "Number 22 is transferring me to a better school. It's right over there."

She gestured to the Diamond Cement Factory, whose smokestacks rained gooey pellets that speckled our black coats. Jilin's amphitheater of pine-clad hills was fronted by factories like this, manufacturing poison against the prettiest backdrop of any Northeast city. Some of Jilin's districts still looked like a live-action version of the old propaganda magazine *China Reconstructs*: chemical tanker trucks threaded their way between cooling towers and under steaming pipelines that snaked over the narrow lanes.

"My new school's location is much better than Wasteland," Ms. Guan said, but I couldn't see how.

Jilin is a second-tier metropolis, with four million people—and sleepy by Chinese standards. A century ago it had flourished as a shipyard and trading post. An English traveler passing through in 1903 found "shops and main streets bright with the beloved northern colour, vermillion red, [selling] beautiful carved wood, all manner of stamped leather, furs, bear-skins, tiger and leopard skins from the Eastern forests, and curious colored silks." The old walled city was made of wood; a Japanese poet, arriving in the winter of 1918, described it as "breathtakingly beautiful, fully warranting its reputation as the 'Kyoto of Manchuria.'" Fire destroyed most of wooden Jilin in 1930. Industrialization took care of the rest.

Our bus stopped every fifty yards to fill the remaining seats, then the padded engine cover at the driver's right hand, then the aisle. Bundled as we were in layers, every added body felt like additional protection from a crash. The interior became a human airbag.

Immobile in the crush, I was happy to be rolling, to feel the thrum and hear the grinding gears as people gossiped about apartment prices and school fees. Everything cost more. Had I seen the prices at the new apartment high-rises named Moca, Loire Town, and the Fifth Avenue? So *gui* (pronounced *gway*). Expensive. Forget what the zodiac said about the rabbit: this was really the Year of the Gui.

I looked out the window at the winding Songhua. The river did not freeze here even during the fortnight called Severe Cold, and when its water vapor rose into the frigid air, the droplets crystallized on the branches of willows and pines. This rime ice (called *shugua*, pronounced *shoe-gwa*) transformed the riverbanks into a photo backdrop of national renown.

In the late nineteenth century, an English explorer described the phenomenon: "We saw one morning one of the most perfectly lovely sights I have ever seen. I have never seen a similar sight, either before or since. It was a frozen mist. As the sun rose we found the whole air glittering with brilliant particles sparkling in the rays of the sun—and the mist had encrusted everything, all the trunks of the trees and all the delicate tracery of their outlines, with a coating like hoar frost. The earth, the trees, and everything in the scene was glistening white, and the whole air was sparkling in the sunlight. It lasted but a short time, for as the sun rose the mist melted away, but while it could be seen we seemed to be in a very fairyland."

A century later the description held.

The bus passed a building site for an apartment complex named Warm City. In English, its billboard said: IF WHITE AMERICA TOLD THE TRUTH FOR ONE DAY ITS WORLD WOULD FALL APART. That's the title of a song by the Welsh rock group the Manic Street Preachers. How did it end up here? And why would anyone buy an apartment near the shiny, steaming spires of Jilin Ethanol? Its billboard promised CLEAN ENERGY FOR A BETTER ENVIRONMENT. Which ad told the lie?

Next came a Purina feed factory, then a Wahaha brand mineral water plant. At a village named Lower Frog, the bus, sagging on its axles, climbed over the new high-speed railroad tracks, and then the view showed open fields. We had crossed the line from industry to agriculture, from urban to rural. The bus passengers visibly relaxed as after take-off, when an airplane levels and the FASTEN SEATBELT sign chimes off with a *ding!*

An old man sitting beside his grandson, said, "Tell Teacher Plumblossom all the English words you know."

"Banana!" the plump boy yelled. "Apple!"

"If he can eat it, he knows how to say it," the grandfather said proudly.

"Hamburger!" the boy yelled. "Pizza! KFC!"

The other passengers laughed. The grandfather recognized me, but some of the other riders did not. The grandfather explained to them: "He married a woman from here, but she left for work." Passengers whom I had never met nodded empathetically. We were like many rural households, they said: one spouse became a migrant worker, leaving the other behind.

An old saying holds that if you go three miles from home, you are in another land, but the distance was shorter for a foreigner. Outside Wasteland, people stared at me with friendly, cautious curiosity, the way you might if a kangaroo joined your commute.

I read that the comedian Steve Martin used to hand autograph seekers a signed name card that confirmed the person had met Steve Martin and found him to be "warm, polite, intelligent and funny." At times—like on this bus—I wished I had a similar card to present that would answer the usual questions strangers asked of me, in this order:

> I am an *American.*
> I have been in China *a long time.*
> I was born in the *Year of the Rat.* I am *1.86* meters tall.
> I *do not have* a salary. I am a *writer and volunteer teacher.*
> Chinese is *not hard. It is easier to learn than English.*
> Yes, *I can* use chopsticks. *We eat Chinese food in*
> America, *too. But often it is expensive and orange.*

On rare occasions someone started me off with a curveball: a gruff construction worker, hard hat in hand, once asked if anyone had ever told me that my beard was beautiful; a gentleman in a business suit standing on a country lane wondered if morality was more important than wisdom.

Saying that I was American always brought a smile; regardless of political ups and downs, that reaction had not changed since I first arrived in China in 1995. Though sometimes—when interrupted mid-slurp over noodles, or facing a drunkard—I tired of giving honest replies that would only lead to more questions. *I am from Mars,* I would say. *What are chopsticks? I just started learning Chinese yesterday—what a breeze!* Kids caught on faster than adults; sarcasm, via movies and the Internet, was a recent American import.

Ms. Guan pulled a child onto her lap. She asked me to guess his age, and I—forgetting the Inverse Rule—guessed too low instead of too high.

"He's eight," I said, honestly.

"No! He's twelve."

So many of the village kids looked smaller and younger than their years, in contrast to the adults, who accelerated to middle age.

"How old am I?" Ms. Guan demanded.

"Thirty," I tried, safely, although I knew the truth.

"I'm forty-two!" she laughed.

"Forty-two and you're still without a husband?" the woman standing in the aisle teased. I knew this talk stung Ms. Guan, but she gamely parried back. Later she told me she hated living in Wasteland, where there were no secrets, unlike in town, where she could blend in and be anonymous.

The boy on her lap studied my face in silence.

"*Gan sa?*" Ms. Guan said, dialect for "What's up?"

"Can I ask Teacher Plumblossom a question?" the boy said, seriously. "I want to know: Do you hate Osama bin Laden?"

"Can you hate a dead person?"

The boy blinked. "Do you hate Hitler?"

"I hate eating cabbage." I was talking to a twelve-year-old and trying to lighten the subject.

The boy didn't take the bait. For the remainder of our ride to Wasteland, we discussed not food but the nature of evil. It was 7:30 in the morning when the boy got off at the intersection of Red Flag Road.

"I have one more question!" he yelled to the driver, who idled.

"Teacher Plumblossom, do you miss your mom?"

The full bus watched, expectant.

"Yes, I miss my mom."

"Do you miss her so much that you cry?"

"Yes," I lied. The boy had boarded the bus alone and was exiting alone, and I guessed he needed assurance. "Sometimes I miss her so much that I cry."

"Ha ha!" the boy crowed. "What a big baby!" He bounded off the bus as the passengers laughed.

It was a typical Wasteland house. A wrought-iron fence and gate separated its painted yellow brick from the nameless street that crossed Red Flag Road. Forty homes clustered in this corner of the village. All had peaked corrugated tin roofs and gardens for yards; ours was known for its large spring onions. Rows of corn grew in the back.

The entrance's exposed cement floor needed sweeping, while the kitchen conjured thoughts of anything but food. Its soot-coated walls held a rusting cleaver and wok, a single propane burner, a refrigerator, garlic bulbs, and a bottle each of black vinegar and soy sauce. Frost-tipped cabbages filled a waist-high clay pot capped with a marble slab that balanced atop them. Cabbage leaves drooped from the gap, looking like they had tired and given up while trying to escape.

The house had two rooms, both nearly entirely filled with a *kang*, fueled by the stacks of rice stalks piled outside. The platform bed began just inside the door and required a high step to mount; coming home felt like climbing onstage.

The house, like Wasteland itself, straddled the nineteenth and twenty-first centuries: there was no indoor plumbing, but I had broadband Internet, installed by a technician who drove out from Jilin city. "You must like to play online poker," he guessed. Perhaps that explained why I was holed up out here.

"I need Skype to call my wife."

"OK," the technician replied, looking around the empty farmhouse.

I had installed a virtual private network to breach the "Great Firewall" that blocked selected Web sites. In China, one came to recognize the stealthiest Internet on-ramps the way American parents could rattle off the highest performing school districts: *96.44.178.178 is much better than 216.240.128.82.* It turned out I didn't much need the VPN; I could access more forbidden Western media sites in the countryside than in a city. It was as if no one bothered to keep an eye on the single screen glowing atop a *kang* in a village named Wasteland.

I shared the house with Ms. Guan's brother. Mr. Guan was a wiry farmer my age whose temperament reminded me of neighbors in Minnesota: at once taciturn and bemused. He was a bachelor and every day wore baggy army pants and an oversize army jacket. He was thin, tanned, and perpetually squinting, as though the daylight hurt his eyes. He spoke softly, and my voice fell, too, when talking to him. We shared the mud-walled outhouse, and not much else. He had no interest in the Internet, spoke not a word of English, and never asked about my research, my wife, geopolitics, or whether I missed my mother.

He asked his teenage niece, who often dropped by to surf music-sharing Web sites, to write our lease by hand on the back of an English vocabulary exercise sheet. On one side, a list of words—*exhausted, embarrassing, kangaroos*—on the other, a paragraph that stated I was entitled to 750 square feet and half the onion garden for 300 yuan ($49) each month. I took the space—well lit with a wall of windows on either side—but passed on the onions. The only thing I had ever successfully grown was a beard.

The niece, age seventeen, wanted to be a kindergarten English teacher. She showed me her textbook, which explained that a tenet of American pedagogy was "a plan for ending the children's relationships with their parents."

I explained that just because most kids left home after graduating high school, they still had a relationship with their parents, even from a distance. In the countryside, the niece said, "everyone is together with everyone forever."

Outside my back wall of windows, under snow, was the well where Ms. Guan's father had committed suicide during the Cultural Revolution. Mr. Guan didn't remember it; he was a baby then. "We drilled a new well," he said conclusively.

Mostly we talked about fish; he rose before dawn and rode his Flying Pegasus motorcycle to the Songhua River to cast nets. I heard the motorcycle return at daybreak and park near the storage shed, which burbled like a creek. One day I opened its tin door to see a hose, connected to a pump at the well, running into red plastic buckets filled with fingerlings, tadpoles, and writhing eels. Bait leeches dried on string dangling from the wooden rafters. Frances thought this sounded like a set for a Chinese production of *The Silence of the Lambs*. But to me it looked no different than the shed at a Minnesota cabin. Except for the eels. The sound of their contorted thrashing made me shut the door tightly. I dreaded opening it to fill a laundry bucket with water.

Mr. Guan didn't drink liquor or play cards. He fished, sold his catch on rounds to regular customers, then brought the rest home. He was asleep each night by eight. We moved in silent comfort around one another.

Our front door had no lock, though Mr. Guan installed a small padlock on the door to my room. Aside from my laptop and a hot-water kettle, I had nothing worth taking, unless a thief wanted stacks of Japanese-language South Manchuria Railway reports from 1938 with titles such as "An Example of Japanese Free Settlers Primarily Operating Irrigated Paddy Fields Along the Mukden–Kirin Railway."

My first day in the house, a burning smell roused me from a nap. I opened my eyes to see the room enveloped in smoke pouring through the cracks of the *kang*. No one had used it for months, and no one had tested it, either. As I coughed and rubbed my eyes, Mr. Guan came into focus on the other side of the window, standing outside in the fresh air over the bed's fire vent. "*Mei wenti!*" he advised, attempting to damper the smoldering rice stalks. The sleeves of his oversize coat flapped uselessly. "No problem!" he yelled. "Just don't breathe! No problem!"

*

In early March, the solar term with the foreboding name the Waking of Insects indicated hibernation's end. Still the snow remained, and the only thing stirring in Wasteland's air were Fierce Dragon fighter planes. Air force pilots in training flew over the village after taking off from what had been Jilin city's airport, until a new one opened in 2005, closer to Changchun, the provincial capital.

Aside from its functioning single runway and a hangar, the old airport's squat cement terminal building and air traffic control tower sat empty, surrounded by a rusting fence that kept out only tumbleweeds. Dried stalks of volunteer corn smothered the empty redbrick storage sheds, whose painted slogan, in fading yellow, urged Chairman Mao to live forever. In China, seeing those words was like noticing a fallout shelter sign rusting on an American post office. It was a relic of a distant era, even if only a few decades had passed.

My memories of rural students seemed just as outdated. As a Peace Corps volunteer in southwestern China fifteen years earlier, I had taught college students who still worked the land beside their parents. They were eager to move away but unsure how the wider world worked. It was an ideal introduction to China, since they were as confused as I was about how to sign up for a pager, let alone find a job, rent an apartment, and live independently. Tales of villagers who migrated to work on the coast filtered back to the campus, but making that leap meant turning down the security of a government-assigned teaching job. Most of my students were their parents' only child and felt enormous pressure to provide for them as they aged. Once, when I visited a student after graduation, she remembered my explanation of mascots, which Chinese schools didn't have. The middle school where she worked should be called the Mules, she said, because the kids—and teachers—were driven hard like one.

Wasteland's students were more mobile, more prosperous, and more connected. None of them had used a scythe; aside from household chores, they were expected to work on their studies, not in the fields. The team name that would best describe the cell phone–toting Number 22 Middle Schoolers was not the Huskers but the Texters. And their parents expected them to move away, beginning with testing into a Jilin city high school, then advancing to university elsewhere in China, or finding work on their own. Who looked to the state to provide a job anymore? That was another fading memory of a faraway time.

My former Peace Corps site was no longer surrounded by rapeseed fields and bamboo-shaded hillsides. In 1997 a student had described the walk out the back school gate to her parents' farmhouse:

"Dusk, on a Country Road"

> Sun is setting
> Earth veiled
> With soft light
> Water brightening
> Cooking-smoke rising
> And, shepherdess coming
> With her song
> What a wonderful thing!

Now that spot held billboards for high-rise apartments named Seattle Gold Mountain, California Blue Harbor, and a development whose signs receded around the river bend: VIP VIP VIP VIP.

If that happened in comparatively moribund rural Sichuan, what would well-off Wasteland look like in fifteen years?

Yet, when it came to teaching in the countryside, some things hadn't changed. The classroom still held thirty students sitting in rows. The back line of desks showed not alert faces but nests of black hair rising rhythmically in sleep. The English textbook's vocabulary list still read like a game of free association: *Unfortunately. Go down. Politely. Overslept.*

Wasteland's teens wondered, as my college students had fifteen years before, if it was true that American teachers were not allowed to assign homework. They constantly asked what time it was in the U.S., and—since China only had one time zone—what time it was in various cities. *New York!* Eleven p.m. *San Francisco!* Eight p.m. *Washington, D.C.!* Eleven p.m. *Wait, that's the same as New York!* The boys questioned me on NBA rosters; the girls fretted over choosing an English name.

I didn't require students to select one; it was easier for me to memorize a single list of names, in Chinese. But some students wanted an

English-speaking identity. One day, before lunch, Hu Nan, a shy girl with bangs combed over her eyebrows, told me she had decided to call herself Phil.

"How about Nan, or Nancy?" I suggested.

"I like Phil."

"But Nan sounds like your Chinese name. It's unique and special."

"I am not special. I am just Phil."

"If it's short for Phyllis, I like it."

"Just Phil," she said.

After lunch, two of the boys who had slept through my lesson challenged me to one-hundred-meter dashes over the packed snow. Phil stood at the finish line, outshouting her peers yelling "*Jia you!*" Pronounced *zha yo*, it literally means "Add fuel," or "Come on!"

That was what teaching in tranquil, pastoral Wasteland sounded like: air force jets thundering over a pack of pubescents screaming at me to hustle. More boys stepped to the starting line. After ten minutes of this, Phil surprised me with an offer to switch places and it was my turn to shout. Looking serious, she outran each of her male challengers, high-fiving me with the hint of a smile on the way back to class.

At March's end, the insects awoke, and our part of the world spun into the solar term named the Vernal Equinox. Finally the snow began to melt. Next came early April's Qingming—Pure Brightness—the fortnight named for China's tomb-sweeping festival. After banning it post-Liberation as a relic of the old society, the central government made Qingming a national holiday in 2008. Now it is a tradition anew.

Wasteland's tombs had been destroyed, so my students instead read descriptions of the festival in their Beijing-issued textbook. In English class, we translated the poem "Qingming," written twelve hundred years ago:

> *A drizzling rain falls on Mourning Day,*
> *The mourner's heart is breaking on his way.*
> *Enquiring where a tavern is,*
> *A herder points to Apricot Blossom village, far away.*

When I told Frances that the kids translated the famous poem by Du Mu, she asked, "Who?"

"The Tang dynasty poet. Du Mu."

"You mean Du Fu?"

"No, Du Mu, the poet."

"Du Fu was the famous Tang dynasty poet."

"Du Mu! He wrote the poem about Qingming!"

"Oh! Du MU. You said it wrong."

Frances relished my missteps just as I did her (comparatively rare) ones in English. I still teased her about the time she pronounced *Yosemite* in two syllables: *Yose-mite*. Or the time she said she liked the band named the Dixie Chickens.

My utterance of *Du Mú* (a rising tone) meant nothing to her, not when the writer's name is pronounced *Du Mù* (a falling tone). To me, this inability to use context to guess at my intended meaning was as ridiculous as a traveler stopping on Interstate 70 to ask if this was the way to "Dansas City" and hearing the confounded listener reply, "Dansas City? Never heard of it."

"That's a beautiful poem," Frances said over the phone as I walked north on Red Flag Road, raindrops running off my glasses. "It rhymes in Chinese, you know. Try to make it sound that way in English."

In the original, the lines ended with characters pronounced *fen/hun/you/cun*. "It's assonance, dummy," she said, mystifying me further. I changed the subject to her father and how she had honored him on Qingming.

He had passed away the previous autumn in Shenzhen, the southern coastal city that borders Hong Kong. Frances's oldest brother had moved there on his own in 1989, after turning down an assigned accounting job. Instead, he started at the bottom rung of one of China's first brokerages. He rose to a seat on its board of directors and bought their parents a house. Frances's father had loved being able to leave the Northeast's cold and return to his southern China roots. He died, surrounded by family, after complications from an intestinal obstruction.

His ashes, placed in a carved marble casket the size of a large shoe box, sat on a shelf in a columbarium, awaiting entombment. On Qingming, Frances went there to take her father "out for some air." She lifted the casket from the shelf, carried it out into the warm sunshine to a designated area for burning paper money and incense, and raised the gold cloth covering its lid. Emblazoned there was her favorite picture of him—black-and-white, wearing a black sport coat and white dress shirt, with one corner of his mouth turned up in a half grin. She let out an "airport cry," as if she had just seen him at Arrivals after a long journey.

Frances, her brother, and their mother talked to her father as they had during a holiday meal. "I made your favorite, braised pig knuckle," her mom said, placing the dish by the casket. "Have a smoke, Baba," Frances said, lighting a cigarette and placing it on the ground. Her brother poured a shot glass of sorghum wine, raised a toast, then set the filled cup next to the smoldering cigarette. The dead, Frances noted, got to live it up once each year.

Her mother burned paper gold coins and a stack of paper money that was legal tender in the afterworld. She uncovered more cooked dishes, urging him to eat. She narrated the family news since he had departed, telling him not to worry, that everyone was fine. I had even moved to Wasteland, she said. "Everyone there misses you," Frances added. "They ask about you all of the time. But you'll stay here now, where it's warm."

For two hours the family sat beside him in the sun.

"It does seem strange, not having any tombs around here," Auntie Yi said on her *kang*. "The dead just vanish."

She wore a black padded silk jacket, black cloth shoes, and a worn black bucket hat. Curls of gray hair spilled from its sides. As she spoke, a single snaggletooth jutted over her lower lip. She looked like a hip librarian, and was as vivacious as her brother San Jiu was taciturn. She often papered over my social faux pas, telling me only after she felt my unknowing offense would no longer sting (which it still did): "Go pay a visit to Auntie Zhu," she would advise, "and maybe bring her some pork. Ask her to cook it for you. You walked by her house a few weeks ago and didn't stop to see if she was home, to say hello."

If I had any clout, Auntie Yi would be my consigliere. As I did not, she was simply my favorite aunt. She lived in the first house off Red Flag Road, a half mile from the middle school. It was the most solidly built home in the area, made from reinforced concrete instead of brick. "I was never a farmer," she said. Her father, a Communist cadre, had been assigned to Wasteland in the 1950s to oversee construction of the state-owned granary that now rusted, abandoned, near the train station. Before reaching the mandatory retirement age of fifty-five for female civil servants (men could stay until they turned sixty), Auntie Yi worked as an administrator in the village government. Her work now revolved around the rows of bright pink and white poppies she tended along Red Flag Road. "I used my own money to buy the seeds," she often reminded me. "Long before Eastern Fortune Rice started spending money on the village, I planted those poppies so the road would look nice."

I usually stopped to see her on my walk home from school. In a way, I had to: little passed Auntie Yi's house without her seeing it from the windows that faced the road.

I enjoyed sitting with her husband, who, like me, had married into the family. He said to call him Uncle Fu, though the correct honorific was "Husband of Third Female Cousin." He had a kind face, with large, inquisitive eyes and a close-lipped smile. He kept his white hair shorn close to a liver-spotted scalp, and his blue serge coat and pants hung loosely on a lean frame.

He liked sports, so we usually sat on the *kang* and watched whatever played on TV. On late afternoons it was often women's volleyball, a replay of Premier League soccer, or snooker. Uncle Fu didn't like that, but I did, because he chatted during the long silences between shots. Yet, every time he began to tell me the story of how he ended up in Wasteland, Auntie Yi—taller, heavier and a bundle of industry—entered the room and interrupted. She was a conversational snowball rolling downhill and gaining momentum.

"You know what we used to say back then?" she asked. "When you got sick, you just had to keep going until you got better or you died. There was no clinic out here. I had an older sister already in school, and your mother-in-law had a younger sister. Both of them died of tuberculosis, or pneumonia—you didn't know what it was back then, you just got sick, and then you died if you didn't get better. There wasn't an in-between, like now, where you can still live with a disease. We were talking about graves when you arrived. Today is Qingming. Where are their graves? Gone! Destroyed! Now they're just fields. Now people are cremated and put near

Jilin city. We used to have a Buddhist temple here, too, but it was pulled down in 1956, when this became an official production zone, and Wasteland became a village."

History started then.

"The wind is huge today," Auntie Yi said. "It comes all the way from Mongolia. Once it passes, the weather will get better. What did your wife say about the weather in Hong Kong? Sunny and hot? Isn't it amazing that one country can have so many climates? Down south you have green trees and flowers blooming, and here it's all snow and my poppies are frozen."

Her husband turned from the television and watched her with obvious affection.

"You know," she continued unbidden, "when I was a little girl, I lived in a village closer to Jilin named Sand Creek. There were rolling hills everywhere, so we made sleds out of branches and scrap and we would be happy to see snow, because we could sled all day. I didn't have winter shoes—I wore cloth shoes just like these—and my clothes were all patched up, and I would come home with my face all red, but only when it was time to eat. Do you know what we ate back then?"

Countryside reminiscences often swung around to food.

"Corn and flour fried with soybeans, and a little pickled radish, and sometimes potatoes. In summer it was cucumber, peppers and eggplant, and cabbage, of course. That's what we could grow. We never had meat except at New Year's, and it was a slice of pork. We never received a red envelope of money as a gift. Where could commoners get money? This was in the 1940s, before Liberation. My grandchildren are living in a different time."

I asked Auntie Yi which of her relatives migrated to the Northeast and when. "I'm here because my ancestors were hungry!" she said with a laugh. "They were in Shandong province, and it was a famine. What year? There was always a famine down there; the year doesn't even matter. Famine Year. How's that?"

Uncle Fu laughed and shot me a look that asked, *Isn't she something?*

"Two brothers left the village carrying only their knapsacks and walked for a year until they crossed the Great Wall and entered the Northeast. They got into a fight; no one can say why. No one can even say the village they came from. They split up, and one kept walking north, ending up in Jilin city. I don't know what happened to the other brother. The one in

Jilin hauled corn and sorghum on his back, transporting it. He saved enough to buy a horse and cart, and he could transport more. He bought land around here and rented out huts to other laborers."

This was her grandfather, who grew corn. "We were fortunate. We always had corn flour, and under our roof's thatch and tree branches we stuffed corncobs for insulation. But it was still cold; every spring around this time, we'd coat the walls with new layers of mud. In winter the walls would bubble from frost, and mice infested the ceiling."

Auntie Yi's raised her hands, wiggling her fingers like ten busy creatures.

Her grandfather opened a grain store in a town near here, but across the Songhua River. "He told me that this land where our house is now used to be underwater. He said they used to weave reed baskets and pole over here in a little skiff to trap carp in the shallows. The water was clear and you could see right to the sandy bottom. In winter they would break the ice and reach down to pluck frogs and sleeping bullheads. Like this!"

Her hand darted at my knee. Uncle Fu flinched in surprise, too. We both laughed.

"You sound really tired of telling these stories," I teased Auntie Yi. But my sarcasm eluded her.

"No!" she said, suddenly serious. "I never tell these stories. Who would I tell them to?"

Everyone out here, Uncle Fu added, already knew everything.

CHAPTER 6

GRAIN RAIN

NO ONE COULD say when winter would finally end, or what Eastern Fortune rice had planned for Wasteland. A cold drizzle continued through the end of April. San Jiu said this year's planting would be later than any in his lifetime; usually the rice seedlings went into the ground before May. But ice still filled the paddies' furrows. Then the rain stopped overnight, and the landscape turned from silver white to black mud. Only the distant foothills showed a hint of green.

A worker who didn't recognize me on Red Flag Road asked the usual questions—*American*, I answered. *1.86 meters, Year of the Rat*—then said he was from Mud Town. He came to prune the Manchurian ash trees lining the road. After a winter of pummeling gales, the branches bowed in one direction. He worked alone, with a handsaw and wooden ladder. Eastern Fortune Rice hired him to make the road look nice, he said. Three days later he had completed all two miles of the trees, on both sides of the road, which was now marked with a sign pointing the direction to the company's office—NEW AGRICULTURE/NEW COUNTRYSIDE/NEW FARMERS—and its Shennong (Divine Farmer) Hot Spring, named for the mythological emperor who bestowed agriculture to the Chinese.

Auntie Yi, standing off the road amidst the tall stems of her unopened poppies, said with a snort: "A private company is taking care of our Socialist road and named its resort after a god."

But I liked the hot spring's name, which sounded better than Red Star, or Laborer's Number Seven Leisure District, or other clunky

Communist-era monikers. In the 1960s, Wasteland had been renamed the Ninth Platform Commune.

"You watch," Auntie Yi said. "Before long, Eastern Fortune Rice will control everything here. They'll probably even rename the town."

"To what?"

"Who knows?"

Shennong, the legendary Divine Farmer, is also said to be the founder of acupuncture and traditional Chinese medicine and is renowned for testing the effects of herbs by ingesting them and watching their effects inside his transparent body. For an antidote, he drank another of his discoveries, this one accidental: tea. Legend said that burning twigs of a tea bush sent scorched leaves floating upward, landing in his cauldron of boiling water.

I liked that story, too, and how, even if it was via the name on a new hot spring resort off a road named Red Flag, rural China still spun folk tradition. In the cities, most of that had long been razed and forgotten. None of my Beijing students had known about the fox spirit said to live in the old wall towers, or the legend of Beijing's layout itself, resembling the body of a deity who slew a dragon that lived in the area. In a way, even the countryside's recent eras were sliding into that realm. Painted on the redbrick houses around Auntie Yi's, you could make out the fading characters from 1980 announcing the village as a "Red Defender." To the west we could see the rusting gate of the Rejuvenate China Farm, an abandoned collective from the 1970s. One brick wall of its former storehouse remained, punctured by a window missing several panes of glass, framing a horizon of paddies.

On her *kang*, from under a stack of cross-stitching magazines, Auntie Yi pulled out the oversize calendar Eastern Fortune Rice gave to each village home during the Lunar New Year holiday. "It's an advertisement, really," she said. "The company wants farmers to sign over their land and houses and move to the new apartments."

The calendar's pages included the ancient poem "Sympathy for Peasants," a reminder to appreciate the labor that goes into a bowl of rice, still invoked by parents ordering children to finish their meals:

> A peasant weeding at noon,
> His sweat drips to the field soon.

Anyone with rice on a tray,
Owes it to his toiling day.

Yet the accompanying photos were of Eastern Fortune's threshers and polishing machines. Another picture showed seated farmers being lectured. "The company likes to give advice," Auntie Yi explained. Each month on the calendar was headlined with a suggestion, written as a rhyming couplet, such as: *Reflect on the past months / and sign contracts at once.*

Even in rhyme, that sounded pushy. Auntie Yi said she would never move.

The security guard at the entrance to Divine Farmer Hot Spring smiled as I approached. "No one walks here," he said. "Where's your car?"

The driveway ran straight for a quarter mile, past the billboard showing then Chinese president Hu Jintao touching a can of Big Wasteland rice on his visit, then past fallow paddies and a greenhouse until I reached the Manchu Villa Area. Here visitors could dress up in silk robes and coronets and pose in a replica of a traditional Manchu three-sided courtyard home. It was exactly the sort of site I had expected, and I saw why my Manchu roommate and our neighbors never came here.

I entered the humid greenhouse. A middle-aged man emerged from the rows of lush green trellises. He was worried about fungus, he said, by way of introduction. Powdery mildew in particular: it was attacking his organic cucumbers. During the rice-growing season he lost sleep thinking about insects and birds, especially swallows, and what they were wreaking on the insecticide-free fields. This time of year was supposed to be less stressful. But then powdery mildew showed up.

The football field–size greenhouse was a recently added attraction to the hot spring, since visitors from the city liked picking their own organic fruit and vegetables. "Kids don't know how to do it," the gardener said with a frown. "They'll look at a tomato vine and yank on the entire thing instead of gently twisting off each tomato. They kick the melons like they're soccer balls."

I looked at the trellises. "Is this soil from Wasteland?"

He nodded. "Our black earth is the best." But he worried for how long, since recent tests of Wasteland's soil showed levels of heavy metals that were approaching the allowable limit for a crop to be certified organic. "The soil is safe, but I worry a lot," he said. "Farmers are like that. We always worry."

"You said *farmer*, not *gardener*."

He laughed. "At this hot spring I'm called the Head Gardener. Tourists don't want to eat food raised by any old farmer."

We walked around the outdoor springs, steaming in the cold April air. A wide, shallow communal pool the size of a putting green led to smaller, individual soaking areas. Wicker chaise longues were set out before a thatched-roof bar and a bamboo-walled teahouse. It looked like an upscale resort imported from southern, coastal China.

"It's modeled after a Japanese design," the gardener said.

Children's shrieks and splashes echoed from the covered Olympic-size swimming pool. We stepped along its slippery edge—the gardener first checking that our shoe soles were clean—then entered the resort's cavernous reception area. Robed parents in shower sandals tried herding kids wearing rubber flotation rings. They broke free and ran, full speed, into the furniture and potted plants: bumper kids. The posted prices showed that a day in the water cost 120 yuan ($20), while a night in the cheapest hotel room cost 288 yuan ($47). The most expensive went for double that price.

"That room includes a mah-jongg table," the gardener noted.

"The entrance ticket to use the pool costs nearly as much as renting a thresher to cut a paddy of rice," I said.

"But to someone who lives in the city, it's cheap."

"How is this good for Wasteland's residents?"

"As Eastern Fortune profits, the village profits," he replied. "It's true that locals don't come here, but we don't eat all the food we grow, either. We sell it to people in town, in the region, and across our nation. We're not a dead-end street anymore."

Wasn't it better, the gardener added, to build a place where a city kid could come and exercise and eat organic produce instead of going to a shopping mall with fast food?

"Sure, if local kids can use it, too."

"Do you want to get in the water?" the gardener asked. "Wasteland teachers only have to pay half price."

I said I was afraid of leaving a dirt ring around the pool. The gardener nodded and went back to worrying over powdery mildew. As I left, he jogged after me, calling, "Organic tomatoes!" I carried the heavy sack up Red Flag Road toward home. The view showed yellow cranes adding the fifth and final floor to the new apartments.

May turned, bringing the solar term named the Beginning of Summer. Meltwater filled the irrigation ditches, and the tall birches that lined them budded green. For Wasteland, a more fitting solar term name was the Awakening of Frogs. Their pulsing croaks filled the area, loud enough for me to wonder if *frogsong* was a word in Chinese.

San Jiu said no. He didn't even hear the frogs, just as a city dweller stopped hearing traffic. "I dare not say I turn my back on the natural world, because I'm a farmer, obviously," he said. "But farmers worry about nature, about things we can't control. You don't want floods, or drought, or insects, or anything. You want a quiet summer without any trouble. You want nature to mind its own business."

I saw Wasteland's landscape as natural. San Jiu knew it was manufactured. "This was all underwater until the 1950s," he said, waving at the paddies. "Everything you see was shaped or made by a human. The black earth was here, but only after the marshes and shallows were drained. It was tilled by hand, and tilled again, and fertilized, and so on. Look, the road—cement; the electric poles—timber; those houses—brick; the irrigation channels—cement; the pump house—iron and brick."

What I viewed as bucolic, he saw as industrial. I searched for the Chinese vocabulary to explain how, in the West, people started using the word *grower* instead of *farmer*, as it indicated a smaller-scale operation. But in Chinese, a farmer was *nongmin* ("agricultural person") and *nongmin* only. It was often translated in English as "peasant," which to my ear sounded like person tilling mud in a feudal, preindustrial world. In Chinese, *nongmin* did not sound as archaic. Regardless, the terms didn't matter to San Jiu. "We're *nongmin*. But we're really manufacturers. We produce grain."

We walked a mile south of his house, to the intersection with the road that led to Jilin city. At the single-story cement building that was

Wasteland's "rice station," a chalkboard announced a Perpetual Harvest brand thresher for sale and also a slice of land for rent for 10,000 yuan ($1,631) per year.

"I should rent that," I said.

"You can't," San Jiu replied. "No one outside this village can rent it. Even Auntie Yi and Uncle Fu, they're classified as urbanites, so they can't rent it, either. Farmers only."

"You could rent it for me."

"Uh," he said. It meant *No way.* The last time he leased someone else's land, San Jiu found himself in Beijing, petitioning the central government to resolve a dispute.

China's constitution stipulates that land in cities is owned by the state, although urban residents can buy and sell homes, which usually come with a renewable seventy-year leasehold. In contrast, rural land—including housesites—is owned by "collectives," or local governments. Leaseholds on farming plots are renewable and run for thirty years. Until recently, farmers could not transfer the rights to use their assigned field, which averaged one to two acres per family.

The area fluctuated with a household's size. The local government assigned additional acreage when a child was born or a person got married, or subtracted it after a person died or got divorced. San Jiu's family paddies totaled 1.5 acres, a bit larger than an American football field.

New rules allowed leaseholders to rent their assigned plots of farmland so long as the land did not sit fallow or was converted to industrial use. In Wasteland some families leased their entire plots to sharecroppers, leaving them free to open a restaurant or commute to jobs in Jilin city. Other families leased strips of their allotment.

San Jiu had leased a strip of paddy from a fellow villager in need of cash. The local government approved the deal, but after the land produced more rice than expected, it tried to reassign the plot before the next planting. "I had a signed contract between me and the collective," San Jiu said. "They just didn't expect the land to be that good. They thought it should go back into the pool of village land, to be redistributed. To a government official's relative, I suspected."

In 2010, 65 percent of China's "mass incidents," as protests were called, concerned rural land. Often the conflicts were between farmers and developers or the local government in league with them. San Jiu consulted his law books and sought advice from a legal expert on a call-in radio show. The expert, a professor, suggested he view his dispute as contractual, not personal. This, San Jiu said with a self-aware laugh, only angered him more.

"Of course it was personal," he told me, clenching his fists. "Everything in a village is personal."

Still, he had filed a complaint in a Jilin city court, asking that the village government be made to honor the terms of their contract. When the court dismissed it without ruling, San Jiu boarded a train to Beijing.

Petitioning the central government was rarely successful; some supplicants spent years clutching ever-growing sheaves of photocopied documents, waiting to be heard, while others were hauled back by police who followed them from home. San Jiu, however, got lucky.

"I was there only a couple days," he said. "I followed the law handbooks I had collected. The important clause, which I memorized, was: 'Collectively owned land must be registered at the county government, which will issue a land-use contract and land-rights certificate.' I had those. An official read them and wrote a letter for me to bring back here."

The document, called a *gonghan*, told a lower court that the petitioner's grievance had been heard in Beijing and suggested the matter be handled "courteously and according to law." It was, in effect, an upbraiding for wasting the central government's time.

"The Jilin city court heard my appeal right away. The contract was upheld. I can still farm that land."

"So you won."

He shrugged, looking wary of the harvest to come.

San Jiu had refused to contract his crop to Eastern Fortune Rice, and so far it had been a smart bet. His last harvest sold for the equivalent of forty cents a pound, double the previous year's price. Even after expenses, he still earned 50 percent more than what a contract with Eastern Fortune would have paid.

Like Auntie Yi, he also refused to move to the new apartments. The company representative hadn't threatened him or even called him stubborn. The man understood that San Jiu wanted to stay in his home. But when San Jiu cooked dinner every night, the view from his kitchen window showed the cranes and sprouting high-rises silhouetted in the setting sun. "The taller those buildings get," he said, "the closer they seem."

The rice station was a state-owned shop that sold pesticides and seeds. There are more than 140,000 varieties of rice; the station sold two dozen of them, selected for their suitability for these paddies. San Jiu, like all farmers here, hedged his bets and selected five varieties, whose names ranged from boastful (Super Production Number 1) to technical (Agricultural Institute Number 7) to inventive (Jilin Japonica Number 66) and poetic (a Japanese variety that translated as "Small Part of an Autumn Field").

The rice station showed packets of each, hanging from walls adorned with dried rice husks, banner advertisements for herbicides— OUTSTANDING PADDY: SPRAYING ONCE IS ENOUGH!—and posters for seeds named Harvest Leader Number 8 (and 9, and 13, and 14), which promised higher yields. Pictures showed ripe rice hanging heavy off the stalk.

The seed varieties all looked the same to me, but San Jiu described the properties of each like a car salesman touting a new model's features. "This kind takes 145 days to ripen, and this one takes a few less, but the real difference is that this one averages 90 grains of rice per panicle, but some of these other ones can have a third more than that, so you're getting more rice, obviously, but that's if they all ripen and don't get sick. You'll spend all summer worrying about fungus," he said, shaking his head.

The rice station smelled like musty fertilizer, and the walls were painted the same colors as my classroom. But it looked lively after the brutal winter; its opening signaled planting season. A posted chart explained how to prepare a rice paddy according to the solar cycle. Now, during the period named Grain Rain, was the time to plant beds of seedlings.

"I didn't know you transported seedlings to the paddies," I said. "I thought you just walked through the field broadcasting dry rice like this . . ." I demonstrated the Johnny Appleseed toss, flicking my hand left and right.

San Jiu laughed loudly, as did the clerk standing behind the counter.

"You can't plant like that! You'll starve!"

Actually, rice seeds can be sown this less efficient way. But I learned this later. At that moment I heard the many Chinese synonyms for *moron*.

San Jiu called me a dolt, a fool, a hollow head, and more. It was the happiest I had seen him in weeks.

I interrupted to add: "It must be exhausting transplanting the seedlings, bending over all day."

He snorted. "We use a machine! A mechanized rice transplanter! You load trays of seed beds onto it and it plants them in the paddy." San Jiu's tone made it sound like robots had long followed his every command. But when I asked him when the machine first came to the village, he said, "Last year."

Now it was my turn to teach. In California, this type of short-grain rice was planted by a low-flying propeller plane pelting the paddies with dry seed that bounced like hail off the mud. Standing on the ground meant being stung by a post-wedding seed shower: rice in your hair, rice under your collar, rice in your shoes.

The clerk said, "I wonder who isn't working anymore, that they need to use planes."

"Even though the machine plants our field," San Jiu stressed, "we still prepare the seedlings, and weed the paddies. We still labor."

"Young people don't want to work the fields, though," the clerk said.

It was true. On our walk back to his house along Red Flag Road, everyone pacing the muddy fields, or tending seedbeds in their front yards, looked San Jiu's age. He was about to turn sixty-seven.

Unusual for a Chinese company, Eastern Fortune Rice kept its office building's electric accordion gate open, and its front door, too. I walked in and asked to see the boss. He wasn't there, but the company's chief agronomist offered to take me on a tour. Dr. Liu was in her fifties and wore a white lab coat over slacks and a hand-knit sweater. Behind her oversized glasses, her eyes had shown no surprise at seeing me.

"You're the teacher," she said. "I often see you running. How do you know where to go?"

"I just head for the river, and the hills."

"Do you get lost?"

"I try."

"You should make a map. You could sell it at the hot spring. Tourists like to drive around and take pictures."

"I still haven't reached the foothills. That's my goal: ten miles each way."

"That's far! That's like running all the way downtown."

Dr. Liu lived there, in Jilin city, where she taught at the agricultural institute. She told her origin story chronologically and quickly, sounding practiced. In the late 1990s, Wasteland's then village chief hired a man named Liu Yandong—no relation to Dr. Liu—as his driver. When officials visited, the leader would send Mr. Liu to purchase the freshest rice. Mr. Liu always drove to a neighboring township that had its own mill and polishing plant, and better-looking and -tasting rice.

"His brain opened up," Dr. Liu said. "He thought, 'If I have money, I can open my own mill in Wasteland.'"

But he didn't have money. His family was among Wasteland's poorest. And even if he did open the mill, he would have to buy rice to polish. Not just any rice, but high-quality rice.

"He came to the agricultural institute looking for the director, but he was out, and by chance Mr. Liu talked to me. I was doing research on organic rice, which was an initiative that started with the provincial party secretary, who was looking to make a name for himself by doing something experimental. So here comes Mr. Liu and his partner, the other driver. They drove a simple Hyundai. Yes, it was black."

She smiled at my question. Officials, from the president of China down to the chief of a village named Wasteland, rode in black cars.

"I told them what varieties of seeds would be best to try. They left. Then they came back asking if I would teach them how to plant. I came out here and stayed with his family for a few days to see what kind of people they were. They wanted to start something that would be good for the village, something that wasn't being done elsewhere. I told them, 'Look, if you want to make money, that's fine, don't hide it. But I don't care about your money. I care about my research.'"

Dr. Liu smiled at the memory of her conviction.

She told them that the State Council had earmarked funds to develop businesses producing "green food." Dr. Liu suggested they be among the first to raise organic rice.

"Mr. Liu said, 'You can do whatever you want.' That was April 8, 2000. He called the business Eastern Fortune because it combined the last character of his and his partner's names. Then he drove around in his Hyundai seeking approval to start what we called the Eastern Fortune Technological Experimental Site." The adjectives were chosen because they would look pleasing to the agencies that issued business licenses.

"It cost 700 *yuan* [$115] back then to complete the process, but I followed the clerk around the agricultural committee office to make sure she wouldn't pocket the money. I argued that the price was too high, that we were just a small company, and experimental, after all. In the end, she charged me only half the license fee."

It was a modern Chinese business fable: an impoverished village driver, a chance meeting with an agronomist, a farm created from scratch in twenty-two days. I would have been skeptical, until Dr. Liu said she bargained down the price of the business license. That was entirely in the Northeast's character.

"I attended a provincial agricultural meeting in July 2000," she said, "and began my second career, in public relations. For the next year I was an advertisement for the company, telling officials at meetings in Dalian city, in Xi'an, in Beijing, about our farm. Our first harvest brought no recognition. The next one attracted financing from the State Council. Mr. Liu was able to open the polishing mill that had triggered his dream. I'll show you the new one."

We walked past the posted results of a company Ping-Pong tournament and across the road, where, in temperature-controlled silos, the company stored 280 tons of processed rice.

"This all used to be marshland, navigable only by boat," she said, matching what Auntie Yi had told me. "The land was almost perfectly flat already. The marshes were drained, and workers dredged an irrigation canal from the Songhua River. The first rice was planted in 1965."

"My aunt said it was 1955," I corrected. "She lived here then."

Dr. Liu asked who my aunt was. Her eyes narrowed. I felt the end of the tour drawing near. But no, she knew Auntie Yi for her poppies. She pressed a mental Delete key and repeated when rice was first planted with the corrected date.

"Farmers only produced a fraction of what they do now," she said, regaining her footing as we balanced on a strip of raised dirt separating paddies. The Northeast grew 12 percent of China's total rice crop, but nearly half of its output of the short, sticky variety. "It's strong and cold tolerant," Dr. Liu said, "and a good plant to raise organically."

Eastern Fortune used animal feces as fertilizer: organic fertilizer was often made from sheep poop, Dr. Liu noted. The company no longer used river water but extracted it from forty feet below the soil. "It's clean; we monitor it all the time," she said.

As China developed, food safety and pollution rapidly became national concerns. In 2010 the results of a countrywide soil survey were classified as a state secret, but by 2013 a high-ranking official announced that eight million acres—an area the size of Maryland—was so polluted that "farming it should not be allowed." In early 2014 the government released the results of an eight-year survey that found that one-fifth of farmland, mostly in central and southern China, was contaminated.

"Really, our company's biggest concern isn't pollution," Dr. Liu said as we walked to the paddies. I thought of the Head Gardener worrying over recent soil samples, and the string of feed, fertilizer, and ethanol plants on the road from Jilin city to Wasteland. I imagined villagers'—and my— insides pulsing radioactive green.

"Everything is fine," Dr. Liu said. "Don't worry. I'm not worried."

A moment passed. That wasn't true, she admitted. She worried about weeds and bugs. "We've experimented with all sorts of preventions. We put laying ducks in the paddies at planting, in those little wooden houses you see out there. When the ducklings are a month old, they can start swimming around and eating insects. We've tried putting crabs in the water, too: they're always hungry."

I said I liked the ducks. In the silent if croaking countryside, seeing them swim past in a paddy made me smile. Ducks always look content.

Dr. Liu clucked her tongue. "Those ducks taught me a hard lesson! One year I gave them special food—really high-quality organic feed. Well, what do you think happened? They stopped eating the paddy's weeds. They got lazy and just waited for me to bring that gourmet stuff. It was ridiculous. I fed them so well, they wouldn't work. When it rained, they would even stay in their little houses, waiting for me to arrive with dinner." The ducks won that round. Starting the following year, Dr. Liu cut their rations. Now they again fattened themselves on insects.

As in a fable, the ducks taught Dr. Liu a lesson, one she passed down to villagers who contracted their crop to Eastern Fortune.

"Every year after harvest, we call all of our farmers in for a meeting," she said, "even the ones who lease their land to us and no longer work it themselves. We remind them how to choose quality seeds, and what temperature the seedbed soil should be, and how to choose the good sprouts and get rid of the rest. The farmers know this process. We Chinese have been doing it for thousands of years. But every year, no matter what new technology arrives or what machine replaces hands, we reteach the old ways in case they don't remember."

Recalling the snapshot of a lecture shown on the calendar the company had given to Auntie Yi, I said that some farmers must tune out the lesson.

"Of course!" Dr. Liu said with a smile. "So I ordered calendars with the instructions written above the corresponding months. They're big and red and shiny and look really great. We hand them out at Lunar New Year as gifts. My hope is that their children study it, so at least they'll have read of our planting traditions, even if they'll never do it themselves."

CHAPTER 7

THE PILGRIMS' PROGRESS

A UNTIE YI, WEARING her bucket hat, knelt to weed the earth around her poppies along Red Flag Road. She asked what I saw at the hot spring and whether I had learned anything about Eastern Fortune's plans. We squatted and talked. It was a weekday, and the road was empty save for us, pawing at the black earth.

She wondered aloud if there was such a thing as too much development. "How do you know when a place has developed just enough?"

When I had lived in Beijing, I interviewed scores of residents, officials, and urban planners over four years. No one had ever asked this question. And no one—from architects to developers to the government—had ever asked my neighbors what they thought about plans to renovate—or, more commonly, raze—their courtyard homes and community. Many of them would have preferred a new apartment far away from the crowded, dilapidated lanes. Others would have suggested upgrading a house's heat and hygiene, then leaving the people alone to live in a neighborhood that had thrived for six hundred years. As the capital—once a densely textured masterpiece of traditional urban design—transformed into a car-centered sprawl linked by beltways and malls, I often politely pointed out that this was the sort of planning the United States had begun to reverse. Beijing didn't have to make the same mistakes that America had made. With indignant pride, one official replied: "We have every right to make the same mistakes that America made." Widen roads, flatten the courtyards, add subways, build higher: Beijing could never be developed enough.

Its cities' new skylines notwithstanding, China still classified one-tenth of its population as living below the poverty line, earning the equivalent of $1.25 each day. The majority of these 128 million people lived in rural areas.

As villages went, Wasteland was comparatively well-off, with its fertile cropland and train station and businesses and paved streets. As the circumference of my morning run expanded, however, I discovered that, outside the village, Red Flag Road narrowed and crumbled, eventually turning to packed dirt. I ran through hamlets lined not with shops and schools but piles of smoldering trash. Wood-framed houses that needed repainting were fenced by rows of wired-together tree branches. Hanging on them were hand-painted signs announcing GOSLINGS FOR SALE and WELL DIGGING the way poor American towns displayed ones emblazoned with RABBITS and HAIRCUTS. People stood with their hands thrust into the pockets of tattered winter jackets. They eyed me without saying a word as I weaved around standing puddles, feeling like a trespasser caught peeping.

One morning, waking with my roommate Mr. Guan as he set out, I ran to the Songhua River. His fishing spot looked, I imagined, just as it had for centuries. Unlike in Jilin city, here the riverbanks had not been landscaped and smoothed with cement. The fields bordered flat marshland, which ran unimpeded to the channel. Mr. Guan, standing in the current as he threw his nets, seemed an apparition from the past. He said that sometimes the hot spring's day-trippers saw him selling fish in Wasteland and snapped his picture. But he wasn't a character in a rustic rural fantasy; he was Mr. Guan, making his living.

I followed the Songhua's wide bends north for three miles, never encountering a bridge, ferry, or person—not even somebody selling bottled water, which you encounter even on mountainsides in China. A magpie tagged beside me, flitting along electric wires strung between wooden poles that still held their bark.

The fields changed to fresh-planted corn. Pioneer brand seed packets littered the ground. At first I lamented the reach of global agribusiness into local furrows, but in a way these seeds closed a loop. Pioneer, now owned by DuPont, had been founded in Iowa by Franklin Roosevelt's future vice president Henry Wallace. He created the first hybrid corn seed by combining an American strain with one from China.

I turned and ran south through a hamlet named Big Red Soldier. It consisted of soggy redbrick houses that looked like they needed to be disassembled, dried in the sun, and put back together.

"Everything around here used to look like that," Auntie Yi said, back at her poppies.

On the eve of the solar term named Grain Fills, San Jiu raked his paddy's remaining chaff and stubble into piles for burning. The dampness wheezed out plumes of white smoke that smoldered overnight. My walk home after dinner was illuminated by constellations of embers pulsing in the dark.

The next morning a tractor driven by a hired laborer tilled San Jiu's paddy, churning the ash into fertilizer and lifting soil from fifteen inches beneath the dun-colored mud. By lunchtime his field looked like a pan of brownie mix. We softly sank to our ankles in the rich loam.

Organic farming cost too much and required more labor than San Jiu could handle. He paced in rows, spraying a herbicide named Japonica Result 612. Its main ingredient was called pyrazosulfuron-ethyl, and in Chinese the package warned it was not to be ingested by rabbits, guinea pigs, bobwhite quail, bluegill sunfish, or rats. "It's too dangerous for rats!" I exclaimed, but San Jiu said it was safe; everyone used it. In fact, it was a common weed-killer worldwide, sold under brand names such as Diehard and—I laughed at the logic of this one—Nondoctor.

The village pump opened, covering the paddies in an inch of standing water. The mechanized planter plugged the seedlings into the soil and the pump came on again, submerging them. San Jiu's crop was in for the season. He celebrated the same way he celebrated the end of every day: with a meal on his *kang*, sipping beer and watching the nightly national news.

In June, as the solar terms changed from Grain in Ear to Summer Solstice, the landscape turned into an expanse of verdant stalks. Red Flag Road cut a gray wake through a sea of green. After the white winter and rain-soaked spring, sunshine and oxygen returned; I swore I could feel the photosynthesis and taste the chlorophyll. (It could also have been the Nondoctor.)

The paddies sparkled, too: farmers tied compact discs to sticks to reflect sunlight and keep sparrows from landing for a snack. The water's stillness was occasionally broken by the plunk of a frog, a paddling duck, or a leaping fish. San Jiu said the creatures were the best pesticide: the frogs ate insects, the ducks ate worms, and the fish ate fungus.

For the first time since arriving, I understood Frances's attachment to Wasteland. Unlike in Chinese cities, the geography had remained largely unchanged. The view from her former home, now San Jiu's, looked the same. In Beijing most of our favorite places, including entire neighborhoods where we once taught and lived and dated, had been remade. We had little to revisit there; that past lived only in our memories, which were fading, making it feel like that time had irrevocably passed, if it even had happened at all.

The countryside did not provoke that type of nostalgia, Frances said. There were no good old days, only good old families enduring the conditions together. But still she beamed on her return for a weekend, running to show me where, as a little girl, she had sat and kneaded the wet black earth, watching her grandmother bend to plant rice seedlings. The old woman had gently sung the folk song that begins, "Little sparrow, your clothes are so colorful! Why do you come here every spring?"

Thirty years later, Frances pointed to the spot. She could see the past clearly through eyes welling from joy.

How much development was enough? Eastern Fortune's billboard advertised its goal to BUILD THE NORTHEAST'S TOP VILLAGE, but Auntie Yi reminded me that my neighbors, including San Jiu, had themselves built it with their own hands. Fifty years ago, most of Wasteland had been dunes and marsh.

A century before that, explorers traversing the surrounding region described the land in journals that called to mind those of Daniel Boone hacking through Kentucky or Lewis and Clark crossing the American West, slathering their skin in bacon fat as a barrier against palm-sized mosquitoes. One of Manchuria's first extensive surveys was written by an Indian civil service officer who arrived in 1886 to collect specimens of flora and fauna. Mostly he found bugs. "I have not words to express to you the multitude of mosquitoes, gnats, wasps, and gadflies that attacked us at every step," Henry E. M. James recorded. "Each of us, armed with a horse's tail fixed on an iron prong, endeavored to strike them, and this weak defence only served to render the enemy more vicious in his attacks. As for me, I was completely beaten, without strength either to advance or protect myself from the stinging of these insects; or if at times, I raised my hand to my face, I crushed ten or twelve with one blow."

To combat the bloodsuckers, which "left wounds as if struck by buckshot," James said that Chinese settlers plowed fields wearing iron circlets on their heads that held smoldering pieces of wood. "If there were a time not worth living," he wrote, "it was summer in Manchuria."

His fellow traveler was a twenty-three-year-old subaltern named Francis Younghusband. Later, during the Great Game between Britain and Russia, the cavalryman would lead a murderous invasion of Tibet, then return to England to become president of the Royal Geographical Society. In 1936, stemming from a bolt of divine inspiration that had struck him while retreating from Lhasa, he founded the World Congress of Faiths, espousing pantheism and free love.

On his 1886 expedition to Manchuria, the young Younghusband battled gadflies, "another form of torture invented for these parts." He described mules covered in blood, driven mad by the attacks. In an attempt to lessen the stings, the explorers slept head to toe with their assistants beside a roaring fire at the peak of summer's heat. "We, of course, got quite inadequate rest, and that period of our journey was a very trying one."

If the midges didn't get you, the Manchurian tigers might. "If any one is missing, after the signal for the return to the troop," another traveler recorded, "they conclude him devoured by the beasts, or lost thro' his own carelessness."

Travelers disappeared into the region's forests, so thick that, during a nine-day crossing, one eighteenth-century party was "obliged to have several trees cut down by the Mantcheou soldiers, to make room for our observations of the sun's meridian." Considering the sights on this leg one hundred years later, Younghusband wrote, "We never saw anything but the trunks of trees."

Accounts of nineteenth-century Manchurian travel were a litany of spirits being broken. An English consul traveling to Jilin city in 1896 wrote that "the road was very unsafe, brigandage was of common occurrence, inns were few and far between, and to go on till dark would simply be to court danger." The next morning he reloaded his revolvers when a bullet came "whistling into the room in which we were seated and scattered the mud from the opposite wall."

As the Manchu's empire waned, bandits evolved into warlords who ruled the Northeast in everything but name. A Chinese miner who struck it rich, known as Han of the Frontier, established a small forest kingdom of 50,000 settlers that existed until his great-grandson retired in 1925. Bandits, known collectively as "red beards" for the opera masks they wore, scoured the postal roads and plains. One brigand, named Ma the Crazy, pillaged towns across the Northeast, requiring Beijing to dispatch an imperial army of four thousand men to hunt and kill him.

In the nineteenth century, the late-summer rainy season turned the tracks carved by mule-pulled carts into a quagmire. "Road-building" consisted of blazing new ruts alongside the existing ones. They froze in winter, making for jolting journeys in springless wagons.

The explorer Henry E. M. James, fitted in sheepskins against snow-storms and minus-40-degree-Fahrenheit temperatures, didn't mind the extreme climate: "As long as the north wind does not blow, it is an honest, dry, invigorating cold." Echoing my punishing winter walks up Red Flag Road, he added, "But, when the north wind does blow, the less said about it the better."

He was pleased when he covered thirty miles in a day. Often, however, the party would at last arrive at a settlement to find a ramshackle inn, a few scrubby mud huts fumigated with cow dung, and a meal that consisted of "some uneatable pork" and "a curry made of salted eggs six months old." His partner Younghusband's prose brightened at the sight, in a garrison store, of a can of Singapore pineapples.

Yet most journeys include delay and regret. Younghusband, after complaining of natives' stares, added, "But these are the ordinary experiences of every traveler in China, and I am only repeating what has been described a hundred times." His sanguinity may have come from his discovery, on the trip, of opium. ("To my mind, it is one of God's good gifts.") He also, like travelers to the Northeast today, savored the local specialty, dumplings. He described ones "so beautifully cooked and so light that they almost melted in the mouth like jelly."

The Northeast holds, after the Yangtze, the second largest river system in China, but its silt-laden channels then ran wide and shallow: in some places the Songhua was a mile wide and three feet deep. River traffic was masted junks with high bows and sterns, not steam-powered ships. An American captain, sent by President Pierce in 1856 to test the waters for commercial possibilities, said that the sound of pilots crying the river depth to the steersman was "slow work, as they laboriously poled along the sand bar, or cordelled along the shore, and reminded me of the early barge and keel-boat navigation on the Mississippi and Ohio." Though he felt his idea would be dismissed as an impossibility, the captain presciently recommended a railroad be built instead, linking Europe to Manchuria and then the Pacific.

The rivers were prone to flooding, too. In the seventeenth century, a French priest accompanying the Manchu emperor to Jilin noted a deluge that tore away their fishing nets and damaged their boats, compelling the group to return to land. "The sturgeon has made sport of us," said the emperor. The surrounding alluvial plains were marked with camels and horses dead and half-submerged in the mud, and "even the emperor was compelled to go on foot, lest his horse sink."

In 1886, Henry E. M. James arrived in Jilin city to find its western section "under water a great deal of the year. The inhabitants boat from one place to another just as they do in Venice."

Over their three-thousand-mile journey, James and Younghusband survived pests, tigers, bandits, freezing temperatures, bad roads, and intemperate waterways. For eight months across Manchuria, they met woodsmen, gold miners, soybean farmers, Buddhist monks, and ginseng hunters. All had migrated to the new land, recently opened for settlement in a rush that mirrored the one drawing southern Chinese to California in search of gold. Between 1850 and the century's end, Jilin province's population increased tenfold.

As James and Younghusband advanced north, they would often see, heading in the opposite direction, mule-pulled carts laden with coffins. "These were the bodies of colonists who had died in Manchuria," Younghusband wrote, "and were being brought back to their homes again." A caged rooster perched atop each coffin. "The cock was intended, by his crowing, to keep the spirit awake while passing through the Great Wall; otherwise, it was feared, the spirit might go wandering off somewhere and forget the body, and the body might be brought in and the spirit left behind."

Were this a film, the scene would fade here, on the eve of Manchuria's transition from an isolated imperial frontier to an international railway zone. We hear the creak of wooden carts pulled by mules straining over muddy ruts. The northern wind rustles shoulder-high sorghum. Masked bandits hide amidst the stalks. Westerners advance past retreating Chinese. Roosters crow on coffins, urging the dead awake.

In Jilin city, Frances and I walked down the main road, lined with shops found anywhere in China: Shoe City, KFC, Sock Town, a Korean Spicy Soup restaurant, cell phone retailers, a Malahaha Duck Tongue King take-out window, another KFC, and the clothing stores Valued Squirrel, Gweat, and Rich Boss. But then the view showed something unique: a building that survived the city's great fire of 1930, which had incinerated its wooden buildings. There, on the banks of the Songhua River, stood a gray brick church. Built by French Catholic missionaries in 1926, its Gothic spires looked incongruous against the stolid office building tiled in white squares at its back. Mass was still said here daily, even if most Jilin residents used the church only as a photo backdrop.

We walked along the river promenade, past Ping-Pong tables and basketball courts and zero-resistance exercise equipment, upon which grandmothers stepped and spun. "They should add these elderly playgrounds to city maps," Frances said. "They make good landmarks for giving directions."

Instead our map showed ducks drawn onto the water. We looked at the actual spot and saw: ducks.

"Are they decoys?" I wondered. "This is where the imperial boatworks used to be; that's why the plaza has a ship statue."

"Those ducks are just where they're supposed to be," Frances said, checking the map. "It's really up-to-date."

In faint characters, the map marked something across the river called Holy Mother Cave. Neither of us had heard of it. But just behind the blooming elms we spied a gleaming white steeple.

The cab crossed a bridge and dropped us at the start of a rutted cement road. "I can't drive down to the river on that," the driver said. "I'll never make it back up. You can walk." We stood in front of a small factory that manufactured aluminum windows and doors. I hesitated, waiting for the unseen guard dog to make the first move, but Frances pointed to a small, rusting blue sign: RETIREMENT HOME. "There won't be any dogs, otherwise the old folks would complain about the noise," she guessed.

We walked downhill past vacant houses. No dogs. The road ended at a tall wrought-iron gate for the Catholic Seminary of Jilin Province. It looked vacant, too. A sign posted by the police warned: NO BARBECUING. NO LITTERING. RESPECT THE ENVIRONMENT OF HOLY MOTHER CAVE.

The road tapered into a path and, turning a corner, revealed a twelve-foot opening in the hillside garlanded with strings of plastic yellow chrysanthemums. A slab of granite within the recess represented the altar, overlooked by a statue of the Virgin Mary perched in an alcove. Six simple wooden benches faced the shrine. The trickle of springwater plinked from within the cave.

"That's a surprise," Frances said. "There aren't even Buddhist grottoes in the Northeast. No Buddhas, but a Mary."

A plaque in Chinese explained that the shrine dated to 1920, when a French Catholic priest arrived in Jilin to build the gray Gothic church. By 1938 the Northeast had nearly four hundred Catholic churches and twelve hundred French priests. During the same era, Protestant missionaries—Irish and Scottish Presbyterians, mostly—founded hospitals that still operate. (The rationale of sending medical workers, a priest explained then, was that "a doctor has a great advantage that he may have an opportunity of relieving bodily suffering, and thus gain an entrance." English instruction functions similarly today.) Perhaps because they were trained to take patient notes, the medical missionaries were diligent about recording their impressions of Manchuria.

The thin, fragile books collected dust in the deep recesses of American library stacks, their previous due dates stamped by hand a century before. I was drawn to them: most missionaries wrote surprisingly little about God but rather about being alone and foreign in Manchuria, and being very happy for it.

I would like to have shared dumplings with a woman named Isabel Mitchell. Tall and strong, with pale eyes and frizzy brown hair pinned atop her head, the Belfast-born Dr. Mitchell moved to Jilin city in 1905, at age twenty-two. In her journal she recorded: "I could weep, but not with sorrow, for my heart is filled with a deep, deep joy. I have reached the land at last, the haven where I would be." She arrived in winter and wondered if she would ever see a blade of grass. In spring she recorded that "mud and blue" were the colors of Manchuria: the latter described men's cotton gowns and the "clear, dazzling sky." Although she faced much more deprivation than I had, her letters echoed how I once felt as a Peace Corps volunteer, acclimating to stares, anticipating mail from home, and slowly learning Chinese. "Every day," she wrote, "I feel more and more what a wonderful thing it is that I have been allowed to come out here."

Dr. Mitchell also constantly wondered whether her work made a difference. She decided to stop questioning its significance: "Being here is the meaning."

After succumbing to diphtheria at age twenty-six, Isabel Mitchell was buried in Jilin's Russian cemetery. A shopping center now stood on the site. No trace of her grave remained.

Frances and I were surprised that Holy Mother Cave had survived. According to its plaque, the shrine to Mary was destroyed during the Cultural Revolution, and Red Guards painted anticlerical slogans in the grotto. In 1986, local Catholics donated funds to restore the site "as a quiet place for reflection and prayer." The wishes of supplicants were scrawled in characters whose black ink shone off the white-painted walls of the chapel above the cave. On this day the shuttered church was attended only by furry spiders fattening themselves on webs hanging over messages to Mary, such as:

> I hope I earn a lot of money.
> I hope I grow a little taller.
> I hope I study better.
> I hope for a good job.
> I hope my mother buys me a cell phone with an MP5 player.

"That person is confusing Mary with Santa Claus," Frances said.

I thought perhaps a place had developed enough when its people prayed not for health or safety but for a cell phone upgrade, or:

*I hope my mother listens to me better. I hope I can listen to her
better, too. We need to stop fighting.*
I hope my daughter's temper improves.
I hope my father stops gambling.
I hope for a good husband. Around 30 years old.

I found the words comforting and human, a reliquary of yearning instead
of remains. Frances leaned against me as we read a letter written in dense
characters that filled an alcove's entire wall. It began: *I miss you, oh how
I miss you. Do you know? Do you miss me? Now you won't speak to me—how
did we end up like this? I really didn't want things to end this way. I really didn't.
Life is so short.*

I held Frances tighter. As the short-lived Dr. Isabel Mitchell had
recorded, being here was the meaning.

CHAPTER 8

TO THE MANCHURIA STATION!

THE MANCHU CAME to power on horseback and had shown little
interest in—or understanding of—railroads. The empress dowager
had not allowed tracks to enter Beijing, as they would pierce the city's
wall. In 1888 her ministers installed a small train within the Forbidden
City that ran between her quarters and dining hall. She would ride in it
only if eunuchs pulled the cars. The steam engine's clatter, she said, would
disrupt the palace's feng shui.

But only twenty-five years later, a Scottish missionary stationed in
the Northeast wrote: "There are few parts of the world where the
modern change in ease of access has been more marked than in
Manchuria. One can now leave London at nine o'clock on a Monday
morning, and after a comfortable sleeping-car [train] journey drive
through [Manchurian] streets in the afternoon of Friday, eleven days
later. The contrast with thirty years ago, and indeed with thirteen
years ago, is greater than the contrast between that time and the days
of sailing ships."

By the time the Belfast nurse Isabel Mitchell traveled overland to Jilin
city in 1920, she passed through Harbin, a booming railway hub nicknamed
"the Paris of the East." Residents from fifty-three nations—including the
Far East's largest Jewish community—spoke forty-five languages on its
cobblestone streets.

The imperial court did not have a sudden reformist vision to link their
Manchurian homeland to Europe by train. Instead, it relented to the railroad's construction by foreigners.

The Manchu had tried to bend the Northeast to their design via restrictions against Chinese migration and the building of the Willow Palisade. By the mid-nineteenth century those plans had failed, while their dynasty also began losing its grip on greater China. Beginning in 1850, the domestic rebellion led by the Han Chinese who declared himself the younger brother of Jesus lasted fourteen years and killed twenty to thirty million people; the cost of suppressing the revolt drained imperial coffers. Also during this era, the First and Second Opium Wars with Britain and France forced Chinese ports open to foreign trade, led to the establishment of diplomatic legations near the Forbidden City, and resulted in the Manchu's summer palaces being torched.

"You can scarcely imagine the beauty and magnificence of the palaces we burnt," wrote the young British captain Charles Gordon (later killed in Khartoum). "It made one's heart sore . . . It was wretchedly demoralizing work for an army." Among the spoils: the first Pekingese dog in Great Britain, presented to Queen Victoria. She named it Looty.

Russia forced the Qing court to tear up the first treaty it had signed with a European power, in 1689, ending campaigns that extended Chinese territory further into Siberia. The new agreement moved the border back to the Heilongjiang (Black Dragon, or Amur in Russian)—where it remains—resulting in the loss of a Texas-size swath of land and access to the Pacific shore. In 1860, nearly six thousand miles from Moscow, on a piece of coastline Chinese and Manchu fishermen called Haishenwai (Sea Cumber Cliffs), Russia built the port of Vladivostok. Now it had to get there.

In Chinese, this era is dubbed one of "unequal treaties" and "the mad rush to carve up the melon," but it also resembled a royal-family game of Monopoly. In 1897, Czar Nicholas II forcibly leased the southern Manchurian redoubt Port Arthur. In 1898, his cousin Kaiser Wilhelm II grabbed the central coast port of Tsingtao, compelling the court to sign a ninety-nine-year lease. Under similar terms that year, Wilhelm's grandmother Queen Victoria extended her hold on Hong Kong.

As czarevitch, Nicholas had sunk a ceremonial shovel for the construction of the Trans-Siberian Railway. A Chinese diplomat attending Nicholas's coronation in 1896 agreed to grant Russia a rail concession across Manchuria, cutting its distance to Vladivostok and the Pacific.

The three-million-ruble bribe paid to the diplomat notwithstanding, the railroad's construction actually became possible far from St. Petersburg's Winter Palace, where a war fought just offstage in Manchuria's wings resulted in the Qing dynasty turning to Russia for protection.

The kingdom of Korea had been a tributary state of China. An industrializing Japan wanted it as a buffer zone against foreign encroachment in Asia. During an internal rebellion in 1894, the Korean king requested the assistance of Chinese troops, whose arrival broke an agreement between China and Japan to notify the other side before deploying forces. Japan sent a larger contingent, which seized the royal palace in Seoul and deposed the king in favor of pro-Japanese government.

The First Sino-Japanese War was short-lived and one-sided. One of China's four naval fleets, the North Pacific, had once been Asia's mightiest flotilla, but it was crippled by officers' corruption and embezzlement. Admirals had pawned their deck guns, perhaps because no ammunition had been purchased for the fleet since 1891. The funds were directed to restore Beijing's looted summer palaces, including the construction of a double-decked marble paddleboat that was anything but seaworthy. The empress dowager used it as a veranda for drinking tea.

In September 1894, Japanese warships sank the North Pacific fleet and routed Chinese troops from Pyongyang, pursuing them north into Manchuria. Seven months later, the Qing court signed a treaty that recognized Korea's independence and granted Japan control of Taiwan. (It soon annexed the nearby Senkaku/Diaoyu Islands, which China also claimed, causing saber-rattling to this day.) It also ceded to Japan the Liaodong Peninsula in southern Manchuria.

Russian-controlled Port Arthur sat at its tip. Unlike Vladivostok, the port remained ice-free year-round. The czar persuaded France and Great Britain to force Japan—under threat of war—to hand the peninsula to Russia in exchange for an increased indemnity. In 1898, Russia signed a lease with China for the territory.

"Of course you already know, dear Mama," the young Nicholas II wrote to his mother that year, "the glad news of the occupation of Port Arthur, which in time will be the terminus of the Siberian railway. At last we shall have a real port that does not freeze. Above all I am thankful that this occupation was peaceful, without the loss of any Russian blood! This gives me real joy. Now we can feel safe out there for a long time!"

To the Qing court, Russia sold the idea of a railroad through their Manchurian homeland as part of a secret defense pact against Japan. "In order to facilitate the access of Russian land forces to places under threat," the contract said, "the Chinese government agrees to the construction of a railroad across the Chinese provinces of Heilongjiang and Jilin toward Vladivostok." And also south to Port Arthur, as the czar exulted to his mom.

Echoing the example of the Canada Atlantic Railway, which connected Montreal to Halifax via Maine, Russians engineers drew a track diagonally across northern Manchuria, forming a nine-hundred-mile-long shortcut to Vladivostok on the Trans-Siberian Railway from Moscow. Once completed, an influx of Europeans arrived in numbers the Qing dynasty neither expected nor had the power to curb.

The line was named the Chinese Eastern Railway, and its tracks formed a T-shaped steel suture running across Manchuria's shoulders and down its spine. The empress dowager ordered that the train could not enter existing Manchurian towns or garrisons or pass near graveyards, which would disturb *feng shui*. In 1901, one of its first passengers wrote that he was "weary of gazing off upon the eternal snows, the vast expanses of nothingness which stretch around the crawling train." Time and again it pulled into a desolate station, prompting this exchange:

"What is the name of this place?

"It has not got a name yet."

Heading east from Russia, the first stop in China was Manchzhuriya Station. Its echo is heard in the city's contemporary name: Manzhouli—"Inside Manchuria."

The border town sits on Inner Mongolian grasslands eight hundred miles northwest of Wasteland, and I was eager to see if any relics remained from its founding. From there, I would retrace the journey travelers made a century before, crossing northernmost Manchuria on the Chinese Eastern Railway.

Train 1303 was not a high-speed carriage but one of the antiquated four-number long-haulers that formed a slow-rolling town square. Passengers removed their shoes, stretched out, and passed the hours sipping steaming tea, making small talk, eavesdropping on others' small talk, staring, playing cards, texting, reading, pacing, napping, drinking, and snacking. My package of Drunkard brand fried peanuts came with instructions in English that explained: "You can enjoy it as soon as you open it."

I had a hard berth, one of six bunks stacked off an open corridor. On the opposite bunk, a young man named Lang Shitao stared searchingly out the window. "When I look in the mirror, I don't see me," he said, motioning to the acne that colonized his cheeks. Everyone became close, immediately, on a train, and my foreignness often transformed the berth into a confessional. The twenty-one-year-old was headed for a dermatology clinic near his home in Harbin city. I said I was heading to Manzhouli, looking for traces of history. His parents were different ethnicities, he volunteered. His mother was Han Chinese, his father Manchu. Her parents migrated north on the train for work; his parents traced their lineage to bannermen, the imperial military-administrative system. He wondered how to say this in English, then asked me to explain the difference between saying one is "Manchu" versus "a Manchu."

"I am both," he decided, "but really, I'm a 'mixed-blood.'"

He had taken a leave from engineering school, which he attended on a partial scholarship awarded because his identification card listed him as Manchu; ethnic minorities were eligible for such benefits. Previous generations of Manchu hid their identity, passing as Han Chinese, he said. Now, even though the national census counted only 10 million Manchu, it was one of the fastest-growing ethnic groups as people reclaimed their lineage. Mr. Lang, like every Manchu I had met, could not speak or write Manchu; the language was all but extinct, glimpsed mostly on signboards in former palaces.

As the train picked up speed, lines blurred past the window: telephone poles, apple orchards, smokestacks, and walls bearing painted ads for liquor, motorcycles, and the promise THE PEOPLE'S RAILWAY SERVES THE PEOPLE. Lang watched until the sun sank and the window showed his hated reflection. Then he drew the curtains.

I woke somewhere after Harbin. A striking woman wearing purple long johns that matched her painted toenails lounged in Lang's bunk. For a drowsy moment I thought his skin treatment had been a marked success. The train bore west out of the Songhua River valley, entering wetlands that ran to the horizon. The only movement out the window came at the town of Daqing, where "kowtow machines," as pumpjacks are called in Chinese, rose and bowed, bowed and rose, extracting petroleum from China's largest oilfield.

Passengers padded to the cabin's squat lavatories and open sinks holding toothbrushes. Gurgles and rinse-spits echoed down the corridor. I grabbed a wad of tissues, filled a cup with Nescafé, and walked in the opposite direction to the samovar. The adjoining car was a "soft sleeper," a higher ticket class, but no one stirred behind the cabin's closed doors, and I crept to its Western-style toilet, feeling sneaky. The slam of a door at the far coupling revealed a uniformed attendant. *Waddle casual.* He smiled as we turned sideways to allow each other to pass. Subterfuge on a slow train! I was home free.

Sixteen hours remained to Manzhouli. As the train climbed through a low mountain range and entered the grasslands, the houses changed from redbrick structures to squat huts of mortared boulders topped with peaked roofs. The more desolate the geography, the brighter the stations: blue roofs outshone the cloudless sky and plots of sunflowers waved us onward.

The train outpaced civilization. The roads turned to gravel, roofs to thatched straw, rivers to an unpolluted clarity that showed their bottoms. Beside a hut-size station stood a water tower whose narrow stone base and bulbous wooden basin didn't look Chinese but like a prop from Chekhov's *The Cherry Orchard.* The Russian play about modernity colliding with the pastoral begins: "The train has come, thank God. What time is it?"

1901, said the water tower's keystone.

Manchzhuriya Station opened that year. On the train heading here then, a British passenger recorded sitting bored in the dining car, watching the French consul's wife playing waltzes on the piano as the fat Russian conductor waved along with his "delicate pink handkerchief loaded with perfume." Behind them, in the open-topped boxcars, stood "crammed Chinese humanity, and some horses."

Another English writer pronounced the Chinese Eastern Railway a "pantomime," a Potemkin Pullman. "Has ever the world seen such a spectacle? Some say three or four thousand Russian employees, some say five thousand, to run fifteen hundred miles of railway in an Eastern country. The idea that the railway is going to build up a new Manchuria, peopled with white Russians and carrying on a white man's trade entirely separate from the twenty million Chinese in the country, is the idea of a maniac who has no conception of what the Far East really is."

At last, Manchzhuriya Station! Exiting in 1903, the Englishman found the station square crowded with rickshaws and droshkies, Mongolian horse dealers, lama priests, red-turbaned Sikhs, Russian officers, and Chinese coolies. Boomtown morals, too: "In Manchuria the lady with a past is, with few exceptions, the lady who is always present."

I exited the station to find the unpaved square coated in blowing sand and filled only with tumbleweeds.

A grid of dirt roads led to another wooden water tower. Nearby, a row of birch trees fronted the former Russian consulate, whose lemon-yellow façade brightly reflected the Manchurian sun. I pushed open its tall wooden doors, surprised to find them unlocked. My footsteps echoed off shoulder-high wainscoting, and I stood still in a room where tall gauzy curtains billowed in the breeze. Dusty shafts of sunlight angled toward an emerald-colored rug. I expected to hear a telegraph tapping out the news from St. Petersburg. Instead I heard a gentle voice repeating in Chinese, "What are you looking for?"

"The past."

"Have you seen the Lenin Room?"

I was standing in the city museum. Its docent led me past glass cases filled with hundreds of pewter miniatures of Vladimir Ilyich. He doffed his cap, stared resolute, sat in a rocking chair, touched his lapel, read against a bookshelf, walked with a child, and lay with his hands behind his head. Listlessly, the docent said, "The next room is all samovars."

The museum held few artifacts: a rusting bell, a wooden cart, and black-and-white photos that showed the railroad's construction. Russian soldiers in double-breasted tunics, fur hats, and mustachios oversaw pickax-wielding Chinese with their hair braided in queues.

But history was being made outside, where jeeps bearing Russian plates idled next to Chinese taxis, their trunks ballooning with stuffed animals. Thick Russian traders in tracksuits walked alongside women in black tights and bulbous sweaters, lugging bags filled with plungers and extension cords. A billboard trumpeted: MANZHOULI IS ASIA'S LARG-EST INLAND PORT.

A century before, the Russians built Manzhouli to move goods and settlers to farthest Siberia. Now trade moved the opposite direction. The markets sold everything a person needed, and then some. One stall displayed car seats, boxing gloves, doorknobs, calculators, ice skates, fur coats, box cutters, clocks, and bikes. Its proprietor had migrated from southern China. His neighbor came from the next province over. Chatting with the traders at a dozen stalls elicited ten different regional accents. All had moved to Manzhouli via the train. The advertisements seen most on a walk around town were for long-distance mobile phone plans and domestic remittance rates.

Architecturally, Manzhouli didn't look particularly Chinese the way other Manchurian railway towns were touched up after colonials had handed back the keys. There were no recently added Buddhist temples or tiled roofs upturned at the eaves, or even the Communist aesthetic of cement buildings covered with white bathroom tiles. There was no public square. Everything looked new, right down to the plastic deer grazing in the city park. It had been made by fencing off a patch of grassland.

Given the nationwide urgency to raze old and build new, I was surprised to find remnants of Russian tenancy. Across from the train station and past the former consulate, a dirt lane led to the former headquarters of the Russo-Chinese Bank, which had financed the railroad. No sign identified what the building had once been—or since become—but that morning two pasted strips of white paper made an **X** across its double doors, giving notice of eviction.

On the sidewalk, a tout asked if I wanted to see Russian ballerinas and Chinese hip-hop dancers on a nightclub stage, with the understanding, "my friend," that their tops may be loose. I hailed a waiting cab.

"You want to see *what?*" the driver asked, then repeated my request. "The *old* trains." She looked out the windshield. "If we're going out there"—she gestured to the ocean of dusty grass that lapped at Manzhouli on all sides—"you're going to have to pay an extra ten yuan, so I can have my car washed afterward."

The driver pulled her tiny CityBaby sedan onto a new highway that ran flat off the horizon's edge. In the Chinese way of spelling, she traced her name's characters on my left knee: Sun Di. The wind buffeted the car, pushing us from lane to lane like a boat over choppy seas. As she passed trucks hauling coal, Miss Sun dodged the jagged chunks that spilled in our path, laughed with her head thrown back, and said she loved to drive.

"That's Russia." She pointed at grassland that looked indistinguishable from all the rest. The only object out the window was on the Chinese side: a cathedral, under construction. "Actually, it's fake," Miss Sun said. "The tourism bureau is building it as a backdrop for wedding photos."

Miss Sun was thirty-one and grew up here. "When I was a little girl," she said, "most people worked at the coal mine. After layoffs, they worked in the markets. I wasn't pretty enough to get hired there. So I learned how to drive. No meetings. No boss." Another full-throated, head-tilting laugh.

She earned enough to buy her own two-bedroom apartment and put away savings. "I like driving by myself. I don't listen to the radio or drink tea. I think about what I want to achieve next. I like the American way of thinking: that a person should depend on oneself."

She had never married and worried that time was running short. "It's hard to meet men here," she said, echoing the sentiment of border towns worldwide. "The bars are bad places."

"You offered to take me to one."

The laugh again. "Speaking truthfully, Manzhouli's getting safer and more civilized. Now we even have a stoplight." A five-star Shangri-La Hotel was being built, too.

Miss Sun exited the highway to pass through a series of soot-covered, late-Socialist-era matchbox-style buildings affiliated with the coal mine. The CityBaby fell into, then climbed out of, a pothole. We rolled over cracking bits of coal to the lip of a strip mine whose furthest limit was obscured by blowing dust. It descended five stories into the earth. Each level held train tracks.

"I hear we are one of the last places in the world where you can see those," she said, pointing down. White clouds billowed from steam locomotives pulling coal-topped hoppers. An engineer saw us staring from above, waved back and honored the code, which knew no borders. The steam whistle went woo-WOO. I waved, and the engineer tooted again. The guttural sound of the churning black engines pulsed through us, coal dust clung to our cheeks, and Miss Sun bolted for the car. I stood transfixed by the near-extinct trains, feeling transported, imagining riding one of them at fifteen miles an hour from Moscow to Manchzhuriya Station. A worker sidled up and offered to take my photo for five yuan. We're back in China, now.

It was nine hundred miles to the opposite end of the line, ending at the eastern border town of Suifenhe, en route to Vladivostok. That trip, equivalent in distance to Milwaukee to New York City, would take twenty-eight hours, broken by a stop midway, in Harbin. As my train chugged east, the setting sun cast a pink glow over log cabins, gravel roads, and the rising moon. The train passed a lone man shepherding a row of geese, and then a small elementary school whose fenced-in rectangle of trampled grassland held a basketball court with backboards made from railroad ties, and bicycle rims for hoops. How happy this would have made the game's inventor, James Naismith, who wrote, "I am sure that no man can derive more pleasure from money or power than I do from seeing a pair of basketball goals in some out of the way place."

At sunrise, train relations took on the tinge of a morning after a passionate fling: intimacy had been replaced by embarrassed proximity. Due to a neighboring bunkmate's snoring, I had not slept and could barely look in the man's rested eyes. Outside, the view had changed, too: gravel roads had turned to pavement, thatched straw to cement, unpolluted rivers to murky ones, and grassland became rows of concrete apartment blocks. The train crossed the Songhua River over a bridge built by Russians in 1901. The noise of traffic, of honking, of the crowd: Harbin.

Frances joined me there for a sort of rolling conjugal visit. Our overnight train passed through sooty one-road towns whose names evoked a once-promising past: Jade Spring, Duckweed River, Timbersea, Scenic Summit, Horse Crossing Bridge, and Red House. Anyone can come up with "Northern Capital," Beijing's meaning, but what was so special about that red house that gave that place its name? Frances thought I was reading too much into it; they were just names. "Why is it named Wasteland?" she asked, but other than repeating that it had become a village in 1956, I couldn't say.

For eleven hours, the train limped three hundred miles east to the Russian border. Cockroaches wandered the carriage. The food cart sold deep-fried soybeans, corn stewed with pea pods and a knockoff version of Tsingtao beer, named Qingtao, that tasted like ammonia. The attendant took my crisp notes pulled from a Harbin ATM and for change plopped a wad of limp bills in my hand. The further you go from a big city, the more the money resembles a palimpsest.

Frances shrouded herself in the horse blankets provided to each thin-padded bunk. Hong Kong was making her soft, she said. The carriage reverberated with raspy coughs, irrigating sniffles, and, after the lights went off at ten, rumbling snores. Frances pounded the berth above her. The man woke and yelled, "I'll show you the colors, bitch!"

"I'd like to see you try," she icily replied. The man backed down, rolled over and ceased his performance.

"Hong Kong's not making you soft," I whispered.

In Suifenhe, we exited to see a town clinging to the low hills like it was trying to hold on to China and not slide across the border. Aside from the old train station, nothing looked Russian save for the passengers lugging sacks of plastic buckets, tennis rackets, ski jackets, teddy bears, and swim-suits onto buses that would shuttle them home.

At Suifenhe's small museum, the docent refused to charge us an entrance fee and paced slowly behind us. Aside from color-added photos of railroad workers, the only displayed Chinese Eastern Railway artifacts were pocket watches and inkwells. The docent asked us to please wait. Over the years I've learned that this meant an historian has been called, or a local official who would be eager to showcase his town for a foreigner. It usually pays to wait for whoever will arrive.

In Suifenhe, the roles had reversed: I was the person waited for. "I called the newspaper," the docent said. "They're sending a reporter over."

He had mistaken us for someone else, we said. "No, he wants to see you. We never have tourists here, let alone Americans."

How did he know? He heard our English. He watched a lot of *Friends*.

The reporter arrived, and I made a joke about this being a slow news month. He nodded without laughing and asked us to wait. "The photographer is on his way."

Our visit recorded for posterity, we boarded the train back to Harbin. One thing I loved about the Northeast was its ease of travel. The trains ran frequently, and nearly everywhere. Stations garlanded the tracks like the stars of Orion's sword and belt, from Siberia to the Yellow Sea. There was never a need to take a long-distance bus.

I had sworn off them in 2001 after an overnight ride in far western China while suffering from dysentery. No matter how much I had pleaded, then cursed, the driver would not pull over in the desert night. I percolated back to my bunk, suddenly remembering that, three weeks earlier, I had stuffed a wrapped blanket into my backpack when exiting the airplane. It was a fortunate grab: the blue cloth made a pliant diaper. The smell from my upper bunk had woken the surrounding passengers, including an infant, who howled. "Your baby stinks to death!" a man cursed its mother. I balled up the blanket, pulled up my pants, pushed the fetid bundle down by my feet, and lay still. Always take the airplane blanket. Never take an overnight bus.

"That's the most disgusting story I've ever heard," Frances said as our train carriage rocked with snores. We had been together long enough to know each other's tales by rote, but the worst travel experiences were recalled in the sleepless downtime between stations. Frances shook her head, made a face, and laughed. "Tell it again."

Back in Harbin, beneath the green onion domes of a former Russian Orthodox cathedral turned city museum, we paced past photographs of Caucasians riding in carriages through the city's groomed gardens, trailed by their Chinese servants on foot carrying picnic supplies. Other photos showed the muddy banks of the Songhua River in 1898, when the Chinese Eastern Railway began construction. The caption did not note that, in 1998, Chinese authorities canceled a planned international academic conference in Harbin on the project's centennial lest it endorse the notion that Russians had founded the city. A disgusted local Chinese historian said, "An independent nation that has confidence in itself must not be afraid to acknowledge the positive contributions of foreigners in its history. All foreigners were not necessarily aggressors and criminals."

The museum explained that Harbin was settled first by Chinese. In fact, they were native Northeasterners; *Harbin* came from the Manchu name, which meant "a place to dry the nets." Russian surveyors arrived to find only a small abandoned distillery, evidence of previous encampments.

There was, as academics loved to say, a lot to unpack here—origins that could be traced "deep into the immeasurable past" rather than a specific event, illustrating nationalism's "futile attempt to draw impermeable and permanent boundaries onto landscapes that defy the effort." Harbin's museum displayed what it evocatively called the "vicissitudes of history" through photos arranged to show the city Before, During, and After Colonialism. But the story was not so simply told: Harbin's transitions between those periods could also stand for Manchuria's in the first three decades of the twentieth century, an era bookended by the Russian-built railroad and the Japanese invasion. In between, the Qing dynasty collapsed.

Starting in 1898, Russians in Harbin created what amounted to a concession—technically illegal, as their railway lease allowed for the construction and administration of a "zone" of control rather than an entire city with extraterritorial rights. They argued, however, that the railroad required more than tracks, and built offices, hotels, shops, and restaurants along broad lamp-lit boulevards extending from the station, where Moscow merchants alighted. Other settlers included Russian Jews fleeing first the czar's pogroms, then White Russians fleeing the Bolsheviks. Harbin's Jewish community grew to 30,000 people, with two synagogues, a library, and its own banks and twenty periodicals, including one named the *Siberia-Palestine Weekly*. Among those buried in its cemetery is the grandfather of former Israeli prime minister Ehud Olmert, whose parents had fled here from Russia and Ukraine.

In 2004, the Harbin government restored one of the synagogues, featuring a large domed roof and pinnacled colonnade, into a Jewish history research center—this, despite the fact that the last remaining member of the city's Jewish community emigrated in 1985. In 2013 the city announced it would renovate the other, older synagogue, which had been repurposed as a railway hostel.

Until recently, the Saint Sophia Russian Orthodox cathedral had long been bricked up and used as a furniture storeroom. A journalist visiting in the 1970s found the ten-story onion-domed church with "windows broken, the grilles rusted and the main door sealed with a wooden slat with nails at either end." Its redbrick walls were slathered in yellow slogans denouncing imperialism. But in the 1990s, when economic reforms closed unprofitable state-owned enterprises, Manchurian cities looked for new revenue streams, including tourism, such as Harbin's ice carnival. Saint Sophia was suddenly a priceless piece of Harbin's heritage. Public fund-raising, including telethons, raised $1.2 million for the building's renovation and conversion into a museum/patriotic education base.

Like the synagogues, Saint Sophia was a pretty relic, not a house of worship. It made for a nice photo backdrop and place to sit—no small treat in China, where benches in public spaces were usually forbidden to discourage gatherings (and naps). Today's tranquillity belied the city's past as a tinderbox, peopled with seething factions eager to throw a punch or pull the trigger. Saint Sophia's exhibit of the colonial era concluded with a plaque that read, *The old age is gone with the wind, but the past events are unforgettable.* Yet here, most of them were.

The railroad brought Han Chinese entrepreneurs and settlers as well as foreigners, making Harbin "the world's crossroads," a modern version of trade centers such as Xi'an on the ancient Silk Road. For its location on a Songhua River bend, the city was nicknamed "the Pearl on the Swan's Neck," though its early twentieth-century reputation was that of an "Infectious Pit."

In 1903 the British Sinophile Bertram Lenox Simpson (writing as Putnam Weale) found that Harbin showed a different face after the lighting of the lamps. On the way to the theater, he passed on the street two naked men with their skulls beaten in, and "drunken wretches lurking along full of vodka, cursing deeply as they fell over ruts and stones." For a Russian, he observed, "life in Harbin was so little worth living anyway that debauch was preferable to dullness." The parties in gambling saloons went until morning, while "suicides punctuate time and relieve monotony":

> "We have had two suicides this week," whispered a man, "who is
>   to be the third?"
> "Not yourself, I hope."
> "No," he said grimly, "I have got beyond that."

Simpson's visit left him "thoughtful and a little sad. Harbin is the very center of Manchuria . . . a place which will be reached for at all costs by the enemy. Who is to conquer in the climax of national anger, hatred and greed, which must come some day and tear this fair country?" He hoped the battle would be won by numbers alone: 30,000 Russians lived in Harbin alongside 250,000 Chinese. "Russian Manchuria is something of a myth made possible by a gigantic bluff," he wrote. "It is a remnant of 1900 and China under foreign occupation. Even if there is no force used, Chinese ingenuity alone may push Russia back to the Amur [River]."

Instead it was the Japanese who did the pushing, at least from Port Arthur, at the southern tip of Manchuria, to Harbin in the far north. After the armies of eight Western nations occupied Beijing in 1901 to break a siege of foreign embassies by rebels known as the Boxers, Russia kept an enormous force—177,000 soldiers—in Manchuria long after the other armies had withdrawn. In 1903, Bertram Lenox Simpson arrived in Jilin city to see the Russian tricolor flying and Russian troops patrolling the streets and running the telegraph office. Simpson predicted that Russia's position in Manchuria would overextend the czar's army and drain his treasury.

Japan took a less sanguine view: it suspected Russia had begun a permanent occupation, and opened negotiations with the czar to ensure that Korea became a Japanese protectorate. In February 1904, after talks failed, Japanese ships launched a surprise attack on the Russian Pacific fleet at Port Arthur. His navy crippled, Nicholas II ordered the deployment of the Baltic Fleet, an eight-month voyage away.

Hearst newspapers, fresh off the success of its "Remember the Maine!" coverage of the Spanish-American War, now warned of the "Yellow Peril." Jack London, whose novel The Call of the Wild was a best seller at the time, was dispatched as Hearst's war correspondent. London pursued the battles on horseback but soon realized his access would be too restricted by Japanese and Russian handlers to do any real reporting. Echoing the Western world's prediction, London wrote, "Granting that no revolution arises in Russia, and there is no interference of outside powers, I cannot see how Japan can possibly win."

The Russo-Japanese War was mostly fought in Korea and Northeastern China, though neither were combatants. The war's use of fixed machine guns, trenches, and massive casualties prefigured the carnage to come in World War One. In the battle for the Manchurian city of Mukden (present-day Shenyang), 330,000 Russians faced off against 280,000 Japanese.

Three weeks later: 90,000 Russian casualties, 75,000 Japanese, victory for Japan. The decisive blow came in May when the czar's Baltic Fleet finally arrived to the fight. The Japanese navy sank it within hours.

Jack London's caveat came true: Nicholas II did face a revolution, one started by the shooting of striking factory workers outside St. Petersburg's Winter Palace on January 22, 1905, a day known as Bloody Sunday. Naval commanders and sailors mutinied; the Reuters correspondent riding a train in Manchuria with survivors of the massive Mukden battle said, "[The] ranks have been filled by reservists, mostly married men, who resent being taken away from home and family. Others have adopted the ideas of the revolutionary parties in Russia." The war "has been unpopular from the first," and before the battle a spiritless officer said of the Japanese, "They are going to give us yet another lesson of how things ought to be done successfully."

In August 1905, China requested that President Theodore Roosevelt intervene to prevent the Russo-Japanese War from spreading south of the Great Wall. Negotiations between Russian and Japanese diplomats were held on a ship docked at the Naval Shipyard in Portsmouth, New Hampshire. The resulting treaty obligated Russia to recognize Korea as within Japan's sphere of influence, return Manchuria to Chinese adminis-tration, and cede a portion of the Chinese Eastern Railway. Japan would take control of most of the spur running south from Harbin to Port Arthur, whose leasehold it also acquired. Unlike the Russian trains, which burned wood, Japanese engines were fueled by coal, requiring the opening of mines and other railroad-affiliated businesses along what Japan now called the South Manchuria Railway. In 1910, foreshadowing its intentions in Northeastern China, Japan annexed all of Korea.

Although he was not present during negotiations, President Roosevelt won the Nobel Peace Prize for his role in the Treaty of Portsmouth. His private correspondence showed that he had followed Manchurian affairs since at least 1901, when he mocked Mark Twain and "all our prize idiots" who defended the anti-foreigner Boxer rebels as patriots. In that letter to a friend, Roosevelt wrote approvingly of Russia muscling into the Northeast: "As you know, I feel that it is an advantage to civilization to have a civi-lized power gain ground at the expense of barbarism. Exactly as Turkestan has benefited by Russia's advance, so I think China would be."

By 1903, however, Roosevelt fumed to Secretary of State John Hay over the "mendacity of the Russians" for monopolizing Manchurian trade. "The bad feature of the situation from our standpoint is that as yet it seems that we cannot fight to keep Manchuria open. I hate being in the position of seeming to bluster without backing it up."

In a 1904 letter prefaced, "Personal—Be very careful that no one gets a chance to see this," Roosevelt explained to a British diplomat why the United States should settle the Manchurian dispute. "I hoped to see China kept together, and would gladly welcome any part played by Japan which would tend to bring China forward along the road which Japan trod, because I thought it for the interest of all the world that each part of the world should be prosperous and well policed."

Roosevelt wanted to maintain the "Open Door" policy of free trade in China and to balance Japan's territorial ambitions with America's. Although the United States never took a concession in China, in 1898 it became a Pacific power, annexing Hawaii and adding Guam and the Philippines after winning the Spanish-American War.

"The Japs interest me and I like them," Roosevelt continued. "I am perfectly well aware that if they win out it may possibly mean a struggle between them and us in the future; but I hope not and believe not. At any rate, Russia's course during the past three years has made it evident that if she wins she will organize northern China against us and rule us absolutely out of all the ground she can control. Therefore, on the score of mere national self-interest, we would not be justified in balancing the certainty of immediate damage against the possibility of future damage."

In September 1904, while on holiday in Oyster Bay, Long Island, Roosevelt wrote to Secretary Hay that he was "immensely pleased" with the account of Chinese officials wishing to treat Japanese soldiers entering Port Arthur as conquerors, evincing their disdain for their feeble Manchu emperor. "I am equally delighted," Roosevelt wrote, by the anecdote of a woman standing quayside when the Japanese landed. For the first time in modern history, an Asian army had defeated a European power. "Really," the woman remarked, "I do not think the British Consul will have many people for tennis today."

*

"State of Anarchy Found at Harbin," the *New York Times*'s front page declared in 1908. "Russian Soldiers Do Nothing to Guard It and Few Residents Venture out After Dark; Conduct of the Japanese, Who Are Flooding Manchuria, Angers the Foreign Residents." The story said that the region's "American Consuls are supporting the Chinese against the aggressions of Russia and Japan."

Two men had recently been appointed to the region by Roosevelt, including Willard Straight as consul general at Mukden, then under Japanese control. Straight—who would go on to found the *New Republic* magazine—had a patrician's look, with thin hair flattened to one side over a high brow and jug ears. His vice-consul was a beefy, baby-faced college graduate named Nelson Fairchild, who rode the train through Harbin. "As nasty a place as you can imagine," he wrote in a letter home. "At night one walks in the middle of the street with revolver drawn."

Straight and Fairchild found a vacant Buddhist temple to house the consulate. Both were sympathetic with China's plight, unusual for the pre–*Good Earth* era; memoirists living in Manchuria at this time often wrote about "the fear of turning Chinese." One writer imagined Chinese voices whispering, "You can never escape us. You are forgotten by your kind. Each day you are less a white man."

Straight, however, was a reputed Japanophobe, and argued for increased American involvement in Manchuria. Fairchild, in a letter home, wrote that he found the Northeast beautiful: "I didn't wonder the Chinese want their country for themselves, and hate having foreigners butting in and putting up railroads and telegraphs." Fairchild had arrived in Manchuria in October of 1906 and, despite watching the consulate thermometer's mercury drop "till nothing is left but a small globule rolling round in agony at the very bottom," took five-mile walks, went pheasant hunting for a Thanksgiving meal, began daily Chinese lessons, and wrote, "I certainly like the place enough to stay five or six years."

That winter, however, the front page of the *New York Times* reported: "Consul Shoots Himself." "It is believed that his death was accidental. Much sorrow is expressed here. The funeral will be held tomorrow." In a privately published memorial book of Fairchild's letters, the final entry came from Willard Straight, informing Fairchild's parents that their son's revolver had accidentally discharged. Manchuria lost an admirer, one who wrote that the land was "too rich too fail" and that when its people "have better methods they will be able to do wonders. China is waking up for sure."

Fairchild's superiors in distant Washington, D.C., saw Manchuria more as an important piece of the geopolitical puzzle. In 1908, in exchange for Japan's endorsement of American claims to the Philippines and Hawaii—as well as limits on Japanese immigration to the U.S.—the United States formalized its recognition of Japanese interests in Korea and Manchuria. The pact weakened America's ability to influence Japan's actions there.

The following year in Harbin, a Korean nationalist assassinated the former Japanese prime minister, who as resident-general had become Korea's de facto ruler. In October 1909, Prince Ito Hirobumi rode the train to Manchuria for a conference. Waiting at the Harbin station was a twenty-nine-year-old member of the Korean resistance named Ahn Jung-geun, who fired six shots. Three pierced Ito's chest, killing him. Unlike the assassination of Archduke Franz Ferdinand five years later, Prince Ito's murder did not start a war. Russian soldiers handed Ahn over to the Japanese. At his trial, he said, "I didn't do this as an individual, I did it as a soldier of the Korean Volunteer Army, and I did it for my motherland's independence and for peace in the East." He was found guilty and executed. Japan formally annexed Korea in 1910. (A century later, Ahn's picture was displayed in a small exhibit at the Harbin train station. It was the rare patriotic education base that taught that Japan's incursions were regional and not only targeted at China.)

Republican Chinese overthrew the Manchu dynasty in 1911. The last emperor, Puyi, was allowed to abdicate in the following year, at age six. Rather than move to his ancestral homeland, he retreated to the northern half of the Forbidden City. At age sixteen he cut off his braided queue.

Though nominally a republic, post-imperial China was fragmented; its first president, Sun Yat-sen, famously said that the nation appeared to be "a loose sheet of sand." Warlords controlled entire regions, among them men who had once fought for the Qing imperial army, such as the Manchurian strongman Zhang Zuolin, whose plot to return Puyi to the throne had failed. This, after a different warlord had restored the boy emperor in 1917, a reign that lasted a mere eleven days before being toppled by republican troops.

In 1925, shortly before Puyi turned nineteen, yet another warlord drove him out of the Forbidden City for good. His ancestors had entered Beijing as conquerors on horseback. He departed a civilian, seated on a plush-cushioned train carriage, rolling eighty-five miles east to the port of Tianjin. The city was home to several foreign concessions, whose buildings resembled their faraway cousins: Georgian English homes, Palladian Italian villas, a Gothic French cathedral. In Tianjin the Japanese offered Puyi a garden residence in their concession. He moved in and waited, unaware that six years would pass before he would be called to action, in Manchuria.

The fall of the Qing, followed by the Russian Revolution in 1917, left Manchuria, and especially Harbin, adrift. The accords that created the Chinese Eastern Railway had been signed by governments that no longer existed. Street battles broke out between Bolsheviks and White Russians for control of the railway's offices; Chinese soldiers were caught in the crossfire at Harbin's railway bridge and chose to side with the revolutionaries.

With few other options, White Russians fled east on the train, massing in Harbin. An American traveler reported throngs of exiles, including "princesses in simple but very appropriate garb . . . old generals still wearing their uniforms, blazing from shoulder to shoulder with decorations, and the same haughty expression of men expecting instant obedience as in their bygone days of power and emoluments." But here, too, were the penniless refugees. "There is no way of computing," the traveler wrote, "how many Russian girls, with nothing to live on but the sale of their charms, there were along the Chinese Eastern Railway from [Manzhouli] to Vladivostok, like the little end of the funnel down through which the miseries of Russia had been oozing for years."

The warlord Zhang Zuolin took hold of the Northeast. In photos he looks like an unthreatening schoolmaster, with a thin frame, slumped shoulders, shaved head, and drooping mustache. But his career of brigandage had supposedly began after the young Zhang killed a wounded "red beard" bandit and assumed the outlaw's identity. Later the Qing court made his band of men an official unit to hunt and kill gangs of thieves in Manchuria. Zhang proved adept at playing both sides. After the Qing dynasty fell, the warlord spun Manchuria's spoils as if set upon a lazy Susan, rotating between Beijing, Russia, and Japan when it most profited himself.

Under Zhang, in 1920, Harbin city came under Chinese control for the first time. Shop signs written in Cyrillic were ordered changed to Chinese characters, a Confucian temple was erected, and street signs were repainted. Orthodox Street became Culture Street, while Nicholas Street was renamed Temple Street, for the city's first Buddhist shrine. (Over Leninists' protests, the popular icon of Saint Nicholas remained in Harbin station.) The city's official holidays now included the Chinese New Year, Russian Orthodox Easter, Chinese Revolution Day, and the Anniversary of the Soviet Union.

Despite the appearance of ethnic harmony, Harbin had not become a functioning melting pot. Bandit activity continued, indiscriminate in its targets. Downriver from Harbin, brigands attacked a farm started by an American army major to employ Chinese famine refugees. The outlaws killed the major and a Chinese farmer and kidnapped the American ophthalmologist who had been visiting from his post at Peking Union Hospital. In his book *Ten Weeks with Chinese Bandits*, the doctor recounted his sorrow at the death of his friend, and his enterprise. As his captivity dragged on, however, the chapter titles tilted toward sentiment such as "From the Sublime to the Ridiculous." He bought favor by treating the bandits' syphilis, trachoma, and ringworm, wryly noting: "They had no books or newspapers to read; they did not play games; they were not given to writing letters or biographic notes; nor were they accustomed to spend their waking hours in quiet reflection. But they knew how to talk, and in this they indulged constantly. Their chief topic of conversation was opium." This led to Chapter 24: "In Which I Teach the Bandits English and Refuse to Assist Them in Smuggling Opium into Peking." Deep in the night, he was woken by soldiers, unsure—despite their uniforms—if they were his rescuers or another group after the ransom. They were the warlord Zhang Zuolin's men, and he was saved.

In Harbin, relations between Chinese and Russians splintered. A dramatic performance of an English music hall play at a fund-raiser for the Russo-Chinese Technical Institute saw half the dignitaries in attendance stand up and leave when a Chinese character spoke pidgin English—"Oh dearee me! This is most ostrepulous!"—and a Western character responded: "A Chinaman is never at a loss for a lie."

In 1926, Harbin students rioted after a Russian YMCA team beat a Chinese high school team, 29–17. The post-match stat sheet counted injuries on both sides and broken windows across town.

Russians living in Chinese-controlled Harbin complained of "squeeze," in which they had to pay higher prices. Harbin deserved its nickname as "Paris of the Far East," a visitor wrote, because its prices were on par with it. White Russians—stateless without valid passports—had to pay for exit permits if they had a line to a new life outside Harbin. A British man beaten by police and held on a bogus charge until he paid an exorbitant fine was released by a city official who told him, "We are very sorry. We were under the impression that you were Russian." *Harper's* magazine wrote that Harbin was "the only white city in the world ruled by yellows." This, in a shocking dispatch headlined: "Where Yellow Rules White."

On June 4, 1928, a bomb ripped through the private train carrying the warlord Zhang Zuolin, mortally wounding him. A Japanese colonel had planned the assassination, wanting Zhang replaced by someone more pliant. The warlord's son did not publicly blame Japan for his father's death. Instead, he assumed power in the Northeast and forged a reconciliation with the Chinese republican government, binding Manchuria's interests to the nation's. If the Japanese thought Zhang Xueliang—known as the Young Marshal—would be as bribable as his father, he dispelled that notion in 1929 at a dinner attended by his top officials. The Young Marshal ordered that the two officers sympathetic to Japan be executed by gunshot at the table.

"Russian Mobs Fight Chinese in Harbin," the *New York Times* reported in 1932. "Five Are Killed and 22 Hurt in a Battle of Ice-Encrusted Street Barricades." Following the theft of a small cake by a famished eight-year-old Russian waif, the child was taken to a Chinese police station, where a Russian mob gathered, demanding his release. The police charged; the mob took up positions on Kitaiskaya Street, Harbin's cobblestone grand boulevard of hotels and shops, where usually Russian girls sold lilacs and irises beside Chinese vendors displaying candied hawthorn berries on bamboo skewers, and shoppers, a traveler wrote, walked with a "lighthearted gait as if they were prepared at any moment to break into dance." Now the crowd wrenched furniture, doors, and window frames from businesses and built street barricades. In Harbin, the *Times* breathlessly reported, "tension and clamor reign, recalling the wild days of the French Revolution." For the first time, czarist and Soviet Russians fought side by side. Chinese police turned fire hoses upon them, but it was January and the water froze, "making the barricades as solid as masonry." Next the police charged with rifles, causing the Russians to countercharge, swinging clubs and fists. That round went to the Russians.

Today the street is named Zhongyang Dajie—Central Boulevard—and its cobblestones remain, as does its procession of art nouveau shops, painted pistachio green and lemon yellow. Uniquely for China, plaques on the buildings tell—in Chinese and English, but not Russian—who designed the structure and its original use. Most had been department stores and restaurants begun by Russian Jews. They are still in business, if recast as a Northeast Dumpling King, a McDonald's, the Northeast Fur Store, a shop selling nesting dolls, and a window steamed over from fresh loaves of brown Russian bread.

The street is a pedestrian-only thoroughfare and Harbin's chief tourist site. It begins at a Holiday Inn and ends at a Walmart bordering Stalin Park on the banks of the Songhua River, where old men flying kites fill its promenade. One man shuffling along in cloth shoes smiled and showed me the pet goldfish he carried in a transparent plastic bag. "I'm taking him out for a walk," he announced.

Nearby, a tinny bullhorn set on repeat bleated, "Boycott Japanese products!" University students sitting at a table set in front of the Russian-built Modern Hotel passed out flyers urging us to stand up for the Diaoyu Islands, claimed by both China and Japan since the First Sino-Japanese War. The students competed for attention with a campaign whose table faced them directly across the cobblestones. Its bullhorn blared a trebly recording that ordered us to "resolutely smash illegal electronic games!" Behind the tables, I spied a fairy-tale storefront obscured by vines in bloom. Its evergreen wood façade framed a plate glass window with lace curtains. I ducked inside, silencing the bullhorns by closing the heavy wooden door. The room smelled of cabbage piroshki and espresso. Black-and-white photos of ruddy Russians adorned the yellow walls. The café's name, Sufeiya, meant *Sophia* in Chinese.

Its owner, Hu Hong, was in his fifties, with short black hair flecked with sawdust. "I was just renovating my new restaurant," he said, raising a shot of vodka in a toast. "I trained as an architect but I'd rather spend my time on the job site, making things. Sitting in a meeting room seeking approval of a design from an official who is not even from your town, but was assigned from far away, is just absurd. It's one correction after another, one suggestion that you have to implement, no matter how ridiculous. Just today, I was chiseling a rose into a slab of oak—hard work. The building inspector came, looked around approvingly, then on his way out stopped at my table and said, 'You should carve a different flower. A chrysanthemum would be better.'" Mr. Hu laughed. "Northeasterners can't help themselves. We're never happy with the present state of things."

Hu grew up in Harbin, the "mixed-blood" child of a Chinese father and a Russian mother. "All of these pictures on the wall are my ancestors," he said. "This was their house." A Tchaikovsky suite tinkled faintly on the stereo as Hu walked me around the room, past his family's old grandfather clock to snapshots of a beautiful woman with bobbed hair and a broad smile that matched the one of the man proudly pointing at her image. "This is my mom," he said. "I built this café in her memory, and named it for her. She died during the Cultural Revolution. The Soviet Union and China had split then. I was sent away." He paused. "Another vodka."

He handed me a newsletter that showed a steam locomotive next to the title *Russia's News*. "I put this together every month. It's sort of an émigré newsletter. I include translated excerpts from my mother's 1920s diary." Mr. Hu said the project was more than just a way to spend time with her memory. It kept Harbin's memory alive, too.

"Everyone in this city—the people who grew up here, the natives—are mixed, if not by blood, then by culture," he said. "It might not be apparent to young people or tourists. Stalin Park? That's the last one in China, maybe even in Russia. Why is it still named that? People have no idea who Stalin was or what he did. We may as well have named it Hitler Park. But all people know is that Stalin is Russian and now Russia is our friend. But Russia was not always China's friend, and history isn't as simple as 'First it was like that, but now it is like this.'"

Hu was an architect and showed me a magazine article about his design to commemorate Harbin's Saint Nicholas Cathedral, which had been razed during the Cultural Revolution. A traffic roundabout stood on its former site. "We could put some onion domes there as statues, at least, to remind people of what was the city's most prominent building. I doubt that city leaders will agree." They would argue, he said, that Saint Sophia had been restored and opened as a museum. Preserving one relic was the same as restoring many.

Hu studied architecture in Japan, making him, as he put it, "an historical Northeasterner"—Chinese with Russian and Japanese components. I brought up the notion of Chinese one day hyphenating their ethnicities. Hu didn't think a hyphen was necessary. "I'm just Chinese. Most Chinese know that our country is a mix of many cultures and peoples."

The hyphens were silent. Transparent, he said. But in Manchuria, you could see them clearly.

CHAPTER 9

TUNNELS IN TIME, SIDINGS TO SPACE

BEFORE RETURNING TO Wasteland and San Jiu's ripening rice, I followed old railroad sidings to four relics, of a sort, from Manchuria's cosmopolitan era. The first stop was to a ghost town. The second, a ghost village. The third, a ghostly museum. The fourth stop was to meet a man who swore he had sex with an alien.

To the ghost town: two hundred miles west of Harbin, I exited the train at Qiqihar. Saying its melodic name was the best thing about the place. *Chee-chee ha-ER*. The train station was a chocolate-colored monolith built by the Japanese during their occupation. Now it was China's last to wear a crown of red characters greeting arrivals with LONG LIVE MAO ZEDONG THOUGHT.

During the Qing dynasty, Qiqihar was a military garrison and home to a Muslim community whose three-hundred-year-old mosque looked marooned between new wide boulevards in the city center. The Manchu court would not allow the Russians to run their train line near existing cities, so the Chinese Eastern Railway station was built twenty miles southwest of town, linked by a narrow-gauge shuttle train. The shuttle was gone, replaced by an hourlong bus ride over rutted cement-and-dirt roads to a town named Ang'angxi.

Its station still remained, looking like a Black Sea dacha: tall windows, gabled roof, and a bright exterior painted salmon pink. There were no bustling passengers, no tooting trains. Aside from the cicadas' thrumming drone, all was still. Across the street, dirt lanes led past brick cottages with carved wood porticos. The fifty-odd homes—painted yellow and robin's-egg blue—buckled under rotted rooftops. Weeds reached into broken windows.

Volunteer corn filled the former sidewalks. On the main road, which formerly echoed with the clip-clop of horses' hooves and squeaking carriage wheels, four elderly Chinese women squatted next to standing puddles. The blankets before them displayed limp cucumbers and broad beans. Like the vegetables on sale, the women looked wilted. "If you're looking for history," one said, "you've come too late."

Actually, I had arrived just in time. The pink crenellated fortress that was once the Russian Railway Club showed open doors. Inside, playing cards were scattered on tables, with chairs pushed away, suggesting that everyone had folded and run to catch the train back to the fatherland. Standing in this stillness sent a shiver up my spine. I asked aloud if anyone was there, but the question bounced off the thick walls and returned to me in reply.

Now only three passenger trains stopped at the station each day; most of the traffic was passing oil tankers and timber-filled boxcars. The ticket window's lone worker pointed me toward the Chinese plaque hanging on the station's front that said it had been built in 1903 and had "the railroad's best surviving wood platform bridge," roofed against the Manchurian snows. Even today, the barren view was one that would give a traveler pause before getting off a warm train. No wonder the stations on this line were painted in such bright colors.

In 1930 a Harvard graduate named Liang Siyong disembarked here alone. Railway workers had uncovered a tomb containing carved stones that, in their words, "looked old." At the site, Liang performed one of China's first scientific excavations, discovering that the artifacts dated back seven thousand years. Liang was twenty-six.

A small museum devoted to the site sat five miles outside town, beside a road that cut razor-straight through wetlands. In the first exhibit room, a tour guide spoke in practiced enthusiasm before a life-size diorama of Asiatic hunter-gatherers. "This settlement was the cradle of northern fishing and hunting civilization," the guide intoned. "The hominids who lived here created a brilliant culture with their great wisdom and hard-working hands. They made significant contributions to Chinese civilization."

They did not have any concept of what China was; they were sparking fire with stones. But the guide continued, "The Ang'angxi hominid created the harmonious state between human and nature with firm, indomitable, and pioneering spirit. They remind us how we can contribute to the strengthening of our nation." The archaeology site was a patriotic education base. Even hominids could serve the national narrative.

The museum's other exhibit room was shuttered. A docent unlocked the doors, flicked on the lights, then left. Displayed behind glass I saw a hand-knit cardigan, a safety razor, and an inkstone. Initially, I thought that the hominids actually did have great wisdom and hardworking hands. But a black-and-white photograph of a young man with oiled black hair, spectacles, and a starched collar and tie revealed that this was a memorial hall for Liang Siyong, the "father of Chinese archaeology."

From my years researching Beijing's planning, I knew about his brother, Liang Sicheng, considered the father of Chinese architecture. I had interviewed his son and read much about his father, a famous court official who had urged the Manchu empress dowager—unsuccessfully—to modernize. But not once had I heard mention of the brother, Liang Siyong.

I paced past photographs of him through the years, and shots of the dig here at Ang'angxi, before reaching a glass case whose caption tag read: "Treatise and job logging of Liang Siyong." A stack of papers sat within. Neatly typed in English, the top page was titled *Expedition Journal*.

My eyes swelled and I felt, perhaps, similar to how Liang had in 1930, traveling all the way out here and hitting pay dirt on his first dig. I had read Westerners' accounts of traveling through Manchuria, but what had a Chinese explorer made of the place?

The docent, playing solitaire on her cell phone, didn't share my excitement. She couldn't read English, she said, so had never lifted the cover page to see if the rest of the journal was there or if this was a prop, like the books on an Ikea showroom floor. She didn't have the key to open the display case. "Mine only open doors. I don't even know who can open the displays." Her high heels clicked away, leaving me forlorn in the wetlands, outside the ghost town of Ang'angxi.

The original of Liang's journal sat seven thousand miles away, in a rare book room at Harvard. Written entirely in English, it was the sort of artifact that, had it remained in China, could have been burned during the Cultural Revolution, like the papers of his famous architect brother. Liang Siyong died before then, of a heart attack aged fifty, in 1954.

The journal was more personal than scientific, providing a unique glimpse into Manchuria on the eve of Japanese occupation: Liang's train north from Beijing kept getting shunted to sidings to make way for troop trains. His writing covered two months of 1930, navigating the Russian, Japanese, republican Chinese, and warlords who held shifting sway along the route.

The economy was just as splintered. Shopping for supplies in Harbin, Liang wrote: "I was positively bewildered and appalled by the different kinds of bills and paper money. Besides the Big Money and the Japanese dollar, there was the Harbin dollar, the [Heilongjiang] dollar, the Tiau Piau (a written document)," plus two more. "Each had its own exchange rate and the rate was different at each store where one used the money! Further, the last four kinds could not be used outside the limits of the Province."

To dig, Liang first needed permission from both the Russian railway boss and the Chinese provincial governor. The red tape was cut by a letter of introduction written by a local strongman, whose description matched so many men I had met across the Northeast. Of the warlord, Liang wrote: "He was quite a representative specimen. He had the short round head, a squarish face, was bull-necked, thick chested, in short a solidly built man of a little over thirty. He was very domineering in his manner and also very rough, almost coarse, but he was very straight forward and showed even in his way of talking a man of great energy, efficiency, and endurance, a typical man of action of this land. The official side of the matter was finished in less than ten minutes—I had formally obtained the permission to excavate."

Bandits, however, did not read. A gang on horseback chased Liang until he found shelter in a house that was a "veritable fort, with walls 20-30 feet tall and gun holes. Reports of guns sounded all through the night in all parts of town like fire-crackers."

Throughout the expedition, sleep came hard; if it wasn't bandit fire, it was lying on a *kang* that grilled Liang's back and nauseated him with the smell of cow dung burned as fuel. Often he was roused to beat the rats rummaging his supplies. And it was cold: "The northwester was so forceful that it penetrated my heaviest coat. My nose seemed to be frozen and I could hardly breathe. My fingers became so stiff that I could hardly write my notes and take photographs."

His two-hundred-page journal includes eighty-four hand-developed photos showing excavation sites and the people he encountered on the way. Liang is visible only in his shadow, cast from behind the camera into the frame's foreground. I imagined him grinning; the people he photographed smiled widely, unusual for subjects seeing a camera for the first time.

On this part of the journey, to Manchuria's western steppe, Liang—ethnically Han Chinese—was disgusted by Chinese colonization of the Mongols' pastures, which he equated to Japan's encroachment into the Northeast. "I found a great and significant parallel between the Mongol-Chinese and the Chinese-Japanese situation," he wrote. "The facts, the method, and the psychological attitude involved were just the same . . . [T]he Chinese aggression and penetration were very persistent and vital. The Mongols were regarded as backward and uncivilized. Their land was regarded as wasted and sought to be opened to Chinese cultivation . . . The officials coddled them, but butted in whenever and wherever possible. And the merchants cheated them, pure and simple. As for the Mongols, they hated and feared the Chinese, and above all distrusted them. They very gradually but nevertheless perceptibly retreated into the more desert part of the land."

By 1930 the Russians had largely retreated, too, as Japan's position increased. Out in remote Manchuria, seated in an "extraordinarily clean and orderly" third-class carriage, Liang recorded the shift: "Here was seen the Japanese influence," he wrote. "Everything was run after the Japanese manner, from the behavior of the conductor down to the manner of the candy-seller." He passed new stations whose high roofs and large windows in this region of extreme cold showed that "the Japanese architects who designed them had forgotten to take geography into consideration in their plans—one had the feeling of seeing a Spanish summer villa in Siberia."

In the dunes outside Ang'angxi's salmon-pink station he found, in a trough excavated by that persistent northern wind, stone chips and pottery fragments, and then a skeleton. The next day he uncovered "an undisturbed Neolithic burial with the skeleton in comparatively good condition and all the funerary furniture intact."

Around the description of his finds, Liang punctuated the journal with dry humor. He sat atop his overloaded expedition cart "like the Santa going on his Xmas trip." After a day "wading through more than 6000 paces of marsh" in water "that chilled my foot bones until they ached" through "clouds of mosquitoes," he noted that the lack of drainage and flatness of the land "was one of the important factors in hastening railway construction in Manchuria. There wasn't really very much engineering work to do, and the heaping up of dirt for the road-bed and the laying of the rails was extremely easy. Whatever may be said of this it is not a favorable place to hunt for the remains of ancient man."

A recent relic still survived an hour north of Ang'angxi, if only barely. The Northeast's last native speakers of Manchu lived in a village whose name, Sanjiazi, meant "Three Families." Its residents descended from a trio of bannermen—Qing military administrators—dispatched in the seventeenth-century to defend the frontier against Russian incursions.

On the dirt road leading to the village, the cabdriver—an ethnic Manchu—warned that there was nothing to see. "It's a very backward place," he said. "This road wasn't built until the 1950s, so until then, the village really was on its own, which is how the Manchu language survived. There was little contact with outsiders." Out the window, cows and sheep grazed the open grassland. Their herder, a young boy, sat under a willow tree, staring at a cell phone screen.

"During the Cultural Revolution, we were told that people who spoke Manchu could be spying for the Soviets," the driver said. "So any remaining speakers switched to Chinese. Only the old folks kept speaking Manchu, but they're dying off." According to Chinese linguists and historians, only three fluent native speakers, all in their eighties, remained.

Half of the world's 6,800 languages are predicted to go extinct by the end of the twenty-first century, but none were once as prominent as Manchu, the "national language" of the vast Qing Empire. Even though Mandarin had remained its lingua franca, official documents were written in Manchu and Chinese. But an estimated 20 percent of the ten million archived Qing-era documents were penned in Manchu alone, making them unintelligible to all but a handful of specialists.

The road turned to dirt, leading past the first house made of sod that I had seen outside of a Woody Guthrie song. Subsequent houses were fashioned from mud and thatch; Wasteland looked like a boomtown in comparison. The driver stopped at a sign at the village entrance, written in Manchu and Chinese. The latter said:

SANJIAZI WELCOMES YOU!
Here is a tribe of Manchu speakers.
Here are the remains of Manchu culture.

I could read the Chinese, but could make no sense of the Manchu, a phonetic script based on the Mongolian alphabet. To my untrained eye, its thick, dark lines, loops, and dots looked like vertical Arabic. "Does the Manchu caption say the same?"

"I can't read it," the driver said. "Manchu wasn't taught in school."

But here, uniquely, it was. A thirty-four-year-old villager named Shi Junguang had learned the language from his grandmother. After compiling an oral archive of the village elderly speaking it, he received official permission to teach Manchu at the village elementary school for a few hours each week.

In Chinese newspaper stories, I had seen Sanjiazi described as a "living fossil," but today the village looked dead. The elementary school had emptied for summer vacation. It was one of the tidiest rural schools I had seen, and the first whose playing field had pockets of shade, courtesy of willows that made a palisade around its perimeter. Pasted on its notice board was a poster written in Manchu and Chinese that read PASSING ON MANCHU CULTURE BEGINS WITH ME.

A child pointed me to the teacher's house, tucked behind a furrowed front yard growing onions. Shi Junguang opened his front door, and if he was surprised to see a foreigner, he didn't show it. Instead, he asked if I had received official permission to talk to him.

"It's a complicated situation," Mr. Shi said, looking embarrassed.

"Village politics?" I guessed.

"*Uh.*" He nodded. Chinese reporters had recently visited, upsetting the village leader because they had not asked for permission to enter the school and observe the Manchu class. The reporters also had pestered the elderly Manchu speakers, goading them to talk on-camera. Mr. Shi said the reporters had complained to the county, then the provincial, propaganda bureaus. The matter boomeranged back to him, and he caught criticism from the village leader, who himself had been scolded from above. Mr. Shi felt it had been a strike against his experiment. The national slogan had changed from "Build Socialism" to "Build a Harmonious Society," and expressions of minority culture—unless they attracted tourist revenue—could be branded "sensitive," and shut down.

"All I want is to continue teaching the kids Manchu," Mr. Shi said in Chinese. "If I don't help to preserve it, the village children will one day blame their elders—myself included."

How to describe the sound of a dying language? To my ears it was a rapid, more sibilant Korean. As the tutorial ended, I asked Mr. Shi how to say *Farewell* in Manchu. He voiced it, I repeated, and he said it twice more: "*Sirame achaki. Sirame achaki.*" It sounded like a horse galloping away.

Mr. Shi switched to Chinese. "Zài jiàn." Good-bye.

In Harbin, on a gorgeous morning under a high blue sky, I walked past signs for the Harbin Pharmaceutical Group's Old Cadre Hall and the same company's real estate corporation offices. It was a very twenty-first-century-Manchuria walk, never passing the original thing, but rather its suggestion: the restored brass doors of hotels whose keystones said *1903*, the synagogue's repainted façade, Saint Sophia's green onion domes. HARBIN PHARMACEUTICAL GROUP WELCOMES YOU TO HARBIN! read the sign at its plaza. On the cathedral's redbrick exterior you could still just make out the faint outline of the anti-imperialist slogans painted in yellow during the Cultural Revolution.

But history had cycled back to the promotion—not smashing—of Harbin's cosmopolitan past. Two blocks away, at the world's only International Sister Cities Museum, a guide led a group of middle school students past displays for each of their hometown's twenty-seven twins. "Our government's friendship with these cities promotes peace and understanding," the guide intoned. The children stared at silver-plated spoons from Sunderland, Punta Arenas postage stamps, sake made in Asahikawa, and a Zohar from Giv'atayim. "Forgetting about history means betrayal."

The kids shuffled across the museum's polished marble floor and ran their fingers along its walnut wainscoting, evidence of the building's past as the Danish consulate when Harbin had been an international railway hub a century before. The students halted at Rovaniemi's stuffed lemming, sniffed at wool scarves from Daugavpils, then sidled to the jersey of Ping-Pong champion Werner Schlager, proud son of Weiner Neustadt.

"Where is that?" asked a boy, breaking the silence. "What country are these cities in?" Typically for China, the museum displayed no maps, and the students were confused and restless—until the tour guide spotted me, puzzling over the display of Harbin's newest buddy, my hometown of Minneapolis. "Here is our *American* friendship city!" she exclaimed. "This must be our *American* friend!" After the admiring ooohs died down, I explained in Chinese that I was not part of the exhibit, then turned to the jewels the Minneapolis mayor's office had sent to represent my proud city, home of the Walker Art Center, Prince, an elegant skyline, and a chain of lakes downtown. The students and I stared at an arrowhead, Target and Best Buy logos, a stuffed Goldy Gopher, and boxes of Tuna Helper and Betty Crocker angel food cake mix. "It gets very cold there, just like here," I added, seeking common ground. "Winter is long, and many people drink too much." The guide interrupted to recite that Minneapolis had twenty-one universities and thirty theaters. But the children's eyes had already drifted away, to the neighboring puppets of Ploiesti.

China loved friendship, especially the official yet personal sort. Anyone who spent time here heard *weile womende youhao*—"It's for our friendship"—enough to head for the exits before learning what Our Friendship wanted this time. (It's never a quiet night at home with a book.) In the Peace Corps, I learned that—due to an earlier anti-imperialist propaganda campaign—I had been repainted as a "United States–China Friendship Volunteer." For those two years I had been entreated into doing anything—English Corner, karaoke of Carpenters' songs, hot pot, heroin—with the assurance that it was for Our Friendship. You knew a phrase had saturated the masses to the point of meaninglessness when even junkies invoked it.

To attract tourists, both domestic and foreign, Harbin had resurrected its photogenic backdrops. Shaded by trees and set back from a busy downtown street, the International Sister Cities Museum's two-story, lemon-colored building looked like it boarded the train in St. Petersburg, got off in Harbin, and decided to settle down.

Inside, the children filed past the displays over a floor so polished it seemed illuminated, reflecting the chandelier light. The windows were shaded by the heavy red drapes that always caught fire in movies, and the marble stairs ascended in a cinematic sweep; someone in a gown should be stepping down them any second now. As this building had been in use through the Russian, republican, warlord, Japanese, and Communist eras, I was about to ask a schoolgirl if she thought we might see a ghost. The guide hushed us and warned not to "nibble, litter, or spit. Do not take pictures or use your cell phone. Keep silent."

We looked at some coins from Edmonton, and a hoodie with the price tag on it from MacEwan University (Go Griffins!). Arras displayed a rocking chair and a handwritten letter from Mayor Jean-Marie Vanlerenberghe, whose penmanship put that of South Taranaki mayor Ross Dunlop to shame. The last time I had seen handwriting like his was when opening a note passed during eighth grade math. But then I read Mayor Dunlop's looping words—expecting hearts to dot the i's—and learned that not only is South Taranaki home to the world's largest dairy plant, but that its people knew the Sister Cities Museum will "help citizens of Harbin learn more about customs, cultures, landmarks and location of your international friends." To a jaded visitor, this was eye-rolling stuff. But the room was so still, you could hear a child's stomach growl, and felt even quieter because no one laughed.

The sister city movement—"town twinning" in Europe—dates to the ninth century, when Le Mans, France, formed a partnership with Paderborn, Germany. In 1931, Toledo, Ohio, invited Toledo, Spain, to form North America's first twinning. The trend accelerated after World War II as a form of reconciliation and Cold War propaganda. In 1956 the Eisenhower administration founded Sister Cities International (SCI), now a nonprofit organization based in Washington, D.C.

In these post–Evil Empire days, twinning's rationale, according to SCI's mission statement, was to "build global cooperation at the municipal level, promote cultural understanding, and stimulate economic development." In other words, it's for our friendship. American cities often had multiple partners, but SCI's website cautioned against playing the field. "Having more than one sister city should only occur if your community feels that it has the necessary resources to support multiple affiliations." I imagined a personal ad titled DESPERATELY SEEKING CITY: *Single, attractive, mixed metropolis seeking foreign partner for long-term ties and travel. Size matters: No townships, please.*

Since China's first pairing—Shanghai with San Francisco, 1980—sister cities had, like UNESCO World Heritage Sites, become an imprimatur that evinced development. Chinese metropolises clamored to add partners to their rolls (and have them break up with Taiwanese mates: Mobile dumped Kaohsiung to pick up Heze *and* Tianjin). Beijing—with forty-seven sister cities—was the fulcrum of degrees of civic separation; it was how one could connect Islamabad to Tel Aviv. Some of the pairings were intuitive: Lhasa with Boulder; industrial Wuhan with Pittsburgh; the tiny Jilin town of Jiaohe with equally forlorn Folsom, California. Making friends with cities that looked or produced like yours was one thing, but it took chutzpah for the rusting Northeastern port of Huludao to hook up with glamorous Las Vegas. The port was already bringing culture back home via its annual International Swimsuit Festival.

Our tour group trudged upstairs, past a yarmulke meant to evince that Harbin's Jewish community was once the largest in the Far East. We stared at a rusting flatiron, proof that "Harbin flourished as a modern, open, and inclusive city." No connection was made to the synagogues, to Saint Sophia's, to the restored cobblestone street, or the district of former Russian tenement homes crumbling nearby. No mention was made of the czar and emperor and warlords and armies that had battled for Harbin, once home and refuge to people from fifty-three countries, speaking forty-five languages.

Instead we saw displays from Chiang Mai (tapestries), Cagayan de Oro (an ostrich egg), Sunderland (a photo of George Washington, whose parents emigrated from there). Griffith had also sent an egg—an emu's—along with kangaroo skins and bottles, now empty, of Yellow Tail wine. Asahikawa's beer bottles were drained, too, as was the vodka from Sverdlovsk Oblast. The children stared at a boomerang behind glass. The hall was silent, and dimly lit. We were looking at dry bottles, locked-up weapons, and there in the corner, at Rovaniemi, a pile of unopened letters to Santa Claus.

"The most favored person residing in Rovaniemi is Santa Claus," the guide recited. "Every year there are hundreds of thousands of tourists visiting his office at the Santa Claus Village on the Arctic Circle." Those who couldn't make it, such as a child named Max Lee of 139 Boundary Street, Kowloon, sent letters instead. Here was his now, on display in Harbin.

The guide led us downstairs for a summing-up—*Harbin, international city, friendship, development, modern, friendship*—and the children stared at me and smiled, and I thought: *This beats being called laowai.* The museum was closing, the kids filed past Minneapolis, whose items did not disprove critics who sniped that the sister city movement was a gloss on doing business, on increasing trade. But I dropped the sense of wizened expat irony and did as the tour guide asked, enthusing in Minnesota-accented Mandarin how Mill City life on the *Mixixibi* (Mississippi) river was illustrated by the displayed box of Pillsbury Funfetti brownie mix.

I grew up eagerly anticipating the latest issue of *National Geographic* for the maps, which wallpapered my bedroom. When you're from a place like Minneapolis, surrounded by a continent on all, nearly equidistant sides, you naturally wonder what holds you in—one reason Midwesterners make up a disproportionate number of Peace Corps volunteers. It's a ticket Out There.

And here's what it looked like this gorgeous morning in our sister city of Harbin: at Saint Sophia's square, I sat on a green wooden bench next to a planter of yellow marigolds being bothered by black butterflies. A little girl fed pigeons, a boy blew bubbles, women walked past holding parasols, a couple wore matching Angry Birds T-shirts, and bus honks and dialect filled the air: *ayamaya* and *en'e.* Dumpling house employees stood in rows for their post-lunch group exercises and pep talk. Dragonflies buzzed the marigolds, a woman leaned against the former cathedral to be photographed, and a man strutted past with his hand purse tucked in his arm like a riding crop. Another followed him, holding a brown, string-sealed

FILES envelope with both hands. The smell of hot dogs and popcorn wafted from a cart. When you travel, everything can look new, and the mundane becomes interesting. The city is on display, and travelers—in China especially—are also an exhibit. A grandfather cradling an infant hurried toward the marigolds, spread the slit of the boy's pants, and held him as the baby watered the flowers. I watched them; they watched me. Our expressions were exactly the same. We're twins.

I had last seen the lumberjack Meng Zhaoguo at the Red Flag Logging Commune, eighty miles north of Wasteland, set among the remains of a forest of oak, birch, and Manchurian ash that once covered an area twice the size of Wyoming. Back then, he had directed me to find him in the last house on the village lane. Now he told me to come to a Harbin university and walk to the last building on campus. "If you can't find me, just ask anyone," he said. Everyone knew the man who had been abducted by aliens.

I stood at the gate of the Harbin University of Commerce, feeling like I had arrived in another ghost town. The campus was part of a pump-priming project to build a new Harbin city center as large in area as New York City. The scheme had stalled: people simply did not want to move across the Songhua River, and some halted building sites had been reclaimed by rows of corn and soybeans. The university's main classroom building stood empty but for a group of students shouting phrases from a popular textbook series named *Crazy English*, which was an excellent lesson in yelling, if not communication. As I walked past transplanted pines propped up in planters, the voices chorused: "It's better than nothing! You can't please everyone! Time will tell!"

But at the back end of campus, in full grin, stood Meng Zhaoguo. "I am very happy to work here," he said. "It's quiet. I'm in charge of the boiler and watch the steam pipes." It was a better job than felling trees, he said. Logging had been curtailed at his former post; only 10 percent of the trees remained, protected as part of the Dragon Mountain National Forest Park. The workers at Red Flag Logging Commune had either left or stayed to farm soybeans.

Mr. Meng wore a clean white tunic, slacks, and loafers, with short black hair pushed neatly to the side. He looked thinner, healthier, and just as earnest as before. But he was tired of retelling what became known as the Meng Zhaoguo Incident. Talking with him is how I imagined it would be to interview a former adult film star embarrassed about his past. "When students say they recognize me from television," he said, "I tell them that was someone else who looks like me."

But his notoriety had landed this job. "A friend told me about it, and when I came for the interview, the boss had seen me on the news. The college provides an apartment with heating, my wife and daughter are working on campus as well, and my son attends a good Harbin middle school. He's studying English. Life is better for him here than in the forest."

Mr. Meng was the best example of Manchurian self-invention I had ever met. Chinese characterize Northeasterners as bighearted, industrious, and sometimes a bit touched in the head. So it was not a shock when the nation's first person claiming to sleep with an extraterrestrial came from up here.

When I previously visited him at the Red Flag Logging Commune, Mr. Meng was living in a two-room timber-frame house he had built with his own hands. Bare yellow light bulbs dropped from the ceiling, there was no phone—or cell reception—and the wall over the kang's barley-stuffed pillows was filled with a fading map of the world. "I put that up a long time ago," he explained, "when I dreamed of seeing more places."

A big-screen Sony television filled one end of the room. "Out here, it only picks up two channels," he said. "So it's a waste of money, but I didn't buy it. A businessman brought it, after he heard about my story." Another visitor, from Malaysia, had brought him a cow. "I sold that," Mr. Meng told me. "Cows cost money to take care of. What am I going to do with a cow out here?"

We had stepped outside, boots crunching snow, and faced the Dragon Mountains, veiled in purple mist as the day's light faded. Meng said that on a night much like this in 1994, he saw a metallic glint shimmer off those peaks. "I thought a helicopter had crashed, so I set out to scavenge for scrap." He made it to the lip of a valley, spying the wreckage in the distance, when "Foom! Something hit me square in the forehead and knocked me out."

He awoke at home, with no memory of how he got there. A few nights later he woke to find himself floating above the kang. As his wife slumbered beneath him, a three-meter-tall, six-fingered alien woman with thighs coated in braided hair straddled his waist. Mr. Meng and the alien had copulated for forty minutes. "She then disappeared through the wall and I floated back down to bed. She left me with this." He undid his trousers to reveal a two-inch-long jagged mark that he insisted bore only a coincidental resemblance to a scar resulting from a saw accident.

The next morning Meng told his wife what happened. She did not feel betrayed, he said. He had been helpless, after all, abducted in his own bed by an alien.

I asked him to draw the creature, and he took my pen and tore off a sheet from a roll of rough, unbleached paper ("This could be made from a tree I cut"). To my surprise, I recognized the alien. She looked like the carved round-eyed figurines excavated by a young Liang Siyong at the Neolithic sites near here. Actually, she looked more familiar than that. As he made tiny x's on the alien's inner thighs, I realized Mr. Meng was sketching a hairy cousin of the Michelin Man.

His smiling, puffy white face waved from atop an auto repair shop at the base of Red Flag Logging Commune. I thought of that, and the empty crates of Five Star beer stacked just outside Mr. Meng's front door, and the remote loneliness of a Northeast winter. But he told the story calmly, not in an anxious or pleading tone, cajoling the listener to believe. I kept my deductions internal, and Mr. Meng suggested we go outside with his kids and light off the fireworks I had brought for them. That night I slept fitfully on his *kang*.

The government monitored faith in anything but the Communist Party, but an expression of belief in extraterrestrials was permitted, as it fell under the purview of astronomy, and the "scientific socialism" the Party supported. A UFOlogy journal had a circulation of 200,000, and the China UFO Research Center boasted 50,000 members and held annual conferences before splintering—as organized groups of believers tended to do—into rival factions. Once Mr. Meng's story started making the rounds via text messages and the Internet, the media came calling, leading to his appearance in national newspapers and on television. He was even the subject of a debated Wikipedia page, which listed different versions of his story, including being taken to the aliens' home planet of Jupiter, and "ongoing harassment" from the extraterrestrials.

"Journalists look for discrepancies in my story," he told me at the logging commune. "I get tired of telling it. In the end, I'm just a peasant."

But the next morning he had continued the tale: a month after the alien had visited him in bed, he again awoke to find his body passing through the world map over the *kang*. He levitated through the stratosphere and into a spaceship, where a circle of aliens cloaked him in a robe of flesh.

"A robe of what?"

"Of flesh," he repeated. "They said in Chinese, but with a heavy accent so it was hard for me to understand at first, that they were refugees. Like me, they wanted to escape their former lives, so they left their dying home."

That echoed the tales of many migrants to Manchuria.

Mr. Meng asked to see his alien paramour, the one with braided hair on her inner thighs.

"'Impossible,' they replied. But then they said something that made me hopeful. 'In sixty years, on a distant planet, the son of a Chinese peasant will be born.'"

This was a stroke of genius: Mr. Meng had introduced Chinese class-consciousness to interstellar relations. The story transported Mr. Meng and his wife and children from the last house on a logging commune lane to a college campus in the provincial capital. When he retold the tale over our lunch in Harbin, only one detail had changed: now he said he had copulated for an hour, not forty minutes. "I asked the aliens if I would see my child," he added. "They said yes. But they would not tell me where."

I made a joke about sister planets, but Meng didn't laugh. "Once, humans believed that the earth was flat," he said. "Even a decade ago, people would not believe that a cell phone could work. Humans, if we have never seen something with our own eyes, naturally doubt that it exists, or that life could be that way. I was the first to be brave enough to say: 'I saw that.'

"But you know," Mr. Meng said, nodding collegially, "when you live up here, you see strange phenomena all the time."

CHAPTER 10

SUMMER SOLSTICE

I N SUMMER, WASTELAND came alive. Cottony white clouds reflected off the water-filled paddies, which resonated with the sounds of jumping fish, quacking ducks, and croaking frogs. On Red Flag Road I stepped around furry caterpillars and dodged dragonflies. Tractors put-putted past the deep green rice that ran to the foothills. Two months after planting, the stalks, called tillers, reached past my knee. Harvest was two months away. Then the northern wind would come, and the sun would set before four. Summer was a time to savor.

After my travels, the land felt tranquil. At first glance, there was nothing to see, and it was a relief. Compared to Harbin, it was easier to define Wasteland by what was absent than what was here. No museums, no local newspaper, no graveyards, no plaques, no library, no former mansions or battlefields. I understood the pride villagers displayed when speaking of recent developments that allowed a family to sow a plot, sell what they reaped, and live a life outside war, famine, bandits, and shifting politics. When I turned off Red Flag Road and walked into San Jiu's house, the first thing he said was "You're back. You've been gone. Nothing's new."

To me, with a backpack of filled notebooks, that was news in and of itself. But to San Jiu, it just meant everything was fine: no one was sick, the rice was growing, and the weather was regular. He walked me along the berm of earth that separated his ripening paddies—frogs bouncing wildly off our shins—to check for weeds. The formal names of the choking sedges sounded like portmanteaus from *Finnegan's Wake*: Dayflower. Fringerush. Ducksalad.

San Jiu searched for a three-bladed signalgrass that had to be pulled by hand. But the herbicide was working. "The rice is growing just right," he said. "Where's your wife?"

"In Hong Kong."

"That's good. She has a job," San Jiu said. Then he stared at me with a bemused look on his tanned face, crossed with new lines. A tear welled in his left eye; a cataract was forming. From across a field, he still looked like a stout bull of a man with a white crew cut. But up close all of his now sixty-seven years were upon him. I wondered if contracting his crop to Eastern Fortune and moving to a modern apartment wasn't such a bad idea.

"You wander around up here while she works down there," he said. "How do you afford it?"

My expenses were low: trains, dumplings, house rent, and the occasional inn on the road amounted to a few hundred dollars a month. But the figure seemed exorbitant to San Jiu. The price of chives seemed exorbitant to San Jiu.

"Everything is more expensive now," he said. "The three-wheel pedicab from this house to Wasteland's clinic used to cost five yuan, and now it's seven. That's a 40 percent increase in just one year. The cost of seed is up. Pork is outrageous." A year ago one pound of pig cost 12 yuan ($1.97). Today it was 19 yuan ($3.12).

Now we were off the topic of my livelihood—or lack thereof—and onto the Island of Prices, where so many villagers liked to drop the conversational anchor and spend some time. San Jiu listed the rise in everything from soap to milk (up 9 percent from last year) and chives. They were to Northeastern cooking what oregano was to Italian, and he couldn't bargain down their price at the market. "I planted them myself this year. And tomatoes, and potatoes, and onions. I also bought a chicken, because eggs are more expensive now, too."

It was a national trend. On a recent train ride, passengers around me munched sweet popcorn and read books titled *Currency Wars, The Collapse of the Eurosystem,* and *The Upside of Irrationality.* Despite the raft of anti-inflationary measures introduced by the government, the lead article in that morning's paper announced that the price of gasoline was at a record high of $4.91 a gallon. Another article said that a popular Chinese online forum voted 涨—*zhang*, increase—the "character of the year." It outpolled the runner-up, "resentment," nearly six to one.

As the train glided silently past cornfields, I had asked my seatmates, people of varied ages and professions, about *zhang*. They swapped stories of soaring apartment prices, not to mention the *zhang* of cooking oil, the *zhang* of toilet paper, the *zhang* of airplane tickets, the *zhang* of school fees. Voices rose as the passengers blamed "speculators and hoarders" and declared that *zhang* made them "angry to death"—it was always personal in China—and suddenly everything was in the grips of *zhang*, including my formerly tranquil train ride.

So it was not surprising that the annual *Blue Book of China's Society*, compiled by the Chinese Academy of Social Sciences, reported that prices topped the list of the public's concerns. China's consumer price index, a gauge of inflation, rose a record 5.5 percent in the month of March 2011. That was driven by food prices, which, on average, rose 11.7 percent, with vegetable prices doubling in some places.

Master Kong, the nation's best-selling brand of instant noodles, increased its price 10 percent to cover, it said, a rise in ingredient prices—leading the French hypermarket chain Carrefour to pull the product from its 169 stores in China. Say it with Parisian élan: *zhang*! And real estate prices continued to surge: a two-thousand-square-foot apartment in the Hong Kong border city of Shenzhen could cost the equivalent of a four-bedroom in prime New York.

Even the dead were affected by *zhang*. At the privately run Eternal Garden Cemetery in Shenzhen, a saleswoman explained to Frances that 50,000 yuan ($7,547) would secure her father's ashes in a one-square-meter hillside plot for twenty years, with an option to renew for fifty after that, provided the cemetery had not been evicted by a building site.

"If you want the grave to face the pond and valley, which has the best *feng shui*," the saleswoman said, "it will cost 70,000 *yuan* ($10,566). Those are selling quickly; I suggest you buy today. The price will not go down." Frances quickly chose the tomb with a view.

I dared not tell San Jiu the actual cost. Instead, I described to him how Frances knelt beside the grave, updated her father's ashes on family news, placed him in the earth, knocked her head three times on the soil, cried, and said good-bye.

"That sounds proper," San Jiu said approvingly. "Filial piety is a tradition." It was the closest to praise that San Jiu would ever offer, and I softened inside, remembering the feel of the fresh earth on my hands and forehead beside the grave. Then San Jiu said, "So how much did the plot cost?"

I was alone in Wasteland now, with Frances buried in work in Hong Kong. We had been separated for stretches in the past, and bridged the distance with daily text messages and Skype calls. So long as we stayed busy, it didn't feel like we were apart. Thirteen years together had planted her voice, her presence, in my head, anyway; sometimes Wastelanders turned questioningly after the foreigner blurted something aloud to a woman who wasn't there. I considered wearing a Bluetooth headset as a prop to mask my one-sided conversations.

Frances thought that alien-loving Mr. Meng had seen a meteorite crash that night, not a spaceship. (The rest of his story, she said, was a master performance of the Art of Northeastern Bullshitting.) A meteorite had burst into pieces over Wasteland in 1976. San Jiu and Auntie Yi and Uncle Fu remembered hearing the sonic boom and seeing a ball of fire in the March afternoon sky: they thought an airplane had exploded. The debris missed their homes, slamming instead into the paddies in a spray of mud and smoke. The ground quaked—1.7 on the Richter scale, according to the Jilin city museum built to display a microwave-oven-size chunk of the meteorite. It was not a patriotic education base: it spiced up the narrative for schoolkids by describing the rock as a "visitor from outer space." Reading that caption, I thought fondly of Mr. Meng.

The bus from the museum back to Wasteland passed Number 22 Middle School, vacant in late June. Results for the high school entrance exam hung from red banners on its exterior walls, announcing which students tested into the top Jilin schools and who had been relegated to the Physical Education Academy. The serious girl who called herself Phil earned a place at the city's best high school. She aspired to go to university and become an English teacher despite being able to outrun her classmates headed for "P.E. School." They would be groomed for a nonacademic career. Sitting beside me on the bus, Ms. Guan laughed at my translation of Woody

Allen's joke: Those who can't do, teach; those who can't teach, teach gym. "Although," she added, "P.E. teachers don't have to grade homework. So maybe they're the smartest teachers after all."

Around the school, paddies of deep-green rice shone in the morning sun. The landscape had not changed in my absence, but the school's garbage pile rose with empty plastic bottles of Coke, Pepsi, and orange Fanta. Two small billboards papered on the side of the grocery store featured Kobe Bryant and a team of gowned surgeons concentrating on a prone man. Kobe pitched the Web portal sina.com, while the operation demonstrated KOREAN STYLE CIRCUMCISION. It could be performed in Wasteland's expanded clinic, presently shrouded in scaffolding.

But the biggest change lay ahead.

As the roar of training jets cut through the silent morning, the bus idled at the start of Red Flag Road, waiting for a passenger to offload boxes of flooring tiles. An auntie unknown to me asked the singsong question "*Shei jia'di'ah*"—To whose family do I belong?—and smiled broadly, saying that she remembered Frances as a little girl. I said I was here alone, and she clucked her tongue, exhaling an *aiya wo'de maya* to register her concern. "You two don't have a child yet? When are you going to be a father? You're not a young man anymore. She needs to get pregnant. You can't do it from up here when she's down in Hong Kong."

It was true: Skype didn't feature that button.

The bus howled in laughter, teasing me for being childless, marooned, alone. The jokes paused only when someone said, seriously, "Mixed-blood children look beautiful. Your child will be so good-looking."

"And smart!" another auntie chimed.

"But tell your wife to eat—"

"Apples," I finished.

The bus nodded in agreement, then went back to needling me, whooping over my self-inflicted solitude.

The driver pulled under the new archway stretching over Red Flag Road. It was Wasteland's tallest structure, reaching even higher than the billboard that pledged to BUILD THE NORTHEAST'S TOP VILLAGE. Green sod ringed the archway's foundations, and its legs rose in marble-clad blocks bridged by five gleaming metal tubes. It looked like something, if not from outer space, then at least not from Wasteland.

White decal characters running down one of the arch's legs said: The Roots of Northeast Prosperity. The other side announced: Eastern Fortune Rice.

"The arch doesn't even show the village name," I said.

"The company is acquiring more and more land," Ms. Guan replied.

The driver searched for, then noisily found, first gear, and the bus stuttered under the arch, toward the ripening paddies. The driver said, "Some people joke that we all live in Eastern Fortune Rice now." But no one on the bus laughed at this.

CHAPTER 11

THE BALLAD OF AUNTIE YI

"JULY IS WHEN the rice sunbathes," San Jiu said at his paddy. He used the word *dao* (稻), which meant planted rice, not *mi* (米), the processed product we eat. With his finger he drew the characters in the dirt separating the fields. "Now you do it," he said, and watched patiently until I wrote both correctly. Then he swept the soil away with his rubber boot, plunking the words into water.

Summer brought up to sixteen hours of light each day. "Aside from the bugs, the biggest danger is that the rice will grow too fast and not ripen evenly," San Jiu explained. "If it's growing too fast, you remove the water from the paddy and let the rice stand dry for a few days." Traditionally, draining the fields for a short period mid-growth was said to toughen the roots. Ancient Chinese records called the practice "shelving the rice" or "baking the fields," since farmers waited until the soil dried enough to crack.

San Jiu pointed at the calf-deep water. "That's the most important thing, you know. The water quality. It's more important than the seed or the soil, even. River water is the best, everyone knows that."

"Not me."

"Silt!" San Jiu exclaimed. "River water has silt and clay." Later I learned that it held fertilizing minerals. In the classical Chinese handbook *On Farming*, published in 1149, the writer advised that rice "likes fresh, moving water and fears cold and stagnant water."

An eighth-century poet wrote a verse that San Jiu and his fields fit right into, thirteen hundred years later:

North of the Yangtze River
Ten thousand acres lie flat as a table.
By the sixth month the green rice is plentiful,
In a thousand fields the jade waters mingle.
San Jiu surveyed his crop.

"At this time," he said, "when it's warm in the daytime and cool at night, the conditions are just right. We haven't even had any humidity."

It was perfect weather; highs in the seventies and lows in the fifties, the kind of days made for shorts and a hoodie, though no one beside me wore them. Even the children always had pants on. They spent their summer vacation mostly indoors, watching television, playing video games, or doing homework. The village ran extracurricular English classes each weekday afternoon, where I helped out. During recess, the kids challenged me, one by one, to fifty-meter dashes. Their little legs windmilled across the dirt exercise yard, raising clouds of Roadrunner dust.

One place I never saw children was in the fields, or the seed stores, or at Eastern Fortune's rice polisher and warehouses. This, San Jiu said, was a concern. Parents wanted their child to go to school, and learn white-collar professions. Some also aspired to studying at the agricultural institute, located halfway between here and Jilin city, but what use was learning farm management or seed biology if you didn't have practical experience with animals or soil? China had no equivalent of the 4-H Club. Farming was not a skilled trade in which one apprenticed, then gained professional expertise. It was, San Jiu said, something people were once born into, but seldom would be again.

On television, my students liked to watch sports and the Chinese version of the singing competition *The Voice*. My unscientific sample showed that Wasteland's adults favored the soap operas about gentry during the Manchu dynasty or about heroism during the Japanese occupation. Outside of the news, I never saw a farm on screen. There was no equivalent to *Little House on the Prairie*; the school's bookshelves held no corresponding version of John Steinbeck's stories set on California farms. China's national novel, *Dream of the Red Chamber*, detailed an aristocratic household. Their tenant farmers appeared only to pay rent and present annual offerings. "Country people are such unsophisticated creatures," a character sniffed. "They're just like a piece of yellow cedar made into a mallet for beating the sonorous stones with. The exterior looks well enough; but it's all bitter inside."

One of the first works of American literature appeared around the same time. Written by the French-born J. Hector St. John de Crèvecoeur and published in 1782, *Letters from an American Farmer* was extolled by Benjamin Franklin, Thomas Paine, Percy Bysshe Shelley, and Samuel Coleridge as exemplifying what would come to be called the American Dream. It reads like a sweatier *Walden*: "The father, thus ploughing with his child, and to feed his family, is inferior only to the emperor of China ploughing as an example to his kingdom."

In Wasteland I reread Pearl Buck's *The Good Earth*, wondering if it would interest my students. I also wanted a better reply to Westerners who said my current research was "like *The Good Earth*," aside from pointing out that Buck's book was a novel. Set in central China. Ninety years ago.

It begins with a young farmer named Wang Lung waking on his wedding day. He tears the paper from his shack's window to thrust an arm outside to check the weather, relieved to feel "a wind mild and murmurous and full of rain." Then comes marriage, children, famine, concubines, floods, war, and locusts before greed conquers all. The book concludes with his dying words to his urbane sons: "Out of the land we came and into it we must go . . . [I]f you sell the land it is the end." The sons promise they will never sell, "But over the old man's head they looked at each other and smiled."

It was a tragic ending, but if Wang Lung had lived to see the Communist revolution, he likely would have been branded a bourgeois landlord, and executed. At the very least, his hard-earned acreage would have been seized and redistributed to people like Frances's family, in places like Wasteland.

Forty years after her death, Pearl Buck remained stranded between two worlds. In China she was admired but not read; in America she was read but not admired. William Faulkner once dismissed her as "Mrs. Chinahand Buck." Her most recent Chinese translator, however, told me, "She was a revolutionary. She was the first writer to choose rural China as her subject matter. None of the Chinese writers would have done so; intellectuals wrote about urban intellectuals." Her childhood home, in the Yangtze River port Zhenjiang, which smelled like its famous vinegar, was recently turned into a museum about her life there before she became the first American woman to win the Nobel Prize in Literature. Though, one thing was notably absent from the gift shop: Buck's books.

She wrote eighty of them, but her life story is the most compelling to me. Born Pearl Sydenstricker, she was raised by missionary parents who hired tutors to teach her calligraphy and the classical texts of Confucius and other philosophers in Chinese. "I became mentally bifocal," she wrote in a memoir. "When I was in the Chinese world, I spoke Chinese and behaved as Chinese and ate as the Chinese did, and I shared their thoughts and feelings. When I was in the American world, I shut the door between."

She loved the works of Charles Dickens, whose influence was seen in her descriptions of cultural minutiae. Her father had translated the Bible into vernacular Chinese, and her own syntax often echoed its authoritative run-ons: "The children tugged at Wang Lung then, and Wang Lung led them all back to the hut they had made, and there they laid themselves down and they slept until the next morning, for it was the first time since summer they had been filled with food, and sleep overcame them with fullness."

But that voice, too, sounded familiar to anyone who has spent time listening to Chinese people tell stories, which can come in fits and starts, and then roll, with words spilling fast when freed. Frances got to that point after a few beers, San Jiu when he was angry, Ms. Guan after the stress of a school day. When I would ask my former Beijing courtyard neighbor, an elderly widow, a direct question about a specific date, it could take a few days for her to respond, which she often did while doing something else, such as making dumplings: "The water is almost ready. You must be hungry. My father liked this kind of filling, pork and chives. He said I would have to marry an army officer almost twenty years older, a friend of someone he knew. That's what I remember most about 1931." The voice sounded detached, as if the speaker were telling a tale that happened long ago, to someone else, far away. It was different than an American voice. Frances noticed on arrival to the United States that Americans were their own protagonists, narrating their lives to anyone who would listen, or even when no one was. The Chinese invented many things, Frances said, but only Americans could have come up with blogs, Facebook, and Twitter.

*

Like John Steinbeck, who wrote a series of newspaper stories on visits to relief camps that inspired him to begin *The Grapes of Wrath*, Buck witnessed firsthand the types of scenes she depicted in *The Good Earth*. As an adolescent, she had worked with her mother in soup kitchens during famine, and taught sewing at a school for the poor. At a church picnic she met a newly arrived agronomist named John Lossing Buck. He spoke halting Chinese; she was fluent. After their divorce eighteen years later, she wrote that all they had in common was "Sunday school teaching and Bible classes." But they also shared a love for the Chinese farm.

Pearl moved to his agricultural experiment station in a central China hamlet of mud streets and mud houses, surrounded by mud walls. They explored the surrounding countryside—he on a bicycle; she, per custom, in a sedan chair borne by four laborers. He logged details of farm life: housing, fuel, prices, diet, recreation, funerals, and more. Until then—in a country where 80 percent of the people were farmers—no one had systematically gathered this material.

The result, a book titled *Chinese Farm Economy*, would make him the better-known writer, at least for a year. To a casual reader, the 1930 volume and its sequel are achingly dull, filled with statistical tables. Pearl typed her husband's reports, and his prose could not have helped their marriage. Imagine the woman able to quote Dickens and the great Chinese epics clacking down topic sentences such as "Profitableness of a cropping system depends chiefly upon the yield and price of the crops, the seasonal distribution of labor and the proportion of the most profitable crops in the system."

However, book-ending many chapters were local adages, rendered in Chinese characters, and translated into English, such as: "To learn to be a farmer one need not study. One needs only to do as his neighbor does," and: "One should be cautious not to plant sorghum too close, but at least far enough apart for a cow to lie down."

Some sounded like a fortune cookie that had been parsed into Chinese by Frances: "It is better to let your mother starve to death than to let your crop seed be eaten up."

Pearl Buck had added the sayings. While her husband Lossing talked to the men in the fields, she stayed inside with the women, asking about their lives and lore. Her sister Grace told a biographer, "She entered very much into that project, and she did a great deal of editing." Not long after Lossing's book was finished, Pearl wrote *The Good Earth* in five months' time.

In the 1930s eight different Chinese translations of the novel were "cheerfully pirated over and over again," Buck wrote approvingly. But after the Communist revolution in 1949, her stories were seen as anachronisms from an era toppled by Mao. She had left China—and Lossing—in 1935, eventually marrying her publisher and moving to a farm in Bucks County, Pennsylvania. During the Red Scare era, she wrote five novels set in the American West under the name John Sedges.

In 1972, the year of Nixon's visit to China, Buck's application for a Chinese visa was denied, the rejection letter explained, due to "the fact that for a long time you have in your works taken an attitude of distortion, smear and vilification towards the people of new China and their leaders." She died nine months later and was buried on the grounds of her Bucks County farm in a solitary grave carved with her Chinese name.

I saw many warnings in this tale for a foreigner writing about China, not least of all the possibility of being interred under the characters for Heroic Eastern Plumblossom. Another: a marriage failing because of one partner's single-mindedness in research. "I was busy, busy, busy going back with all this land utilization data," Lossing would admit after their divorce, which took him by surprise. And then there was the chance that one's writing could result in being barred from the country.

But there were other lessons, too, in an age of intensive China watching. The Bucks learned the language. They left big cities. They saw things for themselves, not relying on officials' explanations or intellectuals' critiques. They focused on how life was lived by average people, not the headlines generated by extraordinary ones. "Americans," Pearl Buck wrote in 1970, "have a genuine interest in the Chinese people," but the news media underestimated "the general intelligence of their reading public and the range of its interest." The Bucks focused on the slower story, observing changes to individuals and the land over time.

And they loved the farm. In a speech to American pilots shipping out during the Second World War, Pearl said what *The Good Earth*'s plot had obscured, and made many readers think the title was meant to be ironic. "What if you land in the Chinese countryside?" Buck asked. "Well, then, you are lucky, for the Chinese countryside is beautiful."

Summer headlines in Jilin city newspapers included:

"Expressway Tollbooth Revealed as Corrupt"
"67-Year-Old Woman Leaps from Thirteenth Floor"
"Nine-Year-Old Boy Runs Away from Home After Mother
    Loses Cat"
"Investigative Report of Pornography Viewing Rooms"
"Drunk Driver Kills Two"
"Smart Little Dog Can Use a Cell Phone"
"Corpse Found Beaten, Lying in Pool of Blood"
"Drunks Toss Buddy from Second Story Window"
"Farmer's Prize Pig Mysteriously Murdered"

China always looked different after reading the paper. On the bus back to Wasteland, I suddenly wondered what each passenger was capable of. Corruption? Pornography? Pig murder?

Online, I read Western headlines such as:

"China Sees Food Needs Rising"
"China Snaps Up Farmland in Argentina"
"Brazil Uneasy over China's Interest in Land"

The nation was on a "global commodity hunt," the *Wall Street Journal* reported. China was the biggest purchaser of Argentine soybeans, mainly used as livestock feed, a demand that rose with meat consumption. In Brazil, Chinese companies signed a $7 billion agreement to produce six million tons of soybeans each year, part of a series of deals that made China its largest trading partner. Its food and energy purchases had "helped fuel an economic boom . . . that has lifted more than 20 million Brazilians from extreme poverty and brought economic stability . . ." wrote the *New York Times*.

The shift to overseas food sources came as China's surging demand clashed with its arable land being diminished by urbanization. In the past thirty years, farmland equivalent in area to the size of New York State had been developed.

Science and technology wrung increasing yields from the existing land: an average hectare now produced 6.3 tons of rice, four times more than in 1949. "Chasing ever-higher output levels may mean overfertilization and unsafe agriculture," a top agricultural official warned. "Of course, we have to raise output in this area but our techniques and resources can't keep up."

China classifies corn, wheat, and rice as key grains, and keeps the planet's largest stockpiles of these foods, totaling 40 percent of annual consumption. Once the world's largest exporter of soy, China is now the largest importer. The Brazil deal alone would meet 10 percent of its annual demand. At the start of the twenty-first century, China imported a few tons of corn each year. In 2012 alone, it bought two million tons. Chinese demand, coupled with drought and increasing consumption by the U.S. ethanol industry, pushed the grain's price to an all-time high.

Among the largest beneficiaries of Chinese consumption was the American farmer. Food accounted for $1 of every $5 China spent on American products between 2010 and 2012, led by soy, whose sales totaled $15 billion annually. Exports of all goods doubled from 2005 to 2010, but food—including dairy, pork, and fruit juice—more than tripled. Pecan sales rose twentyfold. An elated grower in Georgia told the *Wall Street Journal* that, thanks to the Chinese belief that the nuts were good for the brain, "we're in a situation of finite supply and seemingly infinite demand." The price of a pound of pecans doubled in a single year.

China kept outsourcing: in 2013 it signed a fifty-year agreement with Ukraine to lease three million hectares of farmland, more than doubling the two million hectares it had previously held overseas. The produce and pigs raised in Ukraine would be sold to two Chinese state-owned grain conglomerates. One was known as Bingtuan, a quasi-military organization founded in the 1950s to strengthen the Chinese border with the Soviet Union. Now it brandished a checkbook, writing on the memo line: *Food*.

"We can send them a trainload of pigtails," Auntie Yi said.

"Is that a Chinese saying?"

She looked up from weeding her poppies. "What?"

"'We can send them a trainload of pigtails,'" I repeated. "What does it mean?"

Auntie Yi laughed, her long gray curls bouncing under her bucket hat. "It means a trainload of pigtails. That's what it means. *Aiya wo'de maya*." She shot me a playful look. Her snaggletooth peeked out from her upper lip. "You just told me that China is buying food from the former Soviet Union."

In August 1945, the Red Army looted Jilin city's cement factory, she said. It was located at the site of Diamond Cement, the plant that now rained gooey pellets on passerby. "It had a bunch of advanced machinery that the Japanese had built, and we finally got rid of them and could use it; but the Red Army stayed after war's end and took whatever it wanted. Stalin said he was keeping the factory safe in the USSR so the Americans couldn't take it. He ransomed it back; Premier Zhou Enlai paid him in apples and soybeans. 'We have no pork,' he said, 'but we can send them a trainload of pigtails.'"

"So there weren't any pigtails?"

"China was broke!"

Auntie Yi veered into a story about her younger brother, who had gone to school in Jilin city. The old town's gates were still standing then, she said, but none of its wall or wooden architecture remained. "A few months ago you asked me about the Japanese occupation, and I've been meaning to tell you what I remember," she said, leading me inside her house, where Uncle Fu poured bowls of hot soymilk.

"You asked me what it used to be like here," Auntie Yi said from the edge of the *kang*. "I remember [the puppet state named] Manchukuo well. I was a little girl when the little Japanese devils occupied this place. Why did they come here? I hear now people say they came here for the mines, and to build a dam, but we Chinese built the dam and worked in the mines. If you didn't work, they would beat you and toss you in the pit of dead bodies."

"Did you ever see Japanese people?"

"They lived in one part of Jilin city. I remember seeing Japanese women wearing kimonos and carrying their babies on their back. They wore wood shoes, and the sidewalks were wood then. The shoes went *ta ta ta ta ta*. They powdered their faces and ate so well; they looked beautiful in all that silk. We Chinese wore old cotton clothes we wove and dyed ourselves. The crotch of my pants kept ripping, and the blankets at home were rough cloth and full of fleas.

"I was in elementary school then, and every morning we had to sing the Manchukuo national anthem. It was about the colors of the Manchukuo flag and went . . ."

She sang a stately tune with Japanese lyrics:

"Our national flag flutters, flutters, flutters.
Red, blue, white, black, yellow.
I love my flag, the flag that flutters, flutters, flutters.

"The teacher would smack your palm three times with a wooden pointer if you didn't sing correctly," she explained. "I hated having a swollen hand. So I still remember some Japanese." She counted to ten in the language without pause.

The flag's five colors represented the five ethnicities living in Manchukuo, which comprised the entire Northeast, from the Great Wall to Siberia. The mustard-yellow field mimicked the Manchu's Qing dynasty flag, but instead of a spindly blue dragon, it featured a square in its upper-left corner that showed a red stripe (representing Japanese) over a blue stripe (Han Chinese), white (Mongolians), and black (Koreans).

"We were taught we were 'Manchukuoans,' not Chinese," Auntie Yi said. "The Chinese language was called the Manchukuo language. You couldn't say China; nothing could be Chinese. They taught only Japanese at school. Every morning we stood up and saluted the teacher and said 'Hai!' It was like what they show on TV: everything was always 'Hai!' and a salute. At lunchtime, we said 'Thank you' in Japanese over and over. 'Arigato arigato arigato.' At the end of the school day, we saluted and said good-bye, and then, on the walk home, I spoke Chinese again. That only lasted for a year. In 1945, Manchukuo fell."

Before rebel forces made it to Jilin, their Chinese foe arrived first.

"The Nationalist army was really fierce. It was the Seventy-seventh and then the Eighty-eighth Brigade. They would come to our homes and demand labor. They often beat my grandfather for refusing to work. He didn't support them at all. When they came into our house, we had to kneel before them. They were bastards. They cut down our trees for fuel and beat my brother, cracking his head. There were ten soldiers on him. Oh, the Japanese came to our house, too, but on patrols. They just looked inside, but it was still scary, because they had helmets on, and rifles with bayonets. But the worst of all came after that."

Auntie Yi lowered her voice theatrically and murmured: *kata kata kata.* "That was the sound of the Russians marching on the road beside their carts. I would sit in a tree and yell, 'Hairy ones!' and the women would hide. They would shut their doors and get sticks ready. Sometimes a car would pull up with two or three Russian soldiers in it, to inspect our homes. They would open the wardrobe and take whatever they could find, even my mother's watch and her gold ring. One guy pulled a gun on our dog for barking at him, but my uncle got the soldier drunk, plucked a goose for him, and he left."

Another time, she remembered, a Russian man raped a neighbor. "People said that after he finished, he tied her legs to the back of a horse and dragged her until she died."

Seeking refuge, her parents moved her out to Wasteland. But the danger stayed near. "In 1948, the Nationalists and Communists fought each other in a big battle by the river here. I used to duck beside the *kang* when we heard shots. I was so frightened. A bullet came right through the paper covering our windows! We couldn't have any light at night, so the lanterns were out, and we just tried to sleep. I couldn't sleep: my heart beat like crazy all night. We slept on the floor, under the window level. I was seven then."

Then the Communist Eighth Route Army arrived in Wasteland. Unlike the Japanese, the Russians, and the Chinese Nationalist troops, they didn't enter villagers' homes. "The soldiers sat quietly in the yard, and camped outside. They carried their own water and cooked their own food and never bothered us. Our windows had paper glued over the panes, not glass, and sometimes they would poke a hole—*pa pa pa*—and say, 'Don't be scared of us. We're here to help common folks like you. We won't bully you.'"

Auntie Yi broke into song after mimicking the sound of triumphant trumpets:

> "Arise! All those who don't want to be slaves!
> Let our flesh and blood forge our new Great Wall!
> As the Chinese people have arrived at their most perilous time. Every
>   person must expel his very last roar.
> Arise! Arise! Arise!"

The song, "March of the Volunteers," was composed for a 1935 patriotic film about exiles from the occupied Northeast who enlisted in the army to expel the Japanese from Manchuria. It became China's national anthem except during the decade of the Cultural Revolution, when its lyricist was imprisoned.

Auntie Yi said that then, in the late 1960s, "The East Is Red" became the national song. "It played on the loudspeakers every sunrise and sunset. The whole countryside all over China could hear it." She sang:

> *"The east is red, the sun rises.*
> *From China arises Mao Zedong.*
> *He strives for the people's happiness,*
> *Hurrah [hu'er haiyo] he is the people's great savior!"*

The inclusion of *hu'er haiyo* always intrigued me, because they are not words but sounds reminiscent of the *aiya wo'de maya* that Northeasterners exclaim in dialect to express disgust. "The East Is Red" was said to have been penned by a patriotic farmer, who set the words to a traditional rural folk song that began:

> *Sesame oil, cabbage hearts,*
> *If you want to eat string beans, break off end parts,*
> *After three days apart, I miss you so,*
> *Hu'er haiyo.*

Auntie Yi knew the words to that, and many other songs. Her generation had to sing, she said with a sly grin. Uncle Fu rose and shuffled across the narrow space between the *kang* and the windows to turn on the television. Snooker again. He switched it off. The home's south-facing windows stretched from his waist to the ceiling, and potted plants lined the sill. "I'll add some water to these," he said. "You two keep talking."

"Only one more song," Auntie Yi promised, although I was enjoying her performance. Her legs dangled off the edge of the *kang*, not reaching the floor. Under her bucket hat and locks of gray hair, her tanned, unlined face flexed comical or serious as the lyrics dictated, the white snaggletooth rising and falling like a baton.

The last song was "On the Songhua River," a regional anthem as ubiquitous here as "Home on the Range" had been in the American West. It was sung from the perspective of an exile who fled south on the day in 1931 that Japan invaded Manchuria. Auntie Yi sang:

> "My home is on the Songhua River,
> There are timber forests and coal mines,
> Mountains covered in sorghum and soy.
> My home is on the Songhua River,
> My compatriots are there, and aged parents, still.
> September 18, September 18.
> At that miserable moment, I left my homeland,
> Leaving the infinite natural resources behind.
> Wandering and wandering,
> Drifting on the Great Wall's other side.
> What year, what month, can I return to my home?
> What year, what month, can I reclaim its treasures?
> Father and mother, will we ever be together again?

"Everyone knows that song," Auntie Yi said.

"When did you learn it? When you were a little girl?"

"I'm not sure," Auntie Yi said. "It has always been around."

I smiled at her turn of phrase. In the countryside, everything had always existed; everything was already known. September 18, September 18. At that miserable moment I left my homeland. Colonizers whose shoes went *ta ta ta ta ta*. An occupying army marching *kata kata kata*. Soldiers slaughtered on a civil war battlefield by men who carefully poked holes in paper windows—*pa pa pa*—to say we won't bully you. Arise! Arise! Arise! The east is red. *Hu'er haiyo*. In 1956, it became a village.

CHAPTER 12

PUPPETS OF MANCHUKUO

I PREFERRED AUNTIE Yi's telling of history to what is displayed in the Northeast's museums. They show the dates and death tolls of when China, Russia, and Japan collided in Manchuria. But the unnoted personal dramas from that time interested me most.

The story of Puyi, the last emperor, mirrored his Manchurian homeland: bandied between empires, allied with whoever held the gun. His reign began in Beijing in 1908 and ended in 1945 in Changchun, the provincial capital seventy miles west of Wasteland. There, in photographs hanging in the Puppet Emperor's Palace Museum, Puyi looked like a doll: first as a toddler regent in an oversize silk gown; then as a young man in a tunic weighted with medals bestowed for docile compliance rather than valor; and finally as a gardener with a Chairman Mao pin affixed to his serge work shirt. In the exhibit, not a single photo, across his life span, showed him smiling.

The two-story museum looked more like a workers' sanatorium than a palace. It would not have qualified as a storage shed at the Forbidden City, Puyi's former residence. There were no vermillion walls, no awe-inspiring gates, no elaborate gardens, no throne room. The swimming pool held only rotting leaves, the rockery masked a tiny bomb shelter, and the puppet palace's displays included captions such as "Puyi sometimes played the piano in here in order to let off his depression and discontent as a puppet emperor." And: "To kill time after getting up, Puyi would sit on the toilet reading the daily newspaper." A copy of the *Manchurian Daily News* sat, folded, before his lesser throne. The museum was, of course, a patriotic education base.

Outside, in the warm summer sun, a low thunder grew louder. I turned a corner to see five chestnut horses rounding a bend. This being contemporary China, patriotic education included running a sideline business. At the Puppet Emperor's Palace Museum Horse Riding and Stables Club, visitors could saddle up and loop the dirt track where Puyi once made circles. The horses trotted past, powdering my face in Manchurian dust.

Puyi's life hinged on a fateful miscalculation, unnoted in the museum, that had reined him to Japan. In a memoir, his childhood English tutor wrote that Puyi was "a very 'human' boy, with vivacity, intelligence, and a keen sense of humor." He found him "mentally active and anxious to learn," taking interest in world news and geography, and reading multiple newspapers each day. "Moreover, he has excellent manners and is entirely free from arrogance. This is rather remarkable in view of the extremely artificial nature of his surroundings and the pompous make-believe of the palace-routine." His tutor felt Puyi's post-Beijing destiny was to attend, and perhaps live out his days at, Oxford.

In 1924, when a warlord expelled Puyi from the section of the Forbidden City granted to him after abdication, the tutor drove him to the Legation Quarter. He chose not to deliver him to the British embassy, as its staff had indicated it would not interfere in China's internal politics. Instead, the tutor brought him across Canal Street to the Japanese legation, an action he later regretted as an "enormous mistake."

For three months, Puyi squatted at the Japanese embassy with his retinue—wives, dozens of attendants, concubines, eunuchs, maids and scullions—who continued to prepare breakfasts featuring twenty-five dishes. (In his memoir, Puyi wrote of the stay: "I was actually relieved to be able to live like a normal citizen, free from the palace.") In 1925, Japan put him on the train to Tianjin, eventually installing him at a mansion named the Garden of Serenity.

"Although he was now thoroughly Westernized—wearing European clothes, eating European food and dancing to European music—Puyi still thought of himself as emperor," his tutor wrote, "and the expatriate community in Tianjin delighted in playing along with this delusion for the [six] years he languished in exile there." Photos showed Puyi as a dandy wearing a diamond tiepin and ring, carrying a walking stick. "My body," he recalled, "would emit the combined odors of Max Factor, eau de cologne and camphor and I would be accompanied by two or three Alsatian dogs and a strangely dressed wife and consort." From around the world arrived letters containing "proposals from unknown females who desired to enter the imperial harem."

Tianjin in 1928 was thick with factions, secret societies, and intrigue. Puyi heard whispers of restoration and assassination attempts. Rumors said a warlord would put him on a Manchurian throne and secede from the Chinese republic; others warned the Japanese wanted him, the most powerful Manchu, dead. When a Japanese-planted bomb killed the Manchurian warlord Zhang Zuolin that year, Puyi feared he was the next target.

If he was unsure of his friends, he was certain of his enemy. In 1928, Nationalist Chinese troops systematically plundered the Eastern Qing Tombs for three days, excavating the treasures buried with the Manchu emperor Qianlong—in power at the dynasty's eighteenth-century peak— and Cixi, the empress dowager who had put Puyi on the throne. The soldiers were said to have hacked their remains to pieces and looted their crypts. Puyi heard that China's first lady, Madame Chiang Kai-shek, used the pearls from Cixi's crown to decorate the toes of her shoes. "My heart smoldered with a hatred I had never previously known," he wrote, "and I made a vow before my weeping clansmen, with my face raised to heaven: 'If I do not avenge this wrong I am not a member of the Aisin-Goro clan of the Great Qing Dynasty.'"

Were this a film, one can imagine a montage of a gritting Puyi lifting rice sacks, running beside a steam train, and stabbing pictures of Nationalist generals pinned to cabbages. But no. Puyi remained in the Japanese concession, attending dances that he never joined, preferring, he wrote, to watch from the side of the room.

Manchuria's man of action was Zhang Xueliang, the "Young Marshal," whose warlord father had been assassinated by a Japanese bomb. At the time, Zhang had lived a life as louche as Puyi's. In a private letter, an Australian journalist wrote that Zhang and fellow officers had "nightly orgies with bunches of concubines, singing girls, mahjong and other things not directly connected with affairs of the state. The latter are relegated to the obscure background. Nero fiddling was not a circumstance to these beauties jazzing. They think more of their concubines than their country." In the light of day, Zhang "tries to bang a golf ball about under bogey.

Perhaps the latter redeems him a little. It has done some good for it has brought about the repair of the road to the course. For that we are grateful. He has also fixed up stone seats at the tees, and so we are thinking of making him Patron of the Club in order to get more out of him. He has a lot of ill-gotten gains."

His father's murder, however, spurred a transformation that echoed Prince Hal becoming Henry V. The young Zhang hired the Australian journalist as his chief adviser, who helped him kick his opium addiction. In April 1931, he ceded administrative control of the Northeast to the Chinese republican government. It announced plans to terminate Japan's lease of the South Manchuria Railway.

But it was more than just a train. The South Manchuria Railway was Japan's largest corporation, whose yearly earnings represented nearly a quarter of all Japanese tax revenue. Called Mantetsu in Japanese, it was a state within a state, with administrative and police control of the tracks' "attached lands," leased—according to an agreement resulting from the American-brokered Treaty of Portsmouth—to the Japanese government until 2002. Its roster of companies in Manchuria included coal mines, steel mills, hospitals, hotels, hot springs, public utilities, slaughterhouses, orchards, water supplies, flour mills, fire stations, sugar refineries, libraries, and schools—from kindergarten to universities. In 1931 the railway's workers (and their dependents) made up one-third of the 230,000 Japanese living in Manchuria.

Under the slogan "Military Preparedness in Civilian Garb," the railway also ran a research department staffed by two thousand employees that produced six thousand reports on Manchuria's land, resources, and culture, recording statistics and stories on everything from jute sack shortages to the stateless Russian Jews trapped in Harbin. Researchers collected the minutiae of Manchurian life to better inform its future colonial administrators and settlers.

In the summer of 1931, a Japanese officer in civilian clothes was killed in Manchuria by Chinese soldiers who correctly suspected he was a spy. In a dispute over irrigation rights in a village north of Changchun, Chinese farmers attacked Japanese-backed Korean settlers. No one was killed, but anti-Chinese riots broke out in Japanese-ruled Pyongyang, resulting in 146 Chinese deaths and hundreds of injuries. A boycott of Japanese products in Manchuria followed, increasing tensions.

China called its theater of the Second World War the War Against Japanese Aggression. It began on September 18, 1931, six years before Japan invaded greater China, eight years before Germany invaded Poland, and a decade before Pearl Harbor. Today the anniversary is marked in the Northeast with air raid sirens that howl at 9:18 a.m. on September 18, the date Japanese soldiers detonated a bomb on train tracks outside present-day Shenyang. The small explosion harmed no one. It didn't even disrupt rail traffic. But it was evidence, the Japanese army said, that their railroad zone was under attack. Soldiers overran a Chinese garrison near the tracks, then occupied the entire city.

Zhang Xueliang was in Beijing at the time, and most of his forces were also south of the Great Wall, skirmishing with Communist rebels. Zhang knew that opposing the Japanese was tactical suicide. "There was no way we could win," he said later. "We could only have a shambolic go of it. Non-resistance was the only feasible policy." Over the next five months, Japan took control of every major city along the railway, and all of Manchuria.

In November 1931, one of the officers behind the September 18 bombing called on the last emperor, Puyi, in his Tianjin villa to offer the position of sovereign of a state named Manchukuo.

"But there was one big problem that worried me," Puyi wrote, "and I asked what form the new state would take."

"As I have already mentioned, it will be independent and autonomous, and it will be headed by you."

"That is not what I asked. I wish to know whether it will be a republic or a monarchy? Will it, or will it not, be a monarchy?"

"This problem will be solved after you come."

After Puyi demurred, the Japanese officer promised: "Of course it will be a monarchy; there's no question of that."

Ignoring the warnings of his advisers, Puyi put on a Japanese soldier's uniform and snuck out of Tianjin by ship. Unbeknownst to him, a large drum of gasoline was on board, to be exploded if the boat was captured, leaving no witnesses. Also unknown: Japan's army had replacement candidates lined up to head Manchukuo if Puyi had declined their offer. These included a Manchu prince and a direct descendant of Confucius. Puyi was their first choice, however, as Manchukuo's western flank would consist of Mongolian grasslands now controlled by princes who had ties to the former Qing court.

Puyi had never lived in his ancestral homeland. After three months of isolation in a Port Arthur hotel, he was met by a Japanese officer who delivered the news that Manchukuo would be a parliamentary state. Puyi would become chief executive, not emperor.

"Without waiting for the interpreter to finish translating," Puyi wrote, "he produced from his briefcase the 'Declaration of Independence of the Manchu and Mongol People' and the proposed five-colored Manchukuo flag and put them on the table in front of me. Pushing them aside with a trembling hand, and with my lungs ready to burst with rage, I asked: 'What sort of state is this? Certainly it isn't the Great Qing Empire!'"

The officer told him to accept the offer, or else. "These words, when relayed to me, left me stunned. My legs turned to jelly and I collapsed speechless onto a sofa."

On March 8, Puyi arrived in Changchun by rail, stepping onto a platform scored by the brassy, thumping din of an army band. "Even before the train had stopped," Puyi recalled in his memoir, "I could hear the sounds of military music and the cheers of people on the platform. In the procession there were people wearing the Chinese-style long gowns and military jackets as well as those in Western attire, while others wore Japanese-style dress, all with small flags in their hands." Among the throng, he spied yellow flags bearing the imperial insignia of a spindly dragon. They were held by former bannermen, the Manchu class of military administrators. An attendant told him, "For twenty years they have anxiously awaited a chance to see your majesty."

Puyi wrote, "Hearing these words, I could not repress the warm tears that welled up in my eyes, and my feeling of hopelessness grew ever stronger."

Japan announced the founding of Manchukuo on March 1. The news was bumped off the world's front page by that day's disappearance of a twenty-month-old toddler named Charles Lindbergh Jr.

Puyi was inaugurated in a "ceremony befitting the graduation from a professional school," an attending Japanese diplomat noted with displeasure, adding that "the look of ill fortune that was clearly revealed in Puyi's face." But one of the masterminds of the September 18 bombing that triggered Japan's invasion of Manchuria sized up Puyi and thought: *Perfect window dressing.*

In his office, Manchukuo's chief executive sat behind an empty desk. "I soon discovered that my authority was only shadow without substance," Puyi wrote. "I didn't even have the power to decide whether or not I could pass out of the door to go for a walk."

Were he to stroll outside today, Puyi would recognize a surprising amount of Changchun.

The wide, Japanese pine–lined axial boulevards still lead to roundabouts such as the former Unity Plaza—renamed People's Square—ringed by steel-frame bulwarks of buildings that were meant to signify Japan's permanent presence. All remain in use. The former Central Bank of Manchukuo is now the People's Bank of China, the Manchukuo Telephone and Telegraph Company is a branch of China Netcom, and the Police Headquarters has become the Public Security Bureau.

Changchun is a city of eight million, renowned in post-Liberation China as the home of First Automobile Works, producer of the Socialist era's ubiquitous powder-blue Liberation truck and black, boxy Red Flag sedans. The city is no Detroit, however (or Flint, one of its sister cities): the car factory now makes sleek Audis, and 160,000 students attend the town's twenty-seven universities. Yet the city center is still littered with reminders of the occupation. While Japanese war memorials and cemeteries have been razed, the government has protected over one hundred colonial sites, making the town itself a sort of patriotic education base.

A walk south on People's Avenue from the train station leads past a waving statue of Chairman Mao inside the gates of the former Jade Child (now Victory) Park, then past the spiky pagoda rooftops of the castle-like structure that had been the Japanese army headquarters. The provincial Communist Party bureau now calls it home. Just south of the former Unity Plaza, a Shinto temple to the god of war stands shuttered in Peony Park. Speed skaters on Rollerblades whoosh in loops around its wide, flat apron of asphalt. On its back wall, painted Cultural Revolution slogans fade in the sun. Otherwise, the building's swooping tiled roof and white walls look recently built.

Japan chose Changchun as Manchukuo's capital for its central location and its rail connection to Korean ports and ships to Japan. *Tokyo* means "Eastern Capital"; Changchun was christened Shinkyo, New

Capital—Xinjing in Chinese. It would be unlike other planned capitals, mired for years on drawing boards and budget sheets, as the United States and Australia's had been. Around the time of Xinjing's inception, an English reporter wrote of Canberra, "Londoners may be all too aware of the disadvantages of living in a city without a plan, but these cannot be compared with the rival disadvantages of living in a plan without a city."

Three decades before Brasília, Xinjing was plan and city at once. Unlike Harbin, to which the Russians had added a few churches, private mansions, and a commercial district that mirrored Moscow's, here the Japanese colonial blueprint called for modernist urban planning that looked nothing like Tokyo's tangle of narrow lanes.

Planners drew clean lines, circular plazas, and numerous parks. They added ornate, colonnaded buildings with steam heat and flush toilets—a rarity in Japan, and the rest of China—meant to overshadow older Russian and Chinese structures and attract new settlers.

I walked past the curving lines of the former art deco movie theater, now home to the Great Jilin Medicine Store. KFC was packed, as usual, and I carried my cup of steaming Nescafé past Walmart and the Shangri-La Hotel down Comrade Street to Liberation Road, ending at the expanse of Culture Square, the world's second largest, after Tiananmen. A grand palace for Puyi was to overlook the fifty-acre plaza, but only its foundation was finished when Japan surrendered in 1945. China built the Geological Palace Museum atop the site. Inside, schoolchildren stared up at the skeleton of a dinosaur from the genus *Mandschurosaurus*.

Culture Square bookended Xinmin (New Citizen) Avenue, which is to fascist architecture what Havana is to classic American cars. The road slopes gently like the Champs-Élysées, terminating after a mile at South Lake Park. Under Manchukuo, the boulevard was named Datong (Grand Unity) and lined with eight ministries set back from wide sidewalks shaded by the spindly branches of Japanese pines. The buildings look unlike any other in China—or the world—and their style, with crenellated towers, porticoes, and curving roofs, was called Rising Asia. Now the structures stand as markers of a fall.

Walking south, the avenue's first building is the former Manchukuo State Council, a wedding cake made of granite and marble crowned with a pagoda-style roof of cinnamon-colored ceramic tiles. Its front door is shaded by a colonnaded ramp that once received the imperial cortege. A vertical signboard next to a mature pine says that Puyi planted the tree.

Like the other Manchukuo ministry buildings, the State Council has been repurposed, here as university classroom space. The front doors were open, without a ticket window or security guards forbidding entry. Inside, I passed Puyi's personal copper-plated elevator—CLOSED FOR REPAIRS— and walked under the chandelier to climb the marble stairs. Carved orchids adorn the balustrade; they were Puyi's favorite flower and became the Manchukuoan imperial seal. The stairs lead to an unlit second floor. Reflexively, I stomped my foot, which usually turns on the lights in a Chinese building. The room stayed dark. The only sound was my echoing footsteps wandering the remains of Japan's imperial ambition.

That night, I slept at the former Yamato Hotel, built as part of a chain along the South Manchuria Railway. A 1934 guidebook described the hotel as "quiet and cozy, surrounded by a spacious summer garden." The garden is now a parking lot, and the hotel is dwarfed by a bus station whose rooftop neon sign flashes AMWAY.

The bedding had been updated and a television added, but otherwise the room—with floor-to-ceiling windows and a cavernous claw-foot tub—was a time capsule of the 1930s. The desk phone rang, and I expected to tell the caller I did not want a massage. But it was Housekeeping. I was the building's only guest, the maid said, so she wouldn't be making her regular rounds. She would leave two thermoses of hot water by the door. The front desk had said that Chinese preferred to stay in the hotel's characterless new wing, which cost twice as much. Being an appreciator of history (or, as the clerk called me, *kou men'r*, a cheapskate) had resulted in having the old hotel to myself. Even the masseuses ignored it. The room was quiet and cozy, with original steam radiators running along a wall. At night they hissed low, as if urging me to keep the room a secret.

In the spring of 1932, a group of foreigners disembarked at the train station across the street. They had been dispatched in response to China's plea for diplomacy to push Japan from the Northeast.

"I have just heard that the League of Nations has decided to send a mission to investigate the Manchurian Incident," Will Rogers wrote. "It reminds me of a familiar scene in early days in Oklahoma when the sheriff arrived to inspect the stable after the horses had been stolen."

The Lytton Commission, named for its head, the Earl of Lytton, consisted of four other men—from the United States, France, Germany, and Italy—who toured the Northeast by Japan's hand. They stepped off the train onto a platform plastered in English posters that said MANCHUKUO, THE DEBUTANTE, WELCOMES THE LEAGUE OF NATIONS and CO-OPERATE TO MAKE MANCHUKUO THE GENEVA OF THE EAST. A Japanese military officer mentioned to a reporter, "The weather has been much better since we Japanese came." The propaganda posters, another correspondent noted, were torn to tatters each night and replaced before daybreak.

The commission interviewed Puyi for a mere fifteen minutes. "They asked me only two questions: how did I come to the Northeast and how had Manchukuo been established?" Puyi considered pleading to be rescued, "but as soon as this idea swept into my mind, I recalled that, seated next to me, was the Chief of Staff of the army. I looked at [his] bluish white face and felt compelled to repeat exactly what he had 'reminded' me to tell the Commission: 'The masses of the people of Manchuria begged me to come. My stay here is absolutely voluntary and free.' The members of the Commission all smiled and nodded at my reply. They did not ask for more. Later, we had our pictures taken, drank Champagne and toasted one another's health."

Japanese officers accompanied the commission at every step—even, Puyi later testified, detaining any Chinese officials who spoke Russian, French, or English so they could not meet the investigators.

The Japanese argued to the commission that Manchukuo was in a region that had never belonged to China proper. It showed a map from 1720 that labeled all locales north of the Great Wall in Manchu script and cities south of it in Chinese characters. The president of the South Manchuria Railway presented decorative copies of a Qing emperor's 1743 poem that lauded the Northeast's unique geography and history.

The commission was not convinced. After six weeks of investigations, its report concluded that China should retain sovereignty of the Northeast, even if that meant forming an autonomous region there. However, in an illustration of why the League of Nations was short-lived, in October 1932 members approved the Lytton Commission report by a 42–1 vote (Japan dissented) while proposing no sanctions or military intervention.

Japan withdrew from the league and pressed south into greater China, breaching the Great Wall in a series of battles at the beginning of 1933. One witness was the American scholar Owen Lattimore, who saw the Japanese "overrun 100,000 square miles of territory in ten days. They did it by the use of motorized transport and by cutting through the Chinese forces and driving deep, paying no attention to their exposed flanks." It was, he wrote, the first modern blitzkrieg. "Only the Germans and the Russians seemed to have paid much attention. Other people thought it was just a lot of Japanese overrunning a lot of Chinese, and not worth study by professional soldiers."

The truce that ended the fighting in May 1933 established a demilitarized zone extending sixty miles south of the wall, from the coastal First Pass Under Heaven to Beijing. The Chinese government was forced to accept that Japan controlled the Great Wall as well as the entire Northeast.

"First Emperor Enthroned," heralded the *Manchuria Daily News* in March 1934. "At 8:25 a.m. of a desperately cold but typically sun-bright Manchurian day, Puyi, last monarch of the Manchu Dynasty, became the first Emperor of Manchukuo." In the English-language newspaper's "souvenir supplement," advertisements from General Motors, Shell Oil, Sunoco, General Electric, and Ford offered "congratulations and all good wishes on today's auspicious enthronement."

The article detailed Puyi's four-day fast and purification, meditations and prayers, silk robes and sable helmet. His motorcade of ten scarlet limousines had circled the city before stopping at the "ceremonial altar."

I expected the story to end with the observation that great historical characters appear twice, the first time as tragedy, the second as farce. But no: at the altar, Puyi wrote a message to the gods and set fire to the paper, sending his words skyward to heaven. "His Majesty is understood to have pledged his life to the service of the state . . . A great moment had passed into posterity."

The purple prose was written by the South Manchuria Railway's chief propagandists, an American father-and-son team named Henry and Charles

Bishop Kinney. They left a scant biographical trail before arriving in Manchuria in 1927 to work for the company, producing maps and editing guidebooks that advised travelers: "A silk hat and frockcoat will be needed when making calls on persons of distinction or attending functions, such as the Imperial Garden Parties."

Henry Kinney had worked as a journalist in Hawaii before heading the territory's public school system for five years. In an article he wrote for the *Atlantic* in 1920, he praised the multiethnic harmony of the island, which the U.S. had recently annexed. He composed a song honoring the late Princess Kaiulani that was performed in schools on her birthday, but stressed that the Hawaiian curriculum should endeavor to make Americans out of the natives and settlers, including the large Japanese population. Was the seed of his admiration for Manchukuo's "harmonious society" planted then?

Or perhaps it sprouted after Kinney moved to Japan to edit the magazine *Trans-Pacific*, bankrolled by an American knitting yarn magnate. In a 1924 *Atlantic* article, Kinney mentioned his twelve-year-old son—whom he called, "affectionately," the Shrimp—and their home outside Tokyo, "the big foreign villa on the beach where we lived with the rest of a bachelor's mess." The article described the horrors of 1923's Great Kanto Earthquake—later estimated to have had a magnitude between 7.9 and 8.4 on the Richter scale, flattening Yokohama and killing 140,000 people in the area—and his journey home from his Tokyo office to see if his son had survived. En route, he encountered the yarn magnate, who said the city would rebuild, and the Americans would stay to help. "We owe it to Japan," he said. "The new government has courage. It's going to reconstruct on a vast, progressive scale—so we must forget our losses and lend a hand. America has a mission here."

A decade later, Henry Kinney represented the South Manchuria Railway during the Lytton Commission's visit. He stands beside Japanese military officers in a photo marking the occasion, silver-haired and resembling the actor Joseph Cotten. In a memo sent to Western journalists then, Kinney argued that the region had been "entirely primitive" but now held promise of becoming the "most prosperous part of China and one of the most rapidly developing countries in the world." Why? "It is well known that Japan introduced Western civilization into Manchuria . . . the one part of China which made progress, while the rest of that unhappy country drifted further and further into chaos and destruction."

Kinney did not write that even though Japanese represented only 3 percent of the population, Japanese was the language of school instruction—not Chinese, now called Manchukuoan. There was no mention of the building of Shinto shrines to which all subjects had to bow ninety degrees when passing; the drafting of 2.5 million citizens into compulsory labor; travel restrictions on natives, who were also forbidden to own land or eat quality rice; the six million tons of grain exported to Japan each year; or the six million tons of steel and 223 million tons of coal Japan extracted from 1932 to 1944.

Foreign correspondents dubbed the puppet state "Japanchukuo" and "Mannequinchuria." The *Times* of London correspondent Peter Fleming— the elder brother of James Bond's creator—traveled the region in 1934 and wrote that the Japanese exhibited "ruthless control." At the Opium Monopoly Bureau, an uncharacteristically loose-lipped employee "poured out stuff for two hours," explaining the profitability of the state-run drug trade, which included secretly lacing the tobacco of a best-selling cigarette with opium.

Henry Kinney, on the other hand, reported "not conquest, but development." Travelers could rely on all-American equipment: the comfort of a Pullman sleeping car pulled behind a Baldwin locomotive over hundred-pound Pittsburgh rails. "The shriek of these American locomotives across Manchurian plains and through Manchurian cities is the voice of modern enterprise bringing a rich, modern life, opportunity, hygiene, education and happiness to an ancient people." The railway cities were "amazingly like new western towns in the United States."

The South Manchuria Railway even opened a public relations office in New York City, on East Forty-second Street (today it's the address of the Asian & American Singles Club). On a visit to the U.S. in 1936, Henry Kinney compiled a list of media members favorable to Japan's "policy of aggression." The memo was discovered and published by an American journalist who later wrote: "After the Japanese discovered the leak they gave Kinney an extended vacation, which he was still spending with his Japanese wife on the French island of Tahiti when the war broke out."

His son Charles Bishop Kinney took over, mailing dispatches headed *For Your Own Information* to American journalists and scholars. In them, he labored to correct "distortions," such as reports of the Chinese resistance, which he dismissed as "bandit activity." And the talk of Japanese being "conspicuously boisterous in restaurants and other public places?" Dear sirs, was this behavior not comparable to American visitors to Paris whose "exuberant actions made them themselves anything but popular with the French? Many were abroad for the first time." Manchukuo, he gushed, had 5,500 miles of railroad, compared to 6,000 miles in the rest of China. Forty-eight new towns were planned. Mines were opened. One Manchukuo yuan was worth 28.5 American cents. Not conquest, dear sirs, but development.

In 1933, Henry Kinney wrote, "In view of the gravity of over-population in Japan and for the development of natural resources of this country, Japanese officials commenced to encourage emigration to Manchukuo on a large scale."

Japanese had migrated in numbers before, notably to its northern island of Hokkaido (displacing the native Ainu people) and to Hawaii, where their increasing numbers led, partly, to the United States annexing the islands and, in 1924, to excluding Japanese immigration to America entirely. Similar acts were passed in Australia, New Zealand, Peru, and Brazil.

But previous attempts to encourage agrarian colonization in China had failed; the majority of Japanese living in Manchukuo were attached to the military or the South Manchuria Railway. Fewer than one thousand Japanese farmers moved to experimental farms established in the railway zone before 1931, and all but two hundred had returned home when Manchukuo was founded that year.

For the Home Islands, it was a time of economic crisis. The Great Depression affected Japan's manufacturing sector, sending migrant workers back to their villages. Farming supported half of Japan's workforce, but the rural economy reeled from falling rice and silk prices, then widespread crop failures. As planners drew up the modern Manchukuo capital and an imperial palace, half a million people died from famine in northern Japan. Officials recorded the sale of 11,604 girls into "service," a byword for prostitution.

In 1932, after intense debate and lobbying in Tokyo, the Diet approved a modest budget for trial colonies of Japanese farmers in Manchukuo. The experiment started slowly: 470 farmers were sent over, settling in a far Northeastern Songhua river town. Five hundred would follow them the next year. In 1936, however, the Japanese government would launch the "Millions to Manchuria" scheme, which aimed at relocating one-fifth of Japan's rural population there over the next twenty years.

Previously, Japan had backed Korean migration to the region. The South Manchuria Railway had urged farmers from Japanese-controlled Korea to cross the Yalu River in a "process that would result in a concrete circle of Japanese power in Manchuria." A map in Korean middle school textbooks showed Seoul and Pyongyang linked by a loop of railroad with Harbin and other Manchurian cities. Korean migrants opened rice paddies—establishing the single annual crop as economically viable—and diffused the native population. This was seen especially in the expansion of the existing enclave of Kando (today's Yanbian Korean Autonomous Prefecture), where the Qing dynasty had granted Korean settlers the right to farm in the late nineteenth century in order to populate the northeast corner of Manchuria where China shared a border with Russia.

Among the Korean arrivals was a young man who attended middle school in Jilin city in 1927, joined the underground Chinese Communist Party, led guerrilla campaigns against the Japanese in Manchukuo, and changed his name to Kim Il-sung. His experience in Manchuria, he would later say, laid the foundation of the Korean revolution, and his ideology of *juch'e* (self-reliance) was still brutally adhered to a half century later in the isolated state he founded in 1948, the Democratic People's Republic of Korea.

On July 7, 1937, a clash between Japanese and Chinese forces at the Marco Polo Bridge outside Beijing erupted into full-scale war, enveloping all of China for the next eight years.

How many instances in history has there been massive conquest and suffering that we—in our culture, anyway—barely know about, or have forgotten? Yet in the Northeast, Japan's occupation still feels near. You can sleep in former Japanese hotels, embark at Japanese-designed train stations, and descend into erstwhile Japanese bunkers. In the northwest corner of the region, on the railroad between Manzhouli and Harbin, a thirty-minute walk from the Hulunbei'er station up a grassland plateau leads to a former Japanese base. There, a monument made of piled ramparts says, in Chinese: NEVER FORGET.

Underground, in tunnels constructed along this western front by twenty thousand Chinese prisoners, a row of sodium bulbs casts a ghostly glow in the clammy air. Plaques in Chinese and English—not Japanese—detail the quarters, kitchens, infirmaries, and latrines. In restoring the site, Chinese workers repainted the walls. They took care, however, to trace around the black Japanese characters inked by the former occupants, warning of non-potable water and other dangers. Here, history has been spared the whitewashing brush.

The base was part of a line Japan established to defend the border against Soviet-controlled Mongolia. Over four months in the summer of 1939, Japanese and Soviet forces clashed here after Mongolian cavalry crossed into Manchukuoan territory to graze their horses. Hostilities accelerated from rifle shots to artillery to tanks to a dress rehearsal for the Second World War. A skirmish that began on horseback escalated into the air. Thirty thousand sorties were launched in this, the Soviet and Japanese air forces' first wartime fighter-bombing campaign. A cavalry commander named Georgy Zhukov led the Soviet ground troops, employing tanks in maneuvers he would later use against Nazi forces in the Battle of Stalingrad and the capture of Berlin.

In the end, the Japanese were badly routed in what it called the Nomonhan Incident, named for the village where it started. Puyi visited the wounded, a trip recounted by Charles Bishop Kinney in a story headlined "Nomonhan Heroes Honored": "On this auspicious day their past deadly struggle for over one hundred days against Soviet mechanized corps on the plain were more than rewarded by the Manchukuo Emperor's comforting remarks."

Unnoted, of course, were the rumors of conscripted Chinese infantry who had killed their Japanese commanding officers, as other mutinous troops had done in Manchukuo.

The costume play of Puyi's life continued. On his return from Nomonhan to the capital's train station, "Imperial Guards fired a salute in honour of the returning Sovereign who appeared to be in excellent health." As a military band played the national anthem—*The world has a new Manchuria,*

/ *Manchuria is the new world*—the train steamed to a halt at a platform thronged by officials who included Vice Minister of the Imperial Household Department, the Public Peace Minister, and Lord Keeper of the Privy Seal.

In April 1941, the Nomonhan Incident officially concluded when Japan and the Soviet Union signed a nonaggression pact that freed the latter to mass its forces against Nazi Germany. With Manchukuo's Mongolian and Siberian border now as secure as its Korean and Chinese one, Japan's battle-tested military turned its attention to the rest of China, and the Pacific.

In *Manchuria* magazine's summer issue of 1941, Charles Bishop Kinney reported BUMPER CROPS FORECAST FOR ALL OF MANCHURIA but also SEVEN MORE KINDS OF NECESSITIES TO BE RATIONED. Japan was forging a "new world order," he wrote in a story headlined THE EAST ASIAN SPHERE OF COMMON PROSPERITY. An item about Puyi and the founder of the Gestapo began: "His Majesty was pleased to confer the First Order of Merit with the Grand Cordon of the Lungkuang on Reich Marshal Hermann Goering for kindnesses shown."

On December 7, Japan bombed Pearl Harbor and overran Hong Kong, declaring war on the United States and Great Britain. Puyi announced that Manchukuo was also at war, pledging, "Together as a united people we shall come to the aid of our ally." Yet Puyi would once again sit this dance out, watching from the sidelines until August 1945, when the Soviets broke their nonaggression pact, declared war on Japan, and unleashed a million battle-hardened soldiers into Manchukuo.

Japan, "our ally," abandoned the Northeast and its thirty million people, including three hundred thousand Japanese farmers enticed to move there as "soldiers of the hoe." Little did they know they were also the first line of defense against such an invasion. The Japanese army had secretly called them "human pillboxes." Now they were on their own.

Wasteland students at recess in deep winter.

San Jiu outside his home.

Mr. Guan's backyard as seen from the outhouse. My bedroom windows are on the right.

Workers widen Red Flag Road by hand.

Stretching to the foothills, Wasteland's paddies ripen in summer.

The same fields in autumn, after harvest.

Auntie Yi on Red Flag Road at the spot where her poppies used to be; now it's Wasteland's first lawn. Also new: seedlings and solar-powered streetlights, bearing ads for Eastern Fortune Rice.

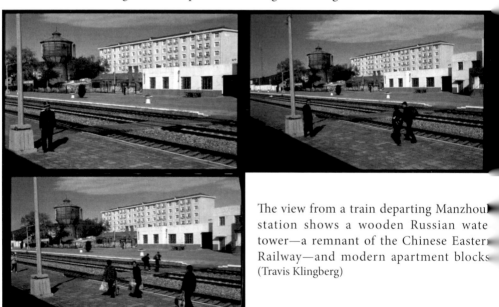

The view from a train departing Manzhouli station shows a wooden Russian water tower—a remnant of the Chinese Eastern Railway—and modern apartment blocks. (Travis Klingberg)

An imperial tomb from the Koguryo kingdom in Ji'an, at China's border with North Korea.

A statue of the chieftain Wanyan Aguda outside Acheng. In 1115, he united the Jurchen tribes and founded the Jin dynasty, which ruled northeast China until 1234. (Creative Commons 3.0, courtesy of Lzy881114)

Nurhaci organized the Jurchen into banners, ordered the creation of a writing system, and died in battle against Chinese forces in 1626. His son, Hong Taiji, renamed the Jurchen the Manchu and founded the Qing dynasty, which ruled China for nearly three hundred years. (Palace Museum, Beijing)

Farmers stand atop the toppled steles marking the remains of the Willow Palisade in western Liaoning province.

Russian remains: Saint Nicholas Cathedral (left) in early twentieth-century Harbin. Pulled down during the Cultural Revolution, its former site anchors the city's largest traffic roundabout. After decades of neglect, including use as a department store warehouse, Harbin's former St. Sophia Cathedral (right) was declared a national cultural heritage site and opened as a city museum/patriotic education base in 1997.

Russian and Japanese claims on China's northeast are depicted on the cover of a 1904 issue of *Puck* magazine. Japan and Russia claw at each other while tied to a rope labeled *Manchuria* with a bow called *Neutrality*. The caption reads: "May the knot hold."

After its victory in the Russo-Japanese War in 1905, Japan built a chain of luxurious Yamato Hotels along the South Manchurian Railway, such as this one in Port Arthur (Lüshun). In 1931, Puyi was hidden here by Japanese officers who revealed their plans to install him as chief executive of Manchukuo.

A century later, the building remains a hotel, albeit a run-down discount inn. No plaque marks Puyi's room or his secret, three-month stay.

Puyi, the "puppet emperor" of Manchukuo.

The Young Marshal, Zhang Xueliang.

Liang Siyong, whose 1930 expedition across Manchuria included an excavation at Ang'angxi. The brother of China's most prominent architect and the son of a leading reformist, Liang is considered the nation's "father of archaeology."

A 1932 editorial cartoon illustrates Secretary of State Henry Stimson's announcement that the United States sided with the Chinese, and would not recognize Manchukuo.

"To Manchuria!" Japanese recruitment poster for pioneer farmers to Manchukuo.

A Manchukuo propaganda poster promises "Japanese, Chinese, and Manchu Cooperation Brings Great Peace to the World." The figures hold the flags of Manchukuo, Japan, and the Republic of China. (Image courtesy of Chapman University, Orange, California)

A shuttered Japanese shrine in central Changchun, a remnant from its era as capital of Manchukuo. This site is popular with in-line skaters for its open pavement.

The abandoned Songhua River docks outside Fangzheng, where, in August 1945, Japanese settlers—mostly mothers and their children—waited for evacuation boats that would never come.

Men with hammers and spray paint attack a memorial to Japanese settlers at Fangzheng's Sino-Japanese Friendship Garden. The following day, the memorial was bulldozed to rubble.

Staff Sergeant Harold "Hal" Leith, a liberator of the Mukden and Xi'an (Liaoyuan) POW camps, whose prisoners included survivors of the Bataan Death March and the generals who surrendered Corregidor and Singapore. (Image courtesy of the family of Hal Leith)

American Navy planes bombing the Yalu River bridge in November 1950. Restricted from entering Manchuria, pilots attacked the bridge on the perpendicular, bombing only the North Korean side. It took six hundred sorties through unrelenting Chinese flak to down the span. Five days later, the river froze.

The Qins and their honeybees occupy the last house remaining in Bursting Lotus valley evacuated due to the unearthing of chemical weapons left by the Japanese.

"I slept with an alien." Meng Zhaoguo stands before Dragon Mountain at the Red Flag Logging Commune. (Image courtesy of Chien-Min Chung)

胡锦涛总书记视察东福米业

Chinese president Hu Jintao inspects Eastern Fortune Rice on a visit to Wasteland in 2007.

New apartments in Wasteland, part of the drive to "Build the Northeast's Top Village."

A dwindling number of Wasteland's farmers dry their harvested rice on the road instead of using Eastern Fortune's imported machines.

CHAPTER 13

OCCUPATION'S AFTERMATH

"Go! Go and colonize the continent!" propaganda posters urged Japanese beginning in 1936. "For the development of the Yamato race, to build the new order in Asia!" The campaign echoed the American nineteenth-century appeal "Go west, young man!" with "Go to the continent, young man! A new land awaits the village youth." Despite the Depression in which rural Japan was sunk, migration to Manchukuo was framed in patriotic terms, not economic ones, and focused on the empire's future rather than its present, racked by food shortages, overpopulation, and an American embargo.

Colonization manuals included articles aimed at men such as "The Joy of Becoming a Progenitor": "What could be better than creating a new country and of becoming the founding fathers to that country?"—and, for women, "The Joy of Breeding." Its accompanying image showed a mother with child standing before a herd of grazing sheep. A 1941 journal promised, "If you become a Manchurian pioneer, you can be an owner-farmer, and you will see permanent prosperity for your descendants. There is no way to revive the [home] villages other than developing Manchuria."

Under the "Millions to Manchuria" plan, Japanese villages would be replicated in Manchukuo, with branch family members—second and third sons, for example—sent to pioneer a satellite outpost sharing the same place name. Unbeknownst to settlers, the majority of these villages were established in bandit-infested areas or along the Soviet border. Photos show Japanese soldiers teaching newly arrived women, infants lashed to their backs, how to fire the single-bolt rifle each household was issued on landing.

Beyond patriotism, tangible incentives enticed civilians to Manchukuo. Skilled professionals such as doctors, teachers, and agronomists earned double their salary at home, while farming households received twenty-five acres of arable land, ten acres of grazing land, equipment, seed, and funds for cows, horses, and hired labor. Men were exempt from the military draft.

The land they were given on arrival in Manchukuo was not, as initially planned, uncultivated swamps and forest that they would open to the plow. Instead, settlers were handed cultivated land belonging to the native population, seized via army-forced evictions and coerced sales—paying as low as 15 percent of the land's assessed value. Dissenters could expect the retribution noted in a Japanese police chief's report: "More than twenty armed men were sent to the area in question, and they either bayoneted farmers who did not comply with their orders or killed their cattle, dogs, and chickens." Often the displaced faced two options: accept a plot of uncultivated land, or become hired labor on their former farm.

While colonization left a visible imprint on Northeast cities, the remains of the Millions to Manchuria movement have all but vanished from the countryside. One of the most publicized migrant villages was a branch of the Japanese hamlet of Ohinata founded in 1938 at Sijiafang (Place of Four Families), forty miles northeast of Wasteland.

A Japanese novelist was paid to document Ohinata's migration, resulting in a popular newspaper series and a book that spawned a film, plays, and songs. The one schoolchildren sang when sending off the settlers went:

> Just plant one grain of wheat
> And the life in our home will prosper
> Work together until everything is beautiful
> In the paradise we will build
> Oh, Ohinata in Manchuria

The writer traveled with the settlers. Now I used his novel as a map to search for the village. The train departed at 5:24 a.m., and once again I had an entire hard-seat-class car to myself. Cool morning air blew through the open windows, and the sun, which rose at four in summertime, shone warmly on my face. For two enjoyable hours the train lumbered through rice paddies and birch groves—flushing out the occasional pheasant—past hamlets with post-Liberation monikers such as Restoring Asia.

Exiting a small blockhouse of a station put me in a broad, empty square. In the Japanese novel, this station was described as being fronted by "four old Manchurian dwellings." The newly arrived Japanese had constructed "houses for a few hundred households," in addition to a police station, school, and hospital. "We are looking forward to a brilliant future," its narrator enthused, "as a medium-sized administrative center."

The town, now named Shulan, had become just that, with offices and services clustered around two intersections. The book's narrator noted the area was already home to four thousand Chinese ("Manchurians") and two thousand Koreans. Those moved off their land had become corvée labor. "Especially for the construction of the new village they come in very handy," the novel's narrator said. "However, for the future I think we have to do some in-depth research about the problem of our leadership of the Manchurian people and our harmonious coexistence."

The writer described the settlers' village as four square miles divided by a river "so clear that you can count the beautiful pebbles at its bottom." A village named Place of Four Families no longer appeared on maps, but a few miles north of the station, nestled between the mountains and that river, was a hamlet called Four Big Families. Perhaps the name had been changed after Liberation? I boarded a minibus heading in its direction.

Fifteen minutes later the driver stopped the bus on a two-lane road hugged by verdant green paddies. I squeezed past the passengers standing in the aisle but hesitated at the door, seeing no sign of life to the horizon. As the bus faded from view, I stood alone, looking at the kind of bucolic landscape that inspired the novel's narrator to say: "I think that we are more than blessed with this settlement place in comparison to other places."

A dirt road led across the railroad tracks, past a row of single-story homes that ended at a cornfield. A sign in a neighboring paddy identified the rice as Japonica #1, a variety also grown in Wasteland. I wanted to tell someone this, but my audience was two cows tethered to a gap-toothed wooden fence. Back at the train tracks, a man stepped out of the crossing house and nodded hello.

"I'm looking for Place of Four Families, where the Japanese farmers lived."

The man frowned. "This is Four Big Families."

"Where's Place of Four Families?"

"Never heard of it. It doesn't matter anyway: you're too late. Those little Japs all ran away. I wasn't born then, but I heard about it. No, nothing remains from that time."

I walked eight miles down a poplar-shaded road, encountering no traces of life except for two signs. One announced Big Tree Village, which had no trees. The other urged the prevention of forest fires.

In the hamlet named Safe and Sound, the lone intersection held only a hand-painted blue plank nailed to a telephone pole, pointing the way to a tiny train station. Its broad plaza was made prettier by the bright green weeds that sprouted between the paving stones. Nothing looked Japanese; the biggest building in town was a Korean-built Christian church and elementary school. Both sat empty on a summer Saturday afternoon.

On the way back to Shulan and my train to Wasteland, the bus driver went off his route to drop me near a new bridge spanning the river, where owners washed their cars while parked in the shallows.

"You're looking for Place of Four Families, but what few people know around here is that this town used to be called that," the driver said. "My father was a teacher who grew up here, that's how I know. The name changed to Shulan after Liberation." (He proved to be right.) "My father told me that this is where the Japanese village was." He pointed at a wide new road, lined with wide new government offices. The only sign said, in Chinese and Korean, SECOND RING ROAD. It was empty.

When the Japanese settlers left for Manchuria, children waved flags, and "the villagers let go of the handkerchiefs and shouted banzai, throwing both hands up in the air" as tears streamed down their cheeks. As their train pulled away from their Japanese home, the settlers heard a farewell song that went:

> *The pioneers of our great Japan*
> *We divided the village of Ohinata*
> *And went to Sijiafang in Manchuria*
> *To build the paradise of the imperial way*
> *We will all march together*

Most of the settlers who woke in the Northeast on August 9, 1945, would not survive the fall of Manchukuo. Many committed suicide, together.

Although they made up only 17 percent of the 1.5 million Japanese living in Manchukuo, settlers accounted for nearly half its death toll, which equaled that at Nagasaki: out of 270,000 farmers in the Northeast, 80,000—mostly women and children—died at war's end.

The Japanese army had abandoned them. The force that invaded northeast China fourteen years earlier had been reduced by the Pacific War, with units transferred south. Settlers took their place; at the end of 1943, 50 percent of farmers had been placed along the Soviet-Manchukuo front line. As Japanese losses mounted in 1944 the army reneged on the draft exemption offered to settlers. It enacted a "bottom-scraping" mobilization in May, calling up all able-bodied men—most without any military training—as Germany surrendered and the Soviet Union turned its forces east. In Manchukuo the army pulled back from their positions vulnerable to the anticipated Soviet advance, leaving three-quarters of the region undefended. No evacuation was planned. A Japanese general bluntly said of the women, children, and elderly left in the settler villages: "Their only alternative is suicide."

In February 1945, the Pacific War was about to turn inexorably to the Allies' favor: after winning Saipan and its airfield, B-29 bombers were in range of Tokyo. The Japanese army continued to draft all age-eligible reinforcements, however. "I had the misfortune of turning twenty that spring," Akira Nagamine told me. "I knew the red paper was coming, and I was obligated to go."

After all of the track I had ridden across the Northeast, and all the museums and colonial buildings I had visited and maps and books I had read, eighty-seven-year-old Akira Nagamine truly brought Manchukuo to life. Shipped from his Japanese hamlet of twenty farming families to defend Manchukuo's eastern frontier, he ended up trapped after the war in China's Northeast for eight years.

"It was my first time out of Japan," Nagamine said. His bushy black eyebrows rose as his tanned face blossomed with a grin. At the time he was drafted, his parents had worked as rice and potato farmers, while he had become a substitute teacher, because the other male teachers had all been called to war. "There were none left to teach."

The army assembled him and other fresh recruits at an inn. "We took off our civilian clothes and put on the army uniform, including cloth farmer shoes, not heavy boots. In February."

A ship carried the recruits across the Sea of Japan. They switched to a train to reach far northeastern Manchukuo. Nagamine and the other conscripts disembarked at the small railroad town of Jixi, then marched to an outlying hamlet whose garrison was the only line of defense between the railroad and the Soviet border, twelve miles east.

For five months Nagamine trained to defend the outpost: "I was taught how to roll under a tank with explosives and blow myself up." His only other weapons were a rifle, grenades, and the unit's light machine gun. "We knew the Russians were coming, and locals were told that if they had to, to use kitchen knives to fight them."

Nagamine still could feel the Northeast's brutal winter. "It was so cold that you had to break the ice on the basin before washing your face," he said, miming the action. During his training, he had no interaction with ethnic Koreans and Chinese living in the area, and thus no language lessons. He also was not issued a compass.

The Soviet Union declared war on Japan three days after the U.S. dropped an atomic bomb on Hiroshima and the same day one obliterated Nagasaki. Commanded by the architect of the Stalingrad counteroffensive, the Soviet's "Manchurian Strategic Offensive Operation"—also known as August Storm—began at the stroke of midnight on August 9.

"Lightning flashed unexpectedly," a Soviet general recorded of the evening. "Dazzling streaks split the darkening sky in half. Thunder sounded, becoming yet louder. The taiga sounded still more menacing. The downpours approached. Already the first drops resounded on the leaves. We entered the dugouts—and glanced at our watches. Sixty minutes remained until the attack. Should we delay the attack? No, under no circumstances!"

The Russians had lost a humiliating war to the Japanese in Manchuria in 1905. Now it would avenge that defeat. August Storm pitted 1.6 million battle-trained Soviet troops against six hundred thousand Japanese, many of whom were green recruits. A pincer movement sent forces pouring into Manchukuo's west, north, and east—the latter heading for second class private Akira Nagamine.

"Their planes bombed the warehouses at our camp," he said. "We had no radio or communications equipment. It was the first time I shot at somebody." Nagamine's white hair was close-cropped, and throughout his story's telling he smiled with his mouth and eyes and gently touched my arm to emphasize his points. "Was I scared? Yes! Everybody was scared."

Soviet forces overran Japanese defenses, which held out despite Emperor Hirohito's broadcast of surrender on August 15. Nagamine and his fellow soldiers did not hear it: by then he and ninety infantry were hiding in the mountains, emerging only to steal ears of ripened corn from local farmers or snipe at the Soviets. Nagamine limped on a broken ankle. His company was pinned down, cut off, and dead to the world.

On a pitted concrete shore ringed by a rusting fence, I studied the Songhua River. Here it ran muddy and wide, with a quick current that made the expanse of water look more like a malevolent lake. Once this site was a busy dock one hundred miles downriver from Harbin.

At Manchukuo's height, the area had been home to Japanese migrants. By 1945, however, their utopian dream had died. Crops failed, false yields were reported, guerrilla attacks increased, and colonial power—forged from native land and labor—ebbed away. A Place of Four Families settler later recalled, "When I first visited Manchuria in 1938, the Manchurians [Chinese] always let us cross the street first. At the train station, we did not have to wait in line at the ticket counter, they let us buy tickets first. . . . When I returned to Manchuria and finally settled in 1943, it was a different story. The Manchurians told me to go to elsewhere because, they said, it was their train station. Looking back, I think they already sensed Japan's imminent defeat. I said to myself that I had come to the wrong place at the wrong time."

On August 10, the day after the Soviets declared war on Japan, the Japanese army evacuated military families from Manchukuo's capital and ordered the bombing of bridges and the cutting of telegraph lines, further severing settlers from evacuation routes.

In memoirs with titles such as *Tombstones in the Frozen Earth*, survivors recounted the horrific journeys made on foot, overcoming starvation, robbery, rape, and revenge killings by the "Manchurians." Several authors survived collective suicides: one woman wrote of killing both her young children, but was captured before she could turn the gun on herself. Others told of walking for days, only to have their escape route dead-end on a riverbank.

I stood on the abandoned Songhua River docks on an August day watching my shadow ripple over opaque water that looked deep and dangerous. There were no plaques, no markers on the site, only rusting skiffs and oil drums. An old man carrying a fishing pole appeared from behind a dune and asked what I was staring at.

"Today's the anniversary of the date the Japanese pioneer families waited here, hoping a boat would come to pick them up."

This was the fisherman's village; he knew the story, even if he hadn't yet been born. The Soviet soldiers drew near. Mothers stared upstream and down. No boat came. Hundreds of Japanese women placed their children—some of them just infants—on these docks, stepped off into the current, and disappeared.

On that date in August 1945, second-class private Akira Nagamine was 125 miles east, retreating on a broken ankle from the Soviet advance. A Korean farmer informed his group that the war was over, but the soldiers could not fathom Japan surrendering. "We were taught that we could never lose," Nagamine recalled. The group pressed on, wading through chest-deep swamps, dodging Soviet patrols, picking lice from their infested bodies. Men in his company were killed in firefights with Soviets, committed suicide after injury, and splintered from the group in the dark confusion. Nagamine was shot through the hand—a bullet fragment remains embedded, he said, rubbing the spot—and finally escaped across the river. For six weeks, down to a single companion, Nagamine survived on pine seeds and pilfered food.

In September, in the mountains, the pair spied a house with smoke wafting from the chimney. Its inhabitant, a Chinese man named Mr. Sun,

convinced them that Japan had lost the war. He gave them Chinese clothing and sliced the bills off their army caps. The man led the Japanese to
a village—talking a mob out of killing them along the way—and turned
them over to the local militia. It put Nagamine to work at a canteen.

In the first year after surrender, an estimated sixty-six thousand Japanese
soldiers died from exposure, cholera, or other diseases in Manchuria. An
equal number was press-ganged into work by the two sides of China's
coming civil war. The Soviets had turned over captured Japanese weapons
to the Communists, doubling their number of rifles and tripling their
artillery. Still, control of the Northeast ebbed between armies. Nagamine's
partner was conscripted by Chinese Nationalists, while he, still recovering
from injuries, was left behind.

A Japanese man, also on the run, clandestinely introduced himself as a
former Manchukuo secret agent who once specialized in infiltrating the
resistance. He told Nagamine their cover story: they were pioneer farmers
abandoned by the army. "He was disguised as an old man," Nagamine said.
"He taught me all the tricks, how to pass myself off as someone else."

The men worked at a sawmill, bartering for rice seed with Koreans and
trading with Chinese. Later, Nagamine milked cows and baled hay for a
family of White Russians who had fled the October Revolution. Nearly
three years passed until, in 1948, the homesteaders—seeing Soviet troops
looting the railroad, even shipping some tracks back home—decided to
stay a step ahead and migrated to Manchuria's wide-open west. "We put
everything on the train, even the cows and hay," Nagamine told me with
a smile.

The homesteaders began anew, building log houses and cultivating fields
north of Qiqihar city before a Chinese policeman "invited" Nagamine and
his erstwhile secret agent friend to town to renovate a city inn. Nagamine
became a porter, learning Chinese. His companion was killed when a loaded
hay wagon overturned.

In 1950, Nagamine tramped further north to work as a lumberjack,
floating logs downriver for two years. He hid in plain sight alongside
Chinese coworkers, never daring to attempt sending a letter home.

The Chinese civil war ended in 1949, and within a year China entered
the Korean War, delaying government repatriation of stranded Japanese.
Not until 1953, eight years after arriving in China, did Nagamine admit

his true identity to officials, who handed him a ticket for a train and ship. In Japan, his parents waited for him at the pier. At first no words were spoken. They welcomed him home with silent tears.

In 1956, Nagamine answered an ad in a Japanese newspaper seeking strawberry pickers for California fields. The state needed farmworkers, and—contravening previous immigration restrictions—one thousand visas were made available. The strawberry farm's hourly wage paid what Nagamine earned for a day's work in Japan. One obstacle remained: after eight years in Manchuria, he had to write an essay for the American visa officer stating that he was not a Communist spy. In fact, Nagamine had wanted to move to the United States since fifth grade. I talked to him—of all places—at a Starbucks near my grandmother's house in Santa Cruz County, where he owned a five-acre organic produce farm located on Freedom Boulevard.

Nagamine had returned to China twice, retracing his journey at the urging of his physician daughter, who had grown up hearing only snippets of his story. "It is a miracle," she said, sitting outside at Starbucks. Her father grinned, touched my arm gently, and repeated the Chinese term that meant nothing and everything at once: *Mei guanxi.* It doesn't matter. *Mei guanxi.* All is well. *Mei guanxi.* Never mind.

On the pitted cement docks along the Songhua River, the fisherman watched the eddies and announced, "This is a bad spot." He pulled up his line, retreated to the shallows, and tried his luck there. I followed the one-lane dirt road that wound through a run-down hamlet of redbrick homes and under a new expressway. Four miles from the riverbank, past the Red Banner reservoir, at the end of a dead-end street, stood a gated grove of birch and pines. It was the only memorial of its kind. The characters on the entrance gate read: SINO-JAPANESE FRIENDSHIP GARDEN. The cemetery held the cremated remains of thousands of Japanese "pioneer farmers."

Across Manchukuo, the majority of surviving settlers—61 percent—waited a year in Soviet-run refugee camps (where many were forced to become "comfort women") and returned to Japan on loaned American ships. The other 39 percent went missing, ended up in Siberia, or waited until 1953, when China began sending them home—a program that continued until recently. Thirty thousand settlers still remained in China when it normalized diplomatic relations with Japan in 1972.

An estimated ten thousand Japanese settlers had lived in the area around this cemetery, in a county called Fangzheng, 260 miles northeast of Wasteland. Of the survivors, 2,300 women—facing no other choice—married local men, and 1,120 children—including those left on the riverbank—were adopted by local families. Their legacy was still seen on the streets of Fangzheng town, where shop signs displayed Chinese and Japanese characters, and there were more Japanese-language tutoring centers than ones teaching English. According to the county government, one-fifth of its 230,000 residents had lived or worked in Japan. Descendants of Japanese settlers made annual pilgrimages here each August, during Obon, the grave-sweeping festival.

The cemetery's roots date to 1963, when a Japanese "remaining wife," as women who married Chinese men were called, struck bones while plowing a field. An excavation unearthed the remains of an estimated 4,500 refugees who had died from suicide or starvation. For three days, on a gasoline-fueled fire, locals cremated their remains. Even though China classified the settlers as "exploitation regiments," in 1963 a monument sanctioned by Premier Zhou Enlai was erected at the tomb containing their ashes. "The people of Japan and the settlers," Zhou said, "were also victims of Japanese imperialism."

Amazingly, given that Red Guards had smashed Wasteland's traditional Chinese tombs, the Japanese cemetery remained intact through the Cultural Revolution. Yet, in order to make way for a reservoir, the graveyard was moved to its present site in the 1980s. A massive carved marble tablet inside its entrance announced that the cemetery was a "provincial-level protected heritage site" (not a patriotic education base). In 1984 the remains of five hundred settlers who committed suicide were moved here from Jixi, the railroad town taken by the Soviet army after it overran Akira Nagamine's garrison.

The Sino-Japanese Friendship Garden cemetery also held the remains of Chinese families who had adopted Japanese orphans. A Japanese officer, expressing guilt for the children left behind, wrote that "the Chinese raised the children of the burglars who had robbed them." But in interview after interview, the foster mothers said that the babies were just like they had been: powerless.

Their charity was enshrined in pavilions painted with images of the Great Wall and Mount Fuji. Cement walkways led through the pine grove to two low concrete domes entombing the ashes of the dead. Folded paper cranes—their silk ribbons wishing, in Japanese and Chinese, for everlasting peace—decorated the pines' lowest boughs, left by Japanese visitors. "We have to ask them not to plant any more trees or we'll have to expand the cemetery," the live-in caretaker told me.

It was a lovely, peaceful place, silent but for the magpies. The *feng shui* was sound: a slope of cornfields shielded the tombs from the malevolent northern wind, and they faced water-filled paddies below.

I had arrived in August to meet a group of descendants traveling from Japan for the grave-sweeping festival. But the war did not end in 1945. The previous week, five Chinese nationalists who met online arrived at the cemetery carrying hammers and a bucket of red paint. Their target: a newly erected monument listing the names of 229 Japanese settlers who were among the thousands who starved to death in Fangzheng. The men crossed the names out with red brushstrokes and chipped at the stone. Internet chat rooms spread the news; within hours a bulldozer plowed the monument's rubble into a hole guarded by forty men. The Japanese grave sweepers canceled their trip. "Our economy profits thanks to people who went to Japan from our county," a local shop owner said, "and I support promoting friendship between China and Japan. But some people criticize residents of our county as if they were traitors."

I rattled the cemetery's locked iron gate. The caretaker warned that he had been told to call the police when visitors appeared.

"*Mei guanxi*," I urged. It doesn't matter.

"I have to call the police."

"*Mei guanxi*." All is well.

The caretaker pulled out a cell phone. History was closed today.

I rode the train 250 miles south of Wasteland to Shenyang to peek through blue tin sheeting that masked another wartime relic. I spied a smokestack, dilapidated barracks, and then the muzzle of a lunging guard dog. Once this site had been an Allied prisoner of war camp. On this date, August 16, in 1945, seventeen hours after Japan surrendered, a young American and four other operatives raced here to save hundreds of lives.

"I was the fourth one out the B-24's jump hole," Staff Sergeant Harold "Hal" Leith told me. "I had the feeling of floating rather than falling." It was his first glimpse of Manchuria. He looked down and saw cabbages.

Now age ninety-two, Leith remembers the day clearly. "The next sound I heard was applause and happy yelling from below. It was a bunch of Chinese farmers who had been working in fields where we were landing. They seemed to be enjoying the air show. It was quite a lot of fun floating down. I hit the dirt fast, tumbled, and spilled the chute."

His mission: liberate 1,443 Allied prisoners of war held around Shenyang (then called Mukden). Also: beat the advancing 1.5 million Soviet soldiers in securing "vital documents and personalities both Japanese and puppet." So came the order from the operation's overseer, the Office of Strategic Services, the precursor of today's Central Intelligence Agency. Dubbed Operation Cardinal, it was one of eight sorties planned that day for strategic targets in China, Laos, and Vietnam. The other mission in Manchuria, code-named Flamingo, was scrapped when the Soviets reached Harbin first.

One of these OSS operations would end with the execution of a missionary turned operative named John Birch. He was to travel overland in coastal China to scout former Japanese airfields that could be used to evacuate POWs. Chinese Communist forces were angered by the Yalta agreements that returned Manchuria's railroad and Port Arthur to Soviet control. A People's Liberation Army detachment stopped and disarmed Birch. "What is the matter with you, anyway? Are you bandits?" he asked his captors in Chinese. The Chinese member of his team told Birch to not antagonize the soldiers, to which he replied, "I want to find out how they intend to treat Americans. I don't mind if they kill me. If they do they will be finished, for America will punish them with atomic bombs." The soldiers opened fire, striking his Chinese colleague above the knee, and Birch in the leg. The soldiers bound his arms and feet, then bayoneted him to death, mutilating his face in an attempt to destroy his identity. The Chinese team member lay beside him, playing dead, until a passerby helped him escape during the night. Birch would later be lionized as the "first casualty of the Cold War" by the right-wing society named for him.

Operation Cardinal was the most dangerous of the OSS missions: Hal Leith and five operatives—armed only with pistols—would jump into territory occupied by thirty thousand Japanese troops about to face a tidal wave of Soviet soldiers. No one knew how the Japanese army would react to the news—if it had even heard—of Japan's surrender. The American POWs could be used as human shields, or as evidence to be liquidated. The nearest American forces were stationed nine hundred miles away.

The war's abrupt conclusion had surprised the OSS: one day after the agency's head, William Donovan—the founding father of American intelligence—arrived in the central Chinese city of Xi'an on August 8, 1945, the Soviet Union declared war on Japan and invaded Manchukuo. The next day the second atomic bomb fell, on Nagasaki. "If we are not in Korea and Manchuria when the Russians get there, we will never get in," Donovan cabled. "Although we have been caught with our pants down, we will do our best to pull them up in time." He ordered his agents to locate American property, prepare dossiers of "potential agents, informants and sympathizers" for the United States, and to secure information on Russian support for Chinese Communists, who were about to engage in full-scale civil war with the ruling Nationalists, the side backed by the U.S.

Operation Cardinal took off at 0450 on August 16, 1945.

For much of its existence, the Shenyang camp had been unknown to the Allies. Its POWs included American, British, Dutch, and Australian enlisted men and officers, including survivors of the Bataan Death March; British lieutenant general Arthur Percival, who had surrendered Singapore; and American lieutenant general Jonathan Wainwright, who had surrendered the Philippines at Corregidor. The survivors of that battle had been shipped to Taiwan—an American submarine fired torpedoes at the vessel, missing both times—before being packed in the holds of "hell ships" that carried them to the Korean Peninsula. There, the men were divided: some were sent to forced labor in Japan, and some were put on trains north to Shenyang, where 260 prisoners died the first winter from disease and cold. Japanese stacked their frozen bodies in a storage shed until the ground thawed. An improved camp named Hoten was built the next year, in 1943, where press-ganged prisoners worked in a tannery and made munitions at the Manchurian Machine Tool Factory.

The Japanese considered Hoten a model camp, with frequent visits from the Red Cross, bearing mail and supplies. Men still tried to escape. The camp commander, Colonel Matsuda, a short, scowling, bald-headed man who wore thick glasses, addressed the assembled prisoners after three prisoners were captured trying to break out. They were executed.

"It is entirely out of my expectations to see the betrayal, the most outrageous and unfortunate trouble that has been caused recently," Matsuda read in English from handwritten notes. "Under the vast virtues of his Majesty the Emperor, all the personnel here have treated you with sympathy. But the very three escapees that have dared to go against my wishes may well be said to be absolutely inhuman . . . You yourselves have quitted your fortune and thrown yourself into the state of Hell."

In photographs before his capture on Bataan, Brigadier General W. E. Brougher looked like a jovial, pipe-chewing hell-raiser. The Mississippi native's diary—hidden inside hollowed bamboo and buried under the barracks—recorded his and the prison camp's deteriorating conditions in 1945. "I am down 14 pounds in three months," read an entry from July. "No meat fats or sugar. Food very poor—everybody hungry." Prisoners' clothing had been reduced to tatters, and the camp guards ordered the digging of more air raid shelters.

On August 8, two days after the bombing of Hiroshima—unknown to Brougher—he noted, "No flags up for first time."

On August 9, when Nagasaki was bombed: "Air raid alarm this morning—men apparently not going to work at factory. Wonder what's up?"

August 15: "Many rumors of approaching end of war. Men being brought in from branch camps. All men discontinuing work at factories."

August 16: "Wildest kinds of rumors all day of end of war. Parachute landing observed near the prison camp about 11:30 am . . . [M]any wild rumors were circulated as to their identity."

Hal Leith looked nothing like Captain America. He was slight, red-haired, and bespectacled, and only selected for Operation Cardinal because he spoke Chinese. After enlisting three years before, the Army had noted his autodidactic fluency in German, French, and Russian, and shipped the Coloradoan to the University of Chicago to learn Chinese for a year. An OSS recruiter visited the campus, soliciting volunteers. Leith was one of a handful of recruits who made it through training on Catalina

Island that taught lock picking, message ciphering, and hand-to-hand combat. One look at a USO hostess named Helen disarmed him. He married her, then almost immediately sailed to Melbourne and onward to Calcutta before boarding a train to Burma and the "hump" flight to Kunming that brought him to Xi'an, and, six hours later, down through the Manchurian sky and into a cabbage patch.

"The first thing I said to the farmers was, '*Women shi meiguoren*,'" Leith told me. "'We are Americans. Do you know where the Japanese are?' We didn't have a compass, or any intelligence, really, not even the name of the camp commander. Our plane turned and started dropping food parcels and supplies, and a Japanese fighter intercepted him and missed. A farmer pointed us in a direction—we hadn't ruined any of their cabbages—and we set off walking. It started raining, and then the Japanese found us."

At the sight of the dozen soldiers, the Chinese member of the team turned and ran. Now Cardinal was down to five. The team's doctor, a Nisei Hawaiian, ordered the Japanese to surrender. They, in reply, clicked their rifle bolts and ordered the Americans to put their hands up.

"No one was yelling," Leith recalled. "It was a quiet exchange. We were the first active American soldiers these men had seen. They didn't know the war was over."

The Japanese took Cardinal's pistols, blindfolded the men, and loaded them in the back of a truck. The engines fired. When the truck stopped and his blindfold was removed, Leith saw not an execution ground but the entrance to the Japanese secret police headquarters. "We were offered sake and whiskey. The head of the police admitted that he had heard a rumor about surrender but didn't know what to do. He knew the Russians were on their way: they were 120 miles north, and closing. He agreed to let us make a quick trip to the prison camp." The Japanese driver said to Leith in English, "I hear you lived in Los Angeles. I've got a brother in LA and wonder if you know him?"

The Cardinal team was lodged in the South Manchuria Railway hotel. The official transmission of surrender arrived from Tokyo the next morning. The highest-ranking Japanese officer asked Leith to witness him commit hara-kiri.

"I asked him not to," Leith said. "I needed him to assure his soldiers that the war was over." The officer turned the camp over to the five OSS operatives. Elated, if emaciated, prisoners besieged Leith with pats, hand-shakes, and questions. *Is Shirley Temple dead? Is Roosevelt really dead, and from what? Who is president now? Who is the British prime minister? Who won the last three World Series? How much pay do the different grades now get?*

In his prison diary, Brigadier General W. E. Brougher wrote: "Happy time for Prisoners of War—the end to our 3½ yrs of misery!" In one of his last entries from the camp, on August 18, he noted: "Getting too much to eat! Great danger of prisoners doing themselves harm by overeating after 3 yrs of starvation." A jerky black-and-white newsreel showed the liberated prisoners laughing, playing guitar, and making the Japanese fill in their foxholes to make a baseball diamond.

For Hal Leith, however, the game was far from over. Missing from the nearly 1,500 freed men were 34 of the highest-ranking officers, including generals Percival and Wainwright, and the governor of the Dutch East Indies. Leith learned that for the past year the men had been sequestered at an unheated, run-down barracks in a town named Xi'an (present-day Liaoyuan). Communications with the camp had been cut off since the Soviet advance and Japanese surrender, air services were grounded, and road travel was unsafe.

With another Cardinal soldier and a Japanese interpreter, Leith set out by train, unarmed. On the ride north, he met a family of White Russians standing on a station platform, wondering where to flee next now that the Red Army had arrived. At the Xi'an camp, the Japanese commander greeted Leith in English; he was a graduate of Oregon State. All the prisoners, he said, were alive.

General Wainwright, gaunt and wearing threadbare clothes, looked like a scarecrow. "He was puzzled at being liberated by the OSS, an arm of service he had never seen," Leith said, laughing.

Three days later the convoy arrived in Shenyang at 12:30 in the morning to find their hotel filled with drunken Red Army soldiers. Many had been under siege at Stalingrad before shipping to Manchuria. A lieutenant told Leith he had been demoted for killing German prisoners of war. In wartime, soldiers became a nation's diplomats, he said, adding, "There are good diplomats and bad diplomats."

A Cardinal report described a binge of Soviet raping and looting across Manchuria, "payback" for Japan's defeat of Russia forty years before.

Revenge extended to the erstwhile Manchukuoans: "Roving Chinese mobs beating and killing Japanese civilians indiscriminately."

Leith witnessed a crowd attack a twelve-year-old Japanese boy, which he stopped by berating the crowd for behaving like their former occupiers. "Some of the Chinese took my side," he wrote in his diary. "And some commented on my good Chinese accent." After he carried the boy to a hospital, Leith returned to break up the mob, seizing their clubs while keeping his pistol holstered. His language ability helped: "The people in the mob again all commented on my being an American and on my good Chinese accent. A number of Chinese sided with me and bawled out the other misbehaving Chinese."

There were screams at night, and machine-gun fire, and the smell of smoke from torched Japanese homes and businesses. Soviet forces, an OSS officer reported, began shipping home "(a) all motor vehicles—even broken ones; (b) all gasoline; (c) small machinery and motors; (d) lumber." The Russians even took vaccine cultures, leaving locals defenseless against outbreaks of typhus and pneumonia.

Twelve days after its launch, news of Operation Cardinal reached America. Leith's mother, living in San Francisco, received a phone call from a local reporter asking for her thoughts on the courageous actions of Staff Sergeant Harold Leith. "That can't be my son," she replied. "He doesn't do things like that."

In Los Angeles, Leith's wife, Helen, read the wire story and said aloud: "That's my Hal."

In October 1945 the Soviets offered Leith a choice: leave immediately or get a free trip to Siberia. William Donovan, the head of the OSS, seethed, "When did Manchuria become part of Russia?" In fact, the Soviets would remain in the railway zone and Port Arthur until 1955. Leith departed but reappeared in Manchuria soon after. Code-named Mr. Williams, he was America's first intelligence agent in China's northeast. After a year in the field, the Communists expelled him for good in 1946. I met him at his home in Golden, Colorado.

With ex-POWs, he had returned to the former camp twice—in 1989 and 2003—to publicize the Shenyang city government's announcement of a museum at the prison site. On my visit I avoided the guard dog by sliding a dead bolt open and sneaking through a side door. The former barracks hall was garlanded with exposed wiring and pocked with standing puddles. A purple banner said: PRESS CONFERENCE OF VETERANS REVISITING SHENYANG WWII ALLIED POW CAMP. The words faced rows of orange plastic chairs occupied by piles of dust.

After the war, the camp's factory was repurposed into an electrical plant and surrounded by worker's housing blocks. Now they were being replaced by high-rises whose billboards promised, in English, LOW DENSITY OF THE HONEY LIFE. Across a ten-lane expressway loomed a new mall anchored by a Pizza Hut.

In Chinese and English, a sign posted outside the camp told nothing of Operation Cardinal, but informed that "only the help of kind-hearted Chinese fellow-workers provided any comfort" to the prisoners. It concluded that the camp "deeply illustrates one aspect of Japanese fascism."

The English translation of the conclusion had been sanded over, however. Since its groundbreaking a decade before, the museum project started and stopped from disagreements over what it would show, what lessons it would teach, what patriotic education really entailed. Construction was ongoing.

After I visited the tombs of Japanese settlers in Fangzheng, a Japanese newspaper interviewed a sixty-two-year-old retired elementary school teacher who the local government had commissioned to write the county's war history. Standing on the Songhua River docks where Japanese mothers had placed their children onshore, then drowned themselves, the teacher told the reporter, "What occurred here reflects the essence of civilian victims of war. Preserving this place can only help the healthy development of Sino-Japanese relations."

He had sought permission to post a plaque retelling the events here and at a nearby tributary, which women had attempted to cross by clinging to torn and knotted kimonos before being swept away. Officials said: "In present circumstances, the plaques are impossible to approve." But, the teacher noted optimistically, "circumstances change."

The Japanese invasion caused 14 to 20 million Chinese deaths, and while Japanese officials continued to pay respects at Tokyo's Yasukuni Shrine—where the nation's honored dead included convicted war criminals—some former Japanese soldiers returned to China to record oral histories of their wartime actions. Others even took the stand. In a Tokyo courtroom in 2002, a veteran soldier testified in a lawsuit brought by the families of 180 Chinese who had been killed by a secret Japanese army unit in Manchuria. For the first time a Japanese court found that its Imperial Army had, in fact, conducted germ warfare in China. Under international law, the victims were not entitled to compensation, but the verdict ended a half century of official denials.

"Forgetting history means betrayal," reads the display at the Japanese Invading Army Unit 731 Museum. "The fascistic guilt of Unit 731 brooks no denial." Japan's biggest bacterial warfare research unit experimented on live Chinese, Russian, Mongolian, and Korean prisoners in a suburb fifteen miles south of central Harbin. Here, Japanese doctors subjected *maruta*— logs, as they referred to the prisoners—to hypothermia, amputation, bullet wounds, and a range of disease and bacteria, noting at which level of suffering a person finally expired.

The museum stood in what remained of the base's seventy-six buildings—covering four square miles—after retreating Japanese had torched all they could. Inside the dimly lit halls, visitors pace past gas masks, bone saws, and viscera hangars. Outside, signs mark the footprint of the Cave for Manufacturing Germ Shell Cases, the Frostbite Laboratory, and the Nursery of Yellow Rats. Children's shouting and laughter carries over the high brick wall from the grounds of the adjoining Number 25 Middle School.

Over thirteen years, an estimated three thousand prisoners were gruesomely killed at this site, in addition to the seven to nine thousand who died in Unit 731–affiliated bases across occupied China under the cover of being "anti-epidemic water supply units"—which, in turn, poisoned local wells, a sickening echo of the mind that thought to post Work Makes You Free at the entrance to Nazi concentration camps.

Japan's version of Josef Mengele was a doctor and lieutenant general named Ishii Shiro, who began his bacterial warfare research in 1932. As the Soviets invaded in August 1945, Ishii ordered Unit 731 and other research bases destroyed and the remaining 404 prisoners killed. It took three days to burn their bodies, after which the ranking officer on-site said, "Now the Emperor will not be hanged."

Ishii and his top staff fled to Japan with crates of files. American troops found him hiding in his home village, where residents had placed a newspaper story saying he had been shot to death and had even held a mock funeral. Ishii was not placed under arrest, only brought to Tokyo for questioning. After nearly two years of off-and-on interrogation of Ishii, a U.S. Army Basic Sciences chief wrote to his commander:

> Evidence gathered in this investigation has greatly supplemented and amplified previous aspects of this field. It represents data which have been obtained by Japanese scientists at the expenditure of many millions of dollars and years of work. Information has accrued with respect to human susceptibility to those diseases as indicated by specific infectious doses of bacteria. Such information could not be obtained in our own laboratories because of scruples attached to human experimentation.

The letter concluded by noting that the army funds spent investigating Ishii's work in China was "a mere pittance by comparison with the actual cost of the studies."

In 1948 the United States granted Ishii and eighteen subordinates immunity from war crimes prosecution. None were ever charged, let alone punished. For three decades the deal was kept secret before it was uncovered by an American journalist. Ishii was said to have opened a clinic in Japan, treating children, before dying of throat cancer at age sixty-seven.

His Majesty the Emperor, Puyi, read the notice dissolving Manchukuo on August 17, 1945. For the second time in his life, Puyi abdicated, then fled his palace. Soviet forces nabbed him at an airfield, boarding a plane bound for Japan. They packed him away to detention in Siberia, where he pleaded not to be returned to China, certain that he would be killed the moment he crossed the border.

In 1946 the Soviets brought him to Tokyo to testify at the war crimes tribunal. Looking frail beyond his forty years, Puyi talked to save his life. Wearing an expensive brown suit and speaking Chinese, he put on a good show: China's last emperor on the stand, striking a patriotic chord. "The people in Manchuria were complete slaves of the Japanese," he averred. "It is almost impossible to describe the pain of the Chinese people in Manchuria. They could not obtain necessities and they could not even get clothing in severe weather. It would be an offense if a Chinese had in his possession any high-grade rice. The Chinese did not have the freedom to say anything without fear of facing death. Manchukuo was a completely darkened country during the term of Japanese rule."

Previously, the looting of his family's imperial tombs by Chinese soldiers had made Puyi vow revenge, hastening his decision to cast his lot with the Japanese. But they had not even allowed him to visit those tombs to make an annual sacrifice. "I had better not go," a general had told him, "because, since my ancestors were all Manchurians, if I went there to worship it would look as if Manchurians stood out unique among other groups of people in Manchukuo."

Why hadn't he told the League of Nations' visiting Lytton Commission investigators the truth and asked for help? "The situation was like myself being kidnapped by bandits, and now my neighbors try to come to my rescue, yet in their presence I could not tell them what actually happened because after my rescuers left I was liable to be killed by the bandits."

So he had bided his time over the next fourteen years, waiting for the right moment to rise against the occupation. "That was my ideal, and so I entered the mouth of the tiger."

In his autobiography, written two decades later, Puyi admitted: "I now feel very ashamed of my testimony . . . I said nothing about my secret collaboration with the Japanese imperialists over a long period . . . I maintained that I had not betrayed my country but had been kidnapped . . . I covered up my crimes in order to protect myself."

Like the Japanese emperor and his family, Puyi was not charged with any crime. In 1950 the Soviet Union handed him back to China. He was shipped to a prison near Qingyuan, the Manchu county along the Willow Palisade whose name meant "Origin of the Qing," the dynasty that had ended when he abdicated the dragon throne.

At the former prison, now a patriotic education base, school groups pause before the former cell of the "living god" who became prisoner number 987. In photos, Puyi darns socks and drinks tea from an enameled mug captioned, "Working Is Glorious." The guide narrates, "In the end, he became a useful friend of China and the Chinese people at large."

Useful, again.

In 1959, on the tenth anniversary of the People's Republic founding, Puyi was pardoned and released. He returned to his hometown of Beijing for the first time in thirty-five years. Dressed in a baggy blue serge Mao suit, he served as a "special guide," leading a one-off tour of his former palace, the Forbidden City. His memoir, published by the state press, did not record his impressions of the visit other than to note that the palace walls had been repainted and the "old and desolate atmosphere" had gone.

The Party assigned him to work in the hothouses at Beijing's Botanical Garden. Always slight and sad-eyed, Puyi looked as delicate as the orchids that had once adorned the Manchukuo imperial seal. His memoir concluded with the first words he learned to write in Chinese, from a Confucian primer:

> People at birth
> Are naturally good
> Their natures are similar
> Their habits diverge
> When foolishly taught

In 1967, as the Cultural Revolution consumed China, Red Guards found Puyi, enfeebled by kidney cancer, and shouted, "We will take you back to the Northeast and smash you, you dog's head!" The cancer took him before they could: he died, aged sixty-one, leaving no heirs or treasure. In its obituary, the *New York Times* called him "a historical leftover." Since he was no longer an emperor, his cremated remains were interred not at the Qing tombs alongside his royal ancestors but at Beijing's Babaoshan Revolutionary Cemetery, the final resting place for Communist heroes.

But in new, market-driven China, Puyi became useful yet again. In 1995 a private cemetery in the capital's outskirts paid his widow an undisclosed fee to move his ashes to one of their plots, aimed at the wealthy elite. The graveyard, named Hualong (Chinese Dragon), neighbors the Western Qing tombs—favoring the interred, its advertisements promise, with imperial *feng shui*. Puyi's presence proves it. Buried under a headstone bearing only his name—written not in Manchu but in Chinese—he remains a symbol for all eternity.

After Japan surrendered in August 1945, the Soviets rolled south through Manchuria, not halting until they reached Korea's Thirty-eighth parallel. The peninsula was divided into north and south, into the Democratic People's Republic and the Republic. The next war was about to begin.

But first the Chinese civil war played out. In 1936 the Young Marshal, Zhang Xueliang, had forced Chiang Kai-shek at gunpoint to form a united front with Mao Zedong. For this, Zhang would never return to Manchuria, spending the next fifty-four years under house arrest on the mainland and Taiwan, and dying at age one hundred in Hawaii. With Japan defeated in 1945, Chinese Nationalist and Communist forces divided and fought each other for four years.

One of the deciding blows for the Nationalists happened in Changchun, site of the erstwhile Manchukuoan capital seventy miles west of Wasteland. Before Japan's invasion, Changchun had 100,000 inhabitants; at the fall of Manchukuo, nearly 900,000 people lived there.

The Communist People's Liberation Army, commanded by Lin Biao, encircled Nationalist forces, and the city itself. Lin—later credited as the creator of the "Little Red Book" of Chairman Mao's sayings—called for Changchun to be turned into a "city of death." His soldiers ringed its perimeter with barbed wire barricades. For five months, from June to October 1948, no civilians were allowed to leave and no supplies were allowed in. Survivors told of eating rotten grain, then corncobs, then tree bark. Others tore open pillows for their corn husk stuffing. Belts were boiled; dead bodies were consumed. Soldiers seized the aid packages dropped by American planes. At least 160,000 civilians perished, equaling the number killed by the first atomic bomb.

"The casualties were about the same," a People's Liberation Army colonel later recorded. "Hiroshima took nine seconds; Changchun took five months." The colonel's book describing the siege, *White Snow, Red Blood*, was published in 1989 but was soon banned for "insulting the Communist Party."

No patriotic education base commemorated, let alone mentioned, the Siege of Changchun. A Hong Kong–based researcher recalled that every elderly army officer she interviewed for a book about China's civil war broke down when recalling the siege. "It's an unspeakable national trauma that has not once been opened up," she said.

"Some refugees threw down their babies and ran away, others hung themselves with ropes right in front of the sentries," the colonel wrote in his book. He cited a cable from a People's Liberation Army officer on the scene, lamenting that soldiers had shown reluctance to follow his orders. "Not allowing the starving city residents to leave and sending other starving citizens back into the city has become difficult to explain to the troops."

You can meet the siege's survivors among the elderly who congregate in Changchun's Victory Park. Originally built by the Japanese, it is now punctuated by a statue of Chairman Mao. There, a former soldier said the Party's official line was that "Changchun was liberated without firing a single shot." He knew how: with 170,000 other Communist troops, he drove back civilians who tried to escape the city. He wished the siege's full story would be made public. Chinese schoolchildren, he said, "only know the propaganda. Maybe if they know how horrible war is, they can try to avoid it in the future."

The war still suppurates into daily life. China estimates that, since 1945, at least two thousand people have been killed by unearthed Japanese chemical weapons. Two million pieces of ordnance were left behind in the Northeast alone, bleeding their contents into the soil and water table, or worse. In Jilin province in 2004, boys aged twelve and eight were burned and sickened after coming into contact with a rusting toxic shell they found in a stream. The Japanese government acknowledged it was one of their weapons but refused to pay damages. Under its obligations as a signatory of the United Nations Chemical Weapons Convention, Japan agreed to send teams to excavate and dispose of the munitions at a facility it would build outside of Dunhua city, where the boys had been injured.

Dunhua was two hundred miles east of Wasteland, and I wanted to check the project's progress. Previously, Japan had pledged to dig up its ordnance by 2007. A Japanese Foreign Ministry spokesman said the cleanup was "extremely important for improving trust." But in 2008 the agency in charge was discovered to have misused $1 million of public funds.

For four hours my bus curved past green foothills over an empty expressway that gently dipped and rose, passing a villa development named the Island of Egrets. I misread it as "Regrets" while under the spell of the Liam Neeson action film blaring on the bus's video player. His vengeful oeuvre was replacing the regional comedic opera *Er Ren Zhuan* on Northeastern buses. I never thought I would miss the opera's clatter, until spending seated hours captive to recorded gunfire and gravel-voiced threats.

Dunhua's street grid still showed traces of a Japanese planner's pencil: in front of the train station, axial roads radiated diagonally off a roundabout, leading to the town center. With a population of 500,000, Dunhua counted as a small Chinese city but felt more like a county seat. Its only fast-food outlets were knockoffs, including CFC, California Fried Chicken.

A local man named Dong Gang offered to take me to the weapons cleanup site where the boys had been injured, twenty miles north of town. Dong Gang was wound tight. He clutched an iPhone hard enough to whiten his knuckles, mirrored sunglasses indented the temples of his shaved head, and his jeans and black T-shirt looked painted on. He told me to call him "brother" and began most sentences with, "Here's my analysis." As he sped down the country road, over the Peony River and past rolling tobacco fields, he turned and looked at me while talking.

"Eyes straight ahead, brother."

"Don't worry. Here's my analysis. The Japs reject any claims for compensation because they think the peace pact signed with us in 1972 settled the matter."

"Watch the road, brother."

"Here's where the Japanese airfield used to be. When I was a kid, we would ride bikes on the runway. Now it's rows of corn. Here's my analysis . . ."

Thirty minutes later we entered a narrow valley, passing signs announcing the activities forbidden in the forest preserve: chopping, burning, barbecuing. The single-lane road looked like a bike trail winding toward the stream where the boys had discovered the toxic shell. The house where they had lived, however, was now deserted.

"Here's my analysis: they moved into town like everyone else."

We continued ahead, stopping to lift a red-and-white-striped pole that served as a gate. A sign warned that we had entered a chemical weapons cleanup site and were not supposed to be here. Yet the road was empty, and the only sound was a faint hum that grew louder as we approached the valley's last house. Through shoulder-high cornstalks we saw a lean-to perched on a slope. A squadron of bees escorted our approach, revealing an apiary. The Qins were the sole remaining family who lived here year-round, and they greeted us with a bowl of boiled water stirred with fresh honey.

The cleanup had paused again, Mr. Qin said, though he couldn't say why. He pointed to the backhoes and bulldozers parked in a clearing. "The trucks are still there, but not the Japanese." As bees buzzed my ears and tickled my arms, Mr. Qin said that the villagers who used to live here in Hualianpao—Bursting Lotus—had met with Japanese officials and accepted their offer of new housing, though the officials had been careful to call its cost a "transformation fee" and not "compensation," which could set a precedent for future war-related claims.

The money had been given to the Dunhua government to contract the building of new apartments in town. When they were completed, Mr. Qin said, the villagers complained of their shoddy quality and accused local officials of pocketing a portion of the funds. Still, they had been forced to move, and their homes razed. "My family never signed the agreement," Mr. Qin said. "I can't grow corn in the city, and I can't have bees. In all these years, I haven't hit any weapons when planting. Hopefully, they're buried elsewhere."

As the tightly wound Dong Gang presented his analysis of Japan, of war, of chemical weapons, of burned children and forced relocation and allegations of embezzlement, I felt the sun on my face and inhaled the scent of ripening corn. Of all things, I thought of Yeats's wish for a small cabin and a life alone in the bee-loud glade, "where peace comes dropping slow."

That poem's ending never sounded peaceful to me: bee stings hurt like hell. I was doing my best to ignore the cloud buzzing around us, sipping the honey water as the bees brushed my ears and tickled my neck.

"They're not going to hurt you," Mr. Qin said, interrupting Dong Gang's analysis. "They have their world and we have ours, but we have to exist together."

CHAPTER 14

GREAT HEAT

B ACK IN WASTELAND, a rumble shook me awake. I brushed a fly off my eyelid and reached for my cell phone. 3:35 a.m. The rumble came again, shaking the house. I rolled off the barley-filled pillow and crawled over the *kang*'s cool linoleum to look out the window. Empty dump trucks sped toward Red Flag Road.

The previous morning, I had sat in the empty house, feeling cut off from the world, thinking: *If I woke with amnesia, could I guess where I was and how I got here? Would I find it backward or beautiful?* My housemate Mr. Guan had puttered up on his motorcycle then, announcing, "Five pounds of eels, four pounds of fish. Not bad." My cell phone whirred with an incoming text message—a different kind of phishing—that said, "One-month MBA/MPA dual-certificate program with a Beijing address on the diploma. Don't worry about the cost! Call Teacher Zhang at 18210557248!" In China, even in the countryside, isolation was short-lived.

Now, before four on a Saturday morning, a convoy of dump trucks shook our little farmhouse.

I pulled the piece of plastic baling string that turned on the room's exposed bulb, but no light came on. The electric kettle, too, would not start. I got off the *kang*, slipped into flip-flops, and tried the kitchen light. Nothing. As Wasteland turned toward the sun, a bit of light crept into our yard. I stepped outside to see our sunflowers turn their heads in the slipstream of each passing truck.

I ducked under the grape trellis and edged past the shed, buzzing with flies that hovered over a mesh tray of drying fish. My head snagged a net, then a spiderweb, and in my murky grogginess I couldn't tell which one I was trying to shake off. Leeches dangled from a string of hooks. If I woke with amnesia in this setting, I'd wonder what horrible thing I had done to end up here. I stepped over the foot-high plank that covered the outhouse entrance to keep the rats out, and squatted. *Don't think about rats in the hole*, I told myself every morning. But then all I thought about was their red eyes shining glassily below.

I stuffed a handful of Nescafé packets in my hoodie's front pocket and set out for San Jiu's. He could burn rice stalks to boil water. Turning south on Red Flag, I saw the dump trucks in a queue that stretched to his house. A Komatsu digger sat parked at Wasteland's intersection. For one mile, past every dump truck cab, I recited the list that began *American, 1.86 meters, Year of the Rat*.

"They're widening Red Flag Road," San Jiu explained, handing me a chopstick to stir the coffee granules. "It's Eastern Fortune Rice's project; they're paying for it. They want better access to the hot spring, I guess. Or there's a high official on his way and they want to impress him and say, 'Look at the road we made.'"

"Does the road need to be widened?"

San Jiu laughed. "The road is fine. It was resurfaced two years ago. I remember when it was dirt, and before that, when it was a footpath. They'll have to tear down that new archway, too. It just went up two months ago."

Sure enough, the arch at the start of Red Flag Road that announced The Roots of Northeast Prosperity came down that morning. The pieces filled a dump truck, which joined the line of mud-filled vehicles exiting Wasteland.

A digger cut a ten-foot-wide gash the length of the road. Previously, it was a drainage ditch. But for a fifty-yard stretch, it had also bloomed with the bright pink poppies planted by Auntie Yi. I found her standing outside her house in her bucket hat, yelling at the machine's operator.

"Eastern Fortune just does whatever it wants," she said. "They didn't even post notices about this project, so I didn't have time to transplant my flowers. I planted those myself, from seeds I bought and raised. Everyone in these villages knows my flowers!"

It was true: their stripe of color on the otherwise barren road served as a local landmark.

We watched the digger cut into the wet, dark soil. "It smells good," I said.

"It smells like dirt," Auntie Yi corrected.

She pointed to the cranes and apartment buildings on the horizon. "Eastern Fortune expects everyone will move out of their courtyard homes and into those. Once you agree, they'll tear your house down and plant rice where it used to stand. I'm never moving there."

Auntie Yi was a Party member and former village cadre; what annoyed her about the development—from the hot spring to the apartments to the road widening—was that a private company was funding it, not the government. "It's all Eastern Fortune," she said. "It's a pilot program, so the state gives some construction subsidies, but the company is in charge. It's their design. To make this into 'The Northeast's Top Village.' You've seen the sign. The government expects companies like Eastern Fortune to lead the 'backward' peasants toward change. That's our nation's direction now."

All politics were personal. Auntie Yi yelled again at the hapless digger operator, who avoided her gaze, instead focusing on depositing a dripping scoopful of mud into a dump truck. Late that afternoon, as the sun cast long shadows that stretched the workers' silhouettes to fifteen feet on Red Flag Road, the trucks returned bearing loads of crushed stone. The rocks clattered onto the excavated area, burying the remains of Auntie Yi's flowers. She cried.

"She really loves those flowers," San Jiu said as we sat down for dinner. "It's her hobby. Everyone has their reason for wanting to stay in their home. For her, it's those flowers. But she can plant them again. They'll finish the road in a week."

I nearly choked on my tofu. "A week?"

"I heard they're bringing in a large team of migrant workers. Must be an inspection by an official coming up." He said it in the same tone that he forecast the weather. *Partly sunny with a party secretary expected. Cloudy with a chance of cadres.*

Despite San Jiu's pragmatic—or fatalistic—view of events, it always stung to see the elderly react to changes in China that were beyond their control, enacted by people who hadn't asked for their input. Auntie Yi was deeply patriotic—*We won't bully you,* the People's Liberation Army soldiers camped in her yard had promised her as a little girl—and sang the revolutionary song "Without the Communist Party, There Would Be No New China" with gusto. So couldn't someone have alerted her to save her flowers?

San Jiu said she hadn't lost a crop, or her home. It was just a bunch of flowers. He glowered at me for a moment, not playfully, as usual.

"What are you looking at? I'll show you the colors," I said.

He snorted, forcing a laugh. "You have to remember. We only grow four months out of the year here. That's our livelihood for all twelve months. I'm paying attention to making a living instead of some flowers. Auntie Yi gets a pension. And you—you just pay rent to your friend, the teacher, and travel around the Northeast."

San Jiu had mentioned, previously, that I should not be paying rent to anyone, since I volunteered at the school.

"I would have paid you if there was space for me to live here."

"Family doesn't charge rent!"

We sat in silence. This was where my Chinese ceased to be fluent. I feared saying something that would make the situation worse. Was he mad that I didn't live with him? Was he worried about money? Did he support the road project, and had he argued with Auntie Yi?

"I don't pay that much rent," I tried.

San Jiu said: "Don't waste your money. You need to have a kid soon. Kids cost money."

"My Chinese name is Sold Son," I said, laughing. "I know all about it."

"No you don't," San Jiu said seriously.

A rumble rippled across the paddies. At first I thought it was more trucks. "Thunder," said San Jiu, meaning, *Go home.* A fifteen-minute walk lay ahead. I thanked him for dinner—he nodded without words—dodged the barking Pekingese tied up in the yard, and cut through the paddies behind his house, angling toward mine.

I called this path Frog Alley, as their croaking filled the air and they leapt into my shins, landing at times on my shoelaces. Clouds of gnats filled my mouth the way plankton got sucked in by a whale. The thunder boomed nearer. The work crews had arrived on Red Flag Road, and I could hear them in the darkness, talking and spreading the crushed rock even as the storm approached. I made it home just as the skies opened. The power was still out, so I climbed onto the *kang* and read South Manchuria Railway reports by the light of my computer screen, until the battery died and it was time for bed.

The chiming tune of "Happy Birthday to You" woke me at dawn. I looked out the window to see the recorded song clanging from roof-mounted speakers on a water truck, spraying away the mess the dump trucks had trailed down our street.

My morning run took me along rain-washed roads, through hamlets named Mud Town and Black Mountain. Its name ended not in *cun* (village) but *wopeng*, a term from imperial times that meant "an inn by the wayside," or a "hunting party base camp." Further on, near the Songhua River, was a *wopeng* named Lower Frog. There, as I gulped a one-yuan bottle of mineral water, the woman who sold it to me asked, "Does your hometown have a river?"

"The Mississippi."

She brightened. "That's a famous river."

I nodded. Then she blurted the area, in square kilometers, of the United States and China. "Your country is just a bit larger," she said.

"Why do you know that?"

"I read a lot."

I bought an apple. She began listing the varieties grown in Jilin province, then the ones commonly found in New Zealand, Chile, and Washington State. To me, all apples tasted like a variety I called Hectoring Auntie: each bite reminded me of Wasteland women chiding me to impregnate Frances and for her to fill up on apples.

I began backing toward the shop exit. But not before one final question.

"Do Americans see the same sun as we do?"

"What? Of course; there's only one sun."

"The same sun, huh?" she said, sounding unconvinced.

I ran until the road turned to dirt, narrowed to tractor tracks, and became the river. By the time I returned to Wasteland, the work crew had arrived, dressed in slacks, sweater vests, and plimsolls. They had been bused in after improving a road in Jilin city. In a single morning they built a new curb, made of mortared stones.

The curb reached from paddy level to the roadbed. Crushed stone and dirt filled the gap, running three miles along Red Flag Road. This all happened within a workweek. The men were at it from sunup until past sundown, working entirely with their hands: no power tools, only trowels, spades and levels. They slept and ate in temporary tin-walled dormitories erected near Eastern Fortune's headquarters. Many would stay on to finish the apartments rising there.

When the work crew reached Auntie Yi's house, she brought out bottles of mineral water, asking if anyone was hungry. They called her *da niang*, a term of respect for an elderly woman, and modestly refused her offers. In her bucket hat and patched hand-knit sweater, she browbeat them to accept by out-humbling them. "I'm just a simple person . . ." her harangue began.

She remained my consigliere: When I handed her a pound of fresh pork, she said, "San Jiu's upset you don't bring him meat like before. He's too proud to tell you that he prefers that to milk, because pork costs a lot more." (I brought the pork; San Jiu again treated me like a son.)

Auntie Yi's grudge lay elsewhere.

"Eastern Fortune Rice expects farmers to give up their courtyard homes and move into new apartments? Then we'll have to pay for heating, for water. We'll have to buy vegetables instead of grow them. We'll even have to pay for rice! It's too ridiculous," she said.

Locals owned their homes, so they would be compensated for the building itself, but not for the land their house sat upon. That belonged to the village collective. "In theory, it's not a bad idea, moving into a modern apartment," Auntie Yi said. "But what if you want to keep things just as they are? What if you prefer the status quo? This is a company telling us what to do—and the police and government will back them up, instead of the way it used to be."

I asked: "Should the government still make decisions when it comes to people's livelihood? Hasn't that been done to death?"

Auntie Yi countered: "Let's say you like your house and plot of land, for gardening. Let's say you want to keep things just as they are. But how did they get that way? Because of government policies meant to make everyone equal, or at least treat everyone fairly. What would you say is fair about this?" She waved her arm at the new road, at the spot her poppies used to bloom.

"People can choose whether to farm or do something else. They don't have to be farmers. That's fair, right?"

"You don't know how to plant anything, so it's easy for you to say," she replied. "It's true that some people no longer want to farm. But many people do, like San Jiu. When we farmed collectively, everyone depended on someone else, since we all worked together. Now, at last, people can work independently. But here comes Eastern Fortune, buying up and controlling our village."

Auntie Yi didn't farm, but she was taking the long view of things. She also sounded more philosophical about developments.

"I'm unhappy about these changes now," she said, "but people are always unhappy when things are new. They say they're unhappy, but really they're unsure. No one explains why the change is happening, and no one can imagine what it means for their family's future. I remember the introduction of 'mutual aid teams' in 1952, then 'agricultural production cooperatives' in 1954, then 'advanced cooperatives' in 1956. These were all stages of collectivizing the land and turning control over to peasants instead of landlords. Were people unhappy then? Of course! *Aiya wode maya!* They quarreled, they complained. And then what happened? Communes. Then the Great Leap Forward, and the famine. At every turn, people were unhappy. But unhappy people can change things."

In the New World, after two years of food shortages at Plymouth, the Pilgrims abandoned communal farming in 1623. Each of the settlement's households tended its own plot and kept whatever it grew. People worked harder than before, with women and children joining men in the field. The colony never starved again.

China's experiment in collective agriculture lasted nearly three decades before—as Auntie Yi put it—unhappy people changed it.

The policies introduced by the Communist Party after Liberation in 1949 winnowed individual farmers into groups. In 1954, after an estimated 800,000 landlords were executed for being "counterrevolutionaries," their land was redistributed to farmers. Auntie Yi's memory of the Land Reform

Policy announcement was eating the canned beef and lamb seized from landlords: it was the first time she had tasted the meats. Two years later China effectively abolished private land ownership, and farmers were organized into 790,000 agricultural cooperatives. Auntie Yi suspected that the former landlords' holdings were simply repainted as co-ops; the numbers nearly matched. The Party called its agrarian restructuring "hammering while the iron is hot," aimed at preventing the reemergence of the gentry.

Rice was first widely planted in Wasteland then. As we sat on her *kang*, Auntie Yi started to recount how the paddies were made before another thought interrupted the story. "Did you notice that the song 'On the Songhua River' mentions the Northeast's forests and coal and sorghum and soybeans, but no rice?"

The lyrics detailed more than Japanese occupation. They also memorialized a vanished landscape. "It's interesting," she said, after belting out a verse. "There's hardly any sorghum planted anymore, and more broad beans than soy, and the forest has mostly been chopped down, and not much coal is mined as before."

Uncle Fu looked away from the televised snooker to add, "Now the song would be about petroleum, corn, and rice."

"It was really hard to open the paddies, though," Auntie Yi said, picking up her previous thread. "We all helped out. We used a horse and sled to turn over the soil, then wore wooden shoes to flatten it, all of us walking back and forth, back and forth. Once the land started to be improved, more and more people were moved here. Our agriculture progressed from a 'beginning collective' to a 'mutual help collective' in 1955. It was for people classified as poor, lower, or middle peasants—not the rich peasants who had hired laborers or owned a bit of their own land. They were excluded, and reeducated."

That last word always sent a chill down my spine, but Auntie Yi was a true believer, and said it with pride. I asked what *mutual help* meant.

"If you have a horse, but I have more laborers in my family, we would exchange: your horse would turn over the soil with a plow, and my family would help you plant and harvest. That changed into the big commune, when we all ate together in a canteen, and when everyone had to bring their hoes and other tools to keep in the yard for anyone to use. We gave our wardrobe to make a table for the canteen. Wasteland became a village then."

"Nineteen fifty-six," I said reflexively, quoting the village stone. By 1958, all of China's co-ops had become "people's communes." The policy triggered the Great Famine, killing at least 20 million people; some estimates go as high as 45 million. Officially, the deaths were blamed on natural disasters, and the period was labeled the Three Years of Bitterness.

"All our personal food was confiscated during the collective times," Auntie Yi said. "We used to grind soybeans mixed with barley in secret at home. Everything was supposed to be for the commune. We didn't even have money. We were paid in work points. At the end of each workday, you had your score assessed and entered into a little handbook for each family. It was casually decided, actually. It wasn't a true commune: whoever had the power to decide the score earned the most points, or rewarded his family and friends. You knew the standard. If you did hard labor, people would murmur, 'Give him six points.' If it was really hard work, you could earn up to ten, even twelve. But the 'rich peasants' could only earn up to eight, and every night they would be reminded it was because they had exploited people in the past. That was our family, you know: my grandfather hired people after he migrated here on foot, starting out hauling grain on his back. And my father ran a granary out here. So I was marked. But really, I was lucky. The people who collaborated with the Japanese in Manchukuo got it the worst. Then you had to sit and eat together after all the points talk! You could have points deducted, too, if you didn't work or made mistakes. There's a saying that proves it: *dao zhao ba fen'r*—you work a whole year and end up owing eight points."

I said that I would not have lasted long.

"You would have talked too much and said the wrong things," she said, swatting my arm in a mock scolding. Then she became a cadre again: "Mostly I hated the points from an administrative standpoint. The system wasn't fair. By the time we got to 'advanced-level collectives' in the 1960s on our road to achieve socialism, we had a good village secretary. But of course he got transferred elsewhere, and we had to start over with new leaders."

That system remained. To advance in the Communist Party was not to stay in one post, like an American mayor working toward reelection, but to do well in one place, then get shuffled up a rung on the portfolio ladder: village to county, county to city, city to province, and so on.

"Whenever we had too much pork," Auntie Yi said, "they transferred that out, too."

It wasn't a saying. Memories often looped back to food. Uncle Fu stood up and, as he made for the kitchen, said I was staying for dinner. He made flash-fried garlic stems and pork over rice. "Eat," he urged me, even after my third bowl. "You haven't eaten enough. You're not full. Eat. Eat. Eat."

When Chairman Mao died in 1976, so did his dream of collective agriculture. By decade's end, farmers were allowed a small, personal plot to supplement crops raised by the village team. The work points system was abolished. "But at every turn, people were unhappy!" Auntie Yi said. "It's in people's nature to complain. But very few people complained when *da baogan* was introduced."

The term meant "the complete allocation of responsibilities," and the policy meant that individuals, like the hungry Pilgrims, no longer had to farm as a team. The change was born not in a ministerial meeting but in a farmer's home in the central China province of Anhui, where *The Good Earth* had been set. A corn-growing village named Xiaogang was starving, suffering under the nation's quota demands. Its residents dug up roots, boiled poplar leaves with salt, and ground roasted tree bark into flour. Entire families left their thatched-roof, mud-walled homes and took to the road to beg.

A farmer named Yan Hongchang, whose studies had ended at middle school, was the deputy leader of the village work team, overseeing production. But there was no production that autumn of 1978. During the Great Famine, a quarter of the county's residents had died. "We knew what it was like to starve, and we would rather die any other way," Mr. Yan later recalled.

On the night of November 24, Mr. Yan summoned the heads of the village's twenty families to a secret meeting. The village accountant was deputized as a secretary, and on paper torn from a child's school exercise book transcribed a seventy-nine-word pledge to divide the commune's land into family plots, submit the required quota of corn to the state, and keep the rest for themselves. "In the case of failure," the document concluded, "we are prepared for death or prison, and other commune members vow to raise our children until they are eighteen years old." The farmers signed the document and affixed their fingerprints.

Thus began China's rural reform.

Today a large stone monument to the pact greets tourists to the village. But in the spring of 1979, a local official who learned of the clandestine agreement fumed that the group had "dug up the cornerstone of socialism" and threatened severe punishment. Thinking he was bound for a labor camp, Mr. Yan rose before dawn, reminded his wife that their fellow villagers had promised to help raise their children, and walked to the office of the county's party secretary. But the man privately admitted to Mr. Yan that he knew, since the pact had been signed, the village's winter harvest had increased sixfold. The official told Mr. Yan he would protect Xiaogang village and the rebellious farmers so long as their experiment didn't spread.

Villagers gossip; farmers talk about their fields. Soon neighboring hamlets copied Xiaogang's model. News reached the provincial authorities, who were unwilling to punish farms that were, at last, producing food. Thus, they did not brand the abandonment of collective farming as counterrev-olutionary but instead endorsed it as "an irresistible wave spontaneously topping the limits once enforced by the state."

In Beijing, three years after Chairman Mao's death, Deng Xiaoping was opening China to foreign trade and liberalizing the economy. Yet originally he ruled against allowing "household farms," afraid that critics would again label him a "capitalist roader," for which he had been purged during the Cultural Revolution. However, the grassroots movement that began in Xiaogang made the decision for him. In a series of policies issued between 1978 and 1984, China formalized the Household Contract Responsibility System (colloquially called *chengbao*). It allowed families to farm their own allocation of land in exchange for turning a portion of their crops over to the state. What remained was theirs to eat, and to sell at unregulated prices. China's communes, brigades, and production teams were renamed as townships, villages, and hamlets, respectively.

Xiaogang was made into a living patriotic education base where a small museum displays a replica of the farmers' pact, since the original was lost. Exhibits praise the bold wisdom of its ringleader, Yan Hongchang, his cosignatories, and the Party. But not everyone bought the high rhetoric. "My father signed that paper because we were starving," Mr. Yan's son told me. "There was nothing heroic about it. He had no other choice. It was human instinct, trying not to die. It's strange the leaders want to celebrate survival."

The reforms continued: in 1984, fifteen-year leases were introduced for family farm plots—then extended to thirty years in 1993. The state stopped requiring grain procurement in 2001 and abolished all agricultural taxes in 2006.

Auntie Yi supported these changes. "But now people are unhappy here again. Why? Because it's not about farmland. It's our individual houses. I don't want to be a tenant of Eastern Fortune Rice."

"You'll own the apartment."

"But they're making me move. It's just a new landlord."

We stood in the July sun on the side of Red Flag Road, watching workers slather golden yellow paint on her house. "There's an inspection coming, now we can be certain," Auntie Yi said. "Whenever the garbage is collected from the side of the road and it's swept, that's when you know someone big is coming. This time they built a new road. How interesting." Three hundred yards ahead, a temporary fence went up at the dirt-road turnoff to San Jiu's house. A call to Frances taught me a new Chinese word: *po'te jin cun*. Potemkin village.

"The land distribution and how we farm it has changed over the years here," Auntie Yi said. "But our houses never did. We lived in one place. The homes themselves improved from mud to cement, but that's all. Your mom"—my mother-in-law—"and wife grew up where San Jiu lives."

She repeated her complaints. If you gave up your home and accepted an apartment, it became part of the collective, which would demolish it and lease the plot to Eastern Fortune for planting. The company would contract to pay an annual rent for the land you previously farmed. "But farmers don't just sell the rice. We eat it, and burn the stalks to heat the *kang*. In an apartment, we'll have to pay for heat. Now, the company said they won't charge for heat the first three years. That's deceptive. Do you expect to be alive three years from now? Yes? You'll have to pay for heat

then. We'll lose our vegetable gardens, our chickens—we'll become dependent on the company. Our house will be razed; there will be no going back."

Using rollers, the painters buttered her home.

"It looks nice."

"I have an idea," she said, ignoring my comment. "If we really want to
know what Eastern Fortune's plans are, you should walk in there and tell
the boss that you want to buy the company. See if the price includes the
office buildings, the greenhouses, the hot spring, and so on. Ask about the
land: how much is under contract now, and how much the company expects
to control."

I gestured at my mud-covered legs, frayed shorts, musty hoodie, and
thick beard.

"But you're a foreigner," Auntie Yi said dismissively. "Also, ask if they're
going to change the village name. Could that really happen?"

Twenty minutes before, her house was unpainted. Now one wall—facing
Red Flag Road—shone freshly yellow.

There is no such thing as a typical Chinese farm. The sizes, geographical
locations, and types of farms—dairy, livestock, produce, cotton, grain—are
as diverse as the number is large. China has 22 percent of the world's
population, on 8 percent of its arable land. Globally, it is the largest producer
of rice, wheat, pork, eggs, cotton, fruit, and vegetables.

But its new agricultural model is easier to summarize: the nation is
turning away from family plots to agribusiness, away from villages to
company towns.

Urbanization brought the challenge of reducing the number of farmers
while simultaneously producing the same amount of food. As in the developed world, the solution was to scale up. Only 5 percent of China's poultry
now comes from "backyard" operations producing fewer than two thousand
birds a year. Instead, three-quarters of chicken meat is produced by commercial farms processing over one hundred thousand birds annually. In the
province where *The Good Earth* was set, and where Xiaogang village's
family-farming rebellion began, the American agribusiness giant Cargill—
which, along with Archer Daniels Midland, controls 80 percent of the
world's grain trade—was building a poultry operation it calls Site 82, which

will breed, slaughter, and process 65 million chickens a year. The output would be "peanuts on the scale of China," the manager said. But the government sees it as a model for similar conglomerations of small farms, and a progression toward "high-tech, efficient and safe farming."

It is harder to monitor safety when a single shipment of food is produced by hundreds of farmers using different levels and quality of feed, antibiotics, and fertilizer. A 2013 government report said that 10 percent of China's rice could be contaminated with cadmium, a heavy metal that causes cancer and kidney failure. It enters the water supply from factory waste, but also from overfertilizing crops: cadmium is an ingredient in the popular fertilizer that San Jiu used on his field.

Farms were more than a workplace, however. In an era of soaring real estate prices, a rural house doubled as a social security policy. Young generations may have migrated to work in factories, but they could always return to their village. Or they could send their children away from a polluted city to be raised on the farm, as Frances had been, here in Wasteland.

Persuading older farmers—and their entire families—to leave that security behind was an obstacle in China's drive toward urbanization. The Party often first tested reforms before implementing them nationwide, as in the creation of capitalistic "special economic zones" such as Shenzhen city, whose model has since transformed other metropolises. In 2007 the central government ran two experimental programs in southwest Sichuan province that could prove as transformative for China's countryside.

The first program set up a "rural property exchange," where interested farmers could transfer use of their land to an agribusiness for an annual rent. This was formalizing what Eastern Fortune Rice was doing—with the central government's imprimatur—on a village scale in Wasteland. Individual households' land would be consolidated, mechanized, and managed by a company, instead of a village government loosely overseeing hundreds of family plots.

The second program allowed rural residents "free migration" into the city, giving them previously forbidden access to schools, employment, health care, and other social services. Since 1958 the household registration system (hukou) had divided Chinese into two strata: rural and urban. The chasm between the two broadened after economic reforms: urbanites earned over three times as much, and city kids were three times as likely to attend high school, and a whopping eleven times more likely to attend university. While China's urbanization rate reached 54 percent in 2013, migrants still officially classified as rural totalled a third of that figure. An estimated 250 million Chinese lived as second-class citizens in the nation's cities.

In the second Sichuan experiment, farmers would retain the right to their plots but could exchange their single-story houses for new apartments in the city, with access to its schools and hospitals. Their former homes would be razed, and the land planted. Consolidating a horizontal village into a vertical apartment block in an already-developed town would result in a net gain of cropland as well as urbanites. It was also similar to what Eastern Fortune offered in Wasteland, although its apartments were located in the village, not downtown.

The central government said the experiments were to test ways of equitably moving people off their farms. But it was also looking for measures to quell dissent against the current system.

China forbids local governments from borrowing to raise funds, so villages cannot sell bonds. Instead, they commonly set up development companies, which use village land as collateral for bank loans. Local debt skyrocketed to $3 trillion in 2013, equivalent to 58 percent of the nation's gross domestic product.

The lucrative deals, and corruption, that resulted from these land transfers caused protests—averaging more than five hundred a day—and headlines such as FARM SEIZURES SOW SEEDS OF SOCIAL UNREST. In 2011, in the southern fishing village of Wukan, three thousand residents attacked the government office after its secret land transfers were revealed. Village officials, in power for forty-one years, had pocketed the proceeds.

A comprehensive nationwide survey released in 2012 found that 70 percent of farmers were unhappy with their socioeconomic situation, with illegal land grabs their top complaint. A rural economist at the state policy advisory body likened tensions over the nation's income gap to that of Spain's on the eve of its civil war. It was an artful dodge: he also could have likened it to China's during its own civil war.

In Sichuan province, the Chengdu city government hailed its experimental program as "the first in the country to break down the long-term barrier hindering the free movement of residents; the first to let farmers enter the city without losing their land; and the first to eliminate inequality in education and health care between urban and rural residents."

Two weeks later the experiment was over. The rural property exchange market was shuttered, without explanation. The only news story I found on a government land bureau website reported that at its recent office party, cadres recited programs, sang snippets of regional opera, and performed a "nunchakus hip-hop skit entitled 'Joking about Land Use Planning.'" At night's end, "the song and dance 'Emancipated Serfs Singing by the Land Reserve Center' brought about a climax."

Another item was headlined: "Poker Playing Competition Closed Successfully." "After six rounds of fierce competition in 20 days, Gao Yang and Zou Mujin from offices of the bureau won the championship with seven victories in seven contests."

But unlike government ministries, private companies had to show their hand. Legal filings and license registrations were accessible to the public. On my *kang*, as Mr. Guan snored loudly in the neighboring room, I read Eastern Fortune's credit report, part of a due diligence dossier on the company.

The destruction of Auntie Yi's poppies aside, the company's hands looked clean: no pending lawsuits, no environmental fines, no muckraking reports of malfeasance. The details matched what the agronomist Dr. Liu had told me in her company office: Eastern Fortune was cofounded in 2000 by Wasteland's current party secretary, a man named Liu Yandong. It started as a small rice-processing workshop with limited facilities. The company's moniker was a blend of characters from the founders' names. Mr. Liu had bought out his partner. There were no shareholders, and his younger brother was the company's general manager. The only news items, from city, provincial and national newspapers, were positive. Mr. Liu was often quoted as saying, "Technically, we are a rice processor, not a rice grower. We provide seed free of charge to farmers, who plant the fields. Those who choose not to farm will have their land tended by laborers and receive an annual payment of 15,500 yuan [$2,530]. Our motto is: 'A stable company, plus farmers, plus technology equals green rice.'"

In 2003, some 2,000 farmers in Wasteland and surrounding villages had contracted their crop to Eastern Fortune. Eight years later the number reached 5,120.

"In the past, farmland here was divided into numerous pieces and contracted to individual households," Mr. Liu told a Jilin city newspaper. "At the beginning of 2011, the village representatives decided to consolidate the farms while preserving farmers' rights to it."

Mr. Liu did not mention that he—and his brother—were among the village representatives, only that "the decision was based on voluntary and legal principals and farmers will get compensated."

Auntie Yi disagreed. "Will anyone replace my poppies?" she asked, watching the road-widening work. "Do you expect me to trust a promise to pay me fairly for my house, let alone to better manage my village? I'm a retired cadre. I know all the policies, all the announcements. But I don't know if we have to move into those high-rise apartments. I told you to go to the office and say you want to buy the company. Did you do it yet? Walk in and get a meeting with the boss. He probably sits in the hot spring all day. Go look for him there."

The sun rose at 4:15 on a Sunday morning, and I was wide-awake to see it. All through the night, cement trucks shook my windows. The electricity had been shut off again. Workers raked wet cement onto the widened road, illuminated by spotlights powered by gasoline generators.

At six, a vendor's pedicab puttered past, calling out types of noodles and also "Seaweed strips for sale!" By seven a crew of men wielding brooms made of willow branches tied to a stalk of dried bamboo swept our driveway. Mr. Guan was still fishing, and I reflexively ducked away from the windows, feeling suddenly foreign amidst the strangers.

I went on a long run, reaching the Songhua River but not finding Mr. Guan. When I looped back through a hamlet named Zhang's Family Outpost, the man who sold me a bottle of water said that his Internet had stopped working and his cell phone reception was spotty. "We're expecting official guests," he said with a smile. *Muggy with a chance of motorcade.*

I turned at the northernmost end of Red Flag Road and ran toward home. Cars never slowed for me on this stretch; they swerved and sped away. But now a Land Cruiser, painted in green camouflage, slammed its brakes and reversed back in my direction. My stomach sank. I pulled out my cell phone and speed-dialed Frances. The diversion, I thought, would somehow render me invisible, or at least look too busy to chat.

Before Frances answered, the driver's tinted window lowered in a whir. A bull of a man—crew cut, aviator sunglasses, thick gold chain around a meaty neck—yelled in Chinese, "Stop filming!"

"I'm talking to my wife," I replied.

His mouth twitched slightly.

"Does that phone have a camera?"

"Nope. I'm cheap. Look." I showed him the old, basic model.

He sneered, the window whirred up, and the Land Cruiser sped away.

At Wasteland's intersection, uniformed policemen halted traffic, preventing anyone from crossing the road. I couldn't go home. Instead I sat in the sundries shop with the rest of the village. "Once the motorcade passes, we can leave."

"Who's visiting?"

"Wen Jiabao." China's premier.

"Incorrect!" a man playing mah-jongg said. "It's a general."

"Someone said it was the minister of agriculture."

"Hu Jintao came in 2006."

"It was 2007," I corrected, and added a brag: once I attended an official lunch for President Hu at the U.S. State Department. The villagers were not impressed.

"He came *here*."

"He ate *our* rice."

The names of other titles, of other officials, rang in the air. In the end no one could agree who was in the backseat of the black Audi that toured Wasteland. The car turned left, edging the concrete drying on the new half of Red Flag Road, and sped away.

At the start of 2013, China's most important policy announcement, called the Number 1 Document, said the central government would "encourage [individual] land contracts to flow to large-scale landholders to develop scale management."

The nation's patchwork of small, single-family plots were to merge into large, company-managed ones. The minister of agriculture said that "gradually transferring land into the hands of efficient farmers and developing moderately sized operations is the direction of the future."

High officials had seen farming's future. It looked like Wasteland.

CHAPTER 15

THE HALF-BOMBED BRIDGE TO WORKER'S VILLAGE

T HE MODERNIZATION OF agriculture followed a transformation of urban life. In the Northeast, the latter began in the 1990s with the shuttering of failing state-owned enterprises. Shenyang, 250 miles southwest of Wasteland, had once been China's leading example of the "iron rice bowl," or jobs that provided housing, health care, and education. One thousand factories operated here, manufacturing everything from bedsprings to airplanes. Employees lived in the nation's model housing project, named Worker's Village. Its three-story walk-up apartments fronted willow-lined roads with names such as Praise Industry, Celebrate Industry, Serve Industry, and Protect and Defend Industry.

I remembered its demise at the turn of the twenty-first century, when the wrecking ball thudded into the apartments, unemployed factory hands trolled for work holding signboards listing their job skills, and the social hall called the Worker's Cultural Palace was the domain of laid-off women. One had pinched my butt and said, "*Privet!*"

"I'm not Russian."

"You don't have to lie," she replied, in Chinese. "You can be frank with me. Let's dance."

She opened the padded door to the ballroom, releasing a burst of alto sax playing on the stereo. The windowless room was completely black; only the smell of her hair spray told me the woman was there. "It's ten yuan for three dances," she said. "You can put your hands anywhere you'd like."

Instead we sat in the hallway with six of her colleagues on a bank of orange plastic chairs usually seen in bus stations. Her factory had closed, and by day she cleaned hotel rooms. "I have a six-year-old son, and my husband is laid-off, too, so we need the money. I dance every night. The community government manages the dance. They earn five yuan for every patron who enters. That's the ticket price. We keep all the money we earn. It's better than nothing. Every bit helps."

"I've been doing this for six months, but it doesn't suit me," a woman said.

Another asked, "Where else can I earn money now? We lost our jobs and there's nowhere to turn."

"Why do farmers want to migrate to cities?" another woman said. "They have it easy compared to us. I wish I had land that could earn money forever."

Despite our surroundings, the women were cheerful and open, talking about how good life used to be, laughing, and taunting one another in dialect—"*Shuo sa?*" They were all mothers to young kids, and explained the shattering of their iron rice bowls to me in language that even a child could understand: the "bad men" took their jobs and one day they would punished for "telling lies."

My would-be dance partner led me upstairs, where the Worker's Cultural Palace computer-training classroom sat dark. Next door, three women in curlers rooted through cases of makeup in a cosmetology class. The lone person sitting at a desk in the English language school asked, in Chinese, what I wanted. I replied in English, but the man dismissed me with a wave. "I don't understand," he grunted. At my back he shouted mockingly: "ABCDEFG!"

The dancers did not deny that sometimes they did more than twirl. "We give our numbers to men if they ask, but most men just come to dance, and to be held. They're going through tough times, too." Back in the darkened dancehall, faces were indistinguishable, and the room had become something felt rather than seen: a mass of laid-off people grasping each other tightly, moving in circles to a wordless song.

Eight years later I revisited the area on a late-August weekday to find that most of the factories had been razed, replaced by luxury apartments. The old street names remained, however, so now people lived on Protect and Defend Industry Road in high-rises named About America and Napa Grove.

A group of well-dressed couples stopped waltzing when I stepped into the former Worker's Cultural Palace. A uniformed security guard asked me to leave: "This is a private club now. It's for people with money."

At a nearby Starbucks, the stereo softly played Chet Baker, and sitting amongst the imported American earth tones made me wonder how any of this indicated I was in Northeast China. The answer came at the door, when I reflexively filled my hoodie's pocket with thick napkins for use in the public toilet that still stood down the lane.

The Worker's Cultural Palace had become a private dance hall, and the former bank owned by the Young Marshal, Zhang Xueliang, had become the Shenyang Finance Museum, telling the "Story of Money." One room contained a bank note from every country—"Eritreans use nakfas," the guide intoned—while in a gilded chapel couples knelt on a pillow, kowtowing to Cai Shen, the god of wealth. In the final exhibit room, Chinese tourists posed for photos beside a replica of Wall Street's bull statue, and a smiling wax likeness of Bill Gates. "He is the living god of wealth," the docent told me.

Across town, in the Japanese-designed plaza facing the former South Manchuria Railway hotel, China's best-known statue of Chairman Mao faces neon ads for Coca-Cola and Hankook tires. The towering likeness was built at the height of the Cultural Revolution and shows Mao riding a flotilla of lantern-jawed proletariat brandishing wrenches and rifles while stomping Buddhist and imperial statuary. Stickers dotted its marble plinth, advertising employment agencies and retirement homes. LOOKING FOR WORK? WHO WILL TAKE CARE OF YOU WHEN YOU AGE? A middle-aged couple, dressed simply in color-faded clothes, entered the plaza. They bowed to the statue, clasped their hands in silent prayer, bowed again, and left a bouquet of cut flowers at Mao's feet. They had once lived at Worker's Village, they said, and had come to ask for help finding jobs. Saint Mao stood silent.

Only seven of the original 157 buildings remain at Worker's Village. The apartments still look inviting, especially compared to the anodyne units rising around them. Cement archways lead to wide staircases stacked with cabbages, boxes of pink geraniums hang outside large windows, and plots of tomatoes and green beans blossom in courtyards between the buildings, where blankets sun on lines strung between poplars.

One building has been transformed into a community-run exhibit. It is not a patriotic education base but an example of how museums can bring history to life instead of burying it under dates and death tolls. The displays show the past glory of Worker's Village through four apartments, re-created to reflect daily routines in the fifties, sixties, seventies, and eighties. Here is the bedroom of Mr. Ren, who moved to Shenyang in 1952 to work at the 3301 Factory. See his rotary phone, propane stove, enamel washbasins, spittoon, antimacassars, and sewing machine, evincing the advanced level of Socialist housing the village provided. Rare for China at the time, his apartment even had electric lights.

Today, however, the power was out, and I toured the two floors alone in darkness, using my cell phone as a flashlight. The museum was open four hours a day, staffed by a single volunteer, who charged no admission. The old woman said her neighbors collected the displayed items: old chopping blocks, coat racks, and the Manchu game *ga la ha* that used pig knee bones as dice. The pictures on old calendars in each room showed the evolution of home entertainment: a black-and-white television (1969), a boom box (1978), a videodisc player (1988).

The granary displayed ration coupons; the school held a blackboard whose chalked characters announced Lesson One: "Long Live Chairman Mao!" The walls of other rooms showed painted propaganda from across the decades, from Mao's exhortation "Dig tunnels deep, store vast amounts of grain, and avoid hegemony" to Deng Xiaoping's "In the future, do not forget what was learned in the past." Seen through the weak glow of a cell phone screen, the slogans looked like cave art from long, long ago.

Just as antiquated as the iron rice bowl was the notion of being assigned to live somewhere, as Auntie Yi's husband had been.

"I was never a farmer," Uncle Fu said as we sat on his *kang* in Wasteland. "I was sent here after the Resist America and Aid Korea War. This certainly wasn't my choice of places to live. I'm a southerner. But in the army you go where they tell you."

Uncle Fu was born in 1934 and enlisted in the People's Liberation Army at age sixteen. As a former soldier, he was the only villager who didn't think running was a waste of time; when he saw me pass on Red Flag Road, he would chug with his arms in place, making his oversize camouflage jacket sleeves flap, urging me on.

"When I was sent here in . . . 1957?—yes, it was 1957—I lived in a little wooden shack at the airfield. The Japanese had used it, but the runway was in bad shape, so we rebuilt it, and that fuel depot you can see out the kitchen window—it's still functioning. We had the granary and the fuel, which may have made farmers feel secure after the war, but as a soldier I knew it just made this place a target. Over here, this was all wasteland. Some grass-and-mud huts, like where your mother-in-law grew up, and your wife lived. There was no electricity, no water tap."

As Worker's Village's opened in Shenyang in the 1950s, villages such as Wasteland still looked as though they belonged to the feudal nineteenth century. One old house like the one Frances was raised in still remained, since converted to a storage shed. Its mud-and-straw walls were missing bite-size chunks, suggesting that a donkey had been nibbling away over the years. Black smoke scarred the dirt floor and interior walls, and the corrugated tin roof bled streaks of rust. Unlike in China's remade metropolises, I had never met anyone nostalgic for old buildings in the countryside. Not when they had looked like this.

"There were no paddies when I arrived here," Uncle Fu continued. "This area was all sorghum. I ate a lot of sorghum in the army; it tasted awful. Mealy and bland. It doesn't have fragrance, like rice."

He had arrived as Wasteland's paddies were being built. "There was no Red Flag Road then; it was all rice out here, and you walked along the dikes dividing the plots. Sometimes you slipped, and you went into the paddies. That upset me: we were living in a field, not a proper village. I hated winter, too. I've never gotten used to it, actually. The first year I had frostbite on my hands and nose. We were always hungry. There were wild chickens and hares here. I used to hunt the chickens: they were everywhere. You chased after them three times. By the third time they were too tired. I was young and in good shape, so I was the one sent to do it. When the chicken surrendered, it ducked its head into the snow. That was its end."

He paused and leaned close to check my powdered soymilk level. "I'll get you some more hot water," he said, rising slowly and shuffling to the thermos set by the window. It was an old-fashioned enamel kind whose large cork emitted a satisfying *tunk* when pulled and the steam escaped.

Uncle Fu talked slowly and softly—Auntie Yi was out on errands and couldn't interrupt him—and told me about his first encounters with Americans.

"My family is from below the Yangtze River, a village named Liangshan. It's southwest of Nanjing. It's very small. But the Japanese still went there in 1943 ... or 1944. It must have been 1943. They torched the whole village when I was a boy. You know, up here the Japanese behaved better. I dare not say they were good, but they needed workers for Manchukuo. In the south, their policy was called the 'three gones': Burn until the Chinese were gone, murder until the Chinese were gone, loot until the Chinese were gone. I was in elementary school at the time."

He took a sip of steaming soymilk.

"I saw my first American then. After the war was over, in 1945, some Americans came to help rebuild our village. They drove up on a tractor." His large brown eyes grew wide at the memory. "I had forgotten about that until now. The Communists liberated our village in May 1949. I volunteered for the army in October the following year, after the Resist America and Aid Korea war started. Every boy at my school enlisted— ninety-six of us from our village. We were between the ages of fourteen and sixteen."

Uncle Fu was then sixteen and away home for the first time, sent to Beijing to train in air force logistics.

"Near the end of 1950, we made it to the border, to the city of Dandong on the Yalu River. They gave us guns and whatever uniform was available. Mine was too big."

It still was, but Uncle Fu's gaunt frame made all of his clothes seem big.

In North Korea, he remembered camping in caves by day and marching through the night. "Once over the border, I could see American planes filling the sky. Frankly, I had no idea where I was; in war, you do as you're told and just think about surviving. We had Koreans in our unit; they had fought against the Japanese in the Northeast, then volunteered with the Communists in the Chinese civil war. We didn't know that Russia wanted

China to fight the Americans for them: Stalin was afraid of America! It wasn't until after the war that I learned that of the ninety-six boys who enlisted from my village, only six of us survived. I was lucky, that's all."

At war's end, Uncle Fu was assigned to Shenyang in 1953. "I knew your Auntie Yi's boss, and he introduced me to her, and then we got married."

I asked if it was love at first sight.

"En'e," he replied—dialect for "Sure"—surprising me with his candor. "Isn't it always that way for a man, when he meets the woman he wants to marry? I don't think that's true for women, though."

Auntie Yi's family was living in Wasteland, so Uncle Fu was transferred to work at the airfield in 1957. "Land reform had finished, so the land had been carved up and distributed to the peasants, but like I said, there wasn't much out here then. When the Cultural Revolution started, the Red Guards didn't have anything to destroy. But our family—my wife, San Jiu—they had a tough time because their ancestors had been labeled 'rich peasants.' I was a soldier, so the Red Guards left me alone, and I could stand in front of anyone they wanted to yell at. But they were ferocious. We didn't know who they were; they came from the city, and it was like an invasion. You can't even imagine it, seeing these strangers in the village, yelling at people. Really, I didn't understand what they were doing; to a soldier, it was completely without discipline."

I asked if there was ever talk of the army subduing the Red Guards—if, after surviving Korea, his unit didn't want to knock the teenagers playing at revolution into the paddies. Uncle Fu smiled. "It's logical to ask that now, but back then everyone was used to following orders—the military but also the farmers, since they had been commanded in the co-ops, then the communes. It was as if we were employees, waiting for the boss to tell us what to do."

Chairman Mao died at three o'clock on September 9, 1976. "A store in Lonely Outpost had a television, so the whole village gathered there. Can you imagine that, all of us standing there, trying to get a look? We all cried, and then someone would get tired and have to step away, so the crowd would move up a spot. You waited until someone got tired from crying, and then you could see the screen better," he said. "But I was genuinely sad. It was three days of silent mourning, and people really were silent. The next year Zhou Enlai died, and Zhu De died after that, but by then I couldn't cry anymore, even if he was the founder of the People's Liberation Army."

Uncle Fu didn't have a single photograph of any of this: his home village south of the Yangtze, his parents, his classmates, his fellow soldiers, his camps in Korea, his airport hut, or the construction of this house. "No one took photographs then," he said, shrugging. "They didn't start recording statistics or taking a census here until 1956, when Wasteland became a village and the administrative office opened. Before then this place had no records. Officially, our history begins in 1956. That's how I understand it. I arrived the following year."

Tunk went the cork thermos stopper, and he carefully poured hot water into my bowl. I wondered if Uncle Fu had ever seen an American up close in the war. His mouth fell. "I forgot to tell you! I was there when the American bombers took out the bridge in Dandong."

The city's name meant "Eastern Peony"; my wife had been named Peony in Chinese because her uncle returned from a trip to the Yalu River town the night she was born. I found this as ignominious as being named Fargo, but Uncle Fu said it linked her arrival to a journey, just like life itself: "When you have a child, put a character from this place in its name."

"*Waste* or *land?*"

He chuckled. "You don't have to ask me that."

Uncle Fu said the fight for the bridge in Dandong was the time he was most scared in the war. "The commanders said we were going to cross that bridge into North Korea," he recalled. "But during that battle, I couldn't imagine it."

You can stand on its remains; the bridge has become a patriotic education base, but one more muted than the museum perched on Dandong's hill, whose entrance greets visitors with that catchy ditty "Defeat Wolf-Hearted America." Its exhibits tell visitors that Chinese soldiers "took good care of every mountain, river, grass, and tree owned by the Korean people" as they repelled the "attack of U.S. imperialists and its running dogs." The War to Resist America and Aid Korea Museum is not for our friendship.

But neither is the minor industry in Chinese gloating that thrummed on Dandong's shore. Every half hour, from dawn to dusk, ferries motored halfway across the Yalu so tourists crowding the railings could snap photos of the North Korean town of Sinuiju. It showed rusting ships, fishermen in threadbare tank tops, and a man pedaling an old bicycle. Chinese passengers said:

"Look at how backward they are! So poor!"

"This is what China looked like during the Cultural Revolution."

"I hear they still use ration coupons to buy food."

"They must think we betrayed communism. But they must admire our development."

Only a generation ago, many Chinese cities looked nearly as moribund. The ferry made a wide turn, and we saw what the North Koreans face all day: cranes building high-rises, billboards advertising banking services, and roads filled with private cars. The War to Resist America and Aid Korea Museum. Along the bustling promenade: a row of telescopes, where people pay to stare at an empty shore.

They also see the black steel bridge that stops mid-river. Built in 1911, the former railroad bridge once linked Japanese-controlled Korea with Manchuria.

Now visitors can walk five hundred yards, halfway across the Yalu, where the bridge ends at an observation deck. Four concrete pilings draw a dotted line to the far shore. Tourists pose next to a disarmed bomb, and a plaque that says the United States bombed the bridge from November 8 to November 14, 1950. The story ends there.

But Uncle Fu had said he was most scared then.

In late 1950, the war had seemed all but over. North Korean troops had been pushed out of Seoul and back across the Thirty-eighth Parallel; United Nations soldiers occupied Pyongyang, and the North's air force had been destroyed. From his Tokyo headquarters, General MacArthur, commander of the UN forces, declared that his troops would be home by Christmas. Despite OSS reports of Chinese movements toward the Yalu River, MacArthur repeatedly asserted that China would not cross into North Korea. The Communists had just won China's civil war and inherited a crippled economy. Its army could not even invade Taiwan, let alone take on the United States.

Chairman Mao, in turn, saw that America's post-world-war commitments stretched from Berlin to Tokyo, and now into Korea. China could put four times as many men on the ground as the UN forces, which it did, nearly surreptitiously, in October 1950 by having them march at night and hide in caves during daytime. A sixteen-year-old Uncle Fu was among the 120,000 troops that flanked the American Eighth Army. An additional ninety thousand soldiers were en route.

Meanwhile, MacArthur had cabled Washington, D.C.: "The defeat of the North Koreans and of their armies was thereby decisive." In fact, the war was about to be extended another twenty months.

Until November 1950, UN forces had been fighting "under wraps," ordered to "stay clear of Manchurian and Soviet boundaries." American naval pilots, taking off from carriers in the Yellow Sea, could not pursue Chinese pilots in Soviet-supplied MiG jets or attack antiaircraft guns stationed across the border. This mandate created "MiG Alley," a zone of airspace along the Yalu River where American pilots played a deadly game of cat and mouse. Chinese fighters took off from Dandong's airfield, climbed to thirty thousand feet, dove with guns blazing on American planes, then darted back across the Yalu and safety. Among their targets was a young ensign named Neil Armstrong. Before he took one giant leap for mankind on the moon, Armstrong was shot down over Korea, evading capture and flying a total of seventy-eight combat missions before leaving the Navy at age twenty-two to become a test pilot.

MacArthur pressed President Truman to allow pilots to engage in "hot pursuit" over the Yalu. Truman, fearing China's entry into the war, instead prohibited any air strike within five miles of the border.

In his memoir, MacArthur wrote that these restrictions made him feel "astonishment" and "inexpressible shock." He told his chief of staff: "For the first time in military history, a commander has been denied the use of his military power to safeguard the lives of his soldiers and safety of his army."

MacArthur threatened to resign, but Truman—facing down McCarthyism, criticism that he had "lost China to the Reds," and a predicted Democratic defeat in congressional elections—relented on the five-mile exclusion zone. MacArthur could bomb the Yalu River town of Sinuiju, the seat of Kim Il-sung's fugitive government. In reply to his request to destroy its bridge, severing it from China, he was ordered: Only take out the span's "Korean end."

It is easy to imagine MacArthur's jaw clenching as he read the cable. Had the joint chiefs—including General Omar Bradley, commander of

Allied forces in western Europe during World War II—forgotten how difficult it was to level a bridge from the air? The flooring itself was easy to drop, but also easy to replace. Even when poorly defended, taking out a bridge by plane required multiple low, pinpointed bombs at key supports. Furthermore, because the United States "did not want to be in the wrong war, at the wrong place, at the wrong time, with the wrong enemy," General Bradley and the Joint Chiefs authorized the Yalu River bridge mission only on the condition that American airmen attacked the structure on the perpendicular, not by the more effective approach of lining up their planes along the bridge's axis and releasing their bombs.

The pilots would have to fly into a hail of antiaircraft flak and Chinese fighters, and try to hit the bridge on a pass. At a preflight briefing, an admiral told his men: "Our naval pilots have been given a most difficult task. Our government has decided that we cannot violate the air space over Manchuria or attack on Manchurian territory regardless of the provocation. If such attacks were made, the world might be thrown into the holocaust of a third world war."

On November 8, American B-29s used napalm and incendiary bombs to level 60 percent of Sinuiju. Sixteen other cities were hit as well. "All of North Korea would be cleared in ten days," MacArthur promised. "Unfortunately, this area will be left a desert."

In history's first all-jet air battle, Chinese planes intercepted Americans targeting the Yalu bridge. Remarkably, no pilots on either side were downed. Neither was the span.

The next day Navy pilots tried again, with Panther jets hitting the bridge under the cover of propeller-driven Corsairs, which fired at the antiaircraft guns. From twenty-seven thousand feet, through unrelenting flak, "we came down in a high-angle attack, probably around in a 70-degree dive," a pilot recalled. "I remember I went down on my target with my wheels down. You did that in a Corsair for high angle dives in order to keep your speed down. Otherwise you'd get up to too much speed and you couldn't use your flaps as the speeds were so fast you'd just blow them right off. The landing gear was designed to take the high speeds encountered in steep dives."

The bridge remained standing.

Back in the United States, Harry S. Truman followed the results of the 1950 congressional elections aboard the presidential yacht. Truman was "drunker" (on bourbon) and "more dejected," his official biographer wrote, "than anyone had ever seen him." Earlier that week he had been the target of a botched assassination attempt by Puerto Rican separatists, and now the election brought further woe: Republicans had gained five seats in the Senate and twenty-eight in the House.

President Truman missed the next day's meeting with the Joint Chiefs (his memoir noted only that he was "unable" to attend), where they concluded that MacArthur wanted an all-out war with China. They favored a political solution to Korea, such as the one proposed by Great Britain, that UN forces retreat and the countries stay divided at the Thirty-eighth Parallel. General Bradley later wrote that they should have stood up to MacArthur then. "We read, we sat, we deliberated and, unfortunately, we reached drastically wrong conclusions and decisions. We let ourselves be misled by MacArthur's wildly erroneous estimates of the situation and his eloquent rhetoric, as well as by too much wishful thinking of our own."

MacArthur had refused to salute Truman at their last face-to-face meeting, on Wake Island the previous October, but the president had not disciplined him, writing: "You pick your man, you've got to back him up." Nor did he confront the general after he wrote the House Republican leader to criticize Truman's management of the war, having ignored his suggestion of opening a second front in China using Nationalist troops from Taiwan. Now MacArthur would not call off attacks on the Yalu bridge even after Chinese forces had realized the Americans could not cross into their territory. They had even stopped camouflaging their antiaircraft guns.

American pilots flew headlong at them, soaring low along the spine of the bridge, then banking up hard to avoid entering Chinese airspace.

Still the attempts continued, into the gales of flak and ninety-five-mile-per-hour crosswinds. After six hundred sorties, the "Korean half" of the Yalu bridge finally fell on November 14, 1950.

Five days later, the river froze.

Chinese forces, including Uncle Fu, marched over the ice to join the war. For MacArthur, "the wine of victory had turned to vinegar." The conflict would last for another twenty months, but MacArthur wouldn't be there at the end: Truman sacked him for insubordination in April 1951. A cease-fire would divide the Korean Peninsula at the Thirty-eighth Parallel. The war solidified Chairman Mao's control of the Party and China.

It also claimed his eldest son, killed at age twenty-eight in the November air raids by a napalm bomb dropped from a South African plane.

Under a withering sun on the day I visited, a group of South Korean tourists toting umbrellas crowded the end of the Yalu River Broken Bridge, getting to within five hundred yards of that forbidden shore. I stood apart, imagining propeller planes diving at seventy degrees with their landing gear down, dodging dogfighting jets. Antiaircraft guns flashing along both riverbanks. Water spraying. Thunderous explosions. Against a twisted steel support, tourists posed beside the bridge's plaque that explained only: *During the war, the United States bombed it from November 8 to November 14, 1950.*

CHAPTER 16

BEGINNING OF AUTUMN

I N AUGUST, WASTELAND ripened green. The rice nearly reached my hips, and its broadening stalks cloaked the paddy's water. Walking down Red Flag Road felt like cutting through a plush carpet that needed to be combed for frogs. Their pulsing croaks reverberated from the fields.

It was the solar term named the Beginning of Autumn, and, San Jiu said, the most stressful time for a rice farmer. Harvest was only thirty days away, and he walked through his plants checking for diamond-shaped yellow lesions made by a fungus called rice blast. Historically, it was the grain's deadliest pathogen, and one that could destroy an entire crop. "It's always a threat," San Jiu said, "but it usually appears about three-quarters of the way through the growing season."

He checked each plant, whose fuzzy seedpods crumbled like damp chalk when cracked. "One more month," he said. He pulled weeds from the irrigation ditch, explaining that soon he would drain some water to strengthen the rice's roots. "Now the days are hot and the nights are chilly. When the days cool down, too, we can harvest."

I noticed that he never added the Chinese equivalent of "Knock on wood."

"Superstitions are useless," he said. "You have to do the work."

But every day fresh fruit appeared before his home's statue of Shennong, the bald, long-bearded icon representing the founder of Chinese agriculture. "That's not a superstition," San Jiu said, seriously. "That's a tradition."

Mr. Guan had no icons in our house, or much of anything. No ticking clocks, no alarms, no television or radio. It was the quietest place I had ever lived: my cell phone ring often startled me, which, when I yelped, Mr. Guan thought was hilarious. I changed its setting to silent.

My runs had lengthened to ten, then twelve, then fourteen-mile loops. Compared to the surrounding hamlets, Wasteland looked kempt and cared-for. The official's visit had left the mementos of houses painted harvest yellow, the clean cement of widened Red Flag Road, and solar-powered streetlights. They were the area's first, and while people said they were good, villagers didn't go out much after sundown anyway, because that was time for dinner, television, and bed. Auntie Yi eyed the blue-and-red bunting adorning each lamppost. It advertised Big Wasteland Rice and Shennong Hot Spring.

"Eastern Fortune paid for this road, so now it's their billboard," she said. "What we need is a speed limit sign." It was true: the improved road looked like a runway. Cars tore down it as if attempting to get airborne. It was unsafe for bikers and pedestrians, and I diverted my running route north, onto dirt roads.

Someone had already tagged a few of the poles with graffiti praising Falun Gong, the tai chi–practicing sect that the government had banned in 1999 as an "evil cult." In Wasteland, however, spray-painted stenciled characters proclaimed it "good." It was the only graffiti I ever saw in the village, and soon it popped up on other lampposts and the metal staircase that ascended the new bridge over the high-speed train tracks.

Also posted: a notice announcing Eastern Fortune was hiring men between the ages of twenty-five and forty-five to work in the polishing shop, loading sacks of grain and running the machines. Mr. Guan got the job; his shift began at eight. He was pleased, because he could still fish before clocking in. Just like that, he said, he had a second income. Eastern Fortune was good.

The company planted seedlings to replace the mature Manchurian ashes cut down to widen Red Flag Road. While the easement between the new roadbed and her home had narrowed, Auntie Yi was pleased to see room enough for new poppies. "I'll plant the seeds in September," she said, "and they'll germinate in spring. Poppies are strong, you know. They self-seed, so only a few packets should fill in this stretch of road. I'll plant pink and orange ones." She pointed to the spot before her home's yellow wall where the flowers would bloom. Outside of Keats ("Through the dancing poppies stole / A breeze, most softly lulling to my soul") I doubted anyone held poppies in such high esteem as Auntie Yi. "They're beautiful. They're elegant, not like a sunflower." She made a face. "Sunflowers have a production purpose. Poppies are just flowers."

"They make opium."

"Incorrect! That's illegal now. Lin Zexu threw all the opium into the harbor." We had, as often happened in conversation, stepped back two centuries, to the faraway southern wharf where the defiant act had occurred. Time travel was real when I boarded Auntie Yi's train of thought. After touring the first Opium War, we returned to Wasteland. "Poppies make you smile when you look at them. There aren't many plants like that." She said this while staring at lush acres of rice running unobstructed to the forested foothills in the far distance. That, she disagreed, was not scenery. "It's food."

Turning right out my driveway, I walked fifteen minutes east past paddies and Eastern Fortune's new rice polishing shop, a metal-walled warehouse that faced a billboard showing rows of apartment buildings and the legend: WITH ONE HEART, EVERYONE BUILDS THE NEW VILLAGE. Cranes and dozens of migrant workers helped, too. I passed their temporary dormitories and turned right down a narrow lane that I remembered as a dirt path that ended in paddies. Rows of blue tin sheeting—the kind that concealed construction sites—ran along the lane, blotting out the abandoned mud-walled farmhouses. Unlike urban architecture, nothing in the countryside was ennobled by its age. Tools rust, weeds climb, roads sink, roofs collapse; nature always wins.

On the single-lane bridge fording a foul-smelling stream choked with trash, another billboard announced: REVERE GENTRY RIVER TRANSFORMATION PROJECT. The accompanying schematic showed planted willows along the widened water's promenade. I looked around the sign: fetid canal. Back at the sign: clean river. Around the sign: feces. Back at the sign: lotuses. Time travel, again.

The shells of the apartments were already built. Fresh steel-grey paint coated the four-story walk-ups, even though the driveway was still unimproved mud and the apartments had yet to be wired for electricity. The buildings looked nice, comparable to new construction in Jilin city, or even Beijing. A posted notice said that in this first phase of development, Eastern Fortune spent $2 million to build six hundred units into which it expected villagers to move.

But the apartments felt cramped compared to a typical farmhouse. Narrow windows faced not foothills and fields but other apartments. Rural homes usually had a wall of south-facing windows. The apartments, however, were dim, with low ceilings. Load-bearing walls divided the space into smaller rooms, unlike a farmhouse's great room, where life took place atop the *kang*. There would be no *kang* here, but central heat.

And stairs, too. Even the ground-floor apartments were accessed by a small flight of steps, which could be an impediment to the elderly, especially during winter. Plus they could no longer "absorb the earth's energy" by living with their feet on the ground.

An "oldsters' leisure hall" was being built, along with a covered parking lot and exercise yard. The development backed against the company's first stab at housing construction, the rows of single-story homes that replicated traditional design and included gardens and areas to dry and store rice seeds. When the village chief had offered to rent me his house, I blanched, seeing the structure as a soulless cement bunker. But compared to the new apartments, it looked practical and inviting.

Mr. Guan listened to my field report and said, "I like the new development. I'm looking forward to moving there." He had signed the agreement. "Why do you think this house is so run-down?" he asked. "I'm not going to put any money into fixing it up when they'll tear it down to plant rice."

"When?"

"When they tell me to." He saw my face fall and added, "Don't worry. If we have to leave before your lease runs out, you can live with me in the new apartment."

His family had also agreed to contract their rice plot to Eastern Fortune, choosing to receive an annual rent payment. Mr. Guan had gone full Eastern Fortune: it would farm his land, swap his house for a new apartment, and pay him to work in the shop. He showed me his uniform, a red canvas jacket with the company's name stitched on the left breast. The item would soon become as ubiquitous around Wasteland as the blue Mao suit had been. Only San Jiu's generation wore that now.

"Pretty soon you'll be spending weekends soaking at the hot spring," I teased Mr. Guan.

"*Wo cao!*" he cursed. "I've never been to that place. That's for people with money."

"That's what everyone says at first. Then it's one soak, and you're on the path to ruin."

He said the greater danger to his morality was the nightly mah-jongg game at the corner shop. Fishing meant going to bed early and missing the action, but he would hear the amounts won and lost the next day. "It's easy to get addicted," he said. "You don't just want to win the game—you want to beat a particular person who pisses you off."

The reasons could include: money, family, love, work, and conflicts therein. Or heard/said things about the above. There were no secrets. "My sister hates coming out here now," he said. "It's obvious. People talk about her. She's unmarried, she moved to the city, she has a foreigner living in her old bedroom." He watched me laugh and added, "Don't tell anyone how much rent you pay to us, OK? We just tell them we're doing you a favor, because your family lives here, and they had no room for you, and you teach at the school for free. No one needs to know about the money. It will make them gossip more."

It was more convenient for him, he said, if villagers thought I wasn't a tenant but having an affair with his sister.

"People say that?"

"No," he reflexively replied. "Maybe." He quickly changed the subject to fish.

That weekend, dump trucks again woke me before dawn, rumbling through Wasteland. Our power went off. "They're fixing Red Flag Road," Mr. Guan explained.

"They just finished fixing it."

"Maybe they're making it even wider."

I caught the first bus to Jilin city, queued for a ticket, and boarded the high-speed train to the airport to catch a flight to Frances. The adrenaline of made connections, of continued momentum, of beating the obstacle course of Chinese logistics—*Push to the front of the line! Lug as little as possible! Don't look in that bucket!*—carried me from the ticket counter through the metal detector, up the escalator, down the gangway, onto the plane. As we ascended, I looked for Wasteland out the window. But from far away the villages all looked the same.

The following week, Auntie Yi fumed on Red Flag Road.

"That's what Eastern Fortune Rice did while you were in Hong Kong! I was going to plant poppies in that space!" She pointed with disgust at a stripe of green sod. A strand of gray hair spilled from her bucket hat and down her tanned cheek. "Now I'll have to wait until the grass dies. Or just dig it up and put the flowers in anyway. They'll know I did it. But this is village land, not their land. Look at that!"

We stared wordlessly at Wasteland's first lawn.

Typically for a Chinese conversation, Auntie Yi slipped the bad news in only after asking about my trip to see Frances. "Is she pregnant yet? No? Well, San Jiu had a stroke."

It had been minor, she said, and now he was resting at home. "Don't disturb him," she advised. "He's in a terrible mood. He's rarely sick, let alone experienced something this serious. Tomorrow morning he'll go to the clinic for medicine. Go sit with him there."

I ran the mile to his house at 6:00 a.m. only to find that San Jiu had biked to the clinic. I ran there. Young nurses in starched white uniforms asked me the usual questions—*American, Year of the Rat, 1.86 meters*—as I roamed the hall, looking in doors for San Jiu.

He lay in a room with four platform beds, each occupied by a man on his back, tethered to an IV line. A ceiling fan pushed the limpid air, and flies buzzed against the screened windows facing the village street. The horns of rumbling dump trucks bleated as they passed, sending plumes of dust into the room. When the saline bag emptied, the patient yelled, at the top of his voice, "*Huan yao!*" ("Change medicine!")

San Jiu's eyes lit up as I said hello and patted his arm; there was no hugging in Chinese families, even after a stroke.

"*Mei shi,*" San Jiu said, when I asked what happened. "It was nothing." While out in the paddy checking for rice blast, he had felt "strange." Two fingers on his left hand went numb. "I hoped it was a cramp," he said. But when the sensation remained, he walked a mile by himself to the clinic. The triage nurse recognized his symptoms and called a doctor. An ambulance took him to a Jilin city hospital for a CT scan and further tests. He showed no lingering effects, but was to come to the clinic three times a week to receive an infusion of rehydration formula mixed with medicine. San Jiu did not know what kind. "*Mei shi*," he repeated. ("No big deal.")

A man with a hand bandaged in white gauze slung around his neck asked where I had been. Another man, who had taken a liquor bottle to an eyebrow now sutured shut, shouted, "*Huan yao!*" A starched nurse entered and said, "Our clinic must look really poor to an American." I replied, truthfully, that the clinic looked well-supplied, attentively staffed, and affordable, even for a farmer. But no one believed me.

I wondered how much San Jiu's medical care cost and how I could let him know, in a roomful of people, that he should not worry about the bill.

Paying in China represented more than a financial transaction: merely picking up a restaurant check could lead to tableside scrums, climaxing with hand-slapping dashes to the register to toss down money first. Paying was a show of respect—and a deposit in the ledger of favors that balanced relationships. As a *laowai*, a foreigner, this account was all but closed to me. San Jiu had known the men in the room his entire life. He had lived through six decades of history with them. Through marriage we were family, but in situations like this I remained an outsider.

After I asked about the bill at the front desk, the clerk said the account had been settled. At lunch later that day, San Jiu's cousin, who ran a local dumpling house, relayed the news that San Jiu had canceled our weekly dinner. "He told me to tell you it's not convenient."

"I told him he doesn't have to cook. I'll bring takeout from his favorite restaurant, the Korean barbecue."

"It's not convenient."

Why? Was it about money, about face, about a joke I made, or something the clinic staff had said? I was baffled, and would have preferred San Jiu call me *shagua*—moron—as he often did, and say what I had done wrong.

I carefully mentioned the encounter to Auntie Yi. She clucked and said, "Everyone calls San Jiu *qiuzi*—slippery. That's been his nickname for decades."

I had never heard it before.

"You can never tell what's going on with him," she said. "Just show up for dinner and pretend nothing happened."

I sat with him during his next appointments—flattering the nurses, humoring his wardmates—then did as Auntie Yi had instructed, arriving at his house for the meal carrying offerings of peaches, pork, walnuts, and chrysanthemum tea. Nothing was explained, but that night I ate dinner seated next to a hale and friendly San Jiu on his *kang*, munching flash-fried pork and garlic stems while kids ran in and out, the door slammed, and the Pekingese tried its best to be heard.

In mid-September the shadows lengthened on Red Flag Road, the foothills' grass dried to a sandy brown, and the paddies turned yellow. At Wasteland's elementary school, the children wore jackets at recess, and the blackboards cautioned against the coming frost of the solar term called White Dew. PREVENT HAND, FOOT AND MOUTH DISEASE. Warnings that winter brought the biggest change in temperature could not be far behind.

For the first time since summer, I shaved, so kids wouldn't want to paw and pull their furry teacher's face. As I passed our intersection's corner shop, its owner said hello and added, "There's been a Libyan walking around here with a black beard."

I was incredulous: another foreigner, let alone one from North Africa, had never been to Wasteland. "Auntie, that was me. I wasn't cleaned up. Now I shaved."

The woman narrowed her eyes at me and said, "Really, Teacher Plumblossom? That other guy was much better looking than you."

My runs increased from fourteen- to sixteen- and then eighteen-mile loops, a route that took me further north along the Songhua to the foothills, which seemed to keep receding. The course now edged past drying cornstalks and sunflowers drooping from the weight of their seeds. Although it was autumn, it felt like a second spring: I ran under bright blue skies around pouncing grasshoppers and fiddling crickets, past blossoming thistles and golden dandelions. The fields showed the same colors: green stalks and yellow crowns. After the paddies had been drained, frogs sunned on the drying mud, fattened from their summer bug binge.

Mr. Guan's teenage niece said I looked "unhealthy," which in the countryside meant "thinner." At night she began bringing over her family's leftovers in an oversize stainless steel bowl—piles of rice and tofu and potatoes—that made me feel like a well-kept pet. After patching its cracks with duct tape, Mr. Guan fired up the *kang*. I stuffed rice stalks into its fire vent, curled against the bed's warmth on my belly, and dozed like a contented dog.

Low on cash, I walked to the crossroads and pressed the buttons on the Agricultural Bank's ATM. As a Peace Corps volunteer the previous decade, I had had to fill out multiple tissue-paper slips, then queue at a bank counter and all but beg the teller to release funds from my account. A few times the bank told me to come back later, as it had run out of cash. Now the transaction took one minute: Wasteland's machine dispensed yuan, still making me feel like I had found a magic portal into money, eight thousand miles from its source.

A man named Mr. Wang managed Wasteland's bank. He was short and plump and always smiling, though Auntie Yi said his grin concealed marital troubles. I asked how she knew, and she replied, "Everyone knows everything."

Mr. Wang said that the bank recently tried a pilot program to lend money to farmers to improve their equipment or to start a side business. "The problem is that they have no collateral," he told me. "They can't put up their assigned plot of land. We decided they could use their home, but that isn't worth much. The loans were restricted to such small amounts. Really, if a farmer wants to buy a bunch of chickens and build a coop, he's not going to come to me and fill out an hour's worth of paperwork to borrow 300 yuan. He can borrow that from family and friends. What this village needs is more threshing machines. They cost 20,000 yuan [$3,200]. That's double the cost of an average house here."

For the past week, Uncle Fu had urged me to buy a fleet of harvesters. "You can rent them daily," he said. "Your business would be excellent. Now people wait their turn for the machines to come. There's a list."

"But outside of this season, the machines would need to be stored, and maintained."

He considered this. "On second thought," he said, "Eastern Fortune will soon be responsible for harvesting everything."

The company rebuilt the arch at the start of Red Flag Road. A new billboard announced that Wasteland was an "eco-agriculture industrialization demonstration region." San Jiu couldn't say what that meant, nor could Mr. Guan or any other farmer I asked; none of them had even bothered to read the sign. Then I remembered Dr. Liu, Eastern Fortune's agronomist, explaining that the company had first labeled its fields a "technological experimental site" because the government had favored those adjectives in 2000. Now the terms had changed, and the company's scope had expanded.

Eastern Fortune's workers, clad in matching red jackets, surveyed the ripened fields with reaping knives, selecting seed grain for the next year. The rice reached above their waists, and the men moving amidst it looked like swimmers in a yellow sea.

The push was on to harvest before Mid-Autumn Festival, a September family-gathering meal that brought the year's highest demand for the freshest rice. Farmers reaped and threshed across Wasteland. San Jiu finally gave in to his family's concerns for his health and hired a two-man crew. Their harvester mowed his paddies in a single afternoon.

The drawback to harvesting by machine was that, once the grain was bagged, it needed to be dried and sold lest it turned rancid. Grains cut by hand, however, left the rice kernels attached to their stalks, which could be kept longer and sold when prices rose. But cutting by hand was back-numbing work, done with a forearm-long scythe. The tool was light and sharp, and the strain came not from pulling the blade through the stalks—yanking as much as slicing—but from bending low to cut just above the roots.

Both processes sent plumes of chaff into the air, clouding the horizon, powdering our clothes, and caking our eyes and lips. But in contrast to the machine-harvested fields, the hand-cut stalks were tied into sheaves and piled in shaggy mounds the shape and color of kneeling lions. Wasteland's prides filled the fields, facing the setting sun.

After threshing the kernels, the rice was spread to dry on cement driveways and lanes—but not on Red Flag Road, or the hot spring's parking lot, filled as they were with tourists' cars. In our driveway, for the last time, Mr. Guan smoothed the rice harvested from his family's plot. Next year the grain would go to Eastern Fortune and be fed into a dryer, then milled and polished by Japanese machines. But now Mr. Guan stepped carefully around his grain's golden patch. He turned it over with a rake, moving as meditatively as a monk in a Zen sand garden.

At September's end, a flatbed truck deposited a sedan-size pink granite slab beside Red Flag Road. Drivers about to enter our hamlet now saw, in carved characters painted red: *Wasteland Village*. On the reverse, in smaller characters painted green, I read: *Brief Introduction*.

The rock said the village was founded in 1722, during the reign of Kangxi, the Manchu emperor who established the Jilin city shipyards. The next carved date was a century later, in 1823, when a temple was built to a goddess that attracted revelers from across the plains to its New Year's carnival.

The following entry leapt ahead another hundred years, to 1931, when Japanese occupied the region. From 1946 to 1947, the Chinese Nationalists took over administration, falling in 1948 to the Communists. *In 1956, it became a village.*

I expected history to end at that familiar line. But three more dates were listed below it. Kneeling in the squishy new sod to see them, I read that in 1958 Wasteland became part of the Ninth Platform People's Commune. In 1962 its name changed to the Wasteland Battalion.

I was on all fours now, tilting my head low and sideways. The final entry said: *In 1984, Wasteland was named a village yet again.*

Like its fields, Wasteland's history spun through seasons, cycling back to the start.

CHAPTER 17

DALIAN'S DISPLAY CASES

T HERE WAS ONE last museum I wanted to see, located at Manchuria's southern tip. For the past century, the cities of Dalian and neighboring Lüshun (Port Arthur) passed between Russia, Japan, and China, while the Northeast's rail traffic had funneled down to its terminus. History and artifacts had accumulated here over time, I assumed, like residue caking a drain.

After four hundred miles, the slow train from Wasteland dropped me at Dalian's station, still the austere white stone building erected during Japanese occupation. Axial roads connected the dots made by roundabouts, leading me to the former South Manchuria Railway hotel. The century-old structure showed its age: the concierge asked if I would share a cold-tap bath, as the building's pipes kept bursting, and few rooms had functioning plumbing.

The hotel was part of a chain of Japanese-designed buildings ringing the city's central plaza, previously crowned by a memorial for the soldiers who died in the Russo-Japanese War. In her memoir a young daughter of a Japanese clerk recalled watching a parade through the plaza in 1932 to celebrate the founding of Manchukuo:

"The marching high school students following their school bands waved Japanese flags in the daytime, but at night they held up lighted paper lanterns, which, with big red dots painted on a white background to represent the Japanese flag, lit up the streets like waves of thousands of illuminated red balls flowing into the park."

The memorial was gone, and glassy office towers overshadowed the plaza's squat, stone colonial buildings. The Japanese memoirist's former house, on the terraced avenues of Singing Crane Heights, was among those being renovated by nouveau riche Chinese. The villas still showed—as she had recorded—cream-colored walls with red-tiled roofs, "as bright as a children's storybook illustration." Her former Japanese elementary school yet sat "quietly in the shadows of tall acacia trees at the edge of the park," only now it taught Chinese.

A sliver of the Russian district survived. Set behind the train station, the block of wooden two-story homes had been repainted in pistachio and lemon yellow and christened Scenic Russian Street. On the pedestrian shopping block, umbrella-toting Chinese tourists bargained over binoculars, Baikal cigarettes, and vodka.

A scrap of the original settlement, built in 1903, hid behind the stores. Slipping between panels of blue tin sheeting, I stepped squarely into the past, and a puddle of sewage. The onetime mansions had rotting wood frames and weather-beaten brick; lean-tos filled former gardens. A neighborhood built for one hundred families now held ten times that number.

A group of elderly women chatted beneath the archway of a former carriage house. One invited me inside.

"Did your ancestors live here?" she wondered as the stairs creaked under our weight.

Sometimes, she said, foreigners walked slowly through the neighborhood. Middle-aged people with white skin. Often they could not speak Chinese. She didn't understand Russian. The sun was setting, and bats looped in the dusk. I asked the old woman what the people did.

"They just look," she said, motioning to her walls.

And then?

"And then they walk away."

Back on the other side of the blue tin sheeting, Dalian was filled with beach-holiday tourists, moving in pairs or groups. The worst part of traveling alone was eating solo amidst a crowd. The sun was setting, and women in dresses and heels stepped from doorways to whisper, "Massage?" in English, followed by "Lady bar?" I missed the tamer pitches of Jilin city, where aunties selling hosiery innocently attempted: "Hello socks?"

On Tianjin Street I popped into a bookstore to buy a city map, passing a shelf of new releases that included *Practical English for Badminton*, parenting books titled *Don't Be Scared, My Child* and *Failure Is Not an Option*, before stopping to flip through *Fifty Selected Letters Between U.S. Presidents and Their Beloved*. Who knew that Rutherford Hayes was such a softie? The book ended with a missive to Bill Clinton: "Dear Handsome. I feel disposable, used and insignificant."

Me, too, Monica. Me, too.

In one long tracking shot of lonesome road fatigue, I ate oyster pancakes and chicken-heart kabobs from street vendors, boarded a public bus to Starfish Beach, bought a cold beer, took off my shoes and socks, and walked over the cold, grainy sand into the Yellow Sea. Standing calf-deep in the pulsing waves, I felt homesick for the paddies of Wasteland.

Remarkably, Dalian has no civic history museum/patriotic education base. In the 1990s, when the city was run by the reformist mayor Bo Xilai, it strove to present itself as China's most modern metropolis, the "Hong Kong of the North." An oceanfront scenic drive that had been open only to officials was made public; beaches were cleaned and linked to town by a new trolley; statues of revolutionary martyrs were replaced by ones of soccer balls; Dalian was then home to the country's best team. Mayor Bo had promised a city free of traffic jams, adding left-turn signals (then a rarity in China) to stoplights, and creating a corps of horse-mounted traffic cops. The all-woman squad, dressed in tight white blouses and navy skirts, drew media attention from around China, and the world. Dalian was not your average Chinese city. Dalian was different. Its annual festival was a Fashion Week.

Mayor Bo built a museum not to the city's variegated past but to its future. Set near Starfish Beach, the white columns of the Dalian Modern Museum echoed the Japanese design of Dalian's train station. Mayor Bo was said to have vetted the plans himself, right down to the degree of shine on the black marble floors. He was the son of a famous revolutionary general and raised in the system. He knew that museums were, in essence, advertisements for the Communist Party. But Dalian's would pitch development instead of orthodoxy.

I had visited in 1999, its inaugural year. "Welcome to the future," the smiling docent had said then. The future looked simulated. The docent whispered encouragement at video screens as I used a joystick to steer a tanker into the city's port, sped a car down empty streets, and soared on a flying carpet above its coast. From this perspective Dalian shrank amidst its rolling hills. My carpet rose higher, away from the Modern Museum's displays of tomorrow: Romantic Beach City, City of No Traffic Jams, Fashion City, Soccer City, Seafood City. Who wanted to see Dalian's past? The screen showed only a boundless, cloud-free sky.

Mayor Bo's makeover campaign brought foreign investment, a UN-Habitat Scroll of Honour Award for greenswards and affordable housing, and accolades for transforming what had been an industrial port into a tourist draw. After seven years running Dalian, Mayor Bo was promoted to provincial governor, then to China's minister of commerce, then appointed to run China's largest city, a southwestern Yangtze River town named Chongqing. In 2012 the city's police chief fled town and sought refuge in the region's American consulate, alleging that Bo's wife had murdered a British businessman over a broken business deal. She confessed and received a suspended death sentence. Prosecutors charged Bo with bribery and abuse of power as mayor of Dalian. In 2013 he was sentenced to life in prison.

So it was not surprising that the Modern Museum's new director was scrubbing the building of Bo. The mounted policewoman mannequins went into storage, as did the flying carpet simulator, UN award, and soccer balls. (The tycoon who owned the city's team had been charged with bribing the former mayor, including gifting his wife a $3 million villa in the south of France.) Gone, too, were the few South Manchuria Railway artifacts, including rusting signs and station bells.

Instead, I looked at a room filled with traditional Chinese paintings and another of cloisonné vases. The museum's four floors swallowed these small displays; even the exhibit of National Significant History Themes—paintings and sculptures depicting "Feudalism," "Privation," "War," and "Liberation"—felt dwarfed.

"The Modern Museum served its purpose," its newly appointed director told me in his gallery-size office. "Even before Comrade Bo met his troubles, I hoped to change the museum into a true museum, not a public relations campaign."

I sank in a plush chair adorned with an antimacassar. Steam rose from the porcelain teacups set wordlessly on the long polished mahogany table before us. I regretted wearing shorts.

The museum director, an officious middle-aged man named Liu Guangtang, spoke rapid-fire Chinese. He pointed at my bare legs and said, "You're wet."

"I didn't pack a change of clothes."

"It's raining out."

"That's why I was late. I'm very sorry."

"Did your driver get lost?"

"I took the public bus."

Director Liu's sixty-year-old face broadened into a smile. "Where are you staying? The Nikko? The Shangri-La? The Conrad?"

"Home Inn," I said. It was China's equivalent of a Motel 6.

Director Liu shot me a grin, keeping the laugh within. "You're a cheapskate!" he exclaimed. "Come, come, come, let's have lunch. You need to eat. Do you like sushi? There's a very good place next door."

Ten minutes later, we sat side by side with our shoes off. "No drinking during work hours," Director Liu said to his menu. He ordered barley tea.

I had traveled to Dalian to meet Director Liu because for thirty years he had run the history and art museum in nearby Lüshun (Port Arthur). I was curious what Manchuria's upheavals looked like when viewed through a display case, changing the exhibits with every shift of the political winds.

Lüshun's museum was particularly vulnerable to revisionism. After sinking the czar's navy off this coast and winning the Russo-Japanese War in 1905, the Japanese transformed Port Arthur's former officers' club into evidence of its appreciation for Chinese culture—a colonizer's PR campaign not unlike the Dalian Modern Museum.

"You've never visited the Lüshun Museum?" Director Liu asked between bites of yellowtail.

"The last and only time I went to Lüshun was in 1999. I was picked up by the cops and fined for being there without a permit."

Director Liu laughed. "Yes, that was a scam they used to run then. Where did they find you?"

"Exiting a public toilet."

He snickered. "Did you pay? How much?"

"I bargained them down to 200 yuan and made them take me to the post office to wire the fine so I'd have a receipt for an expense claim."

Director Liu exploded in laughter. "Very wise! You're a cheapskate!"

His assistant scampered to settle the bill, and he dispatched me to his former post with her, saying I should "return with questions." A staff car took us twenty-five miles down the coast along a scenic, snaking two-lane road and into a long tunnel that ejected us into Lüshun. Manicured lawns led down to the waterfront and naval yard. I recognized the latrine where the police had busted me. Old buildings got razed in China, but not old toilets.

"There's no profit in tearing them down and building new ones," the assistant guessed. "Public toilets are free."

Our driver stopped at the center of town, a tidy grid of three-story masonry buildings that made a bookend with those lining Harbin's cobblestone street, six hundred miles north. I stepped into the former South Manchuria Railway hotel where for three months the Japanese had hidden Puyi before bringing him to Changchun to install him as sovereign of Manchukuo in 1931. The hotel looked like its staff had departed with him; cigarette butts and stiff roaches carpeted the creaking wooden floors. No plaque marked Puyi's former room.

At the Lüshun Museum entrance, I crunched over a driveway of groomed pea gravel. "It looks like we're in Vienna," I said, and the docent agreed.

"The Japanese wanted to show how civilized they were when they took over the city from Russia," she said. "This building was unlike anything in China—or Japan, even." It reminded me of a Hapsburg palace. Tall, arched windows lined both stories of its unadorned marble façade, bracketed by towers resembling rook chess pieces. Only the surrounding cypress trees looked Asian.

Inside, we—the only visitors on this rainy Tuesday—passed through twenty galleries showing a *Colonizer's Greatest Hits* collection of Chinese civilization. Ancient bronzes! Oracle bones! Sanskrit sutras! Silk Road mummies! Paintings of Genghis Khan! Delicate Qing ceramics! The museum's sixty thousand objects were housed in chandelier-lit rooms in tall, polished walnut cases inlaid with chrysanthemums: the Japanese imperial crest.

Once again I was struck by how much of the past one can enter—and touch—in Manchuria. Next door, in the former Japanese army headquarters, I ran my finger over their maps of Manchukuo. There was the First Pass Under Heaven through which the Manchu stormed the Great Wall

and all of China, and there was where the Willow Palisade made a wish-
bone over the region that had peaked just above Wasteland. Here was
Manchzhuriya Station and the railway to Vladivostok. There was Harbin,
and here was Port Arthur, renamed Ryojun after Japan sank the czar's
fleet off its coast. Changchun became Xinjing—at map's center—the
capital of Manchukuo. Over here was where a young private named Akira
Nagamine was sent to defend the border, and there was the town where
Japanese mothers left their babies on the Songhua riverbank. Here was
where Hal Leith floated down into a cabbage patch to free POWs, and
over there was the Yalu River's broken bridge. The red You Are Here
dot marked the city of Dairen, soon renamed Dalian, where a man named
Director Liu waited in his museum office for a cheapskate wearing shorts
to return with questions.

I asked him how, over the decades, the Lüshun Museum had managed
to escape damage, or looting, or eviction, or even remodeling? Had an army
never bivouacked there? Had no stray bombs ever fallen? Had the Cultural
Revolution's Red Guards somehow forgotten that there, in sleepy Lüshun,
was a treasure chest filled with examples of the "Four Olds"—customs,
culture, habits, and ideas—they sought to destroy? Had Premier Zhou Enlai
placed a phone call ordering Red Guards to leave the Lüshun Museum
alone? After hearing that apocryphal anecdote repeated at heritage sites
across China, I had always wanted to ask a museum curator if it was true.

Director Liu smiled. "That's a popular story, but it's not what happened
in Lüshun. We crated up all the priceless artifacts and put them in storage.
We emptied most of the display cases. Then my staff and I painted revolutionary slogans on the building's façade, strung up some red banners, and
locked the front doors. I came to work every day during that time, going
in through a side entrance, waiting for the Red Guards to come. When
they finally did, they wanted to smash the statues outside, but the staff
had already put barricades around them. Then they wanted to come inside.
I told them they were too late, the place had been gutted. I handed over
some comparatively worthless artifacts, which they made a show of smashing, then left."

Director Liu didn't sound boastful or even proud; he spoke in the tone
of a foot soldier who had survived being drafted to war.

"I spent my entire career, my entire life, protecting that museum and everything inside," he said. "In the final analysis, I love my country, and the meaning of that is that I am an historian. I love China's history, all of it, good and bad, glorious and low. The Lüshun Museum—its grounds, its building, its contents—represents so much of the Northeast's unique history, and Chinese history."

It was the first time I had heard an official speak of history in an endearing and not bombastic tone. "What are museums for?" Director Liu asked. "Are they advertisements? No. They are living stories of what our ancestors created."

Now tasked with transforming the Modern Museum into a lowercase modern museum exhibiting art and artifacts, Director Liu said that the one thing he wished he could have brought from Lüshun was not its collection but the tall standing cabinets that displayed it. In their glass a viewer leaning close to see a relic often was startled to notice someone staring back: the faint reflection of his or her own face.

CHAPTER 18

FROST'S DESCENT

T HE DEW ON the rice straw piled against our home froze at October's
end. Around the outhouse, the flies buzzed languidly. For the first
time all year, I could swat them. "The flies have fighter genes from the
days of resisting the Japanese," Frances said via Skype, "but no one can
defeat the cold."

Mr. Guan admitted that he preferred spending his days at his new
workplace instead of at home. Eastern Fortune's warehouse was centrally
heated, whereas our bedroom windows bled frigid air. He suggested buying
a new roll of duct tape to patch my *kang*. "This will be the last winter
spent in this house," he said, sounding relieved.

My morning walk to school had me pulling a sweatshirt's hood tight
against my ears. I imagined Wasteland's version of the mistral gathering
force in Siberia. "Prepare to weep and be grievously distressed when the
wind blows from the north," a traveler to Jilin wrote in 1903, "for you are
about to suffer an agony of nose and eyes and finger-tips not easily
surpassed." Now it puffed in short, chilling bursts, building endurance for
its winter-long marathon across Manchuria.

Past drying cornfields not yet cut for silage, I finally ran the ten miles
to the foothills. Up close they looked smaller than they did from home.
The road ended in a smoldering garbage pile. After a summer of training,
that was the finish line. From out here I couldn't see Wasteland at all. On
the run home, a strong breeze stripped a copse of poplars, showering me
in a confetti of yellow leaves.

The only reminders of summer's colors were the cabbages drying on fences. Stacks of dried rice stalks rose next to the homes they would heat through winter. The fields showed mud. Frogs burrowed into the fallow paddies to hibernate until spring.

Auntie Yi stood on Red Flag Road, staring in disgust at the latest poppy prevention. Over the sod stripe, a work crew had erected a thin wall, five feet tall and painted harvest yellow. In red characters, it said: Build a New Socialist Countryside.

The workers had told her the wall was to protect her home from car accidents. Speed bumps would have been more effective. Vehicles tore down the improved road so fast that you could see the drag on their bodies. For the first time Wasteland had large-scale roadkill. Unfortunate voles and frogs never saw what hit them.

"This wall will also conceal destruction of our homes from passing cars, too, if we have to move to those apartments," Auntie Yi guessed. She studied the wall, and I thought she was reading its painted slogan like a fortune. Instead, she grimaced and said she would plant her poppies along the wall's base. She eased down on both knees and started digging.

Often a cold rain would send me sprinting toward shelter, which was hard to find on the open landscape. After a cloudburst halted a run, I waited under the overpass that bridged the train tracks. The sleek white express running from Jilin city to Changchun whooshed by, moving too fast for passengers to read Wasteland's station sign. Most passengers had lowered their window shades anyway.

The platform sat empty. The station's salmon-pink walls looked pretty in the rain. It was Wasteland's brightest and cleanest building, though weeds began swallowing its disused storage sheds, and the entranceway had turned to mud. A rusting sign said Public Telephone. Farmers—and their children—had cell phones now. Under the new overpass, I read spray-painted phone numbers for well diggers, more stickers proclaiming that Falun Gong was good, and a poster showing the blisters caused by hand, foot and mouth disease. Why did I always look?

The rain turned to rice-size hail.

I ran to the clinic, pushing through double doors with decals that said Open 24 Hours and Wishing You Good Health. The nurse said that San Jiu had just left, and I found him across the street at a table, watching Chiang Kai-shek wring his hands over his failure to dislodge the Japanese from Manchuria. He would be forced to unite with the Communists.

"I know how this soap opera ends."

San Jiu said "*Uh*" for hello.

As the television blared, we shared a plate of *chun bing*, the Northeast's burrito, pinching chopstickfuls of sliced scallions, pickled carrots, and fried spicy pork onto thin, oily wrappers. We didn't order rice. A cooker full of the staple sat plugged in on a sideboard, and we could fill our bowls as we wished. There had been no celebration at harvest's end, no gathering to eat the crop's first bowl. When I asked why not, San Jiu said, "It's just rice."

He stood with some difficulty and shuffled across the restaurant to grab a horse blanket folded on a chair, which he then wrapped around my shoulders with another "*Uh*," adding, "Don't get sick."

Sitting with him in the empty restaurant, saying nothing, clicking chopsticks and crunching into the scallions as the television blared military commands and gunfire, I reminded myself to savor the moment. San Jiu had been my constant, the unchanging variable of my life here. Now that time was slipping away.

I asked about the harvest, and he rattled off the yield and prices as quickly as if he were repeating a phone number. The land produced more than he had expected, and wholesale prices were up, though so was the wholesaler's markup, which San Jiu predicted could be 50 percent when it hit the shelves for consumers. "*Zhang*," I replied.

"You don't have to say it," San Jiu said. "Increase, increase, increase. Everything costs more. China has too many people."

After harvest, the village was reduced by two. In another rainstorm I sheltered under a tin portico over a home's front door. A boy I recognized from the elementary school ran out under an umbrella, yelling, "Teacher don't stand there, don't stand there, Teacher!" Between gasps he said the home's exterior had been painted red because a woman's body was being stored inside, until her funeral. I flinched, realizing the front windows were painted over, too, save for a cross-shaped opening. "Let's go," the boy urged, "before her ghost attaches itself to you."

"What about you?" I said. "Why wouldn't the ghost cling to you?"

"I'm a kid!" the boy yelled.

"So what? Do ghosts hate homework? They don't want to go through school again?"

The boy pulled at my arm and said, "Stop joking. We have to move, before it's too late." He handed me the umbrella, and we huddled beneath it on the walk to his house.

The following week, I woke to the sound of a *nazi* (pronouncd *nah-zuh*), the long horn that produced a sound reminiscent of a grown-up kazoo. The instrument was played at weddings and funerals, accompanied by a gong and drum to scare away evil spirits. The music boomed from a home down a dirt lane that I had never visited. Mr. Guan said the deceased woman had been eight-six, with a loving family who would sit vigil with her body, lying in situ for at least one night, and perhaps more. He was going to the wake. "If you come, make sure you don't say 'Nin hao' in greeting," he advised. The words, used for "Hello," literally meant "You are well." Instead, I was to say, "*Nin buhao*," or "You are not well."

I walked with him to the house, but stopped in its yard. I had never met the departed and didn't recognize her family's name. Suddenly I imagined San Jiu lying in state, and a stranger stepping over the threshold, introducing himself to the bereaved. That the stranger was a foreigner, prone to disrespectful, face-losing faux pas, made the scenario even more upsetting.

Mr. Guan said I was talking logically, but this was an emotional event. "Come show your face," he said. "Don't take notes; you don't have to write about it. If you're uncomfortable, I'll tell the family you have to be somewhere. I know the ways." I could just be, and not record. Mr. Guan led me inside the family's house, and closed the door.

In the final week of October, when the fortnight of Frost's Descent approached the Beginning of Winter, the police called, telling me to appear at the station. My stomach sank; in Beijing such a call had resulted in a lengthy plea to remain in my courtyard home, which the police had insisted wasn't safe. It was, but they had allowed me to live there only after I taught them a list of swearwords in English, so they would know when a foreigner was cursing them. That horse trade wouldn't be much use for a cop in Wasteland.

I had never even seen a policeman out here until the official's summer visit, when an officer had halted Wasteland traffic for the motorcade. The village's two-story brick police station was painted white with blue trim just as in Beijing, though its parking lot was filled with drying corncobs and a pair of wrestling puppies.

The clerk directed me past windows whose plaques said:

BIRTH REGISTRATION

MARRIAGE REGISTRATION

CORRECTION OF ERRORS

"Wait at the last one," she instructed.

The officer, his uniform clean and pressed, called me "Teacher Plumblossom" and apologized for asking me in. He looked as old every other cop I had seen across China, a perpetual forty. They never seemed to age. The man said that the village chief had reported me as living with Mr. Guan. Was it payback for not renting his house? I would never know, but according to a national regulation, foreigners had to register when lodging at hotel or in a home. "In urban areas you have to do it within twenty-four hours or you get fined," the officer said. "But in the countryside you have seventy-two hours. How long have you been living in Wasteland?"

"Seventy-one hours," I replied with conviction.

"*Uh.*" The officer smiled.

I exhaled.

He directed me to a desk where another officer sat at a computer. I expected her to fill out the postcard-size tissue-paper registration form by hand, but instead she opened a Web browser, logged in, and asked to see my passport. Entering its number produced my photograph on the screen.

"There you are," she said.

Now a cop in any far-flung station had access to a database of every identity card. "Here's your visa," she said, clicking a tab. "It shows that your last entry came last month, when you crossed the border from Hong Kong into Shenzhen."

"I was visiting my wife."

Living in the countryside—free of surveillance cameras, checkpoints, security screening—made me forget China's bureaucracy and its rules. Out here, I had never given paperwork or asking for permission a second thought. Just as, on a trip to see Frances in Hong Kong earlier that summer, I had neglected to check when my Chinese visa expired. The previous day, it turned out. I had to miss my train back north and apply for a new one.

In the police station, the officer stopped typing. "There's a field to enter a house number, but we don't have those out here," she said. "I'll say you live in Wasteland." My address was just a place name, like Santa's.

The officer made small talk, asking why I didn't yet have a child. She wondered what I was really doing in Wasteland, alone. Her tone changed from warm to icy: Was I a missionary? "You must be a missionary. Do you understand that proselytizing is illegal? Understand? What religion are you? Can you prove you're not affiliated with a church group?"

I pleaded innocent. "Enter my English name into Baidu."

On the popular search engine's Web page, the officer saw pictures of my dilapidated Beijing courtyard, and snapshots of me teaching English to retirees in the neighborhood. News items in Chinese described the book I had researched there.

"Oh, you're just a writer," the woman said, sounding relieved. It was the first time I had heard someone say that in China.

"Let's talk to the boss," Dr. Liu said, pulling out her cell phone. Eastern Fortune's agronomist was leading me through the hot spring's greenhouses, reeling off statistics from the harvest. After growing six acres of rice at its founding, the company had just harvested 1,200 acres. "The boss can tell you what we're planning next." She put her phone to her ear. A "*Wei!*" in greeting, followed by a series of "*Uhs*" in rising inflection settled the matter. "He'll meet us in the garden." She led me past banana trees, under grape trellises, to a thatched-roof pavilion and wicker chairs. Recorded birdsong filled the air. Dr. Liu stooped to pick a ruby strawberry.

Liu Yanfeng stepped through the plants and shook my hand. He was Eastern Fortune Rice's general manager, the second-in-command after his older brother, the company's cofounder. Boss Liu motioned to a carved wood table and said, through a self-effacing giggle, "Sit down, please," in heavily accented English. "That's about all I remember how to say," he admitted, switching to Chinese.

Boss Liu looked the part: barrel-chested, with black crew-cut hair carpeting a round, ruddy face and a pug nose. "I'm a simple guy," he said, pulling with thick arms at the T-shirt he wore belted into black slacks. "I wear these clothes every day, unless I have a business meeting."

Two waitresses appeared bearing plates of peeled bananas, watermelon, and strawberries. "We grew these here," Boss Liu said, lighting a cigarette. He smoked Red Pagoda Golds, which cost more than the Red Pagoda regulars, but not as much as a pack of Pandas. They were a brand popular with bosses—not ostentatious, but not proletarian, either. I declined his offer.

"That's right, I see you running all the time." His arms mimed a jog. "I like to run, too. I wanted to talk to you about organizing a race here. A marathon, maybe."

"It's a perfect place to run: flat, little traffic, places to get water. You would have a hotel and hot springs at the finish line."

Boss Liu smiled. "Yes, let's talk about that. I'm in charge of promotions. The other day, Zhang Yimou was here filming a commercial for us." He named China's most famous film director, the man who staged the opening ceremony of the 2008 Beijing Summer Olympics.

"He is a good friend. It would have been nice if you had met him. Next time."

I nodded, remembering that Northeasterners were known as champion exaggerators. Boss Liu mentioned a famous pop star. "He came here last year. I sang a song with him."

I thought of Auntie Yi's order to proclaim my intention to buy Eastern Fortune Rice in order to learn its true worth. Boss Liu looked far too savvy for that ruse. He told me to ask him anything, calling me his *gemen'r*—his bro.

"Will everyone have to move out of their homes and into the new apartments?"

"The problem that the central government wants to solve now," Boss Liu said, suddenly officious, "is how farmers can generate a second income. We've tried the production team model of agriculture. That didn't work as well as the Household Contract Responsibility System, which we've used since 1984, actually 1983 here in Wasteland. We were piloting reforms even then. I was born in 1972 and remember that time."

I said we were the same age.

"Brothers!" He smiled, sliding the plate of sweet watermelon closer. "Have more. There is no shortage.

"The current system worked much better. Families here could farm a piece of land and earn a living. When our house made 10,000 yuan [$1,641] in a year for the first time, we felt like we were prosperous. Not rich, but stable. Now that's not enough—not when you have a child to put through school, or a car to buy, and other daily expenses. People want to generate a second income. Out here, we only farm less than half the year. And that's a second problem: Who is going to plant the fields in the future? People our age don't want to farm; they want to be in cities, making as much money as they can. No one wants their child to farm. This is an urgent problem."

Boss Liu stubbed out his cigarette, replacing it in his mouth with a slice of watermelon. Between crunching bites, he slurped, "Our company—you know how it started, right? Now we have eleven enterprises under the original brand. It began as a village enterprise, and the village party secretary is on the board of directors."

"Your brother, the company's cofounder."

Boss Liu nodded. "Our goal is to lead Wasteland to prosperity."

"Will everyone have to move out of their homes into the new apartments?" I asked again. "Or will they have a choice to stay?"

Boss Liu lit another cigarette. "We formed a holistic mechanized collective," he said. I looked to Dr. Liu for help.

"It means cutting out manual labor."

"'Liberating the laborers' is how we say it," Boss Liu corrected. "This is where Chinese agriculture is going, and we were among the first to experiment with it. It's why the leaders come visit: to see and encourage this model. By farming collectively, we have a lower overhead cost. The central government subsidizes some of it: we buy the equipment and pay a family 13,000 yuan [$2,133] annually to lease one *shang* [1.6 acres] of their land. The government provides another 2,500 yuan [$410]. It's a three-year contract at those rates, adjusted the next cycle if the price of rice changes. A family has guaranteed income and can generate secondary income through other work."

Boss Liu saw my mouth forming the question again.

"The central government likes this model," he continued, "because a collectively sown crop can be better managed for safety and grown more efficiently. Farmers shift off the land and the younger generation can find other work that contributes to national growth. Risk is shifted away from the farmers and village government and onto the shoulders of companies looking for a return on their investment."

I opened my mouth.

"I'm going to answer your question," he said. "Improving farmers' living environment is also a goal. If they are not working the land, why do they have to live on it? They can move to a high-rise building with central plumbing and heat. Have you seen the new apartments we're building? Those are for the farmers. The former farmers. It's true that many people are not ready to accept a move into those buildings. Our job is to ease their worries and continue to develop the village so they will be willing to make the move, because they will see that their quality of life—their happiness index—will rise if they live there, such as having access to health care in the senior center. They can depend on receiving help. People will help them."

"Many people enjoy having a garden to raise their own vegetables," I said.

"In the future, they'll want to buy better-quality ones," he replied. "Is this good watermelon?" he asked, pointing at the plate. "Better than any other you've had in October?"

"Yes, but watermelon isn't usually eaten in October—"

"Now it can be," Boss Liu interrupted. "In the city, people go to Walmart and buy any fruit or vegetable year-round, imported from all over China and even the world. We can eat pineapple today, and apples, and mangoes. Shouldn't farmers eat like we do? Instead of cabbage all winter, and only cabbage? I grew up eating cabbage, and those days are behind us just like my parents' generation no longer has to live on sorghum and *wowotou*," the rough cornmeal cakes.

Boss Liu had gathered steam, and I appreciated his willingness to talk frankly. Developers in China rarely discussed their plans. When I asked what Wasteland would look like in five years, Boss Liu leaned forward on the table, rocking on the balls of his feet in eagerness to reply.

"You won't recognize this place in five years. You're a teacher, so let's start with the kids. What about their schooling? Yesterday I signed an agreement with the principal of North China University in Jilin city. They'll move their affiliated elementary and middle school out here to a new campus we'll build. That's how we bridge the urban-rural gap. Now farmers want their kid to go to school in town, so they move away, our population decreases and gets old, and before you know it, our village is dead. That's happening across China."

One-quarter of China's villages had emptied since 2000. The nation targeted an urbanization rate of 60 percent by 2020, an increase of 100 million people. But migrating to a metropolis would not mean an instant upgrade in living standards. The government forecast that by 2020 only 45 percent of China's overall population would be granted city-dweller status, with access to social services such as schools and hospitals.

Boss Liu had a better idea. "We'll bring the town out here," he said. "We'll build a modern campus run by city-experienced teachers. If the students test into the nation's top universities, they'll go there, but if not, they'll have guaranteed enrollment at North China University downtown. It's known for its foreign language department and also traditional Chinese medicine studies. Both degrees will help them find jobs.

"I'm also working on other ways to grow our population so people won't migrate. This is a big issue in China now. The cities are filled with migrants, and the central government wants urbanization to happen at the village level. 'Don't move to a city, build a city.' We'll do it here. First, we can merge the area's villages so our population number is higher. We could probably have 30,000 people total in fifteen years, instead of 2,000 here in Wasteland and a few thousand more in Lonely Outpost, and so on. A higher population can attract investment, because the work pool is larger, and the central government would help support infrastructure costs.

"The urban real estate market is saturated, and city people have nowhere to invest their money, because there are limits on how many apartments you can own. At the same time, city people want to come to the countryside to relax on the weekends. The logical next step is to develop real estate here. We'll build a resort village like they have in Europe. That will require a supermarket, so I have plans for that, and also a stadium, and a theater."

"It sounds just like the city," I said, watching Boss Liu nod. "Why would people buy a vacation home in an area that looks like where they live during the workweek?"

"A lake," Boss Liu replied. "We're going to build a big lake, and beside that, a hill. We don't have hills out here, right? It's totally flat."

"The foothills are nice. Have you been out—"

"So I'm building an artificial hill," Boss Liu continued. "The lake will have boats on it in summer, and in winter people can ski on the hill. We will be at the forefront of agricultural tourism."

I told Boss Liu it was a terrible idea. It was neither renewable nor sustainable, and Chinese consumers faced an array of destinations across their enormous country and, increasingly, abroad. I didn't say that he sounded like a little boy playing make-believe in a sandbox, building a magical world named Rice Land.

"You're wrong," Boss Liu said, smiling. "I'm telling you, I just returned from Hong Kong, where I found an investor for the entire plan. His company will invest; we'll provide the land and get the approvals from the government. Officially, this will all turn into a development zone."

The designation would bring government financing for new roads. "We want an expressway to link us to Jilin city, so we'll only be twenty minutes away, not an hour," Boss Liu said. "I want a road eight lanes wide, nothing less. And the old airport? That can be a logistics base where cargo airlines can fly in fresh seafood. We can fly out fresh flowers. I've signed a deal for the flower's greenhouse location. No one grows fresh flowers up here; they're all imported from the south. We'll be leaders in this sector."

I said nothing.

"I heard that you're from a village in America."

"A small town, yes. In Minnesota. Near the Mississippi River. It's cold, like here."

"What does your town look like now? Like Wasteland?"

I had to admit that it resembled much of what Boss Liu was dreaming. Freeway noise filled my childhood home, where my sister now lived, and the surrounding farmland sprouted only malls and McMansions. The town was a tony suburb of white-collar workers commuting to Minneapolis, with an expanded high school that resembled a college campus. The lakes remained, but the remaining farms mostly grew fresh flowers in greenhouses.

Boss Liu beamed an I-told-you-so grin.

"We could be sister cities," I suggested. "For our friendship."

Boss Liu loved the idea.

"I don't want to get rich myself," he said abruptly. "I want all the people from where I grew up to share the fortune. That's what I want to do next. That is to let my farmers have the same life as I do. Someone's writing a television screenplay about me. It will surely get made. Everyone will watch it, because people love success stories."

"You said 'my' farmers."

He ignored me, continuing: "After we complete the macro-level stuff, we'll build two hundred hot-spring villas for farmers to use. That way everyone can enjoy the hot spring."

"Separate from this hot spring."

"Correct. Farmers don't feel comfortable coming here. And we're going to build a big canteen for the village, so in two or three years' time we can all celebrate the Lunar New Year together, like we did in the past."

"In the commune."

"Only now we'll have a spring gala. I'll invite the best singers and dancers to come here."

My head swam with the contradictions. Farmers would become urbanites, but still celebrate the new year together as a village while keeping to their side of the hot spring. A cargo airport and freeway. A made-for-TV movie. It could be called *My Farmers and Me*. "Let's schedule a meeting," Boss Liu suggested. "I really want to talk to you about what farming in America is like, and its most important characteristics."

Subsidies and corporations came to mind. Instead I said what my lawyer wife had impressed on me: that the right of due process was more important than even the Farm Bill.

"In America, farmers own their land. Here, our collective owns the land," Boss Liu said, speaking collectively.

Forget moving into the new apartments, I thought. Auntie Yi, fretting over her poppies, had no idea of the changes to come.

"What if residents don't like your plans?"

"I'll explain that I'm helping them. I'm making their lives better, and their child's life better. You have to understand, this will be a nationwide trend. It can't be stopped. [Chinese president] Xi Jinping has made developing the countryside his administration's priority. Mechanized farming is one method. So is agricultural tourism. We're doing both. I'm going on a study trip to Australia and New Zealand to see how they're managing it. I understand that their model is similar."

I realized that, during our talk, Boss Liu had yet to say the word *rice*. He had grown up in Wasteland's poorest family but had excelled at Number 22 Middle School—where Ms. Guan was among his teachers—and tested into a top high school, then Tsinghua University, China's most esteemed engineering college. Where he majored in Chinese.

Rice, he said, was the agronomist Dr. Liu's field of expertise. She handled the paddies and he focused on growing the business. She smiled and nodded. She had barely said a word since Boss Liu sat down.

"The one thing we are not allowed to lose is the area's 'farming characteristic,'" he continued. "That's what the provincial officials granting approval stress. We can develop the land, but we can't cause a net loss in arable land. So whatever we build on, we have to replace with crops. Replacing houses with high-rise apartments, for example. One day everyone will want to move into them."

That was Boss Liu's way of answering whether Auntie Yi and San Jiu would have to move: *Eventually.*

Boss Liu said that the head of the nation's Politburo had heard of Eastern Fortune's success and sent a team to investigate. Afterward he wrote a letter of praise, saying that if the company's work "continues to go well"— and by that, Boss Liu figured, he meant high yields, safe food, rising incomes, and no unrest—their business model could be promoted nationwide. He also informed Boss Liu that the nation's next annual agricultural forum would be held in Wasteland, at this hot spring.

"We need to build a bigger meeting hall," Boss Liu told me.

Some brick village walls still held the faded painted 1960s slogan *Learn agriculture from Dazhai*, the name of a model commune. I said that across China those could be refreshed to urge farmers to learn instead from Wasteland.

"Actually," Boss Liu said, "I'm thinking of changing the village's name."

"Wasteland is a great name," I said. "Your new history stone out there on Red Flag Road says it dates back to the Qing dynasty in 1722. That's older than the United States."

"I have a better idea," Boss Liu said. He paused dramatically and announced: "The village name will be changed to Eastern Fortune, after our company."

CHAPTER 19

MAJOR SNOW

IN THE MIDDLE of December, I woke at winter's dawn, which broke three hours later than summer's sunrise. Wiping the steam from my bedroom windows revealed three inches of fresh snow atop the piled rice straw that fueled the *kang*. Mr. Guan had already left, carrying his auger—a salvaged piece of rebar—on his motorcycle like a lance to his Songhua River fishing spot. When I had asked how he navigated the bike on the ice sheet covering the road, he said: "Slowly."

Now came the worst part of the day. I pulled on long underwear, jeans, thick wool socks, a hoodie, a jacket, and a hat and stepped outside into the minus-18-degree-Fahrenheit air. Our outhouse's pit had not been emptied before the frost, and a brown iceberg protruded from its hole. It had grown noticeably over the weekend, when the Guan family convened for a niece's wedding, and male relatives bunked with us on our *kang*.

A rural wedding, especially in the depths of winter, was an extended banquet that moved from house to house. Pork-and-sour-cabbage dumplings topped with garlic and black vinegar made the breakfast, served with steaming bowls of the starchy water in which they were boiled. Fruit and peanuts and sunflower seeds were constantly offered. The plate of salty fried silk worms reminded me of Frances's dad and the first time I had come to Manchuria, to meet her parents. Once again I accepted the dish, and once again the room erupted in laughter at the face I made, biting into the worms' pasty mush.

In a caravan of rented cars, the group went to Jilin city to take pictures beneath the silvery, rime-coated trees lining the riverbanks. Vendors sold roasted sweet potatoes and steaming satchels of chestnuts along with bright red candied hawthorn berries, which looked like skewered Christmas ornaments. Strings of white lights decorated the French Catholic cathedral's gray brick façade, while across the street in the park an animatronic Santa Claus shook his hips while playing a saxophone next to his sleigh and reindeer. The sting of every indrawn breath and the clouds made from exhaling reminded me of Minnesota. As did the site of people windmilling their arms to avoid falling on the sidewalk's black ice. Only now the scene was scored by women howling "*Aiya maya*" and men cursing "*Wo cao*" on their way down.

I left the party early and rode the bus back to Wasteland. Passengers slipped on the slop of melting snow mixed with coal dust that puddled in the aisle. Our breath fogged and then iced the windows, and I scraped a porthole to see the bus sliding precariously close to the river. The driver peered through a cracked windshield at the white road, and I wondered whether I had used up my allotment of safe rides. When the driver, with one hand on the wheel, answered his cell phone, sending the bus sharply to the right, the bus plunge that I feared would one day be my demise seemed imminent. The passengers, meanwhile, chatted calmly and stared at their own phones.

Viewed from afar, Wasteland's houses looked pretty under the pure snow. But once back inside ours, I spent an hour sealing cracks in the plastic sheeting that covered our windows and inspecting the *kang* for fractures. I started looking forward to teaching, if only for the classroom's warmth.

On the way to the elementary school, I made a running start and slid past the chickens free-ranging on the road. "Be careful!" a fourth-grader shouted, sounding as serious and grown-up as her mother. She wasn't game for a snowball fight, either: the cold was something to endure, not play in. My lesson that day described a snowman, which none of the children had ever made. The classroom was toasty, but still the children sat in layers of pants and hand-knit sweaters, as plush and immobile as sacks of grain.

As the sun sank before four o'clock, I walked down Red Flag Road to San Jiu's, passing the hot-spring entrance, wondering if one day it would have a Starbucks: Boss Liu had said he liked lattes. Red Flag Road was silent but for the wind. It lashed through the bare poplars, whipping the paddy snow into drifts.

San Jiu poured me a cup of instant coffee; since the stroke, our drinking days were over. He had not shown any emotion at hearing Boss Liu's village vision, only commenting, "That's a lot of plans."

But he also said that Eastern Fortune was good for the area. Merging farmland, improving food safety, and adding infrastructure were positive changes. "As far as I'm concerned, this is the best era I've experienced as a farmer," San Jiu said. "But a new era is beginning."

Thirty years separated China's landmark agricultural reforms, he noted. That brought a major change every two generations. If your grandmother was a sharecropper in 1925, for example, you had your own plot of land in 1955. If your grandfather worked a commune in 1965, you held a thirty-year lease to grow and sell freely in 1995. The problem, according to San Jiu, was that there wasn't a large enough generation to implement the next step. "So by 2025 machines will take the place of many laborers. But that's a natural evolution," he said. "That's progress." Especially when it spanned a single lifetime. San Jiu started out as a teenager, opening Wasteland's paddies by hand with a hoe.

What he didn't like, however, was the continued assignation of farmers to underling or employee status. Or, as he put it: "Someone up here"—he raised his arm—"is always telling us down here what to do." In feudal times, it was landlords. Then came cadres. Now there were managers.

"Village land is collectively owned, but in theory we farmers are the collective," he said. "If you want to lease your land contract to Eastern Fortune and move to the city and work another job, good! You have that option now, and before you did not. Eastern Fortune provides that choice. If you can't afford to improve your house or want to live differently, you can move into the new apartments. Good! Eastern Fortune provides that choice, too."

But what if you wanted to continue working your land and keep living in your one-story home with a garden? That's what worried San Jiu. "I'm just one person," he said as we sat side by side on his *kang*, "but I think every family should be able to choose how they make a living."

The Eastern Fortune model, he said, would be a win-win for an impoverished farming area, but Wasteland was comparatively prosperous. On the rice station's notice board, only one family advertised land for rent next year, the equivalent of 1.6 acres for 10,000 yuan [$1,640]. Eastern Fortune's rebuilt archway at the start of Red Flag Road was papered not with Seeking Work ads but ones offering farmers special rates on holiday tours to warm southern destinations.

"Could you find an empty house to rent?" San Jiu asked. "No. So you gave money to that teacher and moved into her house. How much did you pay them?"

"You know exactly how much I paid them, down to the last yuan," I said.

He laughed and admitted that he did. Everyone in a village knew everything.

San Jiu opted not to sign the three-year contract with Eastern Fortune. That was for families who no longer wanted to farm, he said. The price of rice kept rising, and it would be foolish to agree to a fixed payment, given the year-on-year increase. San Jiu was betting on *zhang*.

He was also sixty-seven and a stroke survivor. His sons ran a village restaurant, and I never saw them in the fields. I wondered for how long he could continue to work his land. For the elderly, Eastern Fortune's offer—along with the "oldsters' leisure hall" and clinic being built in the new apartment complex—could be a lifeline.

In a phrase that was becoming as clichéd as *It's for our friendship*, Party propaganda and Eastern Fortune billboards promised to "unleash the enormous potential of the countryside." The words put the focus not on the farmers but on the land, suggesting that it did all the work. But China had already seen the enormous potential of the countryside unleashed in its coastal factories, where migrant workers fueled two decades of soaring economic growth. Some Chinese academics and researchers were floating proposals to unleash that potential in villages by granting farmers full land ownership rights.

"The Communist Party will never let that happen," San Jiu said without malice. "That's what the revolution was for: land reform. This is a Socialist economy now."

"Socialist with Chinese characteristics," I said, quoting the official term. It covered all the market's vagaries, from state-owned to privately held to publicly traded companies. If this was the start of the mechanized farming era, then the next landmark reform could be an evolutionary transfer of land ownership from the "collective" to individual families.

"Not in my lifetime," San Jiu said. "My grandson's, perhaps. Or yours."

Sitting on their *kang*, Auntie Yi and Uncle Fu watched a women's volleyball match between China and Cuba on television. "Cuba's winning," Uncle Fu said, sounding disappointed.

"But only in volleyball," I assured him.

Auntie Yi had blown off Boss Liu's plans as bluster. "He talks and talks," she said, "but the collective owns the land and no decisions can be made without consulting every resident."

I said that he had sounded awfully confident.

"We'll see," Auntie Yi said. As a retired cadre, she still had a line to local politics, and did not seem overly concerned that a superhighway or ski slope would soon be visible from her living room windows. Now they showed the peaceful view of a flat expanse of snow-covered paddies and an empty Red Flag Road. In springtime, if Auntie Yi's secretly sown seeds survived the winter, the section passing her house would blossom with guerrilla poppies.

"I heard another rumor," she said. "They discovered oil under the Changchun airport. It's a big enough reserve that they may move the airport here, back to this old airfield." Transferring a newly built international airport forty miles seemed entirely rational in present-day China. It could probably be accomplished in a week. Still, I thought the rumor sounded far-fetched. But Auntie Yi's intel had yet to be wrong.

"Of course, we don't want to leave our house," she said. "Those apartments are no way to live. Besides, our family has roots here. All these families do. Your mother-in-law grew up in this village, and so did your wife. Maybe one day your child will, too."

This was an opening for news.

"My wife is pregnant."

Auntie Yi's face spread so wide into a grin, her bucket hat lifted from her head. Uncle Fu chuckled and said congratulations. San Jiu had made the same low, approving laugh earlier. Then he had scolded me for waiting so long to become a father.

Frances had delivered the news early one summer morning. My cell phone flashed her number and I answered, concerned that something was wrong in Hong Kong. Instead, two home pregnancy tests confirmed that things could not have been more right. My first reaction was to burst into laughter and jump up and down, which startled the villagers standing on the road around me. By nightfall my mouth hurt from smiling. Hers had ached the same.

Perhaps we had Wasteland to thank. It had inured me to urban Chinese bureaucracy, making me forget to renew my visa, which meant missing a train back north from a trip to see Frances. During those unplanned, extra three days together, we had argued about settling down; about finally deciding—at ages thirty-four and thirty-nine—whether to try for a baby; about, in essence, if it was time to stop living "in Manchuria." We grappled to a draw, which had settled the argument definitively.

On her *kang*, Auntie Yi whooped and clapped her hands. She didn't ask if Frances was eating apples, only when she was due, and if it was a boy or girl.

I didn't answer the second question, not wanting to hear that we were lucky, because boys continued the family name. We had already decided that his Chinese surname would not be Frances's—from her father—but that of her mother, who was the last surviving descendant on that branch of the family tree. Our son would carry it on, honoring the woman whose scheduled abortion had been canceled by an earthquake, and who could not bear to give her newborn daughter away. Instead she had sent her to be raised in Wasteland, where I answered the phone and heard "Little Extra" say she was pregnant.

Another cycle, complete. The story's twists only made sense in the end. Being here was the meaning.

"The baby is due after Spring Festival."

"It will be born in the Year of the Dragon!" Auntie Yi exclaimed. "That's good. That's going to be a good year."

"Everyone says that about every year," I said with a laugh. "No one ever says, 'Oh no, your baby will be born in the Year of the Rabbit? Surely it will be a dullard and amount to no good.'"

Auntie Yi hopped off the *kang* and reentered the room carrying the oversize Eastern Fortune Rice calendar, looking for auspicious birth dates.

"We just received this," she said. "It's really good quality."

She flipped the thick pages to find the date of the Lunar New Year. "The Dragon starts then," she said. Above each month, the calendar listed the solar terms, the fortnights that described the growing seasons. Winter Solstice began the following week. I had moved to Wasteland during that spell.

Below the calendar's pictures of ripe fields, smiling farmers, and industrious harvesters, the agronomist Dr. Liu had added folk sayings, a touch that reminded me of Pearl Buck brightening her husband's dull field reports with colorful adages. December's sounded less traditional and more like an optimistic fortune cookie: "Major Snow is finally here. End-of-year calculations will fill your wallet with money."

On her first trip to America, only one slip of paper had stumped Frances in our fortune cookie translation game, requiring no editing to sound authentically Chinese: "The course of life is unpredictable; no one can write his autobiography in advance."

That could have been Manchuria's motto. Now I could put away the Northeast's train timetables, maps, and history books, and write my own.

As I said good-bye to Auntie Yi and Uncle Fu, my cell phone whirred with an incoming message. In their yard, I shielded the screen from the sunlight and read: "I hope you are enjoying the *Dongbei* morning. Felt the baby kick in the lower abdomen, like little thumbs gently poking my skin. Awesome. Come home."

In winter the land was frozen and still. A cloudless sky shone off snow-covered rice paddies, reflecting light so bright you had to shield your eyes. A stinging wind pushed me faster south down Red Flag Road, away from a village named Wasteland.

ACKNOWLEDGMENTS

My thanks go first to the residents of Wasteland who welcomed me into their homes, classrooms, offices, and fields. I'm particularly indebted to the Guans, Auntie Yi, Uncle Fu, and San Jiu.

For the research it allowed, I'm grateful for financial support from the Mrs. Giles Whiting Foundation, the John Simon Guggenheim Memorial Foundation, the Rockefeller Foundation Bellagio Center, and the Dorothy and Lewis B. Cullman Center for Scholars and Writers at the New York Public Library.

At the latter, librarians Sumie Ota and Rebecca Federman went above and beyond in hunting down materials, while Marie d'Origny and Jean Strouse gave support and good cheer. 倍儿棒！ I'm also thankful for Mari Nakahara's help at the Library of Congress in locating South Manchuria Railway gazetteers, and to David Ferriero, archivist of the United States, for assistance with Operation Cardinal and Japanese war crimes in Manchuria.

Being a freelance writer in China brings challenges beyond not having a business card, staff, and expense account. I'm grateful to editors who showed interest in stories from a place none had been to and few had even heard of: Don Belt and Oliver Payne at *National Geographic*, Tom Miller at *China Economic Quarterly*, Richard Story at *Departures*, Chris Hill at *DestinAsian*, Jennifer Schuessler at the *New York Times Book Review*, Susan Jakes at the Asia Society's *ChinaFile*, and Miki Meek, Julie Snyder, and Ira Glass at *This American Life*.

In Shenyang, I benefited from Doug Kelly's knowledge and love of the region, along with then consul general Sean Stein. Thanks, too, for conversations with David Douglas, Liu Haiping at Nanjing University, Anke Scherer, Eva Pils, Dan Abramson, Ping Kiang, Jeremy Zwinger, Ron Suleski, Jeffrey Wasserstrom, Rana Mitter, David Spindler, and Tom Gold. Zhu Keliang at Landesa untangled the ball of yarn that is Chinese land rights, Michael Hunt helped with the mystery of Nelson Fairchild's suicide, Mark Elliot taught me the etymology of Manchuria, and Stephen Wadley translated the zidi shu that appears in the epigraph. Peter Conn illuminated Pearl Buck's fascinating life. The New York Times' Jim Yardley lent a hand in locating survivors of the Shenyang POW camp, as did Andrew Jacobs with the siege of Changchun. Thanks to the Asahi Shimbun's Ishida Koichiro for assistance in Dunhua, and Tomoaki Fujiwara for introductions to repatriated orphans in Tokyo. Finally, I'm grateful to Akira Nagamine (assisted by his daughter Janet) and Harold Leith (assisted by his wife, Helen) for sharing their war stories, too.

My mother-in-law, Cheng Zhaohua, and Gillian Riffe helped both in Manchuria and on the home front. I benefited, too, from the friendship and encouragement of Ron Gluckman, Mike Goettig, Ian Johnson, Mark Leong, and Luke Mines. Cheers, too, to (Dr.!) Travis Klingberg for egging me onward. Matt Forney's Fathom China staff helped with due diligence on Eastern Fortune Rice, while Matt—on a visit to a Red Flag Logging Commune with his son Roy—crashed our Red Flag sedan into an oncoming Liberation truck. I stuck to trains after that; thanks, Matty.

For close reading of the manuscript and critical comments, I'm indebted to Nicholas Griffin, Adam Hochschild, and Peter Hessler. Adam, you're the best teacher a student could ever hope for. Pete: Call Molo, because I owe you one.

Likewise, I'm indebted to my agent, Georges Borchardt, and publisher, George Gibson, for unflagging patience, edits, and support.

Frances and I met in 1997, and I find it hard to believe that, as I write this, we're approaching the seventeenth anniversary of our first date. Where did the time go? (Hey, where do these stairs go? They go up.) Words can't express my gratitude for the friendship, support, laughter, and the family we share. I'm typing this with Benjamin, age two, on my lap, ukulele in hand, demanding to hear "The Wheels on the Bus" yet again. Benji,

路客 (aren't you glad we didn't name you Wasteland, 荒地?), one day you'll tire of this song and demand your dad supply other diversions. These pages tell what your parents were up to before you arrived and made our lives even better. You, son, are the meaning. 我爱你们。

Notes

Sources are provided for direct quotations, identified by their beginning words, and for information that cannot be easily found in one—often several—of the most comprehensive books identified at the beginning of the bibliography. If no page number follows a citation, the source is a newspaper article.

Chapter 1: Winter Solstice

3 **Perhaps no other region has exerted** Chang Kia-Ngau (p. 1). I'm not a fan of hedging, but Frances, despite her hometown ties to the Northeast, feels that the southern coastal province of Guangdong (home to Guangzhou/Canton and bordering Hong Kong) could also lay claim to this title. It's a book waiting to be written.

4 **Between 1927 and 1929 alone** Reardon-Anderson, p. 98. He writes that the figure actually exceeded the waves to the United States, though in the peak year of 1907 one million people arrived at Ellis Island. The National Park Service notes that the average annual migration during the peak era was 783,000.

4 **Although it is uncertain where God created paradise** The speaker is Abbé Evariste Regis Huc, who, in his travelogue, added: "Already two ages have passed away since the Manchus made themselves masters of the vast empire of China, and you would say that during these two centuries they have been unceasingly working out their own annihilation. Their manners, their language, their very country—all has become Chinese." He died at age forty-seven; his *New York Times* obituary concluded:

"He leaves behind him no priests more sincere, and few writers more honest or more entertaining than himself."

5 *But Manchuria long predates the Japanese invasion* Elliott 2, p. 635. The Party's organization was crushed in 1937, but Elliott notes that even future premier Zhou Enlai and president Liu Shaoqi used *manzhou* (Manchuria) in their correspondence, suggesting that "the name did not grossly violate everyone's nationalistic sentiments of the time."

Tartary, as Peter Fleming wrote, "is not strictly a geographical term, any more than Christendom is" (p. 14). It referred to peoples from the Caspian to Korea and was used in English for the first time by Chaucer in *The Canterbury Tales*. Perhaps it was born from Tarturus, Latin for the bowels of Hades, and the fiery destruction unleashed by Mongolians in eastern Europe (Elliott 2, pp. 625–26). On English maps, the Manchu domain around Beijing's palace was commonly marked as the Tartar City.

5 An eighteenth-century Jesuit-drawn map of China included ethnographic information and singled out the Northeast as *"ancien pays des Mantcheou qui ont conquit la Chine."* Japanese editions changed that to Manshū, from which London editions used the Manchew. By the early nineteenth century Manchuria (and Mandshuria and Mantchooria) appeared in American atlases, entering common and often romanticized usage (Elliott 2, pp. 626–32).

11 *In 1993, the U.S. Census stopped counting American farmers* From the United States Environmental Protection Agency's "Ag101" page: http://www.epa.gov/oecaagct/ag101/demographics.html. Of the 2 percent of the American population who live on farms, only half actually farm for a living. Thus, less than 1 percent of Americans farm full-time. (A farm is defined as an operation that sells more than $1,000 in goods annually.) There are 2.2 million farms in the U.S., down from 6.8 million in 1935. Conglomeration and mechanization sees 188,000 farms (9 percent of the total) producing two-thirds of America's agricultural output. Size matters: viable crop/livestock operation in the Corn Belt would need between two and three thousand acres of row crops and six hundred sows to be economically viable for the long term.

11 *That number was plummeting* Boehler 1. The total number of villages declined from 368,000 to 269,000 in 2012.

12 *The variety is commonly used in sushi* Wasteland plants the rice variety named *japonica*. Chinese botanists have long been unhappy with the nomenclature for the two subspecies of Asian domesticated rice—*Oryza sativa*—grown in the country: *indica* and *japonica*. The names obscure the process of subspeciation, making the grains sound like

imports from India and Japan. While rice most likely originated in India, China domesticated the varieties of *indica* and *japonica* that it grows, which it instead calls *xian* and *geng*, respectively.

12 **The company provided rice seed** The guaranteed payment was double China's average annual rural per capita income of 7,000 yuan ($1,100; one-third that of urban residents).

Chapter 3: Lineages

32 **In 1976 a nationwide campaign had begun** The so-called one child policy, officially called the "family planning policy," was introduced in 1979 and is credited with reducing China's population growth but also creating a gender imbalance—through infanticide and selective abortions—as couples favored having a boy instead of a girl. Rural residents, members of ethnic minorities, and parents who themselves are single children are allowed to have two children, and the birth of twins to urban residents is permitted, as is the payment of a large fine to have more than one child.

39 **In the 1947 book From the Soil** The book, by sociologist Fei Xiaotong, is subtitled *The Foundations of Chinese Society*. His teacher scolded him for writing "The same as above," but Fei thought, *Every day my life was the same. Get up in the morning, go to school, play and go to sleep at night. What else could I write?* "When the teacher forbade all the students to write the same as above, we had to make up lies" (pp. 57–58).

40 **Indeed, the best "memoir" I have read of a Chinese farm** University of Texas history professor Li Huaiyin's thick academic study *Village China Under Socialism and Reform: A Micro-History, 1948–2008*. It depicts the hamlet of Dongtai, in eastern coastal Jiangsu province.

Chapter 4: Ruins and Remains

46 **The large-scale cemeteries included foundations of solid houses** Nelson, pp. 213–18.

46 **The finds evinced that the people who resided here** Ibid., p. 252.

47 **Some archaeological sites even suggested habitation** Ibid., p. 252.

47   *His handlers brought Shaw to a room*   Condon, p. 20.

52   *When Manchu cavalry*   Elliott 1, on pp. 1–2, has a great description of the battle, which he calls "China's Hastings."

52   *The Great Wall was, in fact, a series of shifting fortifications*   For three centuries Ming rule ebbed and flowed in the Northeast but its dominion included the present-day Liaodong Peninsula, today's Liaoning province, demarcated by a wall that was shifted several times. (Thanks to Great Wall scholar David Spindler.)

53   *In 1754 the Manchu emperor Qianlong described the barrier*   Edmonds, p. 599. The poem is titled "The Qianlong Emperor's Authoritative Poem on the Willow Palisade." The translation is reproduced from Edmonds' article.

53   *A team of British explorers crossing Manchuria in 1886*   James, p. 6.

55   *The boy was orphaned*   Crossley 1, p. 48.

55   *He also ordered that Jurchen women*   Han Chinese traditionally did not cut their hair, seeing it as a legacy inherited from their parents. Under Manchu dominion, however, those who refused to shave their temples faced execution. For nearly three centuries Chinese knew the slogan: "Keep your hair and lose your head; lose your hair and keep your head." Only monks were exempt.

55   *His name was Nurhaci*   I first heard of him as a child, via another story. In the opening scene of *Indiana Jones and the Temple of Doom*, our hero swaps a jade urn containing Nurhaci's ashes with a Manchurian gangster named Lao Che (a play on the name of the famous Manchu novelist Lao She).

55   *His son would establish the Qing dynasty and in 1635 decreed*   Crossley 1, p. 15. The name change contrasted the erstwhile Jurchen from the Mongol and Chinese-martial (*hanjun*) groups that together formed its military administrative organization named the Eight Banners (八旗*ba qi*). The hereditary manorial system, a martial caste akin to Russia's Cossacks, divided territory into plain or bordered red, blue, yellow, and white banners.

55   The contemporary Chinese term 满族(*manzu*) means not "Manchu" but "the Man ethnicity."

55   The son, named Hong Taiji, called the dynasty the Qing ("clarity"), a character associated with water, which subdued the fire-associated Ming. The character for *Qing*

has a connotation with Manjusri's enlightened state as well. The previous Jurchen dynasty, the Jin, built shrines to the bodhisattva, including one from 1137 still standing at Foguang Temple, on central China's Wutai Mountain.

55   The renaming proclamation took place in November 1635 and read: "Originally, the name of our people was Manju, Hada, Ula, Yehe, and Hoifa. Ignorant people call these 'Jurchens.' [But] the Jurchens are those of the same clan of Coo Mergen Sibe. What relation are they to us? Henceforth, everyone shall call [us] by our people's original name, Manju. Uttering 'Jurchen' will be a crime" (Elliott 1, p. 71).

55   Ten days later, the emperor ordered: "The name of the country is called 'Manchu'" (Ibid., p. 401).

55   **Many live in clusters such as the Manchu Autonomous County**   Despite being one of China's largest ethnic minority groups, the Manchu were the last to be granted an area with a modicum of self-governance, in 1983. By then, fourteen of the largest fifteen groups had their own autonomous regions and prefectures. The delay could have stemmed from spite. Or it evinced that the Manchu had—unlike Tibetans and Muslim Hui people—melted into Han Chinese society and didn't warrant an autonomous zone (Shao, pp. 210–11).

59   **A Jesuit priest who accompanied the emperor**   Verbiest, p. 75.

CHAPTER 5: THE WAKING OF INSECTS

64   **An English traveler passing through in 1903 found**   Simpson (writing as Putnam Weale), p. 431.

64   **The old walled city was made of wood**   Fogel, p. 255. The poet was Omachi Keigetsu. Fogel notes that it was one of a number of recurring expressions aimed at familiarizing a foreign place by nativizing it (like "the Paris of the Orient," "the New York of Asia," etc.). But there was no suggestion here of an imperialistic tone: "since Kyoto, especially in winter, was revered by Japanese as the quintessence of beauty, this was extremely high (perhaps exaggerated) praise for Jilin."

64   **In the late nineteenth century, an English explorer**   Younghusband, p. 43. I loved his account, which felt like a portal directly to the past—in part because, at the New York Public Library, I was the first person since 1918 to check the book out. It looked, felt, and smelled of its age. He writes "to many another kindred spirit, who shares with me that

love for adventure and seeking out the unknown which has grown up within me. The great pleasure in writing is to feel that it is possible, by this means, to reach such men; to ... pass on to others about to start on careers of adventure, the same keen love of travel and of Nature which I have received from those who have gone before."

Chapter 6: Grain Rain

83 *In 2010, 65 percent of China's "mass incidents"* Landesa. Its seventeen-province survey, published in 2012, visited 1,791 villages and found that 43 percent had experienced forced appropriations of arable land for commercial use since 1990, when China began allowing developers to operate. It estimated that the land of four million rural residents was taken annually.

87 *Dr. Liu suggested they be among the first* China observes international standards for organic certification, requiring third-party verification that the food was grown genetically unmodified—without artificial fertilizer, herbicides, or insecticide—in soil tested for residue heavy metals.

89 *In 2010 the results of a countrywide soil survery* Ministry of Environmental Protection, quoted from Wong. In early 2013 the Ministry's book *Soil Pollution and Physical Health* said that "more than 13 million tons of crops harvested each year were contaminated with heavy metals, and that 22 million acres of farmland were affected by pesticides." It estimated that one-sixth of arable land was polluted.

89 The official who announced eight million acres were unfit for farming was Wang Shiyuan, vice minister of land resources.

89 *In early 2014 the government* "China Alerted by Serious Soil Pollution, Vows Better Protection," Xinhua, April 17, 2014. The report was issued by the Ministry of Environmental Protection and the Ministry of Land Resources, based on a study done from April 2005 to December 2013.

Chapter 7: The Pilgrims' Progress

92 *Its cities' new skylines notwithstanding* In 2013 the World Bank commended China for being the first developing country to lift half its population out of poverty. Estimates of the number of impoverished vary. China's news agency reported State Council statistics that said the figure fell from 166 million at the end of 2010 to "98.99

million now" ("UN Official Praises China's Poverty Reduction," Xinhua, October 17, 2013).

94 *I have not words to express to you the multitude of mosquitoes* James, quoted in Lee, p. 5.

95 *To combat the bloodsuckers* Uttered by Father de La Brunière, quoted in Simpson (Putnam Weale). James quote in Lee, p. 5.

95 *On his 1886 expedition* Younghusband, p. 12.

95 *If any one is missing* Du Halde, p. 98.

95 *Travelers disappeared into the region's forests* Ibid., p. 96.

95 *Considering the sights on this leg one hundred years later, Younghusband* p. 12.

95 *An English consul traveling to Jilin city* Hosie, p. 23.

96 *A Chinese miner who struck it rich* Lee, p. 92.

96 *One brigand, named Ma the Crazy* Ibid., p. 94.

96 *In the nineteenth century, the late-summer rainy season* Reardon-Anderson, p. 112.

96 *The explorer Henry E. M. James, fitted in sheepskins* James, p. 15.

96 *Often, however, the party would at last arrive at a settlement* Younghusband., p. 11.

96 *Younghusband, after complaining of natives' stares* Ibid., p. 8.

96 *("To my mind, it is one of God's good gifts")* James, p. 168.

96 *He also, like travelers to the Northeast today* Younghusband, p. 18. Also like travelers to the Northeast today, he fell victim to a banquet's beverage selection: "We had been leading a hard, healthy life lately, so had good appetites," he recorded. "But the drinking was terrible. If we had been allowed to keep at one liquor we might possibly have survived; but the mixture of port and beer, and sherry and claret, and

Guinness's stout and vodka, backward and forwards, first one and then the other, was fatal" (p. 34).

96 *The Northeast holds, after the Yangtze* Reardon-Anderson, p. 113.

97 *An American captain, sent by President Pierce* Collins, p. 232. Of the railroad, Collins wrote: "Even if we find it cannot be accomplished through our efforts, we shall have the remembrance (satisfactory to ourselves) of having known the wants of the country only a little in advance of the times" (p. 390).

97 *"The sturgeon has made sport of us"* Verbiest, p. 77. Even after the construction of the dam upstream from Jilin city, the Songhua river's tributaries remained prone to flooding. During my first summer in Wasteland, a flash flood smashed cars, swept away roads, and toppled a warehouse, washing three thousand blue barrels of toxic, flammable chemicals into the river. The municipal taps were shut, leading to a panicked run on bottled water, and—this being a part of China—throngs of onlookers at the riverbanks, observing the collection of the barrels, none of which leaked.

97 *"These were the bodies of colonists who had died"* Younghusband, p. 50.

99 *By 1938 the Northeast had nearly four hundred Catholic churches* In 1838, Rome created a Vicariate Apostolic of Manchuria, after a century of intermittent visits by priests, who sent reports to Europe—such as Jean-Baptiste Du Halde's published in 1741, promulgating the frontier allure of the Country of the Mantcheoux: "The Lands of this Province are in general very good, and abound in Wheat, Millet, Roots and Cotton; they also supply large Herds of Oxen, and great Flocks of Sheep, which are rarely seen in any of the Provinces of China: They have little Rice, but then in recompense they have several of our European fruits, as Apples, Pears, Nuts, Chestnuts, and Filberts, which grow in abundance in all the Forests."

99 *The rationale of sending medical workers, a priest explained* Christie, p. 26. He felt, too, that because his Manchurian patients were migrants, they were more open to new ideas and practices than "their kinsmen whom they left behind in the old run in the China behind the Great Wall" (p. 14).

100 *"I could weep, but not with sorrow"* O'Neill, p. 37.

100 *In spring she recorded that "mud and blue"* Ibid., p. 52.

100 *"Every day," she wrote, "I feel more and more"* Ibid., p. 47.

CHAPTER 8: TO THE MANCHURIA STATION!

102   *The Manchu came to power on horseback*   A short line in Shanghai, built without permission by the Jardine & Matheson trading company, was ordered dismantled after a decade. The Peking–Hankow line was built from 1898 to 1906 but opened in 1915.

102   *There are few parts of the world where*   Christie, p. 64. He arrived in Manchuria as a medical missionary of the United Presbyterian (now United Free) Church of Scotland. In his book, published in 1913, he reflected on the missionaries: "Thirty years have gone by, and what is their record? Hostility and persecutions, our houses and all our worldly goods burned, wars and deadly plague, tragic death among our ranks, partings with children sent away to the homeland—they have not been smooth years, but *it has been worth while.*" The italics are his.

103   *Also during this era, the First and Second Opium Wars*   The Second Opium War was a punitive battle against a Qing court that reneged on the treaty that ended the first one. In 1858, with France and Great Britain—in addition to the United States and Russia—Manchu ministers had signed the Treaty of Tianjin, opening Chinese ports to foreign trade and allowed for the establishment of diplomatic legations in Beijing.

103   *"You can scarcely imagine the beauty and magnificence"*   Charles Gordon's 1860 letter quoted in Elder, p. 246.

103   *The new agreement moved the border back to the Heilongjiang*   In 1858 and 1860, Russia and China signed the treaties of Aigun and Beijing, opening the Songhua River (and Jilin city) to Russian ships while also moving the Chinese border south.

103   The Russians had controlled the river, or thought they did, until the mid-seventeenth century, when the Manchu began pushing back against incursions into what it regarded as Chinese territory. Battles and sieges resulted ended in 1689, when the two sides met to sign China's first pact with a European power. Written in Latin by Jesuit advisers to the Qing court, the Treaty of Nerchinsk, named for the village in which it was signed, set the border at the Argun River, handing the Amur basin to the Chinese.

103   Russia, feeling the river was indefensible, and having twice been routed there by the Qing forces, agreed. The border remained fixed there for two hundred years, until the governor of East Siberia, Nikolai Muravyov, began a Manifest Destiny campaign,

arguing that Russia's future was at the Pacific, just as America's was forming in California. Muravyov sailed a fleet down the Amur, securing the basin through the establishment of forts and the new treaties. Recently, Muravyov's legacy has been revived in Russia; his grave was moved from Paris to Vladivostok, while his memorial statue, once replaced by Lenin's, has returned. Its image adorns the five-thousand-ruble note. (See "Amur's Siren Song, The: The Long River That Marks the Border Between Russia and China Has Proved to Be a Site of Dashed Hopes." *Economist*, December 19, 2009.)

103   Yet Chinese are moving back across the border. After the breakup of the Soviet Union, vast areas of state-run farms were abandoned, and now those lands—potentially millions of hectares—are being leased to Chinese homesteaders and entrepreneurs, including county governments. Dongning, a county bordering the Chinese city of Suifenhe, was leasing two hundred thousand hectares (eight hundred square miles, half the size of Rhode Island) of idle cropland on the Russian side of the border, planting potatoes, onions, radishes and cucumbers for sale locally. (See Cui.)

103   **A Chinese diplomat attending**   Wolff, p. 5. Li Hongzhang, the Qing diplomat, was a reformer who had supported a previous proposal to built a railway through the Great Wall's First Pass Under Heaven. It hauled coal, not passengers, but was a profitable sideline business for Li.

104   **The three-million-ruble bribe**   Ibid., p. 5. Li accepted the money from Sergei Witte, the Russian finance minister in charge of the Russo-Chinese Bank. The business fronted the Chinese Eastern Railway, as the shortcut through Manchuria was named.

104   **The First Sino-Japanese War was short-lived**   In Chinese it is named the War of Jiawu, for its imperial calendar year.

104   **In September 1894, Japanese warships sank the North Pacific fleet**   For the Japanese, the land battles were literally target practice: photos show Qing soldiers in uniforms featuring large solid white circles on the front and back.

104   **Seven months later, the Qing court signed a treaty**   It was named the Treaty of Shimonoseki. John W. Foster, former American secretary of state under President Harrison, drafted the terms as an adviser to China. The diplomat Li Hongzhang survived an assassination attempt by a right-wing Japanese at the signing, in the southern Japanese city for which the treaty was named.

104 ***"Of course you already know, dear Mama"*** Nicholas II, p. 130.

105 ***"In order to facilitate the access of Russian land forces"*** Wolff, p. 7. The defense pact did not stop an almost all-but-forgotten massacre of Chinese by Russians in far northern Manchuria in 1900. Frances and I took the train overnight from Harbin to Heihe, a Heilongjiang/Amur River port opposite the Russian city of Blagoveshchensk. At the outbreak of the Boxer Rebellion in 1900, Qing ships attempted to blockade the river here and attacked Blagoveshchensk. The Russian military governor ordered the expulsion of all Qing subjects—Manchu, Han settlers—from the region who, after the border had been moved, had been allowed to stay. For four days beginning on July 17, Russian soldiers herded thousands of Chinese—women and children included—into the deep, fast-running river. Most could not swim. Once they entered the water, soldiers opened fire.

"The execution of my orders made me almost sick," a Russian officer said, "for it seemed as though I could have walked across the river on the bodies of the floating dead." Estimates ranged from 3,000 to 8,000 dead, with only 40 to 160 survivors; similar attacks occurred along the river. The general who ordered the attacks promised that "the name of the Amur Cossack will thunder through all of Manchuria and strike terror among the Chinese." A Russian writer who sailed down the Amur three weeks after the killings was sickened by the sight of swollen corpses parting before the ship's bow.

His account was published three years later in St. Petersburg, a rare mention of the event in the censorious czarist capital, which instead ran accounts with headlines such as "Last Days in Manchuria" detailing the evacuation of Russian railway workers before the advancing Boxer rebels and Qing troops (who killed one passenger, by gunfire). The single journalistic account of the massacre appeared a decade later, under the byline Anonymous. Thousands of civilian causalities did not mesh with the heroic narrative of opening the Siberian frontier. No military tribunals were held, and the killings were investigated in secrecy. The general was indicted and temporarily relieved of duty, but not jailed. Other commanders were sentenced to few months in prison, while the Cossacks involved were absolved of responsibility. Czar Nicholas II issued medals engraved "For the Military Campaign in China, 1900–1901."

Frances and I found no monument to the massacre on the Chinese riverbank, either. Historical Sino-Russian relations were displayed twenty miles south in the small town of Aihui (Aigun), whose newly built museum held uniformed mannequins with epaulets and bristling mustaches facing ones wearing silk gowns and braided queues. A series of four garish oil paintings depicted the burning of the Qing villages, the settlers' forced march to the riverbank, and their bodies in the water. Typically for this type of museum—a patriotic education base named "Heroic National Defenders' Garden"—history was presented in statistics, not personal stories. The paintings' captions only informed visitors that between July 17 and 21, 1900, Cossacks killed more than five thousand Chinese, and that the Qing had signed over Chinese territory. Unnoted was that the Qing rulers were the ones who had first acquired it.

105   Perhaps the massacre's memorial was placed in a little-visited town because Heihe and Blagoveshchensk now depended on trade. This was why, our cabdriver back to the train station said, the city's trash cans, once painted to look like *matryoshka* nesting dolls, were scrapped when Russians, all the way up to the Ministry of Foreign Affairs, had taken offense. On this winter day, at the spot where the massacre had actually taken place, the only sign we found on the riverbank advised, in English: SLIP AND FALL DOWN CAREFULLY.

105   *In 1901, one of its first passengers wrote*   Shoemaker, p. 67.

105   *"What is the name of this place?"*   Fraser, p. 225.

106   *Mr. Lang, like every Manchu I had met, could not speak or write Manchu*   A common misconception held that Manchu was one of the five languages on China's paper currency, but it was Mongolian. The others were Tibetan, Uighur, Zhuang, and Chinese.

107   *On the train heading here then, a British passenger*   Shoemaker, p. 67.

107–8   *"Has ever the world seen such a spectacle?"*   Simpson (writing as Putnam Weale), p. 397.

108   *"The idea that the railway is going to build up a new Manchuria"*   Ibid., p. 383.

108   *Exiting in 1903, the Englishman found the station square crowded* Ibid., p.139.

108   *"In Manchuria the lady with a past"*   Ibid., p. 93.

111   *How happy this would have made the game's inventor*   Naismith, p. 109. I encountered it via Ian Frazier's citation in *On the Rez*.

111   *The train crossed the Songhua*   This bridge was replaced in early 2014 after 113 years of use. Rather than being torn down, it was listed as a cultural relic and converted into a tourist site.

112 *In Suifenhe, we exited to see a town* The name, like many in Manchuria, meant nothing in Chinese but rather used characters that approximated the Manchu name for the river dividing China from Russia. A place-name gazetteer said that its eddies resembled the symmetrical grooves of a snail's needle-shaped shell. *Suifen* sounded close to the Manchu word for "awl," describing both the snail and the water's current.

113 *The caption did not note that, in 1998* Carter 1, pp. 190–91. The conference was moved to Khabarovsk, its Russian sister city.

113 *There was, as academics loved to say* The Chinese additions to the Russian colonial center reminded me of the British Marxist historian Eric Hobsbawm's notion of "invented traditions." An example was the choice of Gothic-style architecture for British Parliament, allowing the nineteenth-century structure to tap into an historical tradition that "stretched back into the assumed mists of time." Carter's excellent book *Creating a Chinese Harbin: Nationalism in an International City, 1916–1932* explains this, and is from where I drew the first two quoted phrases in this paragraph (pp. 161 and 195).

114 *A journalist visiting in the 1970s* Burns.

115 *Public fund-raising, including telethons* Carter 2, p. 111.

115 *In 1903 the British Sinophile Bertram Lenox Simpson* Simpson (writing as Putnam Weale), pp. 167–71.

115 *"We have had two suicides this week"* Ibid., pp. 169–70.

115 *Simpson's visit left him* Ibid., 148.

116 *"Russian Manchuria is something of a myth"* Ibid., p 149.

116 *In 1903, Bertram Lenox Simpson* Ibid., p. 430.

116 *Echoing the Western world's prediction* London. In a March 19, 1904, letter home, London (stuck in Seoul) complained of not having access to the front: "Have never been so disgusted with anything I have done. Perfect rot I am turning out. It's not war correspondence at all, and the Japs are not allowing us to see any war." On April 1, still in Seoul, he wrote: "I'll never go to a war between Orientals again. The vexation and delay are too great. Here I am, still penned up in Seoul, my 5 horses

and interpreters at Chemulpo, my outfit at Ping-Yang, my post at Anjou—and eating my heart out with inactivity. Such inactivity, such irritating inactivity, that I cannot even write letters" (www.jacklondons.net/writings/BookJackLondon/Volume1 /chapter24.html). In June he wrote the essay "The Yellow Peril," predicting the rise of China and Japan.

116–17 **In the battle for the Manchurian city of Mukden (present-day Shenyang)** *Mukden* was how Western maps recorded the former seat of Manchu power. The term came from the Manchu word *mukembi* (arise). The city was renamed Shengjing (Rising Capital) in Chinese and then changed again to Shenyang.

117 **Naval commanders and sailors mutinied** Brooke, pp. 302–10.

117 **In August 1905, China requested that President Theodore Roosevelt** Prior to hosting the negotiations, the United States showed little interest in Manchurian affairs. Unlike along the Yangtze Delta, no American missionaries worked the Northeast. Financiers such as John D. Rockefeller did not build hospitals there, as in Beijing, nor send surveyors to plan railroads, as teams did in Guangzhou (Canton) under the auspices of his American-China Development Company. A small trade in cotton, railroad equipment, and kerosene (via Rockefeller-owned Standard Oil) had begun with the north, but overall, business with China, including Manchuria, then represented a mere 2 percent of all American foreign trade.

117 **"As you know, I feel that it is an advantage"** Morrison, p. 112. This letter, written on July 8, 1901, was to George Ferdinand Becker, a prominent American geologist who had served in the Philippines during the Spanish-American War.

118 **"The bad feature of the situation"** Ibid., p. 478. This letter was written to Hay on May 22, 1903. Hay had helped negotiate the Treaty of Paris (ending the Spanish-American War) and authored the Open Door Policy, whereby no foreign power would dominate trade or a treaty port in China.

118 **"Personal—Be very careful"** Ibid., pp. 830–32. This letter, written on June 13, 1904, was to the British diplomat Cecil Spring-Rice, who would act as Roosevelt's best man at his wedding and serve as ambassador to the United States from 1912 to 1918.

118 **In September 1904, while on holiday** Ibid., p. 917. This letter, written on September 2, 1904, was to Secretary of State John Hay.

119   *"State of Anarchy Found at Harbin,   the* New York Time's *front page declared* New York Times, April 19, 1908. In Harbin, its correspondent wrote, "a remarkable state of affairs exists. The Russian town is governed and dominated by a private railway company."

119   *His vice-consul was a beefy, baby-faced college graduate*   Fairchild, pp. 86-87.

119   *One writer imagined Chinese voices whispering*   Tisdale, p. 139. Her account included "dialogue" with the natives in pidgin English, such as: "Boy! Boy! You no belong proper boy. You have sleepy. Plenty piecie [bandits] kill two gentlemen, night time no have catchee place sleep." In comparison, Fairchild dedicated himself to learning Chinese.

119   *"I didn't wonder the Chinese want their country"*   Fairchild, p. 111.

119   *Fairchild had arrived in Manchuria in October of 1906*   Ibid., pp. 153 and 136. As with the Belfast missionary nurse stationed in Jilin, it's wrenching to read this diary of a happy person unaware that he was about to die far from home.

119   *That winter, however, the front page of the* New York Times   "Consul Shoots Himself," *New York Times*, December 20, 1906. Fairchild was buried in Mukden's Russian cemetery but was disinterred two months later after the Japanese shuttered it in the 1930s and moved south to the concession of Newchang (Yingkou), where no trace of it can be found today.

119   Coincidentally, another American shooting—this one by the consul general to Harbin—made the front page of the *New York Times* on May 12, 1914, under the headline "Consul Warner a Suicide."

119   *Manchuria lost an admirer*   Fairchild, p. 100.

120   *The following year in Harbin, a Korean nationalist*   "Prince Ito Assassinated," *New York Times*, October 26, 1909. Ito wanted Korea to remain a Japanese protectorate and not be officially annexed.

120   *"I didn't do this as an individual"*   Perlez.

121   *Street battles broke out between Bolsheviks and White Russians*   Chiasson, p. 46.

121 *An American traveler reported throngs of exiles*   Franck, pp. 93.

121 *"There is no way of computing"*   Ibid., p. 101.

121 *The warlord Zhang Zuolin took hold of the Northeast*   Zhang was more than just a thug. Under Zhang's "Colonization for Development Plan," Manchuria's population and arable land doubled, as a new policy aimed at migrant laborers enticed them to stay with an offer of a house that they could own after five years of tenancy, relief from taxes during that period, and fields to sow. A Japanese traveler riding the train through Jilin at this time wrote that "with roughly 30,000 Koreans having moved to northern Manchuria alone and working the paddy lands, the yield of rice will surely rise and may come to occupy an important position in the agricultural produce of Manchuria" (Yosano, p. 58). Prior to these migrants' arrival, the small amount of rice grown in the Northeast was on dry land.

122 *Shops signs written in Cyrillic were ordered changed*   Carter 1, p. 146.

122 *Over Leninists' protests*   Chiasson, p. 127 (showing a photo of the shrine from Dr. Olga Bakich).

122 *The city's official holidays now included*   Ibid., p. 114. An uneasy peace existed between the new Soviet caretakers of the Chinese Eastern Railway until 1920, when the Chinese Republican government announced the assumption of all police and court duties, the revocation of Russian extraterritoriality, and true coadministration of the Chinese Eastern Railway with Russia in the north and Japan in the south. Fluttering over Harbin station was a flag featuring a hammer and sickle added to the red stripe of the five-color Chinese Republic banner.

122 *He bought favor by treating the bandits' syphilis*   Howard, p. 156. The doctor's name was Harvey J. Howard. He had been Puyi's ophthalmologist in Beijing.

122 *A dramatic performance of an English music hall play*   Ibid., pp. 209–11.

123 *The post-match stat sheet counted injuries*   Chiasson, pp. 198–99. Brawls after basketball games still occur in China: in 2011, a game between Georgetown University and a Chinese professional team ended in a chair-throwing melee.

123 In 1924, Chinese farmers attacked a Russian dairy farm, chasing away its tenants, tearing down its modern equipment, and planting their own traditional crops while squatting on the land. Other farmers staged rent strikes.

123 *Russians living in Chinese-controlled Harbin*   "Harbin's 'Squeeze' Highly Developed," *New York Times*, October 23, 1927.

123 *Harbin deserved its nickname as "Paris of the Far East"*   "Visitors to Harbin Find Expenses High," *New York Times*, October 28, 1928.

123 *White Russians—stateless without valid passports*   "Harbin's 'Squeeze' Highly Developed," *New York Times*, October 23, 1927.

123 *A British man beaten by police*   Ibid.

123 *Harper's magazine wrote that Harbin was*   Gilbreath.

123 *A Japanese colonel had planned the assassination*   The Japanese military itself did not know of the assassination plot in advance, so were not mobilized to use the event as a pretext for grabbing more control of Manchuria, in the name of security. Now, with the patriot Zhang Xueliang in charge, Japan would wait three years for its next chance.

123 What had the elder Zhang done to make Japan want to dispose of its erstwhile ally? In 1920, Zhang Zuolin had attempted to overthrow the Chinese Republican government, attacking Beijing before falling back outside the Great Wall and strengthening his hold on Manchuria. In 1926 he succeeded in capturing Beijing, declaring himself grand marshal of the republic. China's Nationalist (KMT) army, led by Chiang Kai-shek on his Northern Expedition to eradicate regional warlords, pushed Zhang out in 1928, the year the Chinese capital was relocated south, to the Yangtze River city of Nanjing. Zhang's Beijing foray angered Japan, which preferred their reliable partner to maintain the status quo in Manchuria, guaranteeing their share of the railroad. Even worse, from the Japanese perspective, was that Zhang had been routed by the Nationalists, allies of the Soviet Union. Both forces wanted Japan out of Manchuria.

123 *"Russian Mobs Fight Chinese in Harbin"*   *New York Times*, January 5, 1932.

123 *The police charged; the mob took up positions*   Yosano, p. 96.

124–5 *The café's name, Sufeiya*   Hu Hong pulled a book from its shelves titled *The Oriental Paris*. The volume of photographs captured Harbin's most prominent existing colonial structures, from smaller cathedrals to the restored synagogue and the former American consulate. It was the best guidebook for wandering around town, and I wondered what made a person chronicle Harbin's colonial fossils long before they became tourist bait.

125 "I came and watched them tear it down," Song Hongyan, a middle-aged photographer, said of her childhood home. "That moved me to start documenting the history that remained." We stood on a narrow lane running through the Daowai district, or Harbin's "Chinatown" during its colonial era, where most non-Europeans lived. The brick buildings adjoined one another, creating a contiguous street wall punctured by carriage entrances that led into courtyards. Wooden balustrades traced the rotting staircases up to the second floor and a balcony lined with apartment doorways. Migrant workers now occupied the tenements, which look uninhabitable. "Isn't it ironic," Miss Song said, "how often the poorest people live in the formerly richest houses."

125 The neighborhood, China's largest remaining swath of colonial-era housing, was being remade into a development named Chinese Baroque. Its brochure showed a map of China, marking historic districts reconditioned into open-air shopping malls in Beijing, Shanghai, Tianjin, Nanjing, Chengdu, Hangzhou, Suzhou, and Changsha. The photos depicted European-style buildings whose gray-brick façades held signs for Starbucks and Häagen-Dazs. "Every city has its unforgettable memories," the salesgirl told me, handing us an investment guide. "Chinese Baroque combines that traditional culture while creating a new future."

125 I enjoyed walking and talking with Song Hongyan, and was shocked when Hu Hong later called to tell me she had committed suicide by jumping from her apartment window.

CHAPTER 9: TUNNELS IN TIME, SIDINGS TO SPACE

129 *The father of Chinese archaeology*   Unnoted was that the sobriquet previously had been bestowed on his contemporary at Harvard, Li Ji, until he fled to Taiwan in 1949 after the Communist victory. Chinese museum plaques didn't have room for parenthetical asides.

129 *The original of Liang's journal sat seven thousand miles away*   I am grateful for the assistance of Janet Steins, associate librarian for collections at Tozzer Library at Harvard, in helping me access the document. She answered my prayers to Saint Librarian.

130   Although I had not heard of Liang Siyong, I had written about the Beijing motorcycle accident that left his architect brother with a lifelong limp. The older brother was driving the bike that got sideswiped by an official car outside their courtyard home on Nanchang Jie; Liang Siyong, riding in the sidecar, was comparatively unscathed. The brothers appeared to remain close: in this journal, Liang Siyong notes that he accompanied "Cheng and Phyllis [his wife, the architect Lin Huiyin]" to the Young Marshal Zhang Xueliang's ball in Mukden.

130   *Shopping for supplies in Harbin*   Liang, p. 6.

130   *Of the warlord, Liang wrote*   Ibid., pp. 23–24.

130   *A gang on horseback chased Liang*   Ibid., p.30.

130   *And it was cold*   Ibid., p. 109.

131   *"I found a great and significant parallel"*   Ibid., p.116.

131   *Out in remote Manchuria*   Ibid., p 13.

131   *The next day he uncovered*   Ibid., p. 9.

131–32   *After a day "wading through more than 6000 paces"*   Ibid., pp. 9 and 14.

132   *Whatever may be said of this*   Ibid., p. 14.

132   *Half of the world's 6,800 languages*   Lague and Yu. Both cite Professor Zhao Anping, director of the Manchu Language and Culture Research Center at Heilongjiang University in Harbin.

132   The only other preserve of Manchu speakers is in China's far west, on its border with Kazakhstan, where thirty thousand descendants of soldiers sent to guard the then Russian border speak the mutually intelligible Xibe language. For more, see Johnson. The story's link includes a Manchu phrase book with audio: http://online.wsj.com/ public/resources/documents/MANCHU-LANGUAGE.html

132   *But an estimated 20 percent of the ten million archived*   "Et Tu, Manchu? One Hundred Years on, Only a Few Native Speakers Remain." *Economist*, October 8, 2011. The writer quoted Wu Yuanfeng, a government archivist, who said that "only about 30 scholars in China are truly expert in the language."

136 *Shaded by trees and set back from a busy downtown street*   Harbin is unique among Chinese metropolises for the explanatory plaques on its colonial-era architecture. The Sister Cities Museum's building has a nearby twin: the former American consulate at 289 Dongdazhi Street, now home to a Harbin Bank branch. The showcasing of its past is a recent, tourist-attracting phenomenon. For more, see Carter.

137 **In these post–Evil Empire days**   One of SCI's current directives is the "Iraq and American Reconciliation Project," which pairs Denver with Baghdad, Dallas with Kirkuk, Philadelphia with Mosul, and other Iraqi cities with Fresno, Tucson, and Gainesville.

137 *The port was already bringing culture back home*   But even long-term relationships can sour. In 2012, Nanjing suspended its thirty-four-year-old relationship with Nagoya after that city's mayor expressed doubts that Japanese soldiers massacred civilians in Nanjing in 1937. In fact, they killed between 250,000 and 300,000 people. A Nanjing government spokesman said the mayor's remarks distorted historical facts and "seriously hurt the feelings of the Nanjing people." A spokesperson with Nagoya's city hall said that Kawamura's words "represent just his own opinions." The city government also said it would abide by the stance adopted by the Japanese government, which is that "Japan's slaughter and plunder against civilians in Nanjing is undeniable."

139 *The campus was part of a pump-priming project*   Barboza 1.

141 *The government monitored faith in anything but the Communist Party*   In fact, China's interest in the heavens wasn't new. Matt Forney at *Time* magazine found a fourth-century text named *Collected Legacies* that described a "moon boat" floating above China every twelve years, while a famous ancient astronomer once saw a "hovering pearl of light" over a Chinese lake.

CHAPTER 11: THE BALLAD OF AUNTIE YI

149 *He used the word* dao   The character for planted rice—*dao*—dates to the Zhou dynasty, formed in 1046 B.C, which, not coincidentally, was the same dynasty that pioneered hydraulic engineering and irrigation. The short-grain type of rice that San Jiu planted had been grown since those Neolithic times. (*Geng*, the Chinese term for the variety known as *japonica*, dates to the first century A.D. See Bray 2.)

149 *Ancient Chinese records called the practice* During the Song dynasty, agriculture was for the first time explained in handbooks—such as Chen Fu's *On Farming*, published in 1149—and circulated throughout the country. The book walked a reader through financing, plowing, topography, crop selection, the preparation of seedbeds, fertilizer, and weeding, citing the advice of the *Book of Songs*, circa 1000 B.C.: "Root out the weeds. Where the weeds decay, there the grains will grow luxuriantly . . . In this manner you will live up to the system exemplified by the ancients." It concludes with a section on concentration, noting: "If something is thought out carefully, it will succeed; if not, it will fail; this is a universal truth. It is very rare that a person works and yet gains nothing. On the other hand, there is never any harm in trying too hard." It's sound advice for a writer, too.

149 *An eighth-century poet wrote a verse* The poem is "Water Fills the Paddy Fields of Circuit Official Chang Wangpu" by Du Fu. Cited in Needham, p. 510.

150 *There was no equivalent to* Little House on the Prairie There was, however, a text that echoed Upton Sinclair's *The Jungle*: pirated copies of a banned muckraking report from the central Chinese province of Anhui titled *Nongmin Diaocha—Peasant Survey*—sold briskly on its publication in 2004, before taxes were abolished. The translated English version is titled *Will the Boat Sink the Water?* The province had been the setting of *The Good Earth*. See Chen Guidi.

150–151 *Their tenant farmers appeared only to pay rent and present annual offerings* A rare positive portrayal of farmers in literature comes in a short scene where *Dream of the Red Chamber*'s main character, the teenaged Jia Baoyu, is told to amuse himself outside. He leads his pages to explore, coming upon a rack of tools:

> He had never seen farm implements before and was thoroughly intrigued by the spades, picks, hoes and ploughs, although quite ignorant of their names and uses. When a page who knew informed him he nodded and remarked with a sigh: "Now I understand the words of the old poet: 'Who knows that each grain of rice we eat / Is the fruit of intensive toil?'"

151 *It reads like a sweatier* Walden It was a fleeting chimera: Crèvecoeur had the 371 acres left to him by his father, and the land brought personal tragedy when his wife was killed and the farm destroyed by Indians while he was away. He ended up back in city life, appointed as the French consul for New York, New Jersey, and Connecticut, then became trapped in Paris during the French Revolution of 1789 and—as Pearl Buck would two centuries later in China—had

his visa to return to the United States denied by ambassador James Monroe. He died in France, on his father's land. The lone memorial to him in the U.S. that I know of is the small Vermont town of St. Johnsbury, whose name was suggested by Ethan Allen.

151   *In China she was admired but not read*   My professor at Berkeley, the novelist Maxine Hong Kingston, urged me to read *The Good Earth* after I mentioned the awful movie version, featuring white actors playing the leads, including the German-born Luise Rainer as the matriarch O-Lan (for which she won the Academy Award for Best Actress). Kingston, however, fondly recalled being assigned Buck. "I was lucky," she told me. "When I was a student in the California public schools, Buck was still required, so I read *The Good Earth* in 1955, when I was in ninth grade. That book was very important to me. Jade Snow Wang influenced me as a writer, but Buck showed that Chinese people were people. She wrote about them with compassion. That book humanized Chinese people. It is written with so much empathy that, for the first time, Americans had to see Chinese as equals."

151   *Her most recent Chinese translator, however, told me*   Liu Haiping at Nanjing University. For a visit to her Chinese home and museum, see my *New York Times Book Review* piece, listed under "Meyer" in the Bibliography.

151   Professor Liu first read Buck in the United States, when he was a student at Harvard in the 1980s, though not in class. "When I would go to friends' homes, it was usually a woman in her sixties who would ask me how I viewed Buck's portrayal of China," he told me. "I felt embarrassed because I had not read her. She was banned. The more I learned about her life, the more I wanted to do her justice."

151   In 1986, Liu organized a literary conference in Nanjing that marked the beginning of Buck's resuscitation in China.

151   In *China Past and Present*, Buck remembered of *The Good Earth*: "'My only criticism of this book,' a famous Chinese writer said, 'is that it should have been written by a Chinese'" (p. 162).

152   *"I became mentally bifocal"*   Buck, Pearl, 2, pp. 10 and 52. Paraphrased nicely in the excellent biography by Spurling.

152   *Her father had translated the Bible*   Buck, Pearl, 1, p. 86.

153 **Like John Steinbeck** He wrote these columns in 1936 for the *San Francisco News*, since collected in a book titled *The Harvest Gypsies*.

153 **After their divorce eighteen years later** Ibid., p. 92. In the city of Nanjing, Lossing founded China's first agricultural economics department, which grew into what was then the world's largest, with a staff of one hundred. But his work fell out of favor after the Revolution; he had recommended mechanization and access to credit to alleviate farmers' burdens, not Marxist land redistribution. Lossing continued to publish research about China from the United States, where he became a specialist at the State Department's Bureau of Educational and Cultural Affairs. The better-known chronicler of Chinese agriculture became William Hinton, author of *Fanshen*, a six-hundred-page portrait of a village undergoing Communist land reform in 1948. It was not published until 1966, after Hinton sued for the return of his notes, seized by U.S. customs agents at the height of McCarthyism.

153 **"To learn to be a farmer"** Buck, John Lossing, 2, pp. 240–41.

153 **Her sister Grace told a biographer** Ibid., p. 166. In *Chinese Farm Economy's* acknowledgments, Lossing cited ten other people—including "Miss G. C. Mertsky particularly for compiling the index; and of all others who have helped for briefer periods of time" before arriving at "For editing I am greatly indebted to my wife." There was no mention of her name, her translations, or her work alongside him in the field.

154 **In 1972, the year of Nixon's visit to China** Buck, Pearl, 4, p. 171. The actual letter appears on the page, dated May 17, 1972. The author, a functionary, wrote that he was "authorized to inform you that we can not accept your request for a visit to China." It's signed, "Sincerely yours . . ." Buck had wanted to visit her parents' graves. She noted, on the last page of the last book she ever wrote, that "I was humbly happy that my parents were also mentioned [in the Nobel Prize citation] in the added phrase, 'and for masterpieces of biography'" (Buck, Pearl, 3, p. 177).

154 Although Buck said that she had assiduously avoided visiting Taiwan or taking any sides in the Chinese civil war, she did, in 1970, allude to her politics, writing: "After I left China permanently in 1933, knowing that Communism would win because of its growing appeal to the peasantry, and knowing, too, not only that I could not live in a Communist-controlled country but also that Chinese Communists would not tolerate Americans who were not Communist, I then devoted my efforts to helping Chinese in the United States not to be deported to Communist China" (Buck, Pearl, 3, p. 294).

154 *I was busy, busy, busy* Spurling.

154 *But there were other lessons, too* I owe thanks to my friend Leslie T. Chang for this pithy notion. See Chang.

154 *"Americans," Pearl Buck wrote in 1970* Buck, Pearl, 3, pp. 294–95.

154 *"What if you land in the Chinese countryside?"* Buck, Pearl, 3, p. 175. She also told the men, "Perhaps the first Chinese phrase you ought to learn is '*Wo shi Mei-kuo ren*,' or, 'I am an American.'" (I hoped her lesson would continue on to one's birth year on the Chinese zodiac, one's height, and one's ability to use chopsticks, but no.)

155 *The nation was on a "global commodity hunt"* Romig. The purchaser of the Argentine soya was Heilongjiang Beidahuang. The company's name was a combination of the northernmost province and Manchuria's former nickname of "the vast northern wasteland."

155 *Its food and energy purchases* Barrionuevo.

155 *The shift to overseas food sources* I calculated the equivalence. The area plowed under came from Zhou Xiaozheng, a professor of sociology at Renmin University of China in Beijing. (See O'Neill.)

156 *"Chasing ever-higher output levels"* Chuin-Wei. Agricultural statistics, like budgetary numbers, made me cross-eyed as I tried to grasp the size of millions of hectares or how large a metric ton of rice was. Learning that 170 of them could fit in an average-size shipping container didn't help; instead I held tight to comparative statistics that floated by, such as the average yield of a hectare of rice in China now at 6.3 tons, up from 1.5 tons fifty years ago. (The world average was 4.3 tons.) Yuan Longping, the "father of Chinese hybrid rice," continued to break his own records with a 2013 yield of 19.4 tons in an experimental field, though seeds of his "super rice" were not yet commercially available. (Zuo 3 and Zhou.)

156 In 1949, when the Communist Party took power, China had 110 million hectares of cultivated land to feed a population of 542 million; now it has 122 million hectares to feed 1.3 billion. The area increased from reclaiming wasteland.

156 *China classifies corn, wheat, and rice* Ibid.

156 *Food accounted for nearly $1 of every $5 China spent* Wessel, and also Carlson.

156 *An elated grower in Georgia* Wessel.

156 *China kept outsourcing* Zuo 4. The project was reported to become China's biggest overseas agricultural project. For decades China had aimed at being self-sufficient in grain production. Recently the target was lowered to 90 percent self-sufficiency.

160 *It became China's national anthem* Lyrics were changed to exult the Communist Party and Chairman Mao following his death, although now the original words have been restored. A 2004 constitutional amendment finally decreed it as China's official anthem.

161 *It was sung from the perspective* Shao, p. 289. I used the excellent translation that appears here.

CHAPTER 12: PUPPETS OF MANCHUKUO

162 *The two-story museum looked more like a workers' sanatorium* Before the Japanese installed Puyi here, the building had been the Bureau of Salt and Tobacco Taxation.

163 *In a memoir, his childhood English tutor* Johnston, p. 166. The tutor's name was Reginald Johnston.

163 *(In his memoir, Puyi wrote of the stay)* Puyi, p. 129.

163 *"Although he was now thoroughly Westernized"* Johnston, p. 241. An excellent recounting of Puyi's in-between years can be found in Scotland, pp. 37–39. In Tianjin, one can imagine him feeling a sense of freedom unlike any he had felt—or would feel again. Looking back on the twelve years he lived in the Forbidden City after abdication, he wrote, "I lived an aimless and purposeless life . . . While others could enjoy modern ways, I continued to breathe the air of the nineteenth century and before. My life was an anachronism, a leftover of the type of life which had already become dust by that time" (Puyi, p. 37).

163 *"My body," he recalled, "would emit the combined odors"* Puyi, pp. 154–55.

164 *From around the world arrived letters*   Johnston, p. 241.

164 *"My heart smoldered with a hatred I had never previously known"*   Puyi, p. 146.

164 *In a private letter, an Australian journalist wrote*   Donald, letter to Harold Hochschild, February 14, 1927. In the It's-a-small-world Department, I found Donald's archives at Columbia University, began reading his correspondence, and then realized his most intimate letters were addressed to the father of Adam Hochschild, cofounder of *Mother Jones* magazine and author of books such as *King Leopold's Ghost* and *To End All Wars*. The younger Hochschild was my professor at Berkeley, a mentorship that continues.

164 The correspondence halted in late 1941 and resumed on May 19, 1945, when Donald wrote to Harold: "I was in an internment camp, and remained there three years." He had wasted away, surviving on foraged weeds, wishing, like many of his fellow starving prisoners, to die. "That I escaped is a marvel."

164 On May 23, Harold replied, in part, "I was married on November 26, 1941, and the marriage has been, as you assume, a great success. We have a boy [Adam] who is now going on three years old."

164 That autumn in 1945, aged seventy and frail, Donald begged off invitations to Manhattan speaking engagements. "As between friends, I do not want to talk any more about China" (September 9). He urged his friend not to cooperate with his biographer and returned to Shanghai, where he died the next year in the hospital. The Nationalists then ruling China gave him a state funeral.

165 *But it was more than just a train*   A succinct overview of the SMR can be found in Young, pp. 31–33. The "one-third" figure comes from p. 33, where she adds that "a large fraction of the rest were involved in commercial operations indirectly dependent" on the railroad. See also Fogel, pp. 124–25.

165 *Under the slogan "Military Preparedness in Civilian Garb"*   Fogel, viii. Goto said, "We have to implement a cultural invasion with a Central Laboratory, popular education for the resident populace, and forge other academic and economic links. Invasion may not be an agreeable expression, but [language] aside we can generally call our policy one of invasion in civil garb."

165 *Researchers collected the minutiae of Manchurian life*   It took the American researcher John Young eight years to track down surviving copies of South Manchurian

Railway reports. In a seven-hundred-page bibliography published in 1966, Young documented 6,284 titles scattered in the Library of Congress, Stanford's Hoover Institution Library, and libraries at the University of California, Berkeley; Johns Hopkins; Harvard; Michigan; Columbia; Oklahoma; Penn; and twenty-five universities in Japan. Many had been discovered by a Japanese-American soldier in the Occupation Army packed on a pier, where they had arrived from Manchuria. "Startled by the bulk and great value of the materials [including Russian and Japanese-language documents] he sent them hastily to the United States just as they had been packed for evacuation."

165 **In a dispute over irrigation** The village was named Wanpaoshan, and the event is called the Wanpaoshan Incident. The killing of the Japanese spy, Captain Nakamura, is known as the Nakamura Incident.

166 **It didn't even disrupt rail traffic** Within an hour an express train from Beijing traveling fifty miles an hour passed the blast site.

166 **"There was no way we could win"** Chang and Halliday, p. 120.

166 Officially, it was the army's sole initiative. On a visit to Tokyo's Yushukan—the war museum on the grounds of the Yasukuni Shrine, dedicated to soldiers who died fighting for the emperor—I understood why contemporary Chinese (and many Japanese) are angered by Japan's official narrative of the war. The museum's Manchukuo exhibit said the "Manchurian Incident" occurred because "resentment toward the overtly anti-Japanese polices of Zhang Xueliang's government, and dissatisfaction with the Japanese government's conciliatory approach to China, smoldered among Japanese residents in Manchuria (especially within the Kwantung Army). Chinese nationalism developed into a campaign for the removal of foreign interests, in violation of the existing treaties. The campaign spread to Manchuria, where anti-Japanese harassment and terrorism erupted. Under such circumstances the Kwantung Army resorted to force."

166 Kanji Ishiwara, the lieutenant colonel who was the incident's co-plotter, thought he would be dishonorably discharged for it. Instead, he was returned to Japan and promoted to chief of operations for its entire army. On returning to Manchukuo six years later, Ishiwara was so disgusted with Japan's blatant colonial occupation that he denounced the Kwantung Army commanders before being put out to pasture near Kyoto. Free of charges, he testified as a witness at the Tokyo War Crimes Tribunal. His co-plotter, Seishiro Itagaki, who surrendered Japan's Southeast Asian forces to Mountbatten in Singapore in September 1945, was found guilty of war crimes and hanged—as was Kenji Doihara, the intelligence officer who oversaw the plot, and would control Manchukuo's prostitution and opium traffic, including the secret insertion of

the drug into the popular Golden Bat brand cigarettes, addling unsuspecting consumers.

166 *"But there was one big problem that worried me"* Puyi, p. 160.

166 *Unbeknownst to him, a large drum of gasoline was on board* Yamamuro, p. 97.

167 *"Without waiting for the interpreter to finish translating"* Puyi, p. 172.

167 *"These words, when relayed to me"* Ibid., p. 173.

167 *"Even before the train had stopped"* Yamamuro, p. 93. This was translated from the Japanese edition of Puyi's memoir. It noted that Puyi arrived at 3:00 p.m. Unlike today—when all clocks are set to Beijing time—the nation then had five time zones. Changchun ran on Changbai Time, named for the Ever-White Mountains at Jilin province's east. In the English edition of his memoir, Puyi said of this time: "Since I had already openly appeared in public there was absolutely no turning back, and besides, I thought that if I could maneuver the Japanese well, they would perhaps support my restoration as emperor" (Puyi, p. 180).

167 *Puyi was inaugurated in a ceremony* Yamamuro, p. 105.

167 *But one of the masterminds of the September 18 bombing* Ibid., p. 97.

168 *"I soon discovered that my authority was only shadow"* Puyi, pp. 181–82.

168 *Tokyo means "Eastern Capital"* At the time, the romanization of the Xinjng's name was Hsinking.

169 *It would be unlike other planned capitals* "Capital Punishments," *Economist,* December 18, 1997. In 1792, George Washington fired the District of Columbia's planner, Pierre Charles L'Enfant, for refusing to water down his extravagant blueprint. The area around Delaware Avenue remained a swamp as late as 1850, while the National Cathedral wasn't finished until 1991.

169 *Around the time of Xinjing's inception, an English reporter wrote* Ibid.

169 *Planners drew clean lines, circular plazas* Buck, David, pp. 74–89. His article gives an excellent overview of the planning and construction, but also of the men who

were drawing its lines. In 1906, Japan appointed Goto Shimpei as the first president of the South Manchurian Railroad. Born into a samurai family but educated in Germany as a physician, Goto planned freshwater and sewage systems for Japan, then Taiwan. As its appointed governor, Goto also oversaw a plan for Taipei that differed from the tangle of dense, narrow lanes that characterized Japanese cities, where urban planning did not exist as a field of study. After arriving in Manchuria, he oversaw the importation of the design in Mukden (Shenyang) and Changchun, whose planners bypassed the Russian and Chinese settlement areas and planned a settlement from scratch. These cities' maps show his fingerprints today, with a grid pattern of streets bisected by diagonal boulevards that lead to plazas and parks.

169 Buck notes that Changchun's first designer was Kato Yonokichi. Xinjing was drawn up by Sano Toshikata. Both were disciples of Goto Shimpei. Other architects who worked in Xinjing include disciples of Frank Lloyd Wright (who was in Tokyo, designing the Imperial Hotel) and Le Corbusier. See also Young, Louise, pp. 249–50.

169 See DuBois for a fascinating side note on the urban plan that built the city's main road around a "filial son" tomb, evincing Manchukuo's embrace of Confucianism.

169 *Inside, schoolchildren stared up at the skeleton* It looked like a smaller, upright brontosaurus. Fittingly, the validity of the *Mandschurosaurus* as a genus has been debated internationally, with some paleontologists branding it a nomen dubium, a scientific name of doubtful application, since only a partial specimen exists.

169 *The buildings look unlike any other in China* These ministry buildings were completed in 1936, a year before Japan launched attacks against greater China, and five years before bombing Pearl Harbor and attacking Hong Kong and Singapore, drawing the United States and its allies into war.

169 David Buck translates the style's name as "Developing Asia," but other authors, including Victor Zatespine, call it "Rising Asia" (p. 66).

170 *"I have just heard that the League of Nations"* Powell, p. 189.

171 *The Lytton Commission, named for its head* After Japan formed Manchukuo in 1932, China appealed to the nascent League of Nations to intervene. It ordered the withdrawal of Japanese troops, a resolution that Japan ignored. The West's attention was diverted by domestic concerns: British sailors mutinied at the Royal Navy yard at Invergordon; the failure of one of Europe's most preeminent banks threatened the entire continent with bankruptcy; the United States remained mired in the Great Depression.

Its Stimson Doctrine, named for the secretary of state, said it would not recognize territorial changes resulting from force, therefore Manchuria remained part of sovereign China. No sanctions were applied; the toothless doctrine's one noticeable effect was to further alienate Japan from American influence and to view the U.S. as a threat.

171   *A Japanese military officer mentioned to a reporter*   Morton, p. 41.

171   *The propaganda posters, another correspondent noted*   Holmes, p. 12.

171   *"They asked me only two questions"*   Puyi, p. 188.

171   *Japanese officers accompanied the commission*   Inventory of the Papers of Roy L. Morgan. Box 1, Folder 6, MSS 93-4. Item 2: Affidavit of Henry Pu Yi, p. 8.

171   *The president of the South Manchuria Railway*   Elliot 2, p. 639. The poem was "Ode to Mukden" by the emperor Qianlong. Japan's argument is still seen at Tokyo's Yushukan war museum, which displays a time line dating back over two thousand years correctly, if elliptically, showing the homeland of the Manchu "with varying official names throughout history," and kingdoms "frequently at odds with the Han Chinese."

171   For more on the Lytton Commission, see Young, Louise (p. 150), Duara (p. 53), and the International Relations Committee, which gives a sampling of world opinion at the time, via newspaper editorials.

171   *The commission was not convinced*   The league stated it would not recognize Manchukuo and that Japan should recall its soldiers to within the South Manchuria Railway zone. *Time* magazine called the report the financially strapped league's "last chance to escape political and moral bankruptcy as well."

171   Japan's representative to the league, Yosuke Matsuoka, pronounced: "Japan stands ready to be crucified! But we do believe, and firmly believe, that in a very few years, world opinion will be changed and that we shall be understood by the world as Jesus of Nazareth was." Matsuoka would soon become the head of the South Manchuria Railway.

172   *One witness was the American*   Newman, p. 21.

172   *The truce that ended the fighting*   The Tangu Truce was named for the Bohai Sea port where the agreement was signed in May 1933.

172   **"First Emperor Enthroned"**   *Manchuria Daily News.*

172   **I expected the story to end with the observation**   Paraphrasing Karl Marx's appending of Hegel's famous quote.

173   **"A silk hat and frockcoat will be needed"**   *Japan Railways Department,* p. oooviii.

173   **In an article he wrote for the Atlantic**   Kinney, Henry, 1.

173   **In a 1924 Atlantic article**   Kinney, Henry, 2. p. 130.

173   **The article described the horrors of 1923's Great Kanto Earthquake.** Since the Richter scale wasn't developed until the 1930s, the quake's magnitude has been estimated to have been between 7.9 and 8.4.

173   **In a memo sent to Western journalists then**   Kinney, Henry W., in Payson J. Treat Papers at the Hoover Institute Archives, Stanford University 1. Memo dated November 30, 1931.

174   **There was no mention of the building of Shinto shrines**   Yamamuro, pp. 187 and 194.

174   **Foreign correspondents dubbed the puppet state**   Ibid., p. 189.

174   **The Times of London correspondent**   Fleming 3, p. 130. This is a funny book. Fleming was twenty-seven years old on the trip, which he recorded in a diary that he did not organize into a book until 1952. His entries sound familiar to a traveler even today: "This hotel is depressing. The men on the desk are devoted to me, vaguely, I suppose, suspecting that I may one day ventilate their obscure and unnumbered grievances . . . A typical Harbin man deduced that I was a correspondent; finally insisted on giving me his name, written on a piece of paper with the word *drunk* after it. The only Russian in Harbin with a sense of humour" (p. 135).

174   **Travelers could rely on all-American equipment**   South Manchuria Railway Company 2, p. 49.

174   **"The shriek of these American locomotives"**   Ibid., p. 69.

174   **The memo was discovered and published**   Powell, p. 309.

175 *And the talk of Japanese being "conspicuously boisterous"*   Kinney, Henry W., in Payson J. Treat Papers at the Hoover Institute Archives, Stanford University 2. Memo dated June 8, 1935.

175 *Manchukuo, he gushed, had 5,500 miles of railroad*   Ibid. Memo dated March 10, 1937, on the fifth anniversary of the founding of Manchukuo.

175 *In 1933, Henry Kinney wrote*   *Manchukuo: A Handbook of Information*, p. 96.

175 *Japanese had migrated in numbers before*   Wilson 2, pp. 251–52. See also Young, Louise, pp. 310–12.

175 *Fewer than one thousand Japanese farmers moved*   Ibid., p. 253.

175 *As planners drew up the modern Manchukuo capital*   Young, Louise, p. 324.

175 *Officials recorded the sale of 11,604*   Ibid., p. 324.

175 *In 1932, after intense debate and lobbying*   Ibid., p. 321.

176 *In 1936, however, the Japanese government*   Ibid., p. 307.

176 *Previously, Japan had backed Korean migration to the region*   Hyun, pp. 36–43.

176 *The South Manchuria Railway had urged farmers*   Ibid., p. 52. The map appears on p. 48.

177 *Puyi visited the wounded*   *Manchuria*, pp. 211–12. In Russian, the Nomonhan Incident is known as the battles of Khalkhin Gol.

177 *Unnoted, of course*   Inventory of the Papers of Roy L. Morgan. Box 1, Folder 6, MSS 93-4. Item 7: Interrogation of Pu Yi (Continued), p. 12. Puyi told the Tokyo War Crimes Tribunal that this occurred at Nomonhan, although I found no other mention of this incident. In his landmark two-volume history of the battle, Alvin Coox reported a 1936 mutiny in eastern Manchukuo by one hundred Chinese troops who killed three Japanese officers, burned their barracks, fled over the Soviet border, then returned with Red Army escorts for further skirmishes. It provides this indelible image: "During the heaviest combat, 'three men of a commanding rank in the Soviet army were unmistakably observed to be directing the deserters with whips'" (Coox, p. 95).

178   *In Manchuria magazine's summer issue of 1941*   Ibid., pp. 215 and 129.

178   *An item about Puyi and the founder of the Gestapo began*   Ibid., p. 175.

178   *Puyi announced that Manchukuo was also at war*   Yamamuro, p. 194.

178   *The Japanese army had secretly called them*   Young, Louise, p. 406.

CHAPTER 13: OCCUPATION'S AFTERMATH

179   *"Go! Go and colonize the continent!"*   Young, Louise, pp. 364–68.

179   *Colonization manuals included articles*   Ibid., pp. 368–69.

179   *A 1941 journal promised*   Wilson 2, p. 278. For an interesting look at how Japanese planners (including Uchida Yoshikazu, architect of the Tokyo University campus) envisioned these settlements, see Tucker.

180   *Skilled professionals such as doctors*   Young, Louise, pp. 400–401.

180   *Instead, settlers were handed cultivated land*   Ibid., pp. 401–4, and Tamanoi 2, p. 29.

180   *Dissenters could expect the retribution*   Wilson 2, p. 267.

180   *One of the most publicized migrant villages*   Scherer. Also noted in Tamanoi 2, pp. 31–32. I rely on Scherer's translations, taken from her dissertation.

180   *Just plant one grain of wheat*   Ibid., pp. 205–6.

180   *The train departed at 5:24 a.m.*   It left from a little-used station in western Jilin city that resembled a German Gothic castle. It was a relic of the Young Marshal Zhang Xueliang's attempt to break the Japanese monopoly and build a competing railway, called the Jihai Line. The station was designed by Lin Huiyin—also known as Phyllis Lin—the sister-in-law of the archaeologist Liang Siyong and aunt of Maya Lin, creator of the Vietnam Veterans Memorial wall in Washington, D.C. Built in 1928, the station's barn-roof, granite-block structure is meant to resemble "a crouching lion, with its tail ingeniously designed as a bell tower," according to a plaque at its entrance. Around me passed crowds entering a temporary waiting room and construction

workers—in yellow hard hats and olive green plimsolls—off to build high-rise apartments named Park Scenery House.

181   *"Especially for the construction"*   Scherer, p. 213.

181   *The writer described the settlers' village* Ibid., p. 211.

182   *When the Japanese settlers left*   Ibid., pp. 205 and 209.

183   *Although they made up only 17 percent*   Chan, pp. 17 and 20. Young, Louise,
citing Foreign Ministry surveys, found that of the 223,000 settlers at war's end, only 140,000
(63 percent) ever returned to Japan. "More than a third of settlers—78,500 people—died
in the wake of defeat" (p. 411). See Also Tamanoi 2, p. 167. Yamamuro cites the same
figures as Chan: "roughly 270,000 settlers" and "some 80,000" dead (p. 282).

183   *The Japanese army had abandoned them*   Young, Louise, pp. 406–8. See also
Wilson 2, p. 283: "No military protection was provided for them and there were no
plans for their evacuation. In fact, Kwantung Army contingency plans against Soviet
entry into the war, made two months before the event, placed the line of Japanese
defense in such a way that the majority of Japanese settlers would be abandoned."

183   *"I had the misfortune"*   I came across Nagamine via a 2010 article in *Nikkei
West*, "Northern California's longest printing Japanese-American newspaper—now in
our 20th year." See Sammon. I met Nagamine with his wife, their daughter Janet, and
UC Santa Cruz professor Alan Christy. Their collaborative book and documentary film
on Nagamine's life is forthcoming.

184   *Commanded by the architect of the Stalingrad*   His name was Aleksandr
Vasilevsky.

184   *"Lightning flashed unexpectedly"*   General Beloborodov quoted in Glantz, p.
44. His landmark and highly readable monograph gave the battle its more mellifluous
name.

185   *Once this site was a busy dock*   The hamlet is named Yihantongxiang.

185   *A Place of Four Families settler later recalled*   Tamanoi 2, p. 48.

186   *Several authors survived collective suicides*   See Chan, pp. 19–22, and Itoh,
pp. 186–87, for examples.

186 **Hundreds of Japanese women** Estimates range from the hundreds to thousands. In a 2006 report, China's state news agency said more than 10,000 Japanese gathered at the docks waiting for evacuation boats, and that "many chose to commit suicide." By spring "more than 5,000 had died." Of the survivors, 2,400 chose to be repatriated, while "more than 2,000 remaining, mostly women and children, were adopted by the local people." (See "War Proves a Mixed Blessing for Some Japanese," Xinhua, August 12, 2006.) Chan writes: "It is estimated that 20,000 Japanese refugees were kept in Fangzheng" in refugee camps. Only 8,649 survived the winter. By spring 2,300 had married Chinese men, 2,360 had died from disease and hunger, 1,120 children had been adopted locally, and 1,200 had tried to walk toward Harbin (Chan, p. 22).

187 **In the first year after surrender** Young, Louise, p. 410.

187 **An equal number was press-ganged** Dower, pp. 50–51.

188 **I talked to him** The farm began by growing flowers, and is named A. Nagamine Nursery. It's in the town of Watsonville.

188 **Across Manchukuo, the majority of surviving settlers** Young, Louise, pp. 410–11. From the beginning, with a housing and food shortage at home, Japan was not officially eager to have settlers return. Even in postwar Japan, returnees receive a subsidized apartment, language and job training lessons, and a monthly stipend of around $1,500, a pittance in Tokyo, one of the world's most expensive cities. An estimated 60 percent of returnees live on welfare (Tamanoi 2, p. 131). For details on the boat lift, see Maruyama.

189 **Of the survivors** A local offspring of a Japanese woman and Chinese man told Xinhua that their parents' union was not voluntary: "At that time, anyone could go there and bring a Japanese woman or child home," said fifty-four-year-old Bi Zhongqing.

189 **According to the county government** "War Proves a Mixed Blessing for Some Japanese," Xinhua, August 12, 2006.

189 **The cemetery's roots date to 1963** Ibid. See also Pulvers; Chan, p. 22; and Itoh, p. 187.

189 **"The people of Japan and the settlers"** Pulvers. I am reminded of the oath some pioneer farmers took before leaving Japan: "I shall not let my family interfere with my decision. I shall sacrifice my life for our colony. I shall make every effort to settle down permanently in Manchuria."

189   *A Japanese officer, expressing guilt*   Itoh, p. 40.

190   *"We have to ask them not to plant any more"*   The caretaker's name is Zhang Lin.

190   *The previous week, five Chinese nationalists*   Lau. Itoh (p. 187) wrote that the cemetery has a caretaker due to previous vandalism.

190   *"Our economy profits thanks to people who went to Japan"*   Nishimura 1. The county has one of the largest amounts of foreign currency being exchanged by a local government, as migrants remit money home in yen.

190–91   *Once this site had been an Allied prisoner of war camp*   In Chinese, it's called *er zhan meng jun zhan fu jizhongying jiuzhi*, and it's located in Shenyang's Dadong district, southeast of the intersection of Pangjiang Jie and Zhulin Lu.

191   *Now age ninety-two, Leith remembers*   I met him after finding his self-published book for sale online, which he mailed to me inscribed: "Dear Michael Meyer! I hope you enjoy my memoirs! I would like to talk with you so call me on the phone." I'm grateful to his wife, Helen, and son Mike for welcoming me into their home in Golden, Colorado, and assisting with the reproduction of photographs Hal Leith took on his mission. Leith passed away on Christmas Eve 2013.

191   *Also: beat the advancing*   Yu, p. 231.

191   *Dubbed Operation Cardinal, it was one of eight*   The others: Operation Magpie (Beijing), Duck (Weixian), Flamingo (Harbin; aborted due to Soviet advance), Sparrow (Shanghai), Pigeon (Hainan Island), Raven (Vientiane), and Quail (Hanoi). The latter was headed by a young captain with the enviable name Archimedes L. A. Patti, who came face-to-face with Ho Chi Minh and found himself calming the five French soldiers who were part of his team and itching to begin a fight with the guerrilla Communist leader. (Imagine if they had.) Ho would soon launch a war of independence against the French colonizers. Ibid., p. 232.

191   *One of these OSS operations would end with the execution*   Ibid., pp. 236–41.

191   *Chinese Communist forces were angered by the Yalta agreements*   Historians debate whether Franklin D. Roosevelt "sold out" Manchuria at these talks, which restored Russia's rights to the Northeast's railroads and shipyards at Dalian/Port Arthur, which it had lost in the Russo-Japanese War of 1905. General Albert Wedemeyer,

commander of U.S. forces in China, felt the Yalta agreement was a betrayal of Chinese sovereignty, as did the American ambassador to China, Patrick Hurley, who tried to convince Winston Churchill to assuage Stalin by ceding control of Hong Kong. Churchill balked, saying the colony "would be taken out of the British Empire over my dead body." Ibid., pp. 241–42.

192   *The nearest American forces were stationed nine hundred miles away*   Clemens, pp. 73 and 77.

192   *"If we are not in Korea and Manchuria when the Russians get there"*   Yu, p. 231.

192   *He ordered his agents*   Clemens, p. 76.

192   *The survivors of that battle had been shipped to Taiwan*   Harris, pp. 162–64. The men were from the "hell ship" *Tottori Maru.*

192   *There, the men were divided*   Yardley.

192   *Japanese stacked their frozen bodies*   Harris, p. 165.

192   **An improved camp**   Brougher, p. 168.

193   *The Japanese considered Hoten a model camp*   Ibid., p. 168. Whereas the average death rate in a Japanese camp was 27 percent—compared to 4 percent in German-run camps—at Hoten, 12 percent of prisoners died, three of whom were executed in 1943 after trying to escape.

193   *"It is entirely out of my expectations"*   Yang Jing, p. 235. Professor Yang (of Shenyang University) reprinted Matsuda's address, which the colonel had handwritten in cursive English.

193   *"I am down 14 pounds"*   Brougher, p. 179.

193   **On August 8, two days after the bombing**   Ibid., p. 181.

193   *August 15: "Many rumors"*   Ibid., p. 182.

193   *August 16: "Wildest kinds of rumors"*   Ibid., p. 183.

194 *At the sight of the dozen soldiers*   The Chinese team member was named Cheng Shiwu and is lost to history. The Nisei doctor, Fumio Ito, lives in Hawaii.

195 *In his prison diary, Brigadier General W. E. Brougher*   Brougher, p. 183.

195 *In one of his last entries from the camp*   Ibid., p. 184.

195 *General Wainwright, gaunt and wearing threadbare clothes*   Clemens, p. 87.

195 *A Cardinal report described a binge*   Clemens, p. 95, and Yu, p. 244.

196 *"Some of the Chinese took my side"*   Leith, pp. 60–61.

196 *Soviet forces, an OSS officer reported*   Clemens, p. 99.

196 *The Russians even took*   "Changchun Mayor Inspires His City," *New York Times*, March 11, 1946.

196 *William Donovan, the head of the OSS*   Yu, p. 245.

197 *Standing on the Songhua River docks where Japanese mothers*   Ishida.

197 *Officials said*   Ibid. The tributary is the Daluomi River, called "Siwangdu" (Ferry of Death) for those swept away and drowned when trying to cross.

197 *The Japanese invasion caused 14 to 20 million*   Mitter 1, p. 5, notes the former figure is a conservative estimate. On p. 363 he says "the numbers are not clear" and adds the latter figure. Mitter notes, too, that the war resulted in massive refugee flight. Official mainland accounts usually use the higher estimate of deaths.

198 *In a Tokyo courtroom in 2002*   Lewis and "China Alerted by Serious Soil Pollution, Vows Better Protection," *Economist*, April 17, 2014. The historian Sheldon Harris (see note below) died four days later.

198 *Over thirteen years, an estimated three thousand prisoners*   Estimate given at the museum. Harris notes that the number actually underestimates people killed prior to the base's inception, since Ishii had begun human experiments in Harbin nine years earlier, in 1932. Nor does the figure take into account the postwar death toll of civilians living around the camps (thirty thousand dead from plague in 1947, for example). Harris, pp. 86–87.

198 **Which, in turn, poisoned local wells** Ibid., p. 99. Earlier, Harris notes that, with a perimeter of six square kilometers, the Pingfang camp rivaled Auschwitz-Birkenau in area (p. 43).

198 **As the Soviets invaded in August 1945** Ibid., p. 245.

199 **American troops found him hiding in his home village** Ibid., p. 246.

199 **"Evidence gathered in this investigation"** Ibid., p. 263.

199 **In 1948 the United States granted Ishii** Ibid., pp. 287–91 and 304–5. See also Drea, p. 37. It summarizes National Archives holdings on the matter, and also that Harris believed immunity was approved not only by Generals MacArthur and Willoughby in Tokyo but by their superiors in Washington.

199 **For three decades, the deal was kept secret** The journalist John W. Powell was a veteran China hand who had published and edited the *China Monthly Review* from Shanghai until 1953. (His father had cofounded it in 1917 as the *China Weekly Review*. He lost both his feet to gangrene in a Japanese prison camp and died in 1947 at age sixty.) Powell had been unsuccessfully tried for sedition after claiming the United States used chemical weapons in the Korean War. His articles on Unit 731—and the American immunity deals—appeared in the *Bulletin of Concerned Asian Scholars* in 1980 and in the *Bulletin of the Atomic Scientists* in 1981 after mainstream media turned him down. See Fox.

199 The allegations were finally confirmed by the American historian Sheldon Harris, author of *Factories of Death: Japanese Biological Warfare, 1932–45 and the American Cover-up*, published in 1994. The book influenced legislation, passed in 2000, ordering American government agencies to release all information held on the Japanese Imperial Army that details evidence of war crimes. In 2007 the National Archives declassified 100,000 pages of records, prefaced with a 170-page guide to their contents, available free online: http://www.archives.gov/iwg/japanese-war-crimes/.

199 Harris notes that the Chinese (KMT) judge at the Tokyo War Crimes Tribunal never mentioned Japan's bacterial warfare, nor were Japanese prosecuted for it on the mainland; Harris reports that Japanese prisoners associated with bacterial warfare held by the Communists were not executed but returned home "singing the praises of their captors" for the leniency they received (pp. 315–16).

199–200   *"The people in Manchuria were complete slaves"*   Inventory of the Papers of Roy L. Morgan. Box 1, Folder 6, MSS 93-4. Item 7: Interrogation of Pu Yi (Continued), p. 6.

200   *"It is almost impossible to describe the pain"*   Ibid. p. 9.

200   *"I had better not go"*   Inventory of the Papers of Roy L. Morgan. Box 1, Folder 6, MSS 93-4. Item 6: Interrogation of Ai-Hsin-Cho-Lo Pu Yi (Henry Pu Yi), 1300–1500 hours, p. 1. At the time of Puyi's testimony, the term *Manchurian* was popularly used in English, instead of today's *Manchu.* The contemporary Chinese term for the ethnicity, *manzu*, had yet to be coined. I'm guessing that, in Chinese, Puyi referred to himself as a *manzhouren*, which literally translates as Manchurian, or a person from *manzhou*, Manchuria.

200   *"The situation was like myself being kidnapped"*   Inventory of the Papers of Roy L. Morgan. Box 1, Folder 6, MSS 93-4. Item 5: Interrogation of Ai-Hsin-Cho-Lo Pu Yi (Henry Pu Yi), 0900–1200 hours, p. 8.

200   *"That was my ideal"*   Ibid., Box 13, Folder 1, MSS 78-3, p. 1.

200   *In his autobiography, written two decades later*   Puyi, p. 329.

201   *His memoir, published by the state press*   Ibid, p. 306.

201   *In 1967, as the Cultural Revolution*   Scotland, p. 10.

201   *In its obituary*   "Pu Yi, Last Emperor of China and a Puppet for Japan, Dies; Enthroned at 2, Turned Out at 6, He Was Later a Captive of Russians and Peking Reds," *New York Times*, October 18, 1966.

201   *In 1995 a private cemetery . . . paid his widow*   Ho, Stephanie.

202   *"The casualties were about the same"*   Pomfret. In Chinese the siege is called *changchun weikunzhan.*

202   *The colonel's book describing the siege*   Ibid. Pomfret reported that President Yang Shangkun delivered the verdict. By then the book had sold 100,000 copies but was pulled from stores in spring 1990. The book also alleged that Communist troops smuggled large amounts of opium during the civil war.

203 **A Hong Kong–based researcher** Jacobs. The professor's name is Lung Ying-tai, and her book is titled *Big River, Big Sea: Untold Stories of 1949*.

203 **"Some refugees threw down their babies"** *Christian Science Monitor* (translated excerpt from the book).

203 **"Not allowing the starving city residents to leave"** Pomfret. "The author quoted cables from other officers asking that the army be allowed to save starving people. The requests were denied."

203 **Chinese schoolchildren** Jacobs.

203 **China estimates that, since 1945** Monahan, and Xinhua reports. Japan disputes the number, saying estimates range from hundreds of thousands to millions (Yamamura, p. 290).

203 **In Jilin province in 2004** Ibid.

203 **Under its obligations** "China, Japan End Excavation of Chemical Weapons," Xinhua, November 7, 2006. Xinhua 1.

203–4 **A Japanese Foreign Ministry spokesman** Monahan.

Chapter 14: Great Heat

212 **In the New World, after two years of food shortages** Philbrick, p. 165.

212 **In 1954, after an estimated 800,000 landlords** Ho, Peter, p. 8. This is a government estimate. Others go as high as two million. (See Lawrence, p. 13.)

213 **Two years later China** Chen Guidi, p. 145. Li Huaiyin put the number at 708,912, rising to 719,438 in 1982 (p. 361).

213 **The Party called its agrarian restructuring** Li Huaiyin, p. 23.

214 **The policy triggered the Great Famine** Dikötter, p. 333.

215 **"We knew what it was like to starve"** Forney. Li Huaiyin notes that Xiaogang has been "mythified" to the point of some contemporary Chinese journalists questioning

its story (p. 268). Also, despite promising to, the remaining men chose not to sign beside Yan's name but beneath it, shunting most responsibility—and potential punishment—to him. Several of his descendants still held this grudge when I visited the village.

216 *In a series of policies issued between 1978 and 1984* Zweig, pp. 47–85. His chapter is a blow-by-blow account of the advance-retreat-retrench steps the central government took in scrapping collective farming.

217 *The reforms continued* Ho, Peter, p 12.

218 *China has 22 percent of the world's population* Lohmar.

218 *Globally, it is the largest producer* Ibid.

218 *Only 5 percent of China's poultry* Ibid.

218 *In the province where* The Good Earth *was set* Herzfelder.

219 *A 2013 government report said that 10 percent* Pang Jiaoming.

219 *In 2007 the central government ran two experimental programs* Miller, Tom, 1. The exchange auctioned land credits to 179 buyers, including national developers and conglomerates such as PetroChina. The words *buy* and *lease* were avoided, because all land in China is owned by the state (in cities) or the collective (in the countryside). Instead, usage rights to rural land were "transferred" (*zhuanrang*) according to a contract of "compensated use" (*youchang shiyong*). The exchange permitted rural governments to swap, or "couple" (*guagou*), rural land into state-owned urban land available for development. (China divides land into four types: urban construction, rural construction, agricultural, and forest, with limits on each.)

219 *The chasm between the two broadened after economic reforms* Hongbin Li (p. 1).

219 An additional note on *hukou*: In 2010, for the first time since the 1989 demonstrations centered at Tiananmen Square, Chinese newspapers defied the Party propaganda department's diktat and published a joint editorial calling for the system to be scrapped. Eleven newspapers published the piece simultaneously, on the eve of China's annual parliamentary meetings. "We hope," it said, "that a bad policy we have suffered for decades will end with our generation, and allow the next generation to truly enjoy the sacred rights of freedom, democracy, and equality bestowed by the

constitution." The editorial was ordered removed from websites within hours, as was its organizer, the deputy chief editor of the *Economic Observer*. (See Canaves.)

220 Ironically, a trend developed wherein college graduates, facing a crowded employment market, began applying to have their classification reverted to "rural" so they could be allotted housing and land. (See Chen, Lulu, 2.)

220 **In the second Sichuan experiment** Ibid. The homes were torn down and the land planted, resulting in a net gain of cropland. The village government then swapped this "land credit" (*dipiao*) with a developer, who could now build on a similar amount of agricultural land. The government saw it as a win-win-win: China's "red line" of 120 million hectares of farmland remained unchanged; farmers had been "urbanized" by choice; and new construction added to national GDP.

220 As is often the case with state-sanctioned policy experiments, informal swaps of this sort had been happening nationwide. Landesa, the leading nongovernmental organization studying land issues in the developing world, found that 15 percent of Chinese farmers had transferred their land by 2008. In the most recent official statistics, the Ministry of Agriculture shows that land transfers tripled from 2006 to 2009, involving 12 percent of total national farmland. (See Landesa and Zhu Keliang.)

220 **Local debt skyrocketed** Wang, Aileen, 2.

220 **The lucrative deals, and corruption** Huang, Cary.

220 **A comprehensive nationwide survey** Landesa. The survey found that only one-third of Chinese farmers had been issued the paperwork asserting their land rights. Furthermore, less than half of those documents contained the required information or complied with the law, e.g., because they did not list women's names.

220 **A rural economist at the state policy** The speaker is Wu Jinglian at the State Council's Development and Research Centre. O'Neill.

220 **In Sichuan province, the Chengdu city government** Miller, Tom, 1.

221 **The only news story I found** http://www.bjgtj.gov.cn/publish/portal1/tab2951/info54411.htm. (The site has improved markedly.) The Ministry of Agriculture issues policy regulations, while the Bureau of Land and Resources is responsible for administering them. Its bureaus draw and measure boundaries and issue ownership certificates to local governments.

221   Poker results at: http://www.bjgtj.gov.cn/publish/portal1/tab2951/info54408.htm.

221   Starting in 2013, the bureau was engaged in a five-year nationwide project to map farmers' land holdings by satellite and issue standardized documents of tenancy. The project was aimed at both preventing land grabs by local officials and providing security for farmers merging or leasing their fields that they would be compensated for every inch of earth they held. An unexpected result of the survey thus far was an increase in acreage and thus the amount of subsidy (about $150 per acre) Beijing had to pay farmers. Previously, land holdings were underreported to avoid grain taxes. (See Hornby.)

221   *On my kang, as Mr. Guan*   Thanks to Fanny at Fathom China for doing due diligence on Eastern Fortune Rice.

223   *At the start of 2013*   "Premier Underlines Developing Modern Agriculture, Scale Farming," Xinhua, April 1, 2013. A survey by the ministry found that 877,000 families, each holding an average of thirteen hectares, qualified as a "family farm." It's difficult to compare this figure to the U.S., which officially classifies many agribusinesses as family farms.

224   *The minister of agriculture said that*   Zuo 1.

CHAPTER 15: THE HALF-BOMBED BRIDGE TO WORKER'S VILLAGE

232   *The city's name meant "Eastern Peony"*   Today's Dandong was called Andong, or Antung, during the Korean War and Manchukuo.

233   *From his Tokyo headquarters*   Marolda, p. 163.

234   *Meanwhile, MacArthur had cabled Washington*   Blair, p. 396. He writes that MacArthur's long communiqués—this one dated November 6—were not only ridiculed by the Pentagon as "posterity papers" but also gave priceless intelligence to Chinese commanders, since they showed MacArthur was ignorant of their positions and numbers.

234   *Until November 1950, UN forces*   Futrell, p. 220.

234   *Among their targets was a young ensign*   On Patrol.

234   *MacArthur pressed President Truman*   Futrell, pp. 222–23. While there were precedents of "two to three minutes" of flying time over an international border in

hot pursuit, the United States could not convince its UN-force allies to allow allow passage into Manchuria.

234 **In his memoir, MacArthur wrote that** Ibid., p. 394.

234 **MacArthur threatened to resign** Blair, p. 395.

235 **Furthermore, because the United States** Ibid., p. 397. At the time, the Joint Chiefs could issue orders to commanders in the field.

235 **At a preflight briefing** Bruning, p. 49.

235 **"All of North Korea would be cleared"** Blair, p. 403.

235 **From twenty-seven thousand feet, through unrelenting flak** Bruning, p. 50.

235–236 **Truman was "drunker"** Blair, p. 401.

236 **General Bradley later wrote** Ibid., p. 402. This, from one of Lyndon Johnson's most hawkish advisers on Vietnam.

236 **MacArthur had refused to salute Truman** Ibid., p. 402.

236 **After six hundred sorties** Marolda, p. 309.

236 **For MacArthur, "the wine of victory"** Blair, p. 402.

Chapter 16: Beginning of Autumn

239 **Outside of Keats** These are lines 566–77 from "Endymion," which begins: "A thing of beauty is a joy forever." Keats, p. 30.

247 **After threshing the kernels** Sun-dried rice is yellowish and results in more broken grains than rice from a mechanical dryer. Eastern Fortune's blower and rice husk furnace shelled the kernel's rough, inedible shell. What remained was brown rice, whose layer of bran produced a chewy, nutty flavor. Removing the bran traditionally required milling it on a grindstone. Eastern Fortune's Japanese-made "vertical whitener" removed the bran and polished the remaining kernel to the white grain that consumers recognize. (Technically, we eat the plant's endosperm, the layer of starch and protein

that protected its embryo.) Most rice sold in markets worldwide is polished, which reduces the grain's level of B vitamins and iron; unlike in China, in the United States the rice must be "enriched," replacing the nutrients. After polishing, the rice would be graded based on placing 500 grams of kernels on a plate and counting the damaged ones, then packaged, or precooked and sold as instant rice.

Chapter 17: Dalian's Display Cases

249 *"The marching high school students"* Kuramoto, p. 19.

250 *The villas still showed* Ibid., p. 18.

Chapter 18: Frost's Descent

257 *"Prepare to weep and be grievously distressed"* Simpson (writing as Putnam Weale), p. 226.

265 *Risk is shifted away from the farmers* As this book went to press, work began on the Jilin Food Zone, a "super farm" located forty miles west of Wasteland, near the Changchun airport. A joint project proposed by the prime ministers of China and Singapore, the 559-square-mile farm, almost the size of the city of Los Angeles, will produce organic rice, vegetables, poultry, milk, and infant milk powder using Singaporean expertise and technology. Additionally, 480 retail shops, a hotel, and exhibition center are planned.

266 *One-quarter of China's villages* Boehler 1. The total number declined from 368,000 to 269,000 in 2012. "China loses 80 to 100 villages to urban migration every day," according to a study by the rural development scholar Yu Jianrong, of the Chinese Academy of Social Sciences.

266 *The nation targeted an urbanization rate* Miller 3.

Chapter 19: Major Snow

277 *"The course of life is unpredictable"* I love that this is quote is not, in fact, Chinese at all. It's from the rabbi and philosopher Abraham J. Heschel, whose mother and two sisters were killed by Nazis. He escaped to America in 1940.

BIBLIOGRAPHY

PUBLISHED SOURCES

(Where a formal English translation appears on the cover of a Chinese-language text, I have listed it. In other cases, the translation is my own.)

"Amur's Siren Song, The: The Long River That Marks the Border Between Russia and China Has Proved to Be a Site of Dashed Hopes." *Economist*, December 19, 2009.

Atiyah, Jeremy. "The Whole Point of Manchuria Is to Make Everything Else on Earth Seem Really Quite Nice." *Independent*, January 16, 2000.

Bakich, Olga. "Emigre Identity: The Case of Harbin." *South Atlantic Quarterly* 99, no. 1 (Winter 2000); Raleigh: Duke University Press, pp. 51–73.

Barboza, David.
  1. "In China, Wholesale Urban Flight." *New York Times*, November 25, 2005.
  2 "Auditor Warns of Risks from Local Debt in China." *New York Times*, June 27, 2011.

Barrionuevo, Alexei. "China's Interest in Farmland Makes Brazil Uneasy." *New York Times*, May 26, 2011.

Bell, John. *A Journey from St. Petersburg to Pekin, 1719–22*. Edinburgh: University Press, 1965.

Benson, Richard. *The Farm: The Story of One Family and the English Countryside*. London: Penguin, 2005.

Blair, Clay. *The Forgotten War: America in Korea, 1950–1953*. New York: Times Books, 1987.

Boehler, Patrick.
    1. "Report Points to Local Opposition to Beijing's Land Reform Efforts." *South China Morning Post*, September 17, 2013.
    2. "Anti-Corruption Scholar Yu Jianrong's Rural Renewal Project Stalls." *South China Morning Post*, October 8, 2013.

Bogan, M. L. C. *Manchu Customs and Superstitions*. Tientsin: China Booksellers, Ltd., 1928.

Bradsher, Keith. "U.N. Food Agency Issues Warning on China Drought." *New York Times*, February 9, 2011.

Bray, Francesca.
    1. *Science and Civilisation in China. Vol. 6: Biology and Biological Technology. Part II: Agriculture* (Joseph Needham, ed.). Cambridge: Cambridge University Press, 1984.
    2. *The Rice Economies: Technology and Development in Asian Societies*. Berkeley: University of California Press, 1986.

Breidenbach, Joana (ed.). *China Inside Out: Contemporary Chinese Nationalism and Transnationalism*. Budapest: Central European University Press, 2005.

Brooke, Lord. *An Eye-Witness in Manchuria*. London: Eveleigh Nash, 1905.

Brougher, William Edward. *South to Bataan, North to Mukden: The Prison Diary of Brigadier General W. E. Brougher*. Athens: University of Georgia Press, 1971.

Bruning, John R. *Crimson Sky: The Air Battle for Korea*. Dulles: Potomac Books, 2005.

Buck, David D. "Railway City and National Capital: Two Faces of the Modern in Changchun." In Esherick, Joseph W. (ed.). *Remaking the Chinese City: Modernity and National Identity, 1900–1950*. Honolulu: University of Hawaii Press, 1999.

Buck, John Lossing.
    1. *Chinese Farm Economy: A Study of 2,866 Farms in Seventeen Localities and Seven Provinces in China*. Chicago: University of Chicago Press, 1930.
    2. *Land Utilization in China: A Study of 16,786 Farms in 168 Localities, and 38,256 Farm Families in Twenty-two Provinces in China, 1929–33*. New York: Paragon, 1964.
    3. *Three Essays on Chinese Farm Economy*. New York: Garland, 1980.

Buck, Pearl S.
    1. *The Good Earth*. New York: John Day, 1931.
    2. *My Several Worlds*. New York: John Day, 1954.
    3. *China As I See It*. New York: John Day, 1970.
    4. *China Past and Present*: New York: John Day, 1972.

"Building Excitement: Can China Avoid a Bubble?" *Economist*, March 5, 2011.

Burns, John. "Harbin, Near Disputed Soviet Border, Retains Vestiges of Russian Influence." *New York Times*, January 3, 1974.

Buruma, Ian. "A Chinese Box: In Manchuria's Boom, Echoes of a Japanese Utopia." *Harper's* 6 (1994): pp. 70–80.

Canaves, Sky. "Editor Who Authored Chinese Editorial on Reform Ousted by Authorities." *Wall Street Journal*, March 9, 2010.

"Capital Punishments." *Economist*, December 18, 1997.

Carlson, Benjamin. "Good News: U.S. Exports to China Soar, Setting New Record." *Global Post*, January 21, 2014.

Carter, James H.
1. *Creating a Chinese Harbin*. Ithaca, NY: Cornell University Press, 2002.
2. "A Tale of Two Temples," in "Harbin and Manchuria: Place, Space and Identity." *South Atlantic Quarterly* 99, no. 1 (Winter 2000).

Chan, Anita, Richard Madsen, and Jonathan Unger. *Chen Village: Revolution to Globalization*. Berkeley: University of California Press, 2009.

Chan, Yeeshan. *Abandoned Japanese in Postwar Manchuria*. London and New York: Routledge, 2011.

Chang Kia-Ngau, Donald G. Gillin, and Ramon H. Myers (eds.). *Last Chance in Manchuria*. Stanford, CA: Hoover Institution Press, 1989.

Chang, Leslie T. "Book Review of *Pearl Buck in China* by Hilary Spurling." *Washington Post*, July 18, 2010.

"Changchun Mayor Inspires His City." *New York Times*, March 11, 1946.

Chatwin, Bruce.
1. *Anatomy of Restlessness*. New York: Viking, 1996.
2. *In Patagonia*. New York: Penguin, 1988.

Chen Guidi and Wu Chuntao. *Will the Boat Sink the Water? The Life of China's Peasants*. New York: PublicAffairs, 2006. Also in Chinese as 中国农民调查。 Beijing: People's Culture Press, 2004.

Chen, Lulu.
1. "Invited to Farm, but Forced off the Land." *South China Morning Post*, August 6, 2011.
2. "Rural *Hukou* Now a Prize for Graduates." *South China Morning Post*, July 25, 2010.

Chen, Stephen. "Chemical Spill Sparks Battle for Bottled Water." *South China Morning Post*, July 30, 2010.

Chen Wenfu. *Northern Paddies: Production Technology Explained.* (北方水稻: 生产技术问答。) Beijing: China Agricultural Press, 2010.

Chiasson, Blaine R. *Administering the Colonizer: Manchuria's Russians Under Chinese Rule, 1918–1929*. Vancouver: University of British Columbia Press, 2010.

"China Alerted by Serious Soil Pollution, Vows Better Protection." Xinhua, April 17, 2014.

"China, Japan End Excavation of Chemical Weapons." Xinhua, November 11, 2006.

"China Quells Reds in Riot at Harbin." *New York Times*, July 19, 1929.

Choi Chi-yuk. "Farmers Are Finally Allowed to Use Land Rights as Loan Collateral." *South China Morning Post*, April 12, 2009.

Christie, Dugald. *Thirty Years in Moukden, 1883–1913*. London: Constable and Company, 1914.

Chuin-Wei Yap. "China Sees Food Needs Rising." *Wall Street Journal*, March 25, 2011.

Clausen, Soren, and Stig Thogersen. *The Making of a Chinese City: History and Historiography in Harbin*. London: M. E. Sharpe, 1995.

Clemens, Peter. "Operation 'Cardinal': The OSS in Manchuria, August 1945." *Intelligence and National Security* 13, no. 4, (1998) pp. 71–106.

Clyde, Paul Hibbert. *International Rivalries in Manchuria, 1689–1922*. Columbus: Ohio State University Press, 1926.

Collins, Perry McDonough. *A Voyage down the Amoor*. New York: D. Appleton and Company, 1860.

"Come Back in Five Years: It Looks Good, Even with North Korea as a Partner." *Economist*, June 27, 1998.

Condon, Richard. *The Manchurian Candidate*. New York: Four Walls Eight Windows, 2003.

Constitution of the People's Republic of China. Beijing: Foreign Languages Press, 1994.

"Consul Shoots Himself." *New York Times*, December 20, 1906.

"Consul Warner a Suicide." *New York Times*, May 12, 1914.

Coox, Alvin. *Nomonhan: Japan Against Russia, 1939*. Palo Alto, CA: Stanford University Press, 1988.

Costain, Alfred. *The Life of Dr. Arthur Jackson of Manchuria*. London: Hodder and Stoughton, 1912.

Crossley, Pamela Kyle.
> 1. *Orphan Warriors: Three Manchu Generations and the End of the Qing World*. Princeton, NJ: Princeton University Press, 1990.
> 2. *The Manchus*. Cambridge, U.K.: Blackwell Publishers, 1997.

Crèvecoeur, J. Hector St. John de. *Letters from an American Farmer*. Oxford, U.K.: Oxford University Press, 1997.

Crow, Carl (ed.). *Japan's Dream of World Empire: The Tanaka Memorial*. New York: Harper and Brothers, 1942.

Cui Haipei. "Russia Land Lease Likely to Draw Foreign Investors." *China Daily*, March 16, 2012.

"Deafening Silence: An Investigation into Wartime Atrocities, but the Media Keeps Strangely Quiet." *Economist*, February 26, 2011.

Demick, Barbara. *Nothing to Envy: Ordinary Lives in North Korea*. New York: Spiegel & Grau, 2009.

Dikötter, Frank. *Mao's Great Famine*. New York: Walker & Co., 2010.

Dower, John W. *Embracing Defeat*. New York: W. W. Norton & Co, 1999.

Drage, Charles. *General of Fortune: The Story of One-Armed Sutton*. London: Heinemann, 1963.

Duara, Prasenjit. *Sovereignty and Authenticity: Manchukuo and the East Asia Modern*. Lanham, MD: Rowman and Littlefield, 2003.

DuBois, Thomas David. "Manchukuo's Filial Sons: States, Sects and the Adaptation of Graveside Piety." *East Asian History* 36 (December 2008), pp. 3–28.

Du Halde, Jean-Baptiste. *The General History of China*. London: J. Watts, 1741.

Duus, Peter, Ramon H. Myers, and Mark R. Peattie (eds.). *The Japanese Informal Empire in China, 1895–1937*. Princeton, NJ: Princeton University Press, 1989.

Edmonds, Richard L. "The Willow Palisade." *Annals of the Association of American Geographers* 69, no. 4 (December 1979), pp. 599–621.

Elder, Chris. *Old Peking: City of the Ruler of the World*. Hong Kong: Oxford University Press, 1997.

Elliot, Mark C.

    1. "The Limits of Tartary: Manchuria in Imperial and National Geographies." *Journal of Asian Studies* 59, no. 3 (August 2000), pp. 603–46.

    2. *The Manchu Way: The Eight Banners and Ethnic Identity in Late Imperial China*. Stanford, CA: Stanford University Press, 2001.

Ellman, Bruce A., and Stephen Kotkin (eds.). *Manchurian Railways and the Opening of China: An International History*. Armonk, NY, and London: M. E. Sharpe, 2010.

Enatsu, Yoshiki. *Banner Legacy*. Ann Arbor: University of Michigan Center for Chinese Studies, 2004.

Esherick, Joseph W. (ed.). *Remaking the Chinese City: Modernity and National Identity, 1900–1950*. Honolulu: University of Hawai'i Press, 1999.

"Et Tu, Manchu? One Hundred Years on, Only a Few Native Speakers Remain." *Economist*, October 8, 2011.

Fay, Stephen. *The Great Silver Bubble*. London: Hodder and Stoughton, 1982.

Fei Xiaotong. *From the Soil: The Foundations of Chinese Society* [*Xiangtu Zhongguo*], trans. Gary H. Hamilton and Wang Zheng. Berkeley: University of California Press, 1992.

Flath, James, and Norman Smith (eds.). *Beyond Suffering: Recounting War in Modern China*. Vancouver: University of British Columbia Press, 2012.

Fleming, George. *Travels on Horseback in Mantchu Tartary*. London: Hurst and Blackett, 1863.

Fleming, Peter.

    1. *News from Tartary: A Journey from Peking to Kashmir*. London: Jonathan Cape, 1936.

    2. *One's Company: A Journey to China in 1933*. London: Pimlico, 2004.

    3. *To Peking: A Forgotten Journey from Moscow to Manchuria*. London: Tauris, 2009.

Fogel, Joshua.
    1. (trans.) *Life Along the South Manchurian Railway: The Memoirs of Ito Takeo*. Armonk, NY: M. E. Sharpe, 1988.
    2. *The Literature of Travel in the Japanese Rediscovery of China, 1862–1945*. Stanford: Stanford University Press, CA, 1996.

Forney, Matt. "It Takes a Village." *Time*, August 15, 2005.

Fox, Margalit. "John W. Powell, 89, Dies; Writer in Sedition Case." *New York Times*, December 17, 2008.

Franck, Harry A. *Wandering in Northern China*. New York and London: The Century Co., 1923.

Frazier, Ian.
    1. *Great Plains*. New York: Farrar, Straus & Giroux, 1989.
    2. *Travels in Siberia*. New York: Farrar, Straus & Giroux, 2011.

Fujita Shigeru. *Kusa no hi: Man-Mo kaitakudan suterareta tami no kiroku* [*Epitaph of Grass: Records of the Abandoned People, the Agrarian Settlers in Manchuria and Mongolia*]. Kanazawa, Japan: Noto Shuppan, 1989.

Fulton, Austin. *Through Earthquake, Wind and Fire: Church and Mission in Manchuria 1867–1950*. Edinburgh: The Saint Andrew Press, 1967.

Futrell, Robert Frank. *The United States Air Force in Korea, 1950–1953*. Washington, DC: Office of Air Force History, 1983.

Garnaut, Ross, Guo Shutian, and Ma Guonan (eds.). *The Third Revolution in the Chinese Countryside*. Cambridge, U.K.: Cambridge University Press, 1996.

Gilbreath, Olive. "Where Yellows Rule White." *Harper's*, February 1929.

Gillin, Donald G., and Charles Ette. "Staying On: Japanese Soldiers and Civilians in China, 1945–1949." *Journal of Asian Studies* 42, no. 3 (May 1983), pp. 497–518.

Gottschang, Thomas R., and Dianna Lary. *Swallows and Settlers: The Great Migration from North China to Manchuria*. Ann Arbor, MI: Center for Chinese Studies, 2000.

Halberstam, David. *The Coldest Winter: America and the Korean War*. New York: Hyperion, 2007.

Han Lin. "War Proves a Mixed Blessing for Some Japanese." August 12, 2006. www.chinaview.cn

Hanson, Victor Davis. *Fields Without Dreams*. New York: The Free Press, 1996.

"Harbin's 'Squeeze' Highly Developed." *New York Times*, October 23, 1927.

Harris, Sheldon H. *Factories of Death: Japanese Biological Warfare, 1932–1945, and the American Cover-up*. New York: Routledge, 2002.

Herzfelder, Richard. "The Long Road to Half Tower." *China Economic Quarterly*, September 2013.

Hinrichs, Jan Paul (ed.). *Russian Poetry and Literary Life: Harbin and Shanghai, 1930–1950*. Amsterdam: Rodopi, 1987.

Hinton, William.
    1. *Iron Oxen: A Documentary of Revolution in Chinese Farming.* New York: Monthly Review Press, 1970.
    2. *Shenfan: The Continuing Revolution in a Chinese Village.* New York: Vintage, 1984.
    3. *Fanshen: A Documentary of Revolution in a Chinese Village.* New York: Monthly Review Press, 2008.

Ho, Peter (ed.). *Developmental Dilemmas: Land Reform and Institutional Change in China.* London: Routledge, 2005.

Ho, Peter, Jacob Eyferth, and Eduard B. Vermeer (eds.). *Rural Development in Transitional China: The New Agriculture.* London: Frank Cass, 2004.

Ho Ping-ti.
    1. "The Significance of the Ch'ing Period in Chinese History," *Journal of Asian Studies* 26, no. 2 (1967), pp. 189–95.
    2. "In Defense of Sinicization: A Rebuttal of Evelyn Rawski's 'Reenvisioning the Qing,'" *Journal of Asian Studies* 57, no. 1 (1998), pp. 123–55.

Ho, Stephanie. "Burial Plot of China's Last Emperor Still Holds Allure." *Voice of America,* October 10, 2011.

Holmes, W. M. *An Eye-witness in Manchuria.* New York: International Publishers, Inc., 1932.

Hornby, Lucy, and Hui Li. "China's Big Step in Rural Reform: Mapping Tiny Plots of Farm Land." Reuters, February 5, 2013.

Hosie, Alexander. *Manchuria: Its People, Resources and Recent History.* London: Methuen & Co., 1904.

Howard, Harvey J. *Ten Weeks with Chinese Bandits.* New York: Dodd, Mead and Company, 1926.

Hsiao Hung, *The Field of Life and Death and Tales of Hulan River.* Bloomington: University of Indiana Press, 1979.

Huaiyin Li. *Village China Under Socialism and Reform: A Micro-History, 1948–2008.* Stanford, CA: Stanford University Press, 2009.

Huang, Cary. "Farm Seizures Sow Seeds of Social Unrest." *South China Morning Post,* October 31, 2011.

Huang, Ray. "Some Observations on Manchuria in the Balance, Early 1946." *Pacific Historical Review* 27, no. 2 (May 1958), pp. 159–69.

Huc, Evariste Regis. *Travels in Tartary, 1844–46.* New York: Knopf, 1927.

Hudson, W. H. *Idle Days in Patagonia.* Stroud: Nonesuch, 2005.

Hunt, Michael H. *Frontier Defense and the Open Door: Manchuria in Chinese-American Relations, 1895–1911.* New Haven, CT: Yale University Press, 1973.

Hutzler, Charles. "U.N. to Extend Life of Tumen Project." *Wall Street Journal,* March 29, 2001.

Hyun Ok Park. *Two Dreams in One Bed: Empire, Social Life, and the Origins of the North Korean Revolution in Manchuria.* Durham, NC, and London: Duke University Press, 2005.

"Invisible and Heavy Shackles." *Economist*, May 6, 2010.

Isett, Christopher Mills. *State, Peasant and Merchant in Qing Manchuria, 1644–1862.* Palo Alto, CA: Stanford University Press, 2007.

Ishida, Koichiro. "Chinese Historian Battling Prejudice to Honor Japanese Settlers Who Perished in War." *Asahi Shimbun*, August 14, 2012.

Itoh, Mayumi. *Japanese War Orphans in Manchuria: Forgotten Victims of World War II.* Hampshire, U.K.: Palgrave Macmillan, 2010.

Jacobs, Andrew. "China Is Wordless on Traumas of Communists' Rise." *New York Times*, October 1, 2009.

James, Sir H. Evan M. *The Long White Mountain: A Journey in Manchuria.* New York: Greenwood Press, 1968.

Janhunen, Juha. *Manchuria: An Ethnic History.* Helsinki: Suomalais-Ugrilainen, 1996.

Japan Railways Department. *An Official Guide to Eastern Asia.* Tokyo: Department of Railways, 1920.

Jia, (Peter) Wei Ming. *Transition from Foraging to Farming in Northeast China.* Oxford: Archeopress, BAR International Series 1629, 2007.

Jikun Huang. "Enough for Everyone." *China Economic Quarterly*, September 2013.

Johnson, Ian. "In China, the Forgotten Manchu Seek to Rekindle Their Glory." *Wall Street Journal*, October 3, 2009.

Johnston, Reginald. *Twilight in the Forbidden City.* Hong Kong: Oxford University Press, 1985.

Jun Jing. *The Temple of Memories: History, Power and Morality in a Chinese Village.* Stanford, CA: Stanford University Press, 1996.

Kao Kang. *The First Year of Victory.* Peking: Foreign Languages Press, 1950.

Keats, John. *Endymion: A Poetic Romance.* London: Taylor and Hessey, 1818.

Kemp, Emily Georgiana. *The Face of Manchuria, Korea & Russian Turkestan.* New York: Duffield, 1911.

Kikuchi Kazuo. *Watashi to Manshu: Tohiko to kaitaku-dan no kiroku.* [*Manchuria and I: The Records of My Escape from Agrarian Colonies*]. Tokyo: Genshu, 2000.

Kilman, Scott. "Farm Belt Bounces Back." *Wall Street Journal*, October 12, 2010.

Kinney, Henry Walsworth.

    1. "Light on the Japanese Question." *Atlantic*, December 1920.

    2. "Earthquake Days." *Atlantic*, January 1924.

    3. *Modern Manchuria and the South Manchuria Railway Company.* Dairen: South Manchuria Railway, 1927.

    4. *Modern Manchuria and the South Manchuria Railway Company.* Dairen: South Manchuria Railway, 1928.

    5. *Modern Manchuria*. Dairen: South Manchuria Railway, 1929.

    6. *Manchuria Today*. Dairen: South Manchuria Railway, 1930.

Kuramoto, Kazuko. *Manchurian Legacy: Memoirs of a Japanese Colonist*. East Lansing: Michigan State University Press, 1999.

Lague, David. "Chinese Village Struggles to Save Dying Language." *New York Times*, March 18, 2007.

Lau, Mimi. "Memorial to Honour Japanese Settlers Razed." *South China Morning Post*, August 7, 2011.

Lahusen, Thomas (ed.). "Harbin and Manchuria: Place, Space and Identity." *South Atlantic Quarterly* 99, no. 1 (Winter 2000); Raleigh: Duke University Press, 2001.

Lattimore, Owen. *Manchuria: Cradle of Conflict*. New York: Macmillan, 1932.

Lawrance, Alan. *China Under Communism*. New York: Routledge, 2002.

Lee, Robert H. G. *The Manchurian Frontier in Ch'ing History*. Cambridge, MA: Harvard University Press, 1970.

Lewis, Paul. "Sheldon Harris, 74, Historian of Japan's Biological Warfare." *New York Times*, September 4, 2002.

Lewisohn, William. *Manchoukou Revisited*. Shanghai: North-China Daily News & Herald, Ltd., 1935.

Li Chong (ed.). A Survey of Puppet-Manchukuo Postcards. (伪 "满洲国" 明信片研究。) Changchun: Jilin Culture and History Press, 2005.

Li Ping. "Rural Land Tenure Reforms in China: Issues, Regulations and Prospects for Additional Reform." *Land Reform*, March 2003.

Li Zhiting (ed.). *Dongbei tong shi* [*A Complete History of China Northeast Borderland*]. Zhengzhou: Zhengzhou Press, 2003.

Ling Fenglou. *Rice Paddy Seedlings: 200 questions*. (水稻育苗。) Changchun: Jilin Science and Technology Press, 2007.

Liu Hongyi. "In Memory of the Japanese Agrarian Colonists." *Boli wenshi* 5 (1988).

Liu Zhiming (ed.). *The Vast Land of Northeast China*. (东北大地。) Beijing: Diyuan Press. 1989.

Lohmar, Brian. "Planting the Seeds of Reform." *China Economic Quarterly*, September 2013.

London, Jack. "Japan Puts an End to Usefulness of Correspondents." *San Francisco Examiner*, July 1, 1904.

Lü Qinwen (ed.). *Changchun: Once Upon a Time at Manchukuo Period*. Changchun: Jilin Culture and History Press, 2011.

Luo Jiewen. A *Dictionary of Old and New Northeast Place Names*. (东北古今地名辞典。) Changchun: Jilin Culture and History Press, 2009.

Lynch, Elizabeth M. "The Wukan Protests—Because Something Is Happening Here but You Don't Know What It Is." *China Law & Policy*, February 2, 2012.

Lyons, Elizabeth. "Home to One Jew, Harbin Synagogue to Be Renovated." *Times of Israel*, June 22, 2013.

Lytton, Victor.

    1. (et al.) "Preliminary Report on Conditions in Manchuria from the Commission of Enquiry Appointed by the Council of the League of Nations." London: His Majesty's Stationery Office, 1932.

    2. *The Lytton Report—and After*. London: League of Nations Union, 1933.

Ma Kun. "Manchukuo Community." *Jilin City wenshi ziliao* 36 (1987), pp. 95–109.

Manchoukuo: Handbook of Information. Hsinking: Manchoukuo Government, Bureau of Information and Publicity Department of Foreign Affairs, 1933.

Manchuria (monthly publication of the *Manchuria Daily News*), June–July 1941.

Marks, Robert B.

    1. *Rural Revolution in South China*. Madison: University of Wisconsin Press, 1984.

    2. *Tigers, Rice, Silk and Silt*. Cambridge, U.K.: Cambridge University Press, 1998.

Marolda, Edward J. (ed.). *The U.S. Navy in the Korean War*. Annapolis: Naval Institute Press, 2007.

Maruyama, Paul K. *Escape from Manchuria*. Mustang, OK: Tate Publishing, 2014.

McAleavy, Henry. *A Dream of Tartary: The Origins and Misfortune of Henry P'u Yi*. London: George Allen & Unwin, 1963.

Meyer, Mike. "Pearl of the Orient." *New York Times Book Review*, March 5, 2006.

"Military Heroes and Legends of Aerospace: Neil Armstrong." *On Patrol*, Fall 2010.

Miller, Judith. "Why Germ Warfare Happened." *City Journal*, Spring 2010.

Miller, Tom.

    1. "Turning Country Bumpkins into City Slickers." *China Economic Quarterly*, March 2011.

    2. "What Happens When the Land Runs Out?" *China Economic Quarterly*, September 26, 2013.

    3. "[China] Urbanization 2.0." *China Economic Quarterly*, March 18, 2014.

Millward, James A. *Beyond the Pass: Economy, Ethnicity and Empire in Qing Central Asia, 1759–1864*. Stanford, CA: Stanford University Press, 1998.

Mimura, Janis. *Planning for Empire: Reform Bureaucrats and the Japanese Wartime State*. Ithaca, NY: Cornell University Press, 2011.

Mitter, Rana.

    1. *The Manchurian Myth: Nationalism, Resistance, and Collaboration in Modern China*. Berkeley: University of California Press, 2000.

    2. *Forgotten Ally: China's World War II, 1937–1945*. Boston: Houghton Mifflin Harcourt, 2013.

Monahan, Andrew. "Japan's China Weapons Cleanup Hits a Snag." *Time*, March 31, 2008.

Morrison, Elting E. (ed.). *The Letters of Theodore Roosevelt*. Cambridge, MA Harvard University Press, 1951.

Mosher, John. *Japanese Post Offices in China and Manchuria*. Lawrence, MA: Quarterman Publications, Inc., 1978.

Myers, Ramon H. "Socioeconomic Change in Villages of Manchuria During the Ch'ing and Republican Periods: Some Preliminary Findings." *Modern Asian Studies* 10, no. 4 (1976), pp. 591–620.

Naismith, James. *Basketball: Its Origin and Development*. Lincoln: University of Nebraska Press, 1996. (Reprint of the 1941 original.)

Needham, Joseph. *Science and Civilisation in China. Vol. 6: Biology and Biological Technology. Part II: Agriculture* (written by Francesca Bray). Cambridge, U.K.: Cambridge University Press, 1984.

Nelson, Sarah Milledge. *The Archaeology of Northeast China*. London and New York: Routledge, 1995.

Newman, Robert P. *Owen Lattimore and the "Loss" of China*. Berkeley: University of California Press, 1992.

Nicholas II. *The Secret Letters of the Last Tsar*. New York: Longmans, 1938.

Nishimura, Daisuke.

    1. "Memorial to Japanese Colonists Sparks Anger in China." *Asahi Shimbun*, August 4, 2011.

    2. "Chinese County Criticized for Pro-Japanese Policy." *Asahi Shimbun*, August 9, 2011.

Norris, Frank. *The Octopus*. New York: Doubleday, 1901.

Oba Kaori and Hashimoto Susumu. *Haha to ko de miru Chugoku zanryu nihonjin koji* [*The History of Japanese Orphans Returning from China, Written for Mothers and Children*]. Tokyo: Kusa no Ne Shuppan-kai, 1986.

"Off the Rails? High-Speed Trains Might Be Forced to Go a Little More Slowly." *Economist*, April 2, 2011.

Official Guide to Eastern Asia, An; Vol. 1: Chosen & Manchuria/Siberia. Second Edition. Tokyo: Dept. of Railways, 1920.

"174 Russians Held, Harbin Report Says." *New York Times*, July 11, 1929.

O'Neill, F. W. S.

    1. *The Call of the East: Sketches from the History of the Irish Mission to Manchuria, 1869–1919*. London: James Clarke & Co., 1917.

    2. *Dr. Isabel Mitchell of Manchuria*. London: James Clarke & Co., 1917.

O'Neill, Mark. "2011—the Centenary of Two Very Different Revolutions." *South China Morning Post*, January 2, 2011.

"Others, The: It Is Becoming Both Easier and More Difficult to Experience the Thrill of Being an Outsider." *Economist*, December 19, 2009.

Pang Jiaoming, Gong Jing, and Liu Hongqiao. "Confronting China's Cadmium-Laced Rice Crisis." *Caixin*, June 5, 2013.

Parritt, Brian. *Chinese Hordes and Human Waves: A Personal Perspective of the Korean War, 1950–1953*. Barnsley, U.K.: Pen and Sword, 2011.

Pei Huang. *Reorienting the Manchus: A Study of Sinicization, 1583–1795*. Ithaca, NY: Cornell University East Asia Program, 2011.

Perlez, Jane. "China Exhibit, Part of an Anti-Japan Campaign, Reflects an Escalating Feud." *New York Times*, February 9, 2014.

Perdue, Peter. *China Marches West: The Qing Conquest of Central Eurasia, 1600–1800*. Cambridge, MA: Harvard University Press, 2010.

Philbrick, Nathaniel. *Mayflower*. New York: Viking Penguin, 2006.

Pils, Eva. "Land Disputes, Rights Assertion, and Social Unrest in China: A Case from Sichuan." *Columbia Journal of Asian Law* 19, no. 1, pp. 235–92.

"Plans Peace for Harbin." *New York Times*, March 6, 1909.

Pomfret, John. "Red Army Starved 150,000 Chinese Civilians, Book Says." Associated Press, November 22, 1990.

"Poor by Definition: China's Government Offers Relief to the Poor and to the Economy." *Economist*, December 3, 2011.

Powell, John B. *My Twenty-five Years in China*. New York: Macmillan, 1945.

"Premier Underlines Developing Modern Agriculture, Scale Farming." Xinhua, April 1, 2013.

"Prince Ito Assassinated." *New York Times*, October 26, 1909.

Pulvers, Roger. "Manchukuo Tragedy Finally Gets a Film Its Spurned Victims Deserve." *Japan Times*, May 10, 2009.

"Pu Yi, Last Emperor of China And a Puppet for Japan, Dies; Enthroned at 2, Turned Out at 6, He Was Later a Captive of Russians and Peking Reds." *New York Times*, October 18, 1966.

Puyi, Henry. *The Last Manchu*. Edited by Paul Kramer. New York: G. P. Putnam's Sons, 1967.

Rawski, Evelyn S.

    1. "Presidential Address: Reenvisioning the Qing; The Significance of the Qing Period in Chinese History." *Journal of Asian Studies* 55, no. 4 (1996).

    2. *The Last Emperors: A Social History of Qing Institutions*. Berkeley: University of California Press, 1998.

Reardon-Anderson, James. *Reluctant Pioneers: China's Expansion Northward, 1644–1937*. Palo Alto, CA: Stanford University Press, 2005.

Regional Handbook on Northeast China. New Haven, CT: Human Relations Area Files, Inc., 1956.

Restall, Hugo. "The Next Revolution? China Braces for Trouble from Angry Farmers." *Wall Street Journal*, July 25, 2001.

Romig, Shane. "China Snaps Up Farmland in Argentina." *Wall Street Journal*, June 20, 2011.

"Russia Would Rule by Chinese Treaty." *New York Times*, July 8, 1909.

"Russian Mobs Fight Chinese in Harbin." *New York Times*, January 5, 1932.

Ryall, Julian. "Did the U.S. Wage Germ Warfare in Korea?" *Daily Telegraph*, June 10, 2010.

Sammon, John. "Resident's Manchurian Story Is One of Survival." *Nikkei West*, December 16, 2010.

Schneider, Laurence. *Biology and Revolution in Twentieth-Century China*. Lanham, MD: Rowan & Littlefield, 2003.

Scotland, Tony. *The Empty Throne*. New York: Viking, 1993.

Seaman, Louis Livingston. *From Tokio Through Manchuria with the Japanese*. New York: Appleton Press, 1904.

Sears, David. *Such Men as These: The Story of the Navy Pilots Who Flew the Deadly Skies over Korea*. Cambridge, MA: Da Capo, 2010.

Selle, Earl Albert. *Donald of China*. New York: Harper and Brothers, 1948.

Shafer, Jack. "The Rise and Fall of the 'Bus Plunge' Story." *Slate*, November 13, 2006.

Shao Dan. *Remote Homeland, Recovered Borderland: Manchus, Manchoukuo, and Manchuria, 1907–1985*. Honolulu: University of Hawai'i Press, 2011.

Shoemaker, Michael Myers. *The Great Siberian Railway*. New York: Putnam, 1903.

Simpson, Bertrand Lennox. *Manchu and Muscovite: Being Letters from Manchuria Written During the Autumn of 1903*. Elibron Classics, 2005. (See also Weale, Putnam.)

Smith, Norman. *Resisting Manchukuo: Chinese Woman Writers and the Japanese Occupation*. Vancouver: University of British Columbia Press, 2007.

South Manchuria Railway Company.

    1. *Illustrated Guidebook for Traveling in Manchoukuo*. Dairen, 1934.

    2. *Manchuria: Land of Opportunities*. New York: SMR Press, 1922.

"Souvenir Enthronement Supplement." *Manchuria Daily News*, March 1, 1934.

Spector, Ronald H. *In the Ruins of Empire: The Japanese Surrender and the Battle for Postwar Asia*. New York: Random House, 2008.

Spurling, Hilary. *Pearl Buck in China*. New York: Simon & Schuster, 2010.

"State of Anarchy Found at Harbin." *New York Times*, April 19, 1908.

Stephan, John J. "Hijacked by Utopia: American Nikkei in Manchuria." *Amerasia Journal* 23, no. 3 (1997), pp. 1–42.

"Studying History Locked in a Black Box." *Christian Science Monitor*, September 27, 1990.

Suleski, Ronald. *The Modernization of Manchuria: An Annotated Bibliography*. Hong Kong: Chinese University Press, 1994.

Tabuchi, Hiroko. "Japanese Begin to Question Protections Given to Homegrown Rice." *New York Times*, January 9, 2014.

Tai Feng (ed.). *Historical Northeast* (岁月东北。) Guilin: Guangxi Normal University Press, 2007.

Talarigo, Jeff. *The Ginseng Hunter*. New York: Nan Talese, 2008.

Tam, Fiona. "At Least Two Killed, Six Hurt in Jiangxi Blasts." *South China Morning Post*, May 27, 2011.

Tamanoi, Mariko Asano.

    1. (ed.) *Crossed Histories: Manchuria in the Age of Empire*. Honolulu: University of Hawaii Press, 2005.

    2. *Memory Maps: The State and Manchuria in Postwar Japan*. Honolulu: University of Hawai'i Press, 2009.

Thubron, Colin. *In Siberia*. London: Penguin, 2000.

Tian Yongyuan, ed. *Peasant Lawsuits*. (农民打官司。) Beijing: China Agricultural Press. 2004.

T'ien Chun. *Village in August*. New York: Smith & Durrell, 1942.

Tisdale, Alice (Hobart). *Pioneering Where the World Is Old: Leaves from a Manchurian Note-Book*. New York: Henry Holt, 1917.

Tucker, David. "City Planning Without Cities: Order and Chaos in Utopian Manchukuo." In *Crossed Histories*. (See Tamanoi, Mariko Asano.)

Verbiest, Ferdinand. "Two Journeys into Tartary." In *History of the Two Tartar Conquerors of China*, edited and translated by the Earl of Ellesmere. London: Hakluyt Society, 1854.

Victoir, Laura, and Victor Zatsepine. *Harbin to Hanoi: Colonial Built Environment in Asia, 1840–1940*. Hong Kong: Hong Kong University Press, 2013.

Vidal, John. "India's rice revolution." *Observer*, February 16, 2013.

"Visitors to Harbin Find Expenses High." *New York Times*, October 28, 1928.

Wadley, Stephen A. *The Mixed-Language Verses from the Manchu Dynasty of China*. Bloomington: Indiana University Press, 1991.

Waley-Cohen, Joanna.

    1. "Commemorating War in Eighteenth-Century China," *Modern Asian Studies* 30, no. 4 (1996), pp. 869–99.

    2. "Religion, War, and Empire in Eighteenth-Century China," *International History Review* 20, no. 2 (1998), pp. 336–52.

    3. "Changing Spaces of Empire in Eighteenth-Century Qing China," in *Political Frontiers, Ethnic Boundaries, and Human Geographies in Chinese History*, ed. N. di Cosmo and D. Wyatt. London: Routledge/ Curzon, 2003.

    4. "The New Qing History." *Radical History Review* 88 (Winter 2004), pp. 193–206.

Walker, Dale. "Jack London's War." http://www.jacklondons.net/Journalism/JackLon donsWar.html

Walsh, James A. *Observations in the Orient*. Ossining, NY: Catholic Foreign Mission Society, 1919.

Wang Chenfu, ed. *The Best of Jilin*. (吉林之最。) Jilin: Jilin People's Press, 2008.

Wang Ning (ed.). *An English-Chinese Chinese-English Glossary of Agriculture*. Shanghai: Foreign Language Education Press, 2009.

Wang, Sally. "20 Years of Anger Unleashed." *South China Morning Post*, January 4, 2012.

"War Proves a Mixed Blessing for Some Japanese." Xinhua, August 12, 2006.

Weale, Putnam. *Manchu and Muscovite*. London: Macmillan, 1904. (See also Simpson, Bertrand Lennox.)

Wessel, David. "Shell Shock: Chinese Demand Reshapes U.S. Pecan Business." *Wall Street Journal*, April 18, 2011.

Wilson, Sandra.

    1. "The 'New Paradise': Japanese Emigration to Manchuria in the 1930s and 1940s." *International History Review* 17, no. 2 (May 1995), pp. 249–86.

    2. *The Manchurian Crisis and Japanese Society, 1931–1933*. London: Routledge. 2002.

Wolff, David. *To the Harbin Station: The Liberal Alternative in Russian Manchuria, 1898–1914*. Stanford, CA: Stanford University Press. 1999.

Wong, Edward. "Pollution Rising, Chinese Fear for Soil and Food." *New York Times*. December 30, 2013.

Woodhead, H. G. W. (Henry George Wandesforde). *A Visit to Manchukuo: A Series of Articles Contributed to the* Shanghai Evening Post and Mercury, *October–November 1932*. Shanghai: Mercury Press, 1932.

Yamamuro Shin'ichi. *Manchuria Under Japanese Dominion*. Philadelphia: University of Pennsylvania Press, 2006.

Yang Bin (ed.). *Dragon River Writings*. (龙江散记。) Harbin: Heilongjiang People's Press, 1985.

Yang Feng. *Manchu Customs*. (满族风情。) Shenyang: Liaoning Minorities Press, 2004.

Yang Jing. *Fengtian Nirvana*. (奉天涅盘。) Shenyang: Shenyang Press, 2002.

Yap, Chuin-Wei. "China Sees Food Need Rising." *Wall Street Journal*, March 25, 2011.

Yardley, Jim. "Shenyang Journal; The G.I.'s Were Japan's Worker Slaves. Believe It." *New York Times*, September 19, 2003.

Yosano Akiko. *Travels in Manchuria and Mongolia: A Feminist Poet from Japan Encounters Prewar China*. New York: Columbia University Press, 2003.

Yoshihisa Tak Matsusaka. *The Making of Japanese Manchuria, 1904–1932*. Cambridge, MA: Harvard University Press, 2001.

Yosuke Matsuoka.

    1. (with Wellington Vi Kyuin Koo). *The Manchurian Question: Japan's Case in the Sino-Japanese Dispute as Presented Before the League of Nations.* Geneva: League of Nations, 1933.

    2. Building Up Manchuria. Tokyo: The Herald of Asia, 1938.

"You Are What You Eat: Can a Country as Modern as Japan Cling onto a Culture as Ancient as Rice?" *Economist*, December 19, 2009.

Young, C. Walter.

    1. The International Relations of Manchuria: Prepared for the 1929 Conference of the Institute of Pacific Relations in Kyoto, Japan. Chicago: University of Chicago Press, 1929.

    2. The International Status of the Kwantung Leased Territory. Baltimore: The Johns Hopkins, University Press, 1931.

    3. Japanese Jurisdiction in the South Manchuria Railway Areas. Baltimore: The Johns Hopkins University Press, 1931.

    4. Japan's Special Position in Manchuria. Baltimore: The Johns Hopkins University Press, 1931.

Young, John. *The Research Activities of the South Manchurian Railway Company, 1907–1945: A History and Bibliography.* New York: Columbia University East Asian Institute, 1966.

Young, Louise. *Japan's Total Empire: Manchuria and the Culture of Wartime Imperialism.* Berkeley: University of California Press, 1998.

Younghusband, Francis Edward. *The Heart of a Continent.* London: John Murray, 1904.

Yu, Maochun. *OSS in China: Prelude to Cold War.* New Haven, CT: Yale University Press. 1996.

Yu, Verna. "A Language Lost." *South China Morning Post*, August 29, 2011.

Yunxiang Yan. *Private Life Under Socialism.* Palo Alto, CA: Stanford University Press, 2003.

Zeng Wu. *All-Embracing Manchu Customs.* （满族民俗万象。） Shenyang: Liaoning Minorities Press, 2008.

Zhang Guoli. *Old Photos of Jilin City.* （吉林市老照片。） Beijing: China Culture and History Press, 2009.

Zheng Changjiang. *Northeast Cuisine.* （东北菜。） Harbin: Heilongjiang Science and Technology Publishing, 1997.

Zhou Siyu. "Super Rice Crop Needs Time for Commercial Cultivation." *China Daily*, September 23, 2011.

Zuo, Mandy.

    1. "Rice King Sets His Sights Even Higher." *South China Morning Post.* September 26, 2011.

    2. "Wen's Land Pledge Gives Farmers Hope." *South China Morning Post*, January 17, 2012.

3. "Grain Law May Leave Farmers in the Cold: Experts." *South China Morning Post*, August 15, 2012.
4. "Beijing Pushes for Bigger Family Farms to Boost Efficiency." *South China Morning Post*, August 17, 2013.
5. "Ukraine to Become China's Largest Overseas Farmer in 3M Hectare Deal." *South China Morning Post*, September 22, 2013.

Zweig, David. *Freeing China's Farmers: Rural Restructuring in the Reform Era.* London: M. E. Sharpe, 1997.

Zweig, David, Kathy Hartford, James Feinerman, and Deng Jianxu. "Law, Contracts, and Economic Modernization: Lessons from the Recent Chinese Rural Reforms." *Stanford Journal of International Law* 23 (1987), pp. 319–64.

INTERNALLY CIRCULATED AND SELF-PUBLISHED SOURCES

Chinese Eastern Railway. *North Manchuria and the Chinese Eastern Railway.* 1926.

"Classified List of the Books Added to the Dairen Library." South Manchurian Railway, 1937.

Donald, W. H. Papers, Columbia University Archives.

Drea, Edward, et al. *Researching Japanese War Crimes: Introductory Essays.* Washington, DC: National Archives and Records Administration Nazi War Crimes and Japanese Imperial Government Records Interagency Working Group, 2006.

Fairchild, Nelson. Collection of letters sent home, 1907.

Glantz, David M. "August Storm: The Soviet 1945 Strategic Offensive in Manchuria." In Leavenworth Papers, Fort Leavenworth, KS: U.S. Army Command and General Staff College, February 1983.

"Guide to Japanese Monographs and Japanese Studies on Manchuria, 1945–1960." Office of the Chief of Military History, Department of the Army, 1962.

Hongbin Li, Prashant Loyalka, Scott Rozelle, Binzhen Wu, and Jieyu Xie. "Unequal Access to College in China: How Far Have Poor, Rural Students Been Left Behind?" Stanford University working paper. 2013.

International Relations Committee. "Public Opinion Towards the Report of the League Enquiry Commission on Sino-Japanese Dispute." Nanking: IRC, 1932.

Inventory of the Papers of Roy L. Morgan, 1941–1966. Special Collections, Arthur J. Morris Law Library, University of Virginia Law School. Interrogation of Ai-Hsin-Cho-Lo Pu Yi (Henry Pu Yi). From the Tokyo War Crimes Tribunal, August 1946.

Jilin Meteorite Shower Exhibition. （吉林陨石雨。） Jilin City Meteorite Museum, 2001.

Kinney, Henry W., in Payson J. Treat Papers at the Hoover Institute Archives, Stanford University.

    1. Box 51 (Research File) Kinney, Charles Bishop (South Manchuria Railway Co.), firsthand reports on the political, military and economic situation in Manchuria, 1934–39.

    2. (South Manchuria Railway Co.), firsthand reports on the political, military and economic situation in Manchuria, 1927–36.

Landesa. Sixth 17-Province China Survey, April 26, 2012. www.landesa.org/china-survey-6/

Leith, Hal. *POWs of Japanese Rescued!* Victoria: Trafford. 2003.

Liang Siyong. "Journal [of the] Tsitsihar Linshih expedition (1930)." Tozzer Library, Harvard University.

"Never an Empty Bowl: Sustaining Food Security in Asia." Asia Society and International Rice Research Institute Task Force Report, 2010.

Pauley, Edwin W. "Report on Japanese Reparations to the President of the United States." Washington, DC: Department of State, Division of Publications, Office of Public Affairs. 1948.

People's Republic of China:

    1. *Land management law.* (中华人民共和国农村土地管理法。) 1999.

    2. *Rural land usage law.* （中华人民共和国农村土地拥抱法。) 2002.

Petitioning Regulations. （信访条例） Beijing: China Law Press, 2005.

Scherer, Anke. "Japanese Emigration to Manchuria: Local Activists and the Making of the Village-Division Campaign." Bochum, Germany: Ruhr-Universität, 2006. Dissertation.

"Summary of Rural Policies." (农村政策简明手册。) Jilin Province "Three Represents" Working Office, 2008.

"Who Owns My Land? Chinese Farmers' Land Rights at the Crossroads." Presentation by Landesa (Roy Prosterman and Zhu Keliang, presenters) at the Asia Society, New York City, May 2, 2011.

Zhu Keliang and Roy Prosterman. "Securing Land Rights for Chinese Farmers." Washington, DC Cato Institute, No. 3, October 15, 2007.

Index

NOTE: The initialism "MM" refers to Michael Meyer, the author.

and Red Flag Road, 78, 206–8,
247
resistance to moving into
apartments of, 12–13, 84–85,
211–12, 217–18
"The East Is Red" (song), 160
environmental issues, 89–90. *See
also* pollution
Er Ren Zhuan (opera), 50
ethnic dissonance in Harbin,
121–24
extraterrestrial abductions,
139–42, 146

factories, Jilin, 63–64
Fairchild, Nelson, 119–20, 297n
Falun Gong sect, 239
family tree terms, 9, 23
Fangzheng town, Manchuria,
188–90, 197–99
Fanshen (Hinton), 305n
farmers
about, 303n
choices of, 273–74
cultural beliefs about, 151
and Eastern Fortune, 12–13, 37
families of farmers, 150, 266
free migration program, 219–20
Japanese brutality in taking
their land, 180
labor shortage, 264
loans for equipment or side
business, 246
migration to urban centers, 11,
266, 284n, 328n
moving restrictions, 32, 37–38

rules for, 13, 83–84, 288n
second income for, 263
and Shennong icon, 238
taxes abolished, 13, 217
U.S. Census and, 11, 284n
in Wasteland area, 4, 24, 82–86
farming
about, 303n
allowing large-scale landholders,
223–24
collective agriculture, 212–14,
215, 324n
commercial/collective land
grabs, 83–84, 288n
commercial farms, 218–19,
328n
corn fields, 92
iron rice bowl concept, 225–28
land transfers, 83, 219, 220–21,
274–75, 324n, 325n, 326n
organic farms, 80–82, 87–89,
93, 288n, 328n
rural reform, 215–17, 323–24n
in Sichuan province, 219–21,
324n, 325n, 326n
yield increases, 155–56, 306n
Fei Xiaotong, 39, 285n
Mr. Feng, 61–62
fishing, 69, 92
Fleming, Peter, 174, 284n, 313n
flooding, 97, 290n
food poisoning remedy, 43
fortune cookies, 18, 27–28, 277
Four Big Families, Manchuria, 181
Frances
childhood, 30, 33–35

NOTE ON THE AUTHOR

Michael Meyer first went to China in 1995 with the Peace Corps. The winner of a Whiting Writers' Award for nonfiction and a Guggenheim Fellowship, Meyer has also received a Society of American Travel Writers Lowell Thomas Award. His stories have appeared in the *New York Times*, *Time*, *Smithsonian*, *Sports Illustrated*, *Slate*, the *Financial Times*, the *Los Angeles Times*, and the *Chicago Tribune*. He teaches nonfiction writing at the University of Pittsburgh, and spends the offseason in Singapore.